Edible
Wild Plants

VOLUME 2

THE WILD FOOD ADVENTURE SERIES

Edible Wild Plants

VOLUME 2

Wild Foods from Foraging to Feasting

JOHN KALLAS, PhD

Gibbs Smith

I dedicate this book to all the people of the earth living and, unfortunately, dying through the recent pandemic. Their continuing sacrifices and losses are great and should be appreciated. I also offer my condolences to all those with preexisting conditions and compromised immunity for the extra isolation they endure while all the variants rage around the globe. I would also like to give my support to the healthcare workers who have experienced both the most nightmarish working conditions and so much death for the last two years.

First Edition
27 26 25 24   5 4 3 2

PUBLISHER'S DISCLAIMER: The author and publisher disclaim all responsibility of allergy, injury, illness, or death resulting from touching, gathering, or eating or ingesting, in any form, the plants listed in this book. Readers assume all legal responsibility for their actions.

Please consult your physician for personalized medical advice, and always seek the advice of a physician or other qualified healthcare provider with any questions regarding a medical condition.

Published by
Gibbs Smith
P.O. Box 667
Layton, Utah 84041

1.800.835.4993 orders
www.gibbs-smith.com

Designed by Maralee Nelson
Printed and bound in China
Gibbs Smith books are printed on either recycled, 100% post-consumer waste, FSC-certified papers or on paper produced from a sustainable PEFC-certified forest/controlled wood source. Learn more at www.pefc.org.

Cover Photograph: John Kallas with cattail, 2007. Courtesy of Aubrie LeGault.

Library of Congress Cataloging-in-Publication Data
James: Kallas, John, 1952- author.
Title: Edible wild plants. Volume 2 : wild foods from foraging to feasting / John Kallas.
LCSH: Wild plants, Edible. | Cooking (Greens) | LCGFT: Cookbooks.
LCC QK98.5.A1 K352 2022 | DDC 581.6/32—dc23/eng/20220228
2022005447
ISBN: 9781423641346 (paperback)
ISBN: 9781423641353 (ebook)

Contents

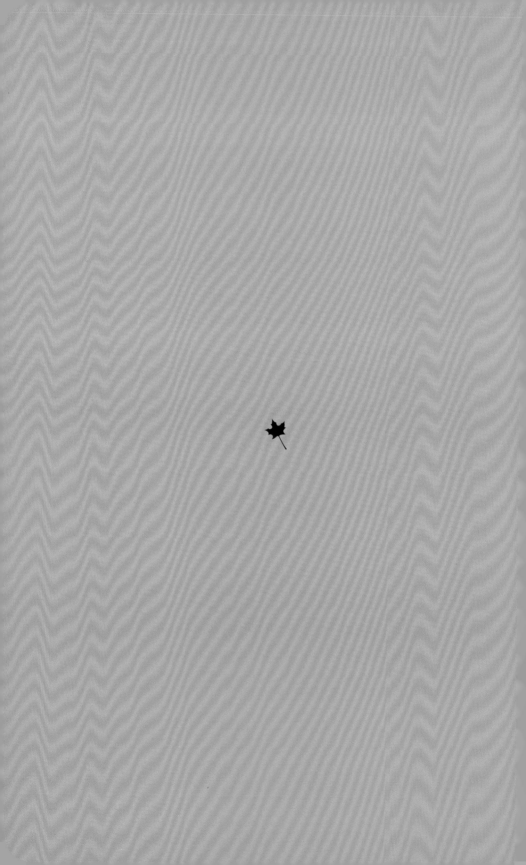

About the Author

I covered my basic bio in the first book so I won't go into the same detail here. Here is a brief summary.

I've researched and experimented with wild foods over the course of the last 40 years in Europe and North America. And this was not in a casual way. Serious study led me to teaching at Michigan State University in the 1980s, and later to starting Wild Food Adventures outdoor school after moving to the Pacific Northwest in the 1990s, where my headquarters have been for researching and teaching ever since. This is my full-time job and career.

I was in college for 17 years, studying everything I wanted, absorbing information like a sponge. The last six of those years focused on wild foods, nutrition, plant systematics, ethnobotany, and foodways across the planet. I have a bachelor's degree in zoology and psychology, a master's in education, and a PhD in nutrition.

While most of my work is now in the Pacific Northwest, I do research and trainings throughout North America. The first half of my career was *mostly* studying plants of the eastern United States, the second half was *mostly* studying those in the West. And the whole time I've been studying those edible plants that are native to humans— the ubiquitous edible weeds.

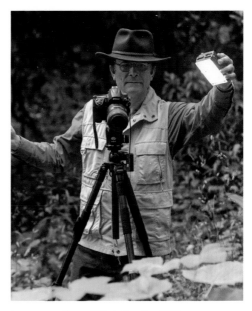

Goals for my own learning have been to identify and then uncover the hidden edible virtues of all the important wild foods. It is my lifelong venture.

Goals for my first three books (the third is yet to be born) are to report on the most common, abundant, and practical wild foods that people should learn about first. And to do so in such a way that you, a researcher in your own right, really "get" it, understand the plants covered, and enjoy them in a practical way.

Disclaimer? Yeah, Right!

If you venture out of your nuclear-proof, earthquake-proof, asteroid-proof bunker into the real world, you might be at risk. Yes, it's true! You may be hit by a bus or get *E. coli* or staphylococcus poisoning from a church potluck. If you kiss someone, you may get herpes, mono, or have a tragic relationship. On the golf course, you may be hit by lightning. If you go ice skating, you may break your neck. If you go on a hike, you may trip on loose rocks, fall over a cliff, and die.

Look, you can curl up under your bedcovers and live a safe, dull, insulated life reading about other people doing things you wish you were doing. Or you can join the real world.

If you venture into the real world, you risk living your life to the fullest. You risk the rush of climbing that mountain, of dancing all night, of scuba diving in reefs of mind-blowing color, of standing in the rain or at an ocean viewpoint, watching huge waves crashing against the rocks, of meeting the partner of your dreams. You risk getting exercise and breathing fresh air. You risk making life worth living.

So if you decide to venture into the world of wild foods, you'd better prepare yourself for some fun, adventure, and risk. Yes, there are risks to eating new foods that you've never tried before. You might make some mistakes or have allergies to foods you haven't been exposed to yet. Nature has its own agenda and is not looking out for the safety of humans—and that fact provides some unpredictability in all things wild. But if you are a reasonable student, if you don't just jump haphazardly into eating everything in sight, and if you pay attention to what your body is telling you, your chances of any real danger are slim. For the vast majority of people, getting into wild foods will be nothing but fun. For that rare person who becomes the exception, we may end up talking about your unusual case in future books.

And while your experiences may be different from mine, I have never regretted eating wild foods, which I have done for over 45 years. I hope your experience will be as good as mine. So be a good student, and you will minimize the chance that you will regret living your life to its fullest.

Students on a Wild Food Adventure at the Oregon coast. Photo courtesy of Chung Li Ramsdell, 2003.

Some Comments About Content

Botanical names are based on the plants cataloged at the Integrated Taxonomic Information System offered through a partnership between U.S., Canadian, and Mexican federal agencies. Plant names were verified at http://www.itis.gov/index.html.

The maps were generated from several sources, including but not limited to the personal experience of the author, Kew's Plants of the World Online (https://powo.science.kew.org), EDD Species Distribution Maps (https://www.eddmaps.org/distribution/), NatureServe Explorer (http://www.natureserve. org/explorer/), Natural Resources Canada (http://www.planthardiness.gc.ca/), the Biology of Canadian Weeds book series—*Reprints from the Canadian Journal of Plant Science*, and plant distribution maps offered by web sites of individual states.

Many of the plants covered in this book have a wider range than the included range maps portray. Range maps rely on scientists, researchers, government workers, and laypersons to report sightings. Since this is not a systematic process, many plants are not looked for or recorded. Expect that even if you are outside the ranges I report, these plants may still be in your area.

Welcome to My World

Lots of people call me a forager. But I am primarily a wild food researcher, educator, and author. Yes, of course, I forage. But, no, I don't live in the woods and cook by a campfire as you are reading this, scratching the text of this book out on some rocks. I live in a normal neighborhood in Portland, Oregon. I eat a primarily Mediterranean-style diet that I forage from regular grocery stores.

That diet is regularly supplemented and enhanced by wild foods in a way that fits nicely into my lifestyle. In fact, this lifestyle is what I recommend to almost everyone interested in adding wild foods to their diet. It is the most practical way to incorporate them into the diet of anyone living in this world today. I forage, harvest, or glean them:

- From my yard and neighborhood
- In the course of doing research on a particular plant
- In the course of teaching
- To gather for fun on occasion with friends
- To harvest some of my favorite foods from annual sites.
- As I travel, I stop my bike or car, jump off or out, and fill my grocery bags when I see a great wild food at its prime just asking to be taken.

Research

Research for me is a joy and a great challenge of imagination. For myself and my students, I favor studying common plants that people are likely to see themselves. What do I mean by research?

To research a plant, the first thing I do is make sure I have positively identified it, beyond a shadow of a doubt. This is not something you do by visiting blogs or Google Images. I use several credible sources, including professional botanical dichotomous keys, until I am satisfied I

LOOK-ALIKES
The more direct experience you have with plants and plant families, the less chance you will confuse one plant for another. The reason I focus so much on plant part detail is that it helps train you to see detail overall. So when you see a new plant, you automatically tune in to its unique features, recognizing how it is different from others.

have positively identified the plant and distinguished it from all potential look-alikes.

It also has to be growing nearby in enough abundance that I can do all sorts of examinations and tests on it. That might involve me growing it myself in research beds like I did for marsh mallow plants.

Researching a plant can be done in weeks or years depending on a variety of factors often unknown when I begin the work. To get a comprehensive understanding of a plant, you have to not only know what it looks like at each stage of its growth, but also what variations those forms can take under different circumstances.

At the same time that I'm learning the growth forms and habits of a plant, I go back into the historical literature. The further back I can go, the more likely, in my experience, that the information reflects a plant's true uses. Since the explosion of books on wild foods after Euell Gibbons popularized the topic, there have been hundreds of books by people who know little to nothing and should not be believed. The exceptions being a few current authors who take a more scholarly approach like I do—Samuel Thayer being my personal favorite.

After reading everything the old ethnobotanical, botanical, cultural, and wild food literature has to offer, I create a summary of that plant's potential. What are the likely edible parts at different stages of growth? One plant may have many edible parts in the form of leaves, stems, flowers, fruits, seeds, roots, etc. They may also have medicinal or poisonous parts. What is the minimum processing required to make each "edible" part edible and tender/pleasant enough to eat? How did people prepare the plant parts in the past? How would I characterize the flavor of each part? Is the flavor, texture, look, feel, or other properties reminiscent of any store-bought food we all have access to today?

Before testing the plant, I then check the toxicological, pharmacological, medical, and veterinary literature to see if there are any contraindications to eating the edible parts of my research plant. If I find any warning signs, I investigate the details until I have a good picture of whatever potential danger there is in eating a plant part. Before I teach about a plant, I have to be confident that any food I am working with is relatively safe and wholesome.

Once I feel that I understand the potential of a plant, I set up some basic experiments. I sample its parts raw and cooked in various ways. What happens when you boil it, steam it, fry it, cook it in a microwave, or dry it?

What happens when you add it as an ingredient to a complex salad (typically five or more ingredients plus salad dressing), sandwich (typically bread with four other ingredients plus mustard or ketchup), or soup of any kind?

What are the flavors, textures, and appearance of each edible part? Evaluation of these traits is somewhat subjective, as I am only one person. My hope as an educator is that I can tune in to what most people might experience.

Given my initial impressions, I ask myself, is this edible plant part reminiscent of any conventional food? If so, what general ways can I use it like the conventional food? Is it like lettuce, broccoli, okra, carrot, potato, blueberry, raspberry, etc? If it fits one somewhat, then I find simple recipes for that domesticated food, and use the wild food in its place. This is where it helps to have a wild imagination and be willing to attempt really new things. For me now, successful culinary experiences often happen right off the bat, but sometimes it requires tweaking to get an excellent result.

While doing all these experiments, my experience grows. Insights develop. I begin to understand why most traditional uses were not random, but done to get the most out of the uniqueness of any plant.

After all this, I pass my experience, understanding, and insights off to you in my books and directly to my students in workshops.

RELATIVELY SAFE

No food, domestic or wild, is totally safe. While mustard seed is considered edible, the condiment mustard can make you sick if you overeat it. Americans are particularly good at overdoing things. The "more is better" syndrome is rampant. This is why historical patterns of use are important guides to how we might eat a plant part. All foods should be eaten in moderation and in the context of a diverse overall diet. Overeating blueberries, for instance, can give you diarrhea. Also, one cannot account for idiosyncratic genetic differences in either humans or plants that may cause reactions in individuals. While these are rare, each person must monitor themselves after eating any new plant part, wild or domestic.

Photography

The photographs in this book are not random. Every image is purposeful to clearly demonstrate or reinforce something, or inspire you to act. What you will see here is clarity. The photographs are so detailed that you can see plant hairs, veins, and even my fingerprints in some of them. All of this takes much more time and expertise and has made me a professional photographer over the years.

I have been taking photographs since 1976. In the beginning that was mostly to document edible plants at various stages of growth for my own interests. Initially, the

This photograph is the culmination of multiple tries over the years, careful gathering and transporting of perfect specimens at perfect stages of growth, designing a stand with holes to support them at the minimum distance apart, perfect background, lighting, focus, and depth of field. With all the tries over the years, this likely took over 50 hours of work to eventually get one perfect photograph.

photographs were mostly used in slide presentations. Once I began publishing, my mission became more purposeful. Each photograph had to show something important.

The wild food literature has long suffered, and continues to suffer, from the following image-related problems: too few photographs, confusing or complex images, blurry images, lack of defining detail, with attention often limited to the flowering stage. My photograph-filled chapters do not have these problems. I include as many photos as necessary to show the detail throughout the plant's life, processing techniques, comparisons, and finished dishes. I use extreme depth of field to have as much of the plant in clear focus as possible. I zoom in on detail that is lost in overall complex plants. And while I show close-ups of flowers, I also show close-ups of leaves, stems, seeds, roots, hairs, veins, and other things that help you know a plant.

Photos are now prettier than they used to be in the overall wild food literature. But don't confuse pretty with useful. Due to digital photography and photo editing software, images you see in modern books are much prettier than in the past. My goal is to have photographs that are pretty, in addition to being clear and sharp, and they teach you something you should know.

Here are some of the considerations when shooting a plant. Is the plant perfect? That is, do you have a specimen that is representative of the standard form of the plant? Is it full of damage or free of defects? Is it a wind-free day so the final image is not blurry from movement? How is the lighting? Harsh sunlight or even bright haze can leach out parts of a photograph. Can you isolate the plant from its background? Complex distracting backgrounds can interfere with the clarity of the subject. It can take years carrying around professional photographic equipment to various habitats and regions in the right seasons, wind, and lighting to get optimal images of what is needed. Then hours on the computer enhancing each image. That is what I try to do.

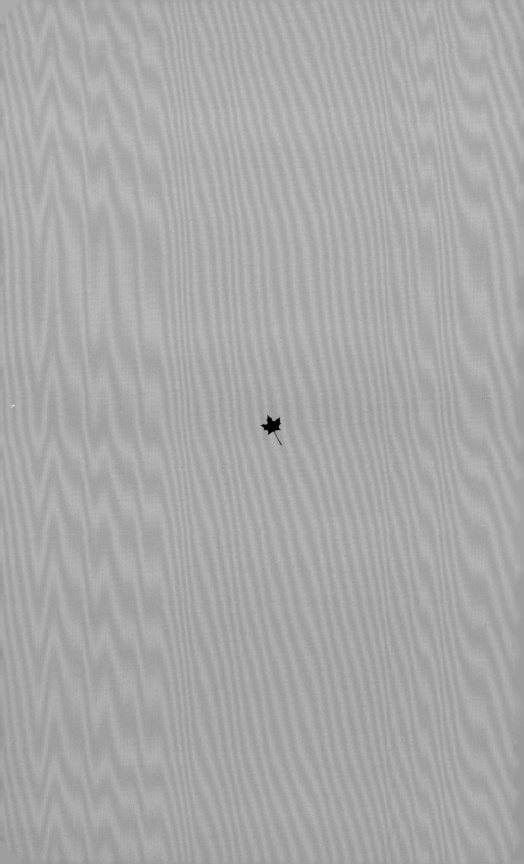

Part I
Understanding
Wild Foods

When I was a young lad, I had a fascination with wild foods. My initial focus on the topic gave me the impression that wild foods were rare, strange, difficult to learn, mostly a survival thing, and not great once you tasted them. There were no experts around and few books. My parents could not help. They humored me in my interests, but showed no interest themselves.

My grandfather, an immigrant from Greece, ate wild foods as a normal part of his diet in southern Ohio. He learned it all as a child from his parents before he arrived in the United States at the age of sixteen in the early 1900s. Since my parents lived a three-hour drive from him in Michigan and visits only occurred at holidays, I did not learn about his knowledge until later in his life. When I eventually tried to learn from him, he wondered why I was looking back and not into the future. After all, I was getting a doctorate in nutrition, what was with the wild foods?

The world I knew as a child no longer exists. Currently, there are tons of resources on wild foods, including books, the internet, and government publications. The difficulty is that while there is great stuff out there, the majority of it is popular garbage, misconceptions, made-up stuff, and material from novices claiming to be experts who know so little it is frightening. If you depend on sloppy inexperienced sources, you have to wade through a lot of confusing content and experience a lot of unpleasant dishes to learn what you need to know to safely identify and enjoy the wild foods you find. Many people give up out of frustration.

This book cuts through all that crap to give you clear, concise, well-illustrated information about the plants covered. No hype, just good practical real-world information to get you doing what you want to do: find, gather, and enjoy eating foods from the wild. Yes, it's a real thing: having fun and wonderful wild food dining experiences without wasted effort and time.

The design of this book and others in the series is predicated on the principle of thoroughness, because if you don't know what you need to know to be successful, you will have disappointing experiences. I cover each plant assuming that you know little to nothing about wild foods. It is a full story, told in a way to build your knowledge gradually over time.

For example, the unprecedented cattail chapter includes about 50 photos, since that is what it takes to cover the most practical aspects and capabilities of the cattail's many edible parts. I dare you to find any book showing the detailed and valuable coverage you will find here. And while I could write a whole book just on the cattail—it's potential is that great—I've distilled that down the most important stuff you can really benefit from.

All of my books are designed to be useful for novices all the way up to modern wild food experts. Wild food instructors, outdoor skill instructors, researchers, nutritionists, dieticians, food suppliers, homesteaders, farmers, and people who want to go beyond their routine lives to experience new things will benefit from what they see here. Want to explore growing these wild foods as a crop? You can start here. Want to understand the nutrient contribution that these plants offer for supplementing the diet? You can start here. Want to write a wild food cookbook? Learn the ingredients and their attributes here.

How is this volume different from the first? Different plants and concepts are covered. The nutrient tables have been updated and expanded to cover plants from both books. Major categories in Part II: The Plants, have been renamed to more accurately describe their contents. In volume 1, plants were divided into categories I called "greens." Volume 2 plants are divided into "plants" featuring these flavors: foundation, tart, pungent or peppery, bitter, distinctive and sweet, and poisonous. While the "greens" label seemed appropriate at the time I wrote volume 1, it contradicted the principle I was trying to convey: that all plants have multiple edible parts at different stages of growth. The fact that these plants provide much more than just greens became lost on many people.

The optimal label for these new Part II sections would be, for instance, "Plants, some parts of which are foundationally flavored." But since that was too long, I just went with "foundation plants."

The plants covered in volume 2, as in volume 1, are universal. They are found almost everywhere in abundance in North America, Europe, and in other places where Europeans have traveled. This makes your job easier. You will likely find almost all of these plants over the next couple of years growing within a short distance of your home. You do not have to drive into the wilderness to find them. They surround you.

Why is this book series important for today—or anytime?

Whether you're rich or poor, wild foods provide variety to the diet that you cannot duplicate in the supermarket. A great variety of nutrient-dense foods, mostly from plants, is what leads to better overall health. And I am sure your gut microflora will love, love, love them.

In this time where many kids are no longer allowed to roam free in their neighborhoods, collecting wild food is a wonderful outdoor activity for the whole family and a great topic for conversation.

In this time of great climate chaos and change, the plants that grow in regions may shift. Drought, sporadic flooding, increases and fluctuations in temperature, and rising sea levels will require some shifts in the foods that can be mass-produced. Many cultivated plants are sensitive to change. They require very specific conditions and will not grow as climatic changes occur. Many wild foods, particularly the ones highlighted in this book series, have much more vigor and flexibility in their needs. They will survive under more circumstances, providing food to both individuals and agriculture.

My hope is that whatever your learning goals, this book will take you there. Good luck and have fun.

For a more complete description of the uniqueness of this book series, look it up at wildfoodadventures.com.

Chapter 1

Introduction

Here is a brief reminder of some important concepts I covered in volume 1 in this *Edible Wild Plants* book series. That is followed by new concepts of importance.

Edible wild plants are endowed with one or more parts that can be used for food if gathered at the appropriate stage of growth and properly prepared.

Concepts from Volume 1

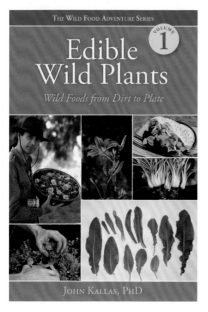

Volume 1 of this Wild Food Adventures series, published in 2010.

DEFINITIONS

Edible wild plants are endowed with one or more parts that can be used for food if gathered at the appropriate stage of growth and properly prepared.

Poisonous plants are plants endowed with one or more parts having chemical or physical attributes that can cause acute or underlying injury or death upon ingestion, touch, or inhalation. Dosage determines the severity of the damage. Poisons can affect some animal species differently than others.

Medicinal plants are plants endowed with one or more parts having therapeutic effects when gathered at the appropriate stage of growth, properly prepared, and properly administered.

Agriotrophytology is my suggested label for the study of wild food plants. A term for academicians and research scientists.

NOT ALL OF AN "EDIBLE PLANT" IS EDIBLE. Edible, poisonous, medicinal, and parts too fibrous to eat can all be found on the same plant, so know the plant's details before you start indulging.

HARVEST PLANT PARTS AT THEIR PRIME FOR EATING. For vegetative parts of edible plants, the areas of rapid growth often define when a part is at its prime—that is, at its most tender for eating. The edible parts of a plant that are no longer growing become tough as development demands they become rigid for structural support or to survive the elements. Reproductive parts like flowers, fruits, seeds, and nuts are typically at their prime when they are fully formed, but many flower buds (like broccoli) and immature seeds (like fresh peas and beans) can be considered at their prime for eating as well.

LEARNING STRATEGY. The best strategies for learning on your own about wild foods include the following: study some common wild plants ahead of time through books and electronic resources; be an observer while walking; when you find something promising, study its situation and life stage in place, take it home and check its identification with my books and other resources, determine if any parts of what you've gathered are edible and at their prime; if so, then sample it. Evaluate your experience and compare it to what it says in my books. Look for more of the plant to play with.

LEARN THE LIFE STORY OF PLANTS. To get the most out of any edible wild plant, you must know its life story, from seedling to maturity. At what stages can you recognize it, and at what stages can you find edible parts?

NATURE IS NOT HERE FOR OUR CONVENIENCE. Plants can vary in shape, size, stage of growth, biochemistry, and flavor depending on the resources (soil nutrients, sunlight, water) they've been exposed to during development. Genetic uniqueness can also play a role. We have no control over that variation. These things can affect our ability to identify a plant and how much we like what we are eating.

THE BEST REFERENCE RESOURCES GO INTO GREAT DETAIL. Great edible plant learning resources include multiple photographs of each plant at multiple stages of growth and discuss identification, edible parts at their prime for eating, important processing techniques, and simple basic recipes so you'll actually enjoy them.

YOU, THE FORAGER, TAKE ON MANY ROLES. If you are getting your food directly from nature, you necessarily take on the following jobs: naturalist, identifier of edible plants at any stage of growth and of edible parts at their prime, harvester-forager, edible part transporter, cleaner, processer, recipe designer, cook, and consumer. With store-bought foods, you only take on the last two and sometimes three tasks.

TOOLS FOR FORAGERS. Tools to carry with you depend on what you expect to gather. They can include: scissors, a digging tool, white or otherwise reflective gathering bags, a spray mister, and a dish towel. Occasionally a fixed-blade knife, water trays, and endless other tools can be useful. Every hand tool you carry, if possible, should be in a holster to free up your hands.

OPEN-MINDED SAMPLING ATTITUDE. Your first exposure to a taste of a new-to-you wild food requires an open-minded, optimistic, forward-looking attitude. More, "What can I do with this?" rather than "That was not nirvana" and "I will only eat flavors I am used to eating." Nothing is nirvana. While you will love many wild foods right off the bat, others may either take time for your sensibilities to wake to them or may reveal their virtues when combined with other foods. You'll love many more wild foods if you experiment with them imaginatively and give them time to grow on you.

FOODS YOU CAN EAT AND FOODS YOU CANNOT. Due to a human genetic variation, some people taste a soapy flavor when eating or smelling cilantro while others do not. New foods need to be adjusted to and figured out for each individual. You've already had a lifetime to figure out which domesticated foods suit you and which do not. Since all wild foods are new, you have to discover, by trial and error, if any are a problem for you. You are less likely to have problems with wild foods if you have little or no problems eating domesticated foods.

On to new stuff . . .

Traditional Foods and Plants Native to Humans

Wild foods have an identity problem with the general public. Somehow, wild foods seem strange, mysterious, rare, and renegade—foods that only rare humans and animals eat. They are something that survivalist and ancient peoples would eat. In fact, contrary to these notions, they are traditional foods that most modernized people have lost touch with.

Further, in the culinary and naturalist worlds, there seems to be a qualitative distinction between native edible plants and edible weeds. The romantic in us likes the idea of native plants. They have a sense of place, they help define a place, they grow here for a reason. They are also perceived as more esteemed, having more value, and deserving more respect. And it is certainly wonderful to walk into an old-growth forest filled with native plants.

Weeds, on the other hand, are mostly considered a nuisance, out of place; they grow in areas where we would prefer more order and control. We pull them, poison them, fight them constantly. At least that is how we were brought up: hating them. We think of many of them as ugly, an eyesore. Unfortunately, delicious, nutritious edible weeds fall into this hate category for most people.

Dandelion (*Taraxacum officinale*) is native to and a traditional food of Eurasia. It is esteemed as a food all over the world, but hated as a weed in the lawns of grass lovers.

ALL WILD FOODS ARE TRADITIONAL FOODS. All wild foods in their land of origin were eaten as traditional foods. So all wild foods, even what we consider weeds, are traditional foods.

WEEDS ARE PLANTS NATIVE TO HUMANS.

All weeds, including the edible ones, follow us around. Weeds love disturbed soil and humans are the champions of disturbing soil. We cultivate land, build, pave, clear forests, bulldoze land, and even bomb countries. All these human activities destroy native habitats and set the stage for weeds to flourish.

If we put two and two together . . .

EDIBLE WEEDS ARE TRADITIONAL FOODS NATIVE TO HUMANS.

I may have to title a book *Traditional Foods Native to Humans*, for this concept to get any traction. I can introduce the idea, but the reality is that virtually everyone already knows what a *weed* is. Only you and one other person reading my book will know what *plants native to humans*, refers to. That forces me to still use the term *weeds* for now.

The bottom line is that all wild foods, native or invasive, have a long history of use. They are not strange, mysterious, rare, or renegade. They are normal foods that we, now a global community, have lost touch with. Wild foods are traditional foods that were perfectly normal to the peoples who ate them. They can become normal to you, too.

Wapato (*Sagittaria latifolia*) is native to and a traditional food of indigenous North Americans.

Wild Fast Food

When you think of fast food, you probably think mostly of greasy burgers and deep-fried foods you can purchase in a drive-through or cheap sit-down restaurant. That is not what I am referring to here. Great fresh food can be fast as well. A fresh, juicy pear is fast food. It is easy to grab and eat. Other foods take more time and work to prepare, like scoring, roasting, and then peeling chestnuts; getting to the edible part of whole artichokes; or grinding wheat into flour.

For most of the plants I present to you, my focus is on the parts that are wild fast food. Of course, since I am

Miner's lettuce (*Claytonia perfoliata*) is a wild fast food. You see it, you grab it, you eat it.

covering each plant in detail, there are parts of each one that may require more work. And there are some that are just fun to make, but take more work, like marshmallows. Making marshmallows from marsh mallow root or its immature seeds is not wild fast food. They are wild amazing fun food, but not wild fast food. However, you can eat the root raw as a wild fast food. See the Marsh Mallow chapter on page 113 for more information.

The thinking behind presenting you with these quick and easy foods is that you will be more likely to eat and experiment with them than with those that require more processing. Look, we are all busy. We've got lives. We have jobs. We are raising families. Time is precious. As an educator, my goal is to break through all of that to inspire you to start learning about and using wild foods, to design your first tries so that they are simple and rewarding. Small, successful first steps show you that cool, fun stuff is happening and that encourages you to do more.

Wild Food Authors Are Not Chefs

Don't assume that any recipe in a wild food book is a good one. Very few wild food authors know what they are doing in the kitchen. Often a recipe we publish is something we tried and liked, but in the right hands it could have been something great! Don't get me wrong. I have been getting better at this over the years, but I have a long way to go. When you try a recipe right out of a wild food book, assume you or someone who knows what they are doing can improve on it.

I remember my first editor for the first volume suggesting that we title this series *The Wild Food Gourmet*. OMG that would have been false advertising, but would have sold more books to unsuspecting people who actually like food. So view my recipes, and any wild food authors' recipes, as a starting point.

Chapter 2

It's How You Eat It

To be a successful wild food consumer, meaning you enjoy what you are doing and eating, it's important *how* you eat a plant part, not just that it is edible.

All wild foods are new to you. So they present more of a challenge to your already established sensibilities. Food is a particularly complicated realm, because we've grown up with our own eating traditions, habits, and practices. We know what we like. We have our favorite foods. We like to eat them over and over.

But it goes further than that. When we say we like pasta (shaped cooked dough), what we really mean is that we like dishes that *include* pasta as an ingredient. The same could be said for almost any food. When people say they like broccoli, they are rarely referring to raw, unadorned broccoli. And when broccoli is served raw, it is often with some thick, savory dip.

Almost all vegetables are eaten in combination with other foods and flavorings. It is the combination of foods that we like. We eat raw combinations like salads, sandwiches, and smoothies. We eat cooked combinations like stir-fries; mixed vegetables with oil, vinegar, and salt; soups; stews; savory pies; etc.

Wild foods are no different than ones you've been eating all your life, except you don't have the combinations of ingredients figured out yet. That is the adventure. Don't let it be a hindrance.

So how then do you discover the combinations you like with wild foods? Follow this sequence. The recommendations here assume it is a green. But use the same principles if you are working with a seed, nut, fruit, or solid vegetable:

1. Be sure you have picked the part at its prime for eating and it is in its edible form. That is, all necessary processing has already been done to make it edible.
2. Microanalyze its flavor and texture in its simplest edible form. Look for ways its flavor and texture are

similar to foods you already eat. If they are very different, use them with wild abandon in the following ways to make great discoveries.

3. Try simple combinations. Mix it in a typical salad you make. Try using it as one-fourth the mass of the greens, while otherwise making the same salad you always make—same accoutrements, same dressings, etc. If it is a bitter green, use it to replace a bitter green you might have put in.

4. Try some of the simple recipes I give at the end of each plant chapter.

5. If you eat foods like spinach, broccoli, celery, kale, lettuce, cucumber, etc., just substitute the wild food for any of them randomly in whatever recipe you are attempting. Or you could try to be more specific in your substitutions, matching similar flavors.

6. At each meal, add a wild food within any dish you are making.

Taking these steps will get you started into seriously integrating wild foods into your normal diet. Marvel in the ones that seem normal and cherish the ones that spark something new. Having open-minded anticipation of your experiments will result in more pleasure. And if you are like me, all sorts of new culinary options will pop into your mind.

If you are like me, you will meet with preference resistance, since you are probably quite happy with your current established domesticated food habits and you don't want to rock the boat. You like your food as it is, and a pox on disturbing something you already like. But if you want to genuinely start incorporating wild foods, all new, into your regular diet, you have to become a culinary adventurer who is not afraid to experiment. You'll be glad you did.

With repeated exposure, even the tries you don't cherish at first might begin to grow on you. My palate has become more sophisticated from incorporating wild foods over the years.

Chapter 3

Indicators of Edibility

The real indicator of edibility of any plant is evidence of a long history of sustained traditional use by some culture. When people lived close to the land, they made efficient use of all their natural resources. If a plant had food potential, they explored, tested, and sustainably ate it over centuries verifying its benefits. Strongly poisonous plants were abandoned or used medicinally.

What you have to be careful about is that there are plants that taste great and seem nutritive that are bad for humans. While showing no overt symptoms, subtle plant toxins over time could damage the kidneys, the liver, the immune system, cause sterility or brain damage without anyone being able to make the connection. It is possible that tribes consuming these damage-causing plants died out over time, while tribes that did not eat those plants survived.

When I come across a common wild plant that has no cultural history of food use, I see that as a clue that there is some problem with eating it, no matter how good it tastes.

For instance, there is a plant in the Pacific Northwest called swordfern. It is the most common fern in our forests. It is evergreen, so you see it all year long—and it's everywhere. It has fiddleheads and a taproot-like rhizome.

Swordfern (*Polystichum munitum*). An evergreen fern with no edible fiddleheads, leaves, or roots.

Among all the numerous indigenous tribes in the region, there is no recorded cultural history of this plant being used for food. It is ubiquitous, easily found at all times of year, and available to everyone, yet no one was using it for food. That lack of a history of use is a warning. The options are that it is in some way poisonous over time, antinutritive, there is just no practical food to find on it, or any combination of the three.

But since it is abundant and easy to identify, people today seem to latch onto any hint that they have discovered something new. A respected ethnographer wrote a paper on this plant, claiming the rhizome was edible. About seven other ethnographers repeated this information. Then it was discovered, if I remember correctly, that the author source was confusing swordfern with some other plant. The consequence of the article being wrong is that the information universe is now contaminated with all sorts of people who think there is food there.

The bottom line to this is: Don't experiment with plants of unknown edibility, no matter how good the taste. Don't trust authors or information sources who assume edibility based on flavor alone.

Chapter 4

Foraging vs Harvesting

How you gather wild foods has implications not only for how to prepare for a trip, but also for what you can expect from that trip and what you will be able to do upon your return.

FORAGING is a treasure hunt, the act of gathering foods as you come across them. And while you can guess based on habitat, season, and region, you don't know exactly what you will find. Mushroom hunting without a specific reliable site is foraging. If you are hiking, stop for lunch, and grab whatever is available around you to add to your meal, that is foraging.

HARVESTING is gathering from known reliable patches of wild food. This can be a seasonal pilgrimage or just to a place where you know a plant is producing right now. If you know of wild cherry trees that are ripe, you travel to them and harvest a sustainable amount of cherries. The vast majority of wild foods gathered by indigenous peoples all over the world were harvested, not foraged. For instance, here in the Pacific Northwest, first peoples knew exactly where the camas and wapato were. They would travel to each plant at the appropriate season and harvest what they needed for the year.

Harvesting is more efficient than foraging. If you are harvesting, you know exactly the tools to take with you. You can plan every aspect of a trip to maximize your time, effort, and quality of your take. You can prep the home front with any processing equipment you would need so the food can be dealt with right away. It is less work for more food. It results in less waste.

Foraging is more random. You do not want to lug a shovel or long fruit harvesting pole with you all the time on the chance you will find something they can be used for. And frankly you may not know you will be foraging until you see those wild fruits in front of you. Then you have to improvise collection and transport, and now adjust your schedule to manage the food that you are bringing home.

CAMAS AND WAPATO

Camas can be one of several *Camassia* spp, **Wapato** can be one of several *Sagittaria* spp.

HARVEST PLANNING

Processing equipment, containers, and storage that you want to prep ahead of time might include sifting, winnowing, grinding, canning, vacuum sealing, freezing, roasting, etc. If you are going to can, pickle, or vacuum-seal, for instance, do you have all the parts to make things happen? Have you cleaned out freezer space? Did you budget time for cleaning, processing, labeling, and storing?

It is important to recognize that, while foraging and harvesting are fun, they are only the beginning. When you get home, you have to process and manage all the food or it will go bad, mold, rot, dry up, or get wasted in some way. I cannot count the thousands of times I gathered a bunch of wild food, only to have it rot in the fridge from neglect because I had so many other things going on. Harvesting sets the stage so you can plan for that return. Depending on the food gathered, foraging requires that you take time that you have not planned for, to manage your bounty upon returning to the home front.

Chapter 5

Weeds, Noxious Weeds, and Food

Many wild foods, including ones in this book, are considered noxious weeds. But, of course, the beauty, benefit, or horrors of any plant are in the eye of the beholder. So let's explore what *noxious* means.

To say *noxious weed* seems redundant. Some might ask, "Aren't all weeds noxious?" Noxious weeds are differentiated in that some regulatory, health, or government agency has labeled them as noxious. They are seen as harmful or injurious to health or well-being, a threat to economic concerns, or a threat to natural habitats or ecosystems. While mostly attributed to nonnative plants, the term noxious can also be applied to native plants if they are becoming a nuisance in some way.

The problems with noxious weeds are many, but there are also benefits, including edibility, food for animals and pollinators, habitat for wildlife, enrichment over time of poor soils, as well as food, medicine, and useful resources for humans. For instance, the well-known noxious weeds Japanese knotweed, garlic mustard, Himalayan blackberry, and pokeweed provide wonderful wild foods. When you find them, you can take advantage of whatever bounty presents itself to you.

I've had all four of the aforementioned plants growing wild in the yards of places I've lived in over the last 30 years. None got out of hand or took over, because I knew how to manage them. The keys are seed and root management. I could have, with diligence, uprooted and disposed of all of them, but did not have to. If you keep them, you cannot let the seed spread or, as in the case of the blackberry, let the seeds or rhizomes spread. This can become complicated and a lot of work if you have lots of land to manage.

So just because a plant is labeled a noxious weed does not mean you cannot enjoy the benefits it offers. Since people in modern society are such poor caretakers of the land, you will find a lot of noxious weeds. If enough people

Japanese knotweed (*Fallopia japonica*) blanketing a stream by an old quarry. Young plants in the foreground, old stems in the background. Lots of great vegetable matter here.

Himalayan blackberry (*Rubus bifrons*), in flower, taking over a hillside and most of the treeless area in the distance. Those flowers are great for pollinators and eventually produce amazing-tasting berries.

knew about the edible potential of wild foods, we would be more likely to embrace many of them. Well, not thistles. Don't embrace thistles or you'll injure yourself, just eat their edible parts.

One major problem that noxious weeds stimulate is that people are constantly attempting to kill them with herbicides. That contaminates the soil and the plants that grow on them. You shouldn't eat from plants in sprayed areas. I'll cover more about this later.

Toss That Survival Manual

If you are learning wild foods from survival manuals, you have my sympathies. Most of what I have seen about wild foods in such manuals is sophomoric, oversimplified, out of context, and, most importantly, would not be useful in a genuine survival situation. The information you really need allows you to efficiently use your time to solve immediate problems when your life depends on it. The poor, mostly incomplete, and out-of-context information in survival manuals would have you spinning your wheels when you don't have time for that.

The original military survival manuals were written by people who had no real experience or expertise doing what they recommend. They were information compilers tasked with trying to figure out what lost military personnel should do to provide themselves with water, fire, shelter, rescue signaling, and food in various regions around the world.

Needless to say, these information compilers had an impossible task, particularly since they did not, at the time, understand the difference between actual survival, where your life is at stake and you are trying to extricate yourself; and outdoor living skills, which Stone Age peoples practiced to make a living off the land. For instance, while Stone Age peoples would take the time, do the hard work, and have the proper tools to process the toxic acids out of

Some survival manuals highlight higher-calorie foods, like acorns. Unless these are sweet, low-tannin acorns (a rare thing), the processing burden is great. They would take lots of time, energy, water, and a way to leach out the toxic tannic acid to make them wholesome enough to eat. Too complicated for a real survival situation. Interesting, and rewarding if you are doing it for fun and have all the time in the world.

acorns, you would be diverted from what you should really be doing—escaping that survival situation.

To be ready if you ever find yourself in a real survival situation, read volumes 1 and 2 of this book series. While the number of plants I cover is limited, the concepts explained are essential. The keys to making effective use of plants in any survival situation are:

1. Studying universal plants that are likely to grow everywhere that humans are (traditional edible plants native to humans).
2. Being able to positively identify these plants at all the stages that produce edible parts, and at those stages that don't.
3. Gaining actual experience using the plants prior to a survival situation.
4. Understanding many of the concepts I cover in general to get the most out of wild foods.
5. Knowing and choosing those plant parts that offer you wild fast food without an unreasonable amount of effort.

Read my books and you will be better prepared food-wise if/when things hit the fan.

The Edibility Test

Another horrific legacy of survival manuals is the edibility test. I cannot think of any circumstance when this test would be more helpful than destructive. What follows is a brief description of the test, when they suggest you use it, and why you should not.

The manuals suggest: If you are not familiar with any plants in an area you find yourself in during a survival incident, the edibility test is one you use to determine what plants are edible. You try small amounts at first, wait a day or some shorter specified time, try larger amounts, wait a day, and so on. Eventually, if you don't experience any ill effects, you assume the plant is edible and add that to your food arsenal. Then you turn to the next unknown to repeat the process. After weeks and months, you will have established many things you can "safely" eat.

Don't do it. Never do it! I would never do it. There are so many problems with this test. For starters, eating unknowns is unnecessary and counterproductive in almost every survival situation. Since there are cell phones, over-population, and roads penetrating most wilderness areas, it takes a unique sort of person to be lost for more than three days anywhere in North America. More important, let's say this test makes you throw up or gives you diarrhea. Guess what? You've just thrown off your electrolyte balance and lost water. You are now sick, useless, dehydrated, and much more likely to die than if you just spent your time trying to get out of there, finding water, or satisfying other immediate needs. With clean water, you can survive for weeks without food. You won't be happy, but you will be alive.

This openness to experimenting with unknowns from survival manuals seems to have given license to testosterone-poisoned wild food enthusiasts who think that all they have to do is taste a plant to determine edibility. If it tastes fine and they have no obvious adverse reaction, they assume the plant is edible. As I've said, flavor is not an indicator of edibility. These people are too lazy or impatient to take the time to learn about plants. Or they suffer from Dunning–Kruger syndrome, overestimating their ability to evaluate plants as food. They are looking for shortcuts to learning. There are even some self-styled ignorant wild food instructors who do the edibility test to demonstrate to the world that they are on the leading edge of wild food research. They are not. Either they don't know how or are not willing to do the actual work required to verify edibility. They declare dubious plants edible on the basis of taste and lack of *obvious* poisoning. They contaminate the cultural knowledge continuum. That is, they pass

TESTOSTERONE POISONING
My tongue-in-cheek way of referring to the fact that testosterone makes males more prone to dumb, dangerous behavior. They are more likely to take unnecessary risks and to take shortcuts due to bravado and impatience.

DUNNING-KRUGER EFFECT
This basically happens when an incompetent individual greatly overestimates their competence, abilities, and skills. In other words, incompetence with bravado, the cognitive bias of the illusion of superior thinking.

on this misinformation via books, articles, videos, or social media and it gets incorporated into the knowledge pool.

The bottom line is that you should determine edibility through expert sources, not by randomly sampling plants you don't know or by believing people who do that.

The connection between wild foods and survival is strong, since many see wild foods as a hedge on surviving disaster. With all of the disasters that can happen, wild foods are a sustenance source that people could depend on. But like any survival hedge, you cannot expect to thrive unless you do your homework before you are in trouble. If you are opening your survival or wild food book for the first time during a survival event, then you will not last long. If you learn plants ahead of time and, more importantly, gain experience using them, then you will be much better off when the unmentionables hit the fan. The added advantage of learning now is that you can enjoy these foods as part of your regular diet even if disaster never strikes.

Chapter 7

Who Gets Poisoned by Plants?

There have been no cases of deadly human poisonings that I am aware of where the person made a reasonable attempt at identifying and understanding the plant prior to eating it.

The vast majority, if not all, of plant poisonings occur because of ignorance, cockiness, laziness, impetuousness, poor source information, and/or unfamiliar terminology. People who put some effort into what they are doing have almost no chance of poisoning themselves. Let's go through these factors, one by one.

Ignorance

Most people who get poisoned by plants have only a vague idea of wild foods and poisonous plants. They have only *impressions* to guide them and can convince themselves, with just a few clues and their own assumptions, that they have found something edible. Sometimes people are lucky; sometimes they are not. Anyone today thinking that they've found wild carrot or any other plant they suspect is edible should look the plant up in a book, on the web, or should ask an expert. The FIRST thing they will see from any responsible source is a warning about poison hemlock. People should not eat anything until they know exactly what they are doing. If they don't want to put the work in, then they should abandon the idea of eating any wild plant.

The typical scenario with hemlock poisoning is: A person sees carrot-like leaves and imagines they have found a wild carrot. They pull up the root, see it is a taproot like a carrot, notice that it is off-white, not orange, and convince themselves its color is due to its wildness. They smell it, getting a carrot-family odor. This intrigues them more. They taste the root, and it tastes good. Sort of carrot-like. Now convinced that they, the genius, have found some new treasure, add the sliced root to their meal and do not live to tell about it. To make these mistakes requires a lack of knowledge, many assumptions about identification and edibility, and a lack of appreciation of the risk.

The remaining reasons listed here all have to do with ignorance of some sort.

Cockiness/impetuousness/laziness

Modern people go to markets where food is set out for you. Everything is pretty much edible and ready to eat. It's easy; you just go in and grab what you want. Novices may believe that wild foods are the same. They believe it should be easy, and they have the brilliance/intuition to identify wild foods without knowing anything or having to do any work. Just find something that "looks" edible, and, if you like the taste, eat it. This seems to happen most often if you are a young, invincible-feeling, testosterone-poisoned male. But this can also happen to *back-to-the-earth* people, who feel that Mother Nature takes such good care of us, and is so nurturing, that our intuition should tell us what is safe. Again, this is nature's way of promoting natural selection. Most responsible people actually do their homework and build wisdom through experience. Great intuition is the result of attaining great knowledge and wisdom.

Poor source information

Nonexpert sources add to general ignorance. Getting your edible wild plant information from survival manuals, ignorant wild food authors (anyone can write a book), or human-interest reporters is dangerous. Seek out real experts and their educational materials. Don't believe something just because someone says it in a book or on the internet. Do homework on your sources.

One of the worst generalizations perpetuated by the survival literature, is that poisonous plants *taste terrible*. In fact, the taste of poisonous plants and their parts ranges from great to mouth burning. The obvious mistake that results from this commonly believed generalization is that if a plant one finds tastes good, it is probably edible.

I repeat: Many poisonous plants taste just fine and you should never assume edibility from flavor.

Misunderstood terminology

Not everyone is familiar with how other cultures refer to food. If a wild food novice hears about *poke salat*, for instance, and finds a plant, they may make a fresh raw salad with young pokeweed shoots and leaves. After eating it, they may have some terrible bowel movements, likely uncontrollably soil their pants, and possibly go to the hospital. A little investigation would have revealed that pokeweed (covered later in this book) is poisonous raw, and that *salat* is an old German/English reference to a cooked dish, not a raw one.

The bottom line for all of this harkens back to the reason for the definition of *edible wild plants* promoted in this series. Once you have properly identified a plant, in order to eat it you must thoroughly research the following: what part or parts are edible, at what stages of growth, and what minimal preparation is required to make the raw material edible. Doing your homework prevents poisonings.

Chapter 8

Avoiding the Chemical Soup

Poisonous chemicals are intentionally sprayed just about everywhere to control weeds and animal pests. In addition, asphalt, railroad tracks, chemical processing plants, heavy metal contamination, like lead, factory effluents, and run-off from farmland pollute much of the land and water we have access to. It is not a pretty picture.

As humans overwhelm the planet, they find more ways to suppress weeds, and especially what they consider noxious weeds. While good land management and mechanical methods of weed removal would be better for the planet, chemicals are easier and temporarily more efficient.

The scientific literature is all over the map about herbicide and toxin uptake by plants. So I will not go into that confusing mess. What I will do is give you some obvious advice about avoiding areas that have been sprayed.

First, let me be clear that almost nowhere on the planet is totally free from pollution in the soil. Organic farms offer much-reduced toxic contamination, but animals and plants grown organically will not be totally free from contamination. All you can do is reduce your intake of undesirable chemicals by making smart choices about where you pick.

The human body is marvelous about detoxifying small amounts of ingested poisonous chemicals. It does not do

The gradient of toxicity in this example runs from highest at the tracks and gravel to less in the ditch, decreasing the farther you get from the tracks. Live plants in the ditch indicate that relatively less toxin has accumulated there than nearer to the tracks. In all cases, whether plants are growing there or not, railroad side ditches are very toxic.

well when you load up on any one of them. You can reduce your intake of any particular toxin by eating a diversity of plants and from a diversity of locations. Washing helps.

Railroad Tracks

The worst place to gather wild foods is by railroad tracks. The older the tracks, the worse the contamination from decades of the following being deposited: herbicides and pesticides, sprayed regularly, to keep the area clear of life that might block the tracks; as well as grease and other petroleum products that drip from engines and all lubricated parts. Toxic creosote, mostly made from coal tar, exudes from the treated railroad ties. Creosote is used to prevent the wooden ties from breaking down. As soon as you see tracks, look for alternative sites to gather.

The distances I am giving you here are my estimates from all the reading I've done on this. But each situation is different, so use your best judgment. The closest I would gather to *still active* tracks is about 20 feet from the bottom of the ditch that runs alongside the tracks. I have less concern about this distance if the tracks are in a low area with hills rising on either side, and more concern if I am downhill from the tracks.

If the tracks cross a small pond, don't gather anything from the pond. If the tracks run alongside a large lake or wetland area, then gather as far from the tracks as possible. If you only eat a rare snack in a thriving green area near railroad tracks, it will likely do you no real harm, but avoid them anyway and don't make a habit of it.

Roadsides

Soft shoulder roadsides are regularly sprayed. A soft shoulder is the hard-packed dirt or gravel along the side of many roads. I used to think that plants did not grow there due to tires regularly compacting the ground. I was wrong. You can often see evidence of this spraying. Sprayed plants

Here you can see that a regularly used multitrack area has a dead zone extending beyond the ditch and up the hillside.

Tanker trucks spray herbicides along soft shoulders to keep plant life away from the road. The white tanker truck here is followed by a van warning you the fresh spray is being applied.

About two weeks after spraying, the dead plants turn brown while ones just a little farther away remain green.

alongside the pavement will be yellow or brown while plants just a little farther from the road will still be green. Recently sprayed plants will be green but wilted, with upper tender stems curved downward. Paved shoulders will also have been sprayed along their edges.

To make matters worse, cars deposit their own toxins along the roadside. Petroleum-based tire wear, leaking batteries, coolant, oil, and other things are constantly being deposited on the roads and washed into the ditches. Then of course there is the exhaust carbon and other matter being pumped into the air. Exhaust gets spread widely, while most other toxins remain near the pavement.

Asphalt itself is petroleum-based and filled with toxins. Cement roads do not contribute toxins like asphalt. So don't collect plants near the edges of parking lots made of asphalt. I would not gather closer than 3 feet from them.

I typically don't gather plants any closer than about 8 feet from the far side of the ditch of a moderately traveled road, and about double that for a more highly traveled road. Small country roads with lots of weeds in their ditches indicate only a small amount if spraying. I am happy to gather just 3 feet on the far side of the ditch on those.

Curbed shoulders in suburban neighborhoods will not typically be sprayed. Under this circumstance, you need to evaluate if it is a highly trafficked area. My neighborhood with curbs has such light traffic that I do not mind occasionally picking from the verge. The verge is that area in between the sidewalk and the road. However, I still evaluate each unique situation.

Never gather plants from roadside ditches. If you don't have a good, clean swamp in your area, the only other place you might see cattails is in roadside ditches. Anywhere you see cattails, there is a great temptation to gather the spikes or pollen. But, before you do so, take into account everything I've said so far. There will be very few if any ditches that are clean enough to gather from.

Right-of-ways along power lines may see a combination of mowing and herbicides to keep the plant life down. These open areas can also promote a greater diversity of species than found under the surrounding trees.

Bases of Utility Poles

Telephone poles and other wooden utility poles are treated with creosote and other chemicals like arsenic. Those toxins seep into the adjacent soil, so don't gather anything near their base. Used railroad ties that people sometimes use for landscaping or to frame raised garden beds are filled with creosote and other antibiologic chemicals to preserve the wood. You should not eat plants growing within about 8 inches of treated landscaping wood. Wooden decks with treated lumber leach their chemicals into the surrounding soil. Since they are raised, material wear-off can spread more. So don't gather closer than about a yard from the base of a deck.

Power grid right-of-ways running across cities, rural areas, and through forests may be sprayed. The power companies have to keep the vegetation down to service the power lines. While there is a lot of mechanical mowing of these areas, herbicides are used when necessary or convenient.

That Damn Grass

If a lawn has no diversity of plants in it, assume that it and the surrounds are regularly sprayed to kill broad-leaf and other weeds. Don't get me started on grass. It is the bane of native plants, taking over many areas, choking out its competition. It takes huge chunks of time, energy, money, and water to maintain. Whoever started this lawn thing was probably the same guy who invented golf courses.

If a lawn has been left for several years and is filled with a diversity of plants, then it is relatively safe to gather from. Years of biological activity will have broken down and washed away most of the toxic contaminants. In fact, one of the standards for classifying land as organic for farmers is three years free of any spray and no indication of unsafe levels of heavy metals. Soil organisms, weather, and time can do wonders for land left abandoned.

Note that not many wild plants will thrive in old grass environments with hard, dry compacted soil. Lots of moisture from rain can improve the wild plant situation greatly. Some plants, like English daisy, can produce great edible flowers in an old lawn, but their leaves are often small and tough.

Spot Spraying

A fellow spraying toxins on a verge next to a parking lot. These weeds would have been sooooo easy to pull. This is a 1978 photo, but it is still a common practice today.

You regularly see homeowners and professional lawn managers holding a tank while spraying plants with herbicides. It is very disturbing to me to see people who could have just as easily plucked a weed—spraying it to death. It is like they are allergic to bending over or interacting at all with the earth. They are toxifying their own lawn and endangering children and pets who play in that lawn.

Beyond that, there are also city, state, and county herbicide spraying crews who target specific plants on public lands. If they see Himalayan blackberry, Japanese knotweed, or just any plant that annoys them, they will spot spray, targeting foliage and roots of undesirables. The surrounding plants and soil remain untouched. This makes it harder for foragers, in that this spraying could be anywhere, on any land, away from other obvious sources of contamination.

So how do you recognize spot spraying? Fresh spray will sometimes be colored with blue, so you can see

These plants have recovered from being sprayed by herbicide. They show irregular bends in the stem that are not explained by growing around obstacles or interfering vegetation. On the left is winter cress, on the right is blackberry. These two images are not at the same size scale relative to each other.

remnants of the blue on leaves and stems, even if dried, and sometimes the ground. But you cannot depend on that since some sprays are clear. If plants are wilting at their tops near to others that are not, that area has just been spot sprayed.

Poisoned plants typically wilt or bend at the tender upper parts of the stem where fiber has not yet been deposited and growth is still occurring. If poisoning is complete, the plant dies. It turns black or light brown and bends completely over where the stem is still tender. Many poisoned plants recover. Recovered plants show irregular bends in the stem that are not explained by interfering vegetation. Bends can occur naturally as a plant grows around obstacles. But if you see bends and there are no obstacles forcing those bends, it is likely that herbicides were sprayed in that spot.

If you see a bare spot surrounded by regular growth with no good reason for the bareness, assume that spot has been sprayed. Bare areas will not be totally bare—you'll see brown remnants of dead herbaceous plants and stems matted down at ground level. If the spot had Himalayan blackberry or Japanese knotweed, new sprouts may be poking up, since their roots are hard to kill.

A relatively bare spot surrounded by some of the Japanese knotweed that spot sprayers were trying to kill.

There is no way to cover all the potential contamination that you will encounter, so just pay attention. Don't just look for plants, evaluate where they are growing.

Now that you know how to more safely gather, let's move on to Part II, the edible wild plants covered in this book.

Part II
The Plants

This part of the book covers just a few of the hundreds of wild plants you could be eating from your yard, garden, neighborhood, woodlot, fallow field, wetland, meadow, and organic farm. The plants covered are important and common wild foods, presented here with the purpose of giving you the detail and photographs necessary to know them well. More plants will be covered in future planned volumes of this series.

These delectable wild foods are widespread in North America, Europe, and most places Europeans have migrated to over the last three centuries. The better the soil conditions and moisture and the more these plants are growing in their own seasons, the lusher their growth.

There are big differences in flavor and texture between parts gathered in their prime and ones that are too old. Some can go from delicious and tender to rank and chewy, so pay attention in the following chapters for how to determine when these plant parts are at their optimal for picking.

Plants are grouped into six sections: foundation, tart, pungent, bitter, sensory-sweet, and poisonous. Each plant within these sections has its own chapter, following the plant from emerging seedling to end-of-life seed production, from foraging to food, from preparation to eating. The content runs from basic to advanced, always with an eye on what you really need to know to make good use of these plants. Each chapter starts out with a brief summary of some facts found within. But, as you will come to learn, the devil and the angels are in the details.

One note on poison hemlock. Young hemlock is compared side-by-side to wild carrot in the carrot chapter since that is when the two plants are confused. What isn't covered in those comparisons is covered in hemlock's own chapter. I try to clearly label it as poisonous whenever it appears. If you want to fully know poison hemlock, you will need to read both chapters.

Foundation Plants

Foundation plants is the category I use to describe those plants that offer mostly mild green flavors when they are at their prime stages of development. These greens, vegetables, roots, flowers, and fruits are suitable for almost every occasion and will be accepted by almost anyone who doesn't hate the sight of vegetable matter. Their mild flavors can serve as the neutral base for dishes containing stronger-tasting vegetables.

Don't let my use of the term *mild* fool you. These vegetables have their own characteristic flavors and textures. They are delicious by almost any standards. Served fresh (all here but pokeweed), they are excellent in salads, eaten as snacks, added to sandwiches, used as garnishes, and made into pestos as well as other greens-based sauces. Cooked, they can take the place of almost any vegetable in any recipe book you have.

Foundation plants can be nutritional powerhouses, packed with nutrients and phytochemicals.

The plants covered in this section of volume 2 include cattail, nettles, marsh mallow, pokeweed, bull thistle, and purple sweet nettle.

For reference, foundation plants covered in volume 1 of this book series are:

- Wild spinach (*Chenopodium album*)
- Chickweed (*Stellaria media*)
- Mouse-ear chickweed (*Cerastium vulgatum*)
- Mallow (*Malva neglecta*)
- Purslane (*Portulaca oleracea*)

Family: Typhaceae
Species: *Typha latifolia*

Cattail

A cornucopia of amazing food all year long.

The male cattail spike at the stage where it is beginning to release its pollen, right around the summer solstice.

Estimated Range

Official Species Name:
• *Typha latifolia* L.

Synonyms:
• None

Common Names:
• Cattail
• Common cattail
• Broadleaf cattail
• Cat-o'-nine tails
• Reed mace
• Bullrush

Herbaceous perennial wetland species that spreads easily by thick underground rhizomes. It's common all over the world, more common north of the equator. Widespread and abundant in North America and Europe.

Edible Parts:
Belowground:
• Rhizome shoot
• Rhizome core
• Corm

CATTAIL

The cattail is one amazing plant. It was a staple food for first peoples all over the planet, and it produces more foods over more seasons than any other wild food I know. It is the first plant anyone serious about self-reliance should learn. It grows fast, spreads easily in shallow wetlands and moist soils, and is just plain fun to harvest and use. Of the ten edible parts I've listed, flavors are mild and range from average to delicious. Some parts you can eat as is; some need processing.

Exact foodways surrounding cattail are historically scarce, but its general edibility is widely known and documented. Our focus is food, but cattails were used for many other purposes too. The seed head fluff serves as insulation for clothing, bedding, and shelters, and are used to stuff diapers as an absorbent. The fluff also makes an excellent flammable tinder for starting campfires. A torch can be made from the brown seed head if dipped in a flammable material. The large strap-like leaves were woven into mats, chairs, shoes, and temporary shelters. Long fibers extracted from the leaves can be used to make natural clothing. The massive biomass of the roots could be used to produce ethanol. And the potential of the mucilage in the roots and the thick liquid between the tightly wrapped lower leaves has yet to be explored. This plant offers great potential.

Briefly, in the 1950s, Syracuse University was the home of the Cattail Research Institute, headed by Leland Marsh, its primary investigator. Without visiting the university archives in person, I could not find any lasting record or papers generated by it. But there are interesting papers describing the potential of cattail for food and many other purposes that are worth a read. (Lovering, 1956, Marsh, 1955, Morton, 1975, Reed, 1955). A whole book could be written about the cattail as food, but I give you the most significant material in this, the longest chapter in the book.

There is only a smattering of nutrient information on various parts of the cattail. It all needs to be expanded and updated. But here are some of the findings. The tender

continued

overlapping leaf bases are higher in fiber than most plants. The pollen is high in protein, carbohydrates, and fiber, low in fat, but hasn't been studied much for other nutrients. The seeds are about 18 percent fat (Reed, 1955), 70 percent of which is linolenic acid (Marsh, 1955), an omega-3 fatty acid.

Knowing Cattail

This chapter will provide you with enough detail to delve seriously into all its important food uses.

This plant can reproduce by seed or by underground stems called rhizomes. Seedlings are grass-like and almost impossible to find. Most of what you will see in nature are rhizomes, providing fast, robust plant growth that vastly outpaces seedling growth.

Rhizomes

Rhizomes are underground stems. They serve to store and transport energy and nutrients to growing parts of the plant. The energy stored by rhizomes comes mostly in the form of carbohydrates, with small amounts of protein.

Here is the rhizome's story. From seed, cattail germinates into a grass-like seedling. As it grows leaf blades up and roots down, a fattening corm begins to form at the base of the plant. Once the plant and its corm grow

Aboveground:
- Basal overlapping leaf bases
- Central flower stem
- Gestational flower spikes
- Immature male flower spike
- Immature female flower spike
- Pollen
- Seeds

CORM WITH AN M

A **corm** (with an *m*, as opposed to corn, with an *n*) is an enlarged stem at the base of a plant, typically at or below the ground. It is continuous with and at the base of the stem.

A cattail plant uprooted, showing new developing rhizomes on the left and a mature rhizome on the right that is storing food. The corm, the starchy base stem, hidden by the roots here, gives rise to the rhizomes and to the tightly packed leaves that reach upward from it. Everything below my thumb is typically growing under the mud, below the water.

large enough, energy goes to producing rhizomes, which emerge outward from the corm. The corm is like the hub of a wheel with the rhizomes being the spokes growing out and away from the plant. Under most conditions, everything except the leaves is under the water and in the underlying muck.

These rhizomes are primarily storage organs so the plant packs them until they are full. They can be up to an inch in diameter and vary greatly in length, from a few inches to a couple of feet long, depending on environmental conditions. Rhizomes grow roots and have the potential to either go dormant to overwinter, or to begin to create a new plant from their tips. Rhizomes are a form of asexual reproduction.

Most new cattails grow from the tips of rhizomes and not from seed. All that stored energy allows a new plant sprouting from it to grow rapidly, outpacing other competing plants. As the new plant grows, the rhizome's contents are cannibalized to promote new growth wherever it is needed. The life literally gets sucked out of it. The depleted rhizome shrivels some and begins to die. In summary, the energy is created in one plant, moves to the rhizome, then moves to create a new plant, which creates new rhizomes,

An excavated cattail patch, exposing the rhizomes that would otherwise be hidden underground (under muck in a pond). This was a patch that was immersed in water for part of the year, but the ground dried enough in fall to make digging by hand very easy. I carefully dug around the existing rhizomes to expose their natural growth patterns. The depth of the hole is about 10 inches. The corm is located where the upright stem and rhizomes meet. The stem grows up and the rhizomes grow out from the corm on each of these plants. The thin fibrous material coming off of them are roots.

each of which creates new plants. Young, newly formed rhizomes are the source of what I call *cattail asparagus*. Mature rhizome cores provide *cattail starch*. Both will be discussed later in this chapter.

The corm grows under the mud, provides an anchor for the plant, stores food, and is the source of rhizomes. I will not be covering the corm as food in this book since I have not had enough time experimenting with it. It is quite hard and fibrous, but may have potential as food.

Young plants

As a new plant grows, many leaves emerge and grow upward from the corm. Leaves wrap tightly around each other forming what I am calling a pseudo-stalk. As the plant grows taller, leaf bases continue to stay wrapped around each other while just above the base they spread out. For the first part of the season, the pseudo-stalk near the base is completely made up of tightly wrapped leaves. It looks like a stem in that it is thick, round to oblong in cross section, and is sturdy enough to hold itself upright. To demonstrate that there is no stem, you can pry the structure apart leaf by leaf.

The leaves spreading out from the plant are strap-like, smooth, and flat, typically anywhere from 3 to 6 feet long. In contrast, similar-looking iris and calamus leaves are often shorter and ribbed into a *V* shape with a central vein.

Young cattail plants emerging from rhizomes under the water. The tightly wrapped leaf bases form a pseudo-stalk while the upper parts of the leaves spread outward.

Cattail has two kinds of stalks, one of just leaves, the other with a flower stalk at its core. On the left: The faux stem, a pseudo-stalk, made up of tightly wrapped leaves on a young plant. No flower stalk is present. On the right: A flower-producing stalk has formed at the corm and is growing up through the center of the tightly wrapped leaves.

Yellow Iris—Poisonous

Iridaceae

Iris pseudacorus

Toxic look-alike

There are many iris species, but the common ornamental yellow iris shares some superficial similarities that might cause it to be confused with cattail. It is also known as yellow flag. At early stages of growth, before the yellow flowers appear, its strap-like leaves give it a cattail look. Iris never gets as tall as cattail.

This iris and cattails inhabit the same exact habitat. They grow along the edges of ponds, both in and out of the open water. Their roots need to be exposed to saturated ground in either case.

Yellow iris grows in dense populations in standing water and along the edges of ponds, just like cattails.

Iris plants are easy to distinguish from cattails after flowers have emerged. In order for the flowers to appear, iris sends up a stalk that, like cattails, arises from between the already-formed long leaves. Once the stalks are 2 to 3 feet tall, buds and flowers appear. The flowers are typically up to 4 inches across. Several flowers can inhabit each stem, arising from where stem leaves meet the stem. The stalks mostly max out at about 5 feet. Cattail stems grow taller, are unbranched, and produce a long, green, unshowy reproductive spike at the tip.

Once in flower, yellow iris is easy to distinguish from cattail.

Left: Cattail leaf bases of the pseudo-stem are rounded. Right: Iris leaves are V-shaped. They wrap around each other in a different pattern than cattail leaves do. These V-shaped leaves clearly overlap each other in a left-right-left-right pattern. Cattail's overlapping leaves together give a rounded appearance in cross section. Iris bases where the leaves all come together give a thin, flatter look.

Iris rhizomes are densely covered with hairy roots. Root removal reveals that the underlying rhizome has a more highly segmented pattern than cattails and is reddish orange on the inside. That color is very apparent once you cut into it.

Iris leaves have similarities and differences to cattail leaves. If you look at the base of each plant where the leaves originate, you see those leaves wrapped tightly around each other. Leaves on one side wrap around leaves of the other side creating a pseudo-stem prior to the real stem emerging. The most obvious difference is in the shape of that wrap.

Cattail leaf bases show that wrap as rounded. Outer leaves encircle inner leaves. Iris leaves clamp over other iris leaves at a sharp angle so that their midrib is pointed outward.

Iris leaves have a hard-angled wrap at their pseudo-stem. In other words, they fold over each other creating overlapping "V" shapes. The older outer leaves clamp over the newer younger leaves. This hard-angled clamping creates a two-dimensional rib that you can see and feel in the leaves as they spread out independently above the pseudo-stem. Long cattail leaves will look and feel flat, with no mid-rib as they spread out above their pseudo-stem.

Iris rhizomes are very different than cattails. They are various shades of reds and yellows on the inside with a fibrous outer covering. Cattail rhizomes are off-white. The only way that a novice would accidently mistake iris rhizomes for cattails is if they know nothing about either one. This is how people get poisoned. They hear that cattails have a rhizome, they see strap-like leaves in a pond, they dig the rhizome, they marvel at how red it is, and eat it. Poisoning occurs. The fact that you are reading this chapter makes you relatively immune to that kind of mistake. It is my assumption that a rare livestock poisoning attributed to cattails was really the animals eating iris rhizomes.

Cattail leaves (the two on the left) are strap-like, smooth, and flat. Yellow iris leaves (the two on the right), in comparison, are angled (V-shaped) at the center creating a ridge when you try to flatten the leaf. If you look close, you can see the center ridge here. Iris leaves are about the same width as cattails, but are more tapered near the tip.

Calamus

Acoraceae

Acorus calamus and *Acorus americanus*

Edible look-alike

Also known as "sweet flag," calamus is a wetland plant with strap-shaped leaves similar to cattail and yellow iris. The native *Acorus americanus* and the introduced *Acorus calamus* are identical for our purposes. They are smaller in stature than cattails, with leaves about 2 to 4 feet long. According to others, the whole plant has an aroma reminiscent of tangerine. My experience with calamus is limited and I have not studied it in enough detail to report about its true edibility. Fernald (1958) reported that the young spring shoots were a vegetable, and the rhizomes were boiled in syrup to make candy.

I mention the plant since it grows where cattails do, has similar leaves, and produces a rhizome. The root is said to be bitter and is banned as a food by the FDA (FDA, 2022). The fact that the rhizome was used medicinally should give one pause. So while calamus is an "edible" look-alike of cattails, it could also have parts that require special attention to be edible. I list it here only to show it for physical comparison.

Calamus grows in shallow water and has strap-like leaves reminiscent of cattail. The leaves spread out from the base, apparently not forming a significant pseudo-stem. Photo Courtesy of H. Zell (User Llez), Wikipedia Commons.

Left: Flower spikes of calamus rising off leaflike stems. The leaves have a midrib and may be smooth or wrinkled. Photo Courtesy of H. Zell (User Llez), Wikipedia Commons.

Above: A calamus rhizome can create new plants at each segment along its length. There are many segments sometimes partially, tightly overlapping each other. This is a young rhizome. Older ones get thick with many rings representing segments. The roots hanging down from the rhizome are often thick and prominent, sometimes coming off like a thick mat of material. Calamus rhizomes are clearly aromatic, having a smell reminiscent of citrus. In contrast, cattail rhizomes typically create new plants at their growth tips (ends), not all along the rhizome. The roots coming off its rhizome are sparse and less prominent. While the cleaned rhizome may smell fresh and plain (never citrus), it can also smell like rotting organic swamp gas under the right conditions. Not to worry, if the cattail rhizome is good, once you peel off the rind, the swampiness will disappear. The same swampy smell can happen on the surface of any material pulled from the muck, including calamus. Photo Courtesy of Dennis Stevenson, New York Botanical Gardens.

Above: Close-up of the flowers on the calamus flower spike. The geometric pattern of tiny individual flowers is striking. Tiny yellow anthers surrounding each green pistil. Photo Courtesy of Dennis Stevenson, New York Botanical Gardens.

The cattail flower stalk

One of the most exciting and misunderstood parts of the cattail is the flower stalk. It alone offers six of the 10 edible parts of this plant. Two or more of those parts are available within a month's period around the summer solstice in Earth's northern hemisphere.

At a certain point of maturity, a solid stem begins growing up from the corm through the center of the tightly wrapped basal leaves. So a real stalk is now growing in the center of the pseudo-stalk. The first signs of flower stalk development are difficult to see in a field of leaves. The

Cattail Flower Spike development. On the left (A), the stalk and immature flower spikes are surrounded by/hidden by leaves. Soon, the flower heads (spikes) emerge and grow past the leaves. Some leaves fall off. Some leaves have been trimmed, particularly in (B) to improve your ability to see spike development. The center stalk (D) shows the immature male pollen spike at the top with the immature female seed spike below it at a prime time for collection. Next, the yellow pollen is released from the maturing spike to drop by gravity and pollinate the lower female spike. On the far right is the iconic brown "cattail" that you see in floral arrangements packed with fully developed seeds and fluff.

leaf-wrapped "stem" begins to stiffen somewhat, and leaves begin originating on the stem rather than just from the corm. This stem is a long, solid cylinder about the diameter of a pencil. You can see this stem in cross section in the image back on page 55.

Eventually you will see a set of short leaves radiating upward from the top of the now true stem. This area of the stem (Stalk A) is somewhat thicker and more substantial than the lower part of the stem because the immature flowers are forming underneath the clasping leaves.

As the stem matures, it develops two flower spikes. The male pollen spike is on the top, at the end; the female spike is directly below it, clearly shown in spike D. The spikes are, with few exceptions, continuous with one another. *Typha angustifolia* (narrow-leaved cattail), a thinner species of cattail, differs from *Typha latifolia* (broad-leaved cattail) in that it has small, much narrower leaves, a smaller diameter stalk (pseudo and regular), and there is a distinct gap between the male and female flower spikes. *Typha latifolia* is the predominant species in North America. Both can be used the same ways outlined in this chapter, but *Typha latifolia* produces more food overall.

While broad-leaved cattail typically has no gap between male and female spikes, it can happen by natural variation. Narrow-leaved cattail is pretty regular about having a gap. And there is always cross-pollinating that can cause hybrids. But, fear not, confusing the two will not have any worrisome consequences, since their edibilities are the same.

The male spike is a tight arrangement of thousands of tightly packed male flowers mostly composed of anthers, the pollen-containing structures of a flower. All those anthers are attached to the underlying plant stem.

Cattail flowers transform from immature to mature once they begin releasing their pollen. Pollen matures starting at the top of the spike, and over several days progressively matures downward. You can see this on the

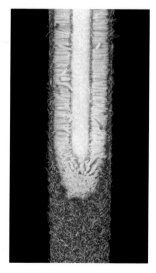

The male pollen spike with some of the anthers cut away to show you the underlying structure. Each anther represents a separate flower.

photograph showing spike development (E and F). The pollen is heavy and drops downward over the female spike. Once all the pollen falls, all that is left of the male spike is the underlying flower stem and empty pollen sacks that were holding in the pollen (top of G). Eventually all remnants of the male flowers fall away except for part of the stem that held the whole thing up.

The immature (unpollinated) female seed spike starts out lighter green than the male spike. It is made up of thousands of tightly packed pistil flowers. Once they receive pollen from the male spikes, seed development can occur. As the seeds mature, the female spikes expand and change from green to brown, resembling a corn dog on a stick. Seeds are fully mature when the spikes are fat and brown. Mature brown spikes are made up of thousands of tiny seeds embedded in a cotton-like fluff. It has been estimated that there are around 300,000 seeds in a single head (Lovering, 1956). As this fat brown seed head is abused by weather, it eventually breaks apart, allowing the wind to propel the fluff carrying the seeds to find new locations in which to plant themselves.

Fully mature female cattail head containing seeds and fluff. That brown corn-dog-like thing breaks apart and fluffs out to release its seeds to the wind. All that remains of the pollen spike is that tiny remnant at the top.

I do not go into the process in depth here, but it is possible to collect a lot of mature seed heads to burn off the fluff and eat the seeds (Harrington, 1933). They are tiny, so you would need a lot of seed heads to acquire any usable mass of food material, like to grind them into a flour. Gathering tons of seed heads is easily done where cattails flourish.

After seed production is accomplished, the cattail leaves and stem eventually pump all their remaining energy from photosynthesis into the rhizomes. The aboveground plant turns brown and dries out. Its rhizomes survive for the next growth season, and the cycle begins again.

Gathering

Foraging in wetlands can be more fun if you do not have to contend with mosquitoes, black flies, and no-see-ums sucking the blood out of you. When I lived in Michigan, these pests were a big problem. In the Pacific Northwest, particularly around Portland, Oregon, these pests are almost no problem at all. In problem areas, I recommend full-body protection: a mosquito mesh hat, thick clothing, and tight-fitting leather gloves. See page 81. Or if you just want to feed the wildlife, gather in your birthday suit.

Where you gather is an important consideration. Make sure the water is not polluted. Roadside ditches will accumulate pollution and runoff from local traffic. Never gather adjacent to railroad tracks or if upland sources of pollution are dumping toxins into the streams feeding the cattail's water. Use common sense when gathering cattails and any wild food.

Cattail seeds are tiny. That is the tip of my first finger in the shot.

Gathering rhizomes

The best rhizomes are fat, straight, and long. Fat means there is more food in the core. Straight and long makes for efficient extraction of starch using methods I'll show you here. Conditions that promote these shapes are soft soil that is immersed in water all year with no obstructions (rocks, tree roots, other rhizomes) that rhizomes have to twist around while growing. So if you want to go for a swim, the growing edge of the cattail patch facing the water of a pond or lake should have the best rhizomes. Digging while floating or standing on muck in deep water makes for difficult gathering. Most of the time you will want to gather in shallow water or on dry land. If you are fortunate to have a patch that dries before seasonal rains, you might be able to carefully lift rhizomes up out of soft, rich dry soil with your bare hands.

Cattail rhizomes are available all year. To gather sustainably (if your supply is limited), do so after seed has been dropped in late summer and don't take more than one-tenth of a stand. Many cattail patches are so large that you can gather all you want at any time of year. Forty to 60 percent of what you find will be old, depleted rhizomes that are best left to decompose in nature. From fall, after the aboveground plants have died to just after the last freeze of winter are the best times to gather rhizomes. During this time, there is more food packed into the rhizomes themselves. Once the growing season begins, that stored food will get distributed into new rhizome shoots and new plants.

Do your best to dig rhizomes by hand so that you do not damage them. Shovels and other metal digging tools are useful for making a starter hole, but after that use your hands to carefully extract the rhizomes. Breaking rhizomes makes them less usable since it allows dirty water to contaminate the broken and smashed cores (where the food is). In water, muck, or soil, work your way around the rhizome until you can free it. Do not pull and tug forcefully or you will break it. If you want to raise the plant upward, do not pull from above; dig down around and below each rhizome and lift upward. Favor keeping straight rhizome segments that are around 1 inch in diameter and more than 7 inches long. Crooked and short pieces are difficult to process for the technique I will explain here.

Once they are freed from the wetland, you will need to clean and process the cattail rhizomes. You can do much

John Kallas, holding a line of cattail rhizomes excavated during a cattail workshop at Wild Food Adventures. Photo Courtesy of Rico Loor, 2011.

of this on-site if there is plenty of water to swish the rhizomes in. To finish the job, it would be helpful to transport them to a clean water source to get the remaining muck off. Several rhizomes spreading out from their corm can look like an octopus and can be unwieldy to move without damage. Since I do not typically use the corm (that is holding them all together), I pizza-slice it into as many pieces as there are attached rhizomes. That leaves a sliced partial corm cap protecting the end of each rhizome during transport for final cleaning.

You do not want them to dry out, so carefully stack them wet in a big plastic bag, spray mist them if they need it, and take them to your processing site as soon as possible. Once home, I power wash them with a hose and trim off all the broken, rotten, and otherwise unusable material. Since nature is not here for your convenience, you will end up having a variety of lengths, some not perfectly straight.

Keep them moist while they are waiting to be processed. Fill some tubs with clean cold water, and submerge the now cleaned pieces. These rhizomes are buoyant, so have bricks to place on top to prevent them from floating up out of the water. For my workshops, I put a little chlorine into the water to kill any toxic pond microorganisms that may be adhering to the plant matter. For this process, the optimal pieces to work with are packed with starch,

Cattail rhizomes at various stages of depletion: full at left and depleted on the right. Full rhizomes have larger cores, providing more food for you. If depleted, they get darker and are more flimsy. The depleted ones have less or difficult to manage food for you.

straight, and about 7 to 10 inches long—not including the corm caps.

There are two steps in my process to extract the starch from the cores. You peel off the outer rind, then immediately squeegee each core.

IMPORTANT: For my technique to work, there needs to be some natural moisture remaining in the peeled cores. Peeled cores dry out fast, so each rhizome must be freshly peeled just before you squeegee; you have to process (peel then immediately squeegee) only one rhizome at a time. And work fast. If you peel a bunch of cores all at once and stack them up for later processing, they will dry out and this technique will not work. So peel one, squeegee it, peel the next one, squeegee it, etc. You can briefly soak a peeled core in water if it dries out, but squeegeeing with too much moisture can get slimy and is a mess. It works but . . . well, you'll see. This process done correctly is extremely efficient once you get the hang of it.

PEELING THE RIND TO FREE THE CORE First peoples all over the world ate the peeled cores raw or roasted them first. Once peeled (there are different definitions of *peeled*), there are three basic techniques for extracting starch from cattail rhizome cores: mashing and soaking the cores in water (Gibbons, 1962); drying, cutting or mashing, then sifting the starch from the cores (Thayer, 2006); and my squeegee technique with fresh material (Kallas, 1999). I only cover mine here, since I prefer it and think it is overall the easiest and most efficient method if you follow the directions exactly.

I am simplifying what you are reading here by referring to the edible part of the core as *starch*. In reality, The core is made up of mostly starch with some protein and a tiny bit of fat. I am referring to the inedible fibers running through the core as *hairs*, since that is what they resemble.

The cut ends of the cattail rhizome reveal a white, starch-filled core surrounded by a spongy rind. Your job is

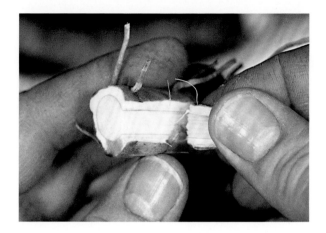

Peeling the rind off the edible cattail rhizome core. Part of the core's hair-like fibers have to be engaged for peeling to work.

to remove the rind and retain as much of the edible core as possible. The core is filled with hairlike fibers running through its length. The spongy outer rind has no fibers. The fibers on the outer edge of the core, where the core meets the rind, can be used to peel the rind just as you would peel a banana. Cut into the end of the rhizome with your fingernail or better, a knife, just barely inside the core. This will engage just enough of the internal fibers to make a clean peel. Pull off and discard the peel. If you cut too deep into the core, you will pull away too much of the core and waste it. If you do not engage the core at all, just piercing the rind, only a small piece of the rind will flake off and no actual peeling will occur. Peel your way around the rhizome until all the rind has been removed. This leaves you with a clean white core with a few stray fibers hanging off.

SQUEEGEEING THE CORE FOR "CATTAIL STARCH" Once the rind has been peeled off, your goal is to press/extract/push off/squeegee the starch away from the hairlike fibers of the core. If you don't remove the fibers—imagine chewing a muffin with fine white hair mixed in—the experience will not be very pleasant. So removing core fibers is important.

APPLY DOWNWARD
PRESSURE HERE

DRAG KNIFE

KNIFE

STARCH
BUILDS UP HERE

CATTAIL RHIZOME CORE

Proper squeegee technique.

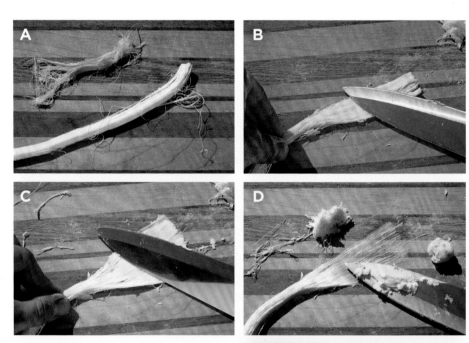

The squeegee process for a peeled cattail rhizome illustrated. (A) The intact core of a peeled cattail rhizome. (B and C) Squeegeeing the core. The starch will begin building up on the underside of the knife until all that is left on the cutting board are fibers. (D) The flipped-over knife shows the starch buildup on the knife. That final chunk (E) represents the starch from about eight cores. To complete the other side of the core you are working on, flip it around, and squeegee away.

Place the just-peeled core on a cutting board, holding down one end. Use any kind of solid, inflexible knife as a squeegee. Either the noncutting side of a butter or chef's knife work well. Use the noncutting edge, because you do not want to cut anything. Your goal is to press, not cut, the starch away from the embedded fibrous material. The core starts out too solid to do this in one sweep.

Here is how you do it as shown by the image with steps A–E: The peeled core (A) ready to squeegee. Hold down one end of the core with your fingers. Place the blade's dull side on the core with the sharp side angled up about 5 degrees *as seen at left*. Press down lightly at first with the dull side of a knife, and sweep across the core as if you are softly petting a pencil (B). With many gentle sweeps, the starch will soften, allowing you to apply more pressure (B and C). As the core begins to soften, it begins flattening out. As you apply more pressure, the starch will begin collecting along the underside of the knife. At some point all of the starch will have been scraped from the core leaving only fibers on the cutting board. Flip that knife over (D) to see the starch that has built up on it. Place the starch in a receptacle or directly into a food dryer. Discard the fibers still on the cutting board, flip the core around to begin squeegeeing its other end. Then move on to begin peeling the next rhizome. This will take some practice.

Troubleshooting: If you press too hard or too soon, fibers will break, mixing into the starch. You don't want that. Broken fibers contaminate the starch. Keep sweeping across, pressing more as the core allows. Occasionally some fibers will get trapped in the starch. Try to pull them out, as they will be annoying later. This takes some practice, so be patient and kind to yourself. Once you "get" it, squeegeeing is fast and easy.

Once you have the starch separated from the fibers, you can use it fresh, or you'll need to dry it right away. If you let it sit in its own moisture, it will begin turning an unsightly tan color. I usually have a food dryer near me

CATTAIL RHIZOME CORE FIBERS

Might cause certain people to begin drooling at the thought of weaving something. While they look promising, core fibers become brittle when dry, so they are not a good raw material for making twine, clothing, nets, or ropes. Their brittleness also means that once the starch you've extracted is fully dried, pulverizing it in a food processor will chop any contaminating fibers remaining in the starch into tiny, imperceptible pieces that can be used as part of the flour you make. These fibers are only good to eat if they get chopped up into minute pieces. Otherwise, you get that hairy mouthfeel.

during the squeegee process, so I can get the starch drying without delay. Once it is dried you can store it in canning jars in this chunky dry form until you need it. The starch must be very dry before you store it. Vacuum-sealing is the best way to keep it from changing in flavor over time.

If you want to make rhizome core flour, you can grind or food-process the dried chunks. If you have a stone grinder specifically designed to make flour, use that. Most people do not have such equipment. Vitamix blenders have a flour blade that is quite good at making flour, but most people do not have that either.

I typically grind the chunky dry squeegeed pieces of rhizome core in a food processor that has four sharp blades. What comes out looks like flour, but it is not. That first grind, when put through a fine filter, reveals how much of it is ground into small enough particles to use like flour. What is left after sifting is all the larger chunks, a lot of them. Unfortunately, food processor blades just bounce small hard pieces around, rather than chopping them up.

Depending on what grinding tools you have, you may find that you have this mixture of various sizes. This is only a problem in that not all of the flour will hydrate at the same rate when you add liquids to recipes. So it would be wise to let food-processor-ground cattail flour sit in its liquids a little bit longer than you would with regular flour, so all the chunks get hydrated fully.

These are the different sizes of grind as the result of using a food processor on dried cattail rhizome cores. There is enough of the two fine grinds on the right to hide all the big pieces on the left when it is all mixed together. For the flour to work like flour, all of your grinding results need to be like the one on the far right, which is fine enough to be sifted through a gold coffee filter.

We've known this starch is edible because first peoples all over the earth have eaten it. To determine its "wholesomeness," first mice, then students at Yale University (Fernald, 1943) ate the starch with no negative effects, except that the students soon after grew long whiskers and tails (see sidebar). Once the core's hairlike threads are removed, that starch is ready to use. You can eat it directly, add it to a recipe as is, or put it in a food dryer. If you add the just-squeegeed core starch directly to a recipe while there is still moisture in it, you will have a problem. The newly squeegeed starch chunks resist blending with other wet ingredients. There is a mucilaginous quality to them that makes them difficult to work with. Try to dry the starch *completely* first; then pulverize it so it can mix with other dry recipe ingredients before you add any liquid.

The raw starch flour is almost flavorless. Once in baked goods, the flavor is reminiscent of potato flour.

In terms of a thickener, the core starch begins to gel in water at around 167°F, and can be used as a substitute for other starches. Its mucilaginous characteristics need to be taken into account for any recipe. Once set/gelled, according to Goering (1968), it has a better cooking and cooling stability than cornstarch.

WHISKERS AND TAILS

Yes, the whisker thing was a joke. If you didn't get that right away, you should reevaluate the choices you've made in your life. But I'll bet those Yale students had more of a penchant for cheese after that experiment.

Rhizome shoots— "Cattail Asparagus"

There is some confusion about the meaning of the term "Cossack asparagus," which refers to cattails in the wild food literature, stemming from the cultural use of cattail by Russians. The term has been applied to the whole plant, to the immature male flower spikes (Medsgar, 1939)—what I would call *cattail corn-on-the-cob*, and more commonly to the edible bases of the leaves (Morton, 1975)—what I call *cattail celery*. The bases of the leaves when blanched are far more mucilaginous than asparagus. If I were to choose a part of the cattail to call *asparagus*, it would be the fast-growing new rhizome shoots. They are solid throughout, edible raw,

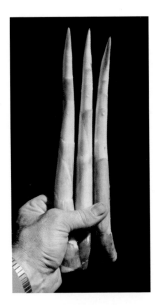

What I consider cattail asparagus, the young growing *shoots* of new rhizomes.

and have no hairlike fibers—an excellent vegetable. Rhizome shoots are the most asparagus-like part of the cattail.

If you want to eat cattail rhizome shoots raw, keep in mind that you just pulled these out of a wetland filled with bacteria and other microorganisms. Some organisms are dangerous to humans. So either wash them thoroughly with soap and water, soak them in a vinegar or bleach solution, blanch them, or cook them before use. Then use them just like asparagus.

To clean and sanitize wetland vegetables that have been exposed to pond water, first rinse them free of any surface dirt and debris then use one of the following:

WHITE VINEGAR: Soak the shoots or rhizomes for 10 minutes in a mix of 1 part of vinegar to 3 parts of water.

CHLORINE BLEACH: Add 1 ounce of bleach to 3 gallons of water. Soak the shoots or rhizomes for 3 minutes. Rinse thoroughly with clean water.

Cattail Celery

Each leaf on a young, pseudo-stalked cattail reaches all the way down to the base of the plant. The lower part of each leaf wraps tightly around the other leaves, creating lots of overlap, giving the illusion of a stem. What I call *cattail celery* is the tender inner white part of the tightly clustered leaves at the base of these plants before a stalk begins forming.

There are two ways to harvest cattail celery: either use a knife to cut low on the plant through the leaves, just above the base, or use the pull technique. Only harvest the fattest rapidly growing young fat stems, since thin ones will not have much food in them.

Freshly cut cattail bases. Some growing a central flower stalk that is solid, others comprising only leaves—encasing the cattail celery. To reach the tender, edible, whitish celery within the leaf-filled stems, the fibrous outer green leaves must be peeled off layer by layer.

For the cut method, go as far down the plant as you can reach and slice directly through it. That gives you the whole plant above the corm. If you cut below the water level, you'll later have to cut off the very end that was exposed to the water.

To use the pull technique, find a suitable thick-based plant. Pry four to six of the outermost leaves outward, all the way down to the base. Then grasp the remaining inner leaves near that base and do a quick pull, snapping directly upward. The tender base of the leaves should snap free, allowing you to pull the plant up. If it does not snap free easily, then you have not pulled away enough of the outer fibrous leaves. Practice will make this an easy, quick harvesting method. This gives you the whole upper plant, minus the few outer leaves you would have peeled off anyway.

Peeling the leaves to reveal the celery

To reveal the edible white "celery," you must peel off the fibrous green upper parts of each leaf. Start by

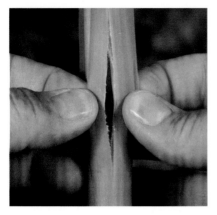

Above: Fully splitting each leaf and peeling them down one at a time prevents damage to the delicate edible parts you are trying to find. Since each leaf wraps tightly around the other leaves, the resistance to pulling is strong. If you split each leaf prior to peeling, only working one-half at a time, the action is much easier.

Above: Cattail celery: what's left after all the fibrous green parts of the leaves have been peeled away. You have layered leaf bases that are white and very tender.

Left: Cattail celery chopped into a salad. The other wild foods include oxeye daisy, cascade sorrel, and lady fern fiddleheads.

removing any outer leaves that are fibrous from their tips to their base. Then, one by one, peel leaves downward until they break away. Each leaf is tender and delicious from that breaking point on down to the base. Keep peeling back leaves until all the upper green is gone and you are left with a white core of leaves, ready to be eaten. If the very base of this piece was exposed to the pond water, then cut it off anywhere you see that dirt has soaked upward.

Tip: Split each leaf lengthwise at the top prior to peeling it down and off—you'll see why this is important with experience. Cattail celery is good for use in salads, soups, and any way you would use regular celery—though this is much more tender. Best eaten raw. It takes on a mucilaginous quality once boiled, which is a great feature if you want to thicken soups or sauces.

Central Cattail Stalk and Gestational Flower Spikes

Since it is buried under layers of leaves, a cattail flower stalk is not easy to see before the flower spikes emerge at the top of the plant. The first clue indicating it is forming is a cluster of upper leaves fanning out. Later, as the spikes emerge, you begin seeing the maturation sequence on page 60. If you locate a stalk prior to the flower parts emerging, you have a chance at finding food from the stalk itself. The younger the stalk, the more of it is still growing and tender. The older/taller the stalk, the more of it becomes too fibrous to eat.

If you find a cattail stem early/young enough, all but the lowest part of that stem will be tender. In fact, if it is young enough, you can even eat the gestational (not quite developed) flower spikes whole. If you find the cattail just as it is beginning to show the flower head, only the center of the stalk will be tender.

To find that edible part, grab a young, still developing stalk and cut it off about a foot above the base. Split and peel off all the leaves. None of the leaves or leaf bases are

A still-growing cattail flower stalk, with all the leaves removed, bending at the center. There is about 10 inches of choice edible stem at the bend in this example. The upper 8 inches, in my left hand, are the fully chewable gestational flower spikes that eventually mature into the male and female flower spikes. At this rapid growth stage, the whole flower area is tender enough to eat.

TENDER GROWING SECTION OF STEM

TENDER GESTATIONAL FLOWER SPIKE

Delicious, crispy, edible growing sections of cattail stalks.

Tender cattail flower stems boiled for 6 minutes, rolled in Italian salad dressing, and sprinkled with Italian spice mix and salt. Garnished with high mallow flowers (*Malva sylvestris*).

tender at this stage. After removing the leaves, you can tell what is tender by where the stalk bends. There is a central point of tenderness where that stem is growing both downward and upward until the flower stalk reaches its full height. Once the flower stalk is at its full height, the whole stem is too fibrous to eat.

To harvest, simply take the stalks, still leaf-covered, home until ready to use. They can last propped up in a bucket of water for a couple of days, but the sooner you peel them, the better. Peel off the leaves using the split-leaf method. Be careful not to bruise the stalks, as they will brown, making them look less appetizing to the finicky connoisseur. Although you can snap them to determine where they are tender, it is best to train yourself to use scissors. First, cut in the clearly fibrous areas, then closer and closer to the tender areas. Once there, the scissors will slice through them like butter. Place the stalk immediately in cold water to slow the browning process on the cut ends. The stalk has a mild, delicious flavor reminiscent of artichoke. Slice stalks into salads or cook them like asparagus.

Male flower spikes

The male flower spikes of cattail are good for eating from the moment they emerge in their gestational stage to the point at which they release their pollen. They change over time. At stage (E) from page 60, they are densely packed flower buds attached to the central stem. They are filled with pollen, becoming fatter and turning a darker green just before they bloat up to release the pollen. They are big pollen-filled sacks. They are fine for eating as a vegetable all the way up to the point where they bloat up.

You can eat them raw, but they are quite dry. The outer coating that encapsulates the pollen grains is hydrophobic (repels water), which results in a dry texture on the tongue. I recommend boiling them for 10 minutes or more. This tenderizes them, eliminates the dryness, and cooks the enclosed immature pollen—making it more digestible,

Raw immature male pollen spike, center. Cattail shavings (anthers/ pollen sacks) on left; shaved spike on far right. Solid or shaved, this makes an excellent vegetable that can be used like broccoli. Shave all spikes with the dull side of a knife.

enhancing flavor, and producing an excellent broth. The flavor is reminiscent of corn silk. The stalk underlying the flowers is too fibrous to eat, so people either pull the cooked flowers off the stalk to add to various dishes, as you would broccoli, or eat them right off the stem like corn on the cob. Use olive oil or melted butter; add some garlic, onion powder, and salt; serve warm. This is a dreamy food. Worthy of a main dish as is, or incorporate it into other things. Delicious.

Female flower spikes

The female cattail flower spikes are good for eating from the time they emerge gestationally from the stem up to just after they are pollinated. Beyond that, they become increasingly fiber-filled, eventually ballooning out into their fat brown corn dog shape. I enjoy them most when they are a bright yellowish green, just prior to pollination—though they are still good before they have expanded much. Conveniently for us, the immature male and female spikes are at their

Left to right: Three edible cattail parts on a dinner plate: central stalks, male flower spikes, and gestational spikes, alongside a wild salad. Served at the 2011 GingerRoot Wild Food Rendezvous.

Boiled female cattail flower spikes, showing the edible parts (pistils) scraped off the underlying stalk. The male spike has been removed and is not in the picture. Scrape using the dull side of the knife.

prime at the same time. The edible "meat" on the female spikes is a thinner layer than on the male spikes.

The raw female spikes are dry, but not quite as dry as the males. They are edible raw. I enjoy them boiled for 10 minutes, like the male spikes. Once boiled, the edible parts are best removed by scraping them off their thick central stalk with the dull side of a butter knife. If you use a sharp side of any blade, you will end up with some fibrous central stalk in the mix, which is miserable to chew. So don't slice; scrape! Both male and female spikes can be used in the same dishes as you would use broccoli. Interestingly, if you soak the scraped-off raw female parts in water, the water will turn reddish.

Freezing cattail spikes

To freeze cattail spikes, boil or steam them for about 4 minutes to kill any enzymes that will break them down during freezer storage. Place them carefully into a vacuum-seal bag, alternating them with large, preferably squarish, chopsticks; then vacuum-seal the bag. The chopsticks provide a framework to prevent the shrinking bag from damaging the spikes.

Cattail spikes interspaced with chopsticks to maintain their shape during vacuum-sealing. A vacuum-sealed canning jar filled with pollen is on the left. I store both in the freezer.

A cattail pollen collector in its proper orientation during use in the field. It should be slightly tilted toward the handle. Practice keeping it in this orientation as you carry it so the pollen does not accidentally spill out of the hole. After many prototypes, this design finally came to me in 2004, and I've benefited from it ever since. (Kallas, 2005a)

Cattail Pollen

Pollen is likely one of the most nutritious foods you can get from plant matter. In general, most calories and a wide variety of nutrients come from the reproductive parts of plants. People sell things like bee pollen for exorbitant prices. Cattail pollen is free. Although new research is needed, years ago it was determined that the pollen of *Typha angustifolia* was made up of 25 percent pollenin (mostly protein), 18 percent sugar, 4 percent stearin and olein (oils), and 2 percent starch. (Maiden, 1889)

The cattail pollen collector

You need to be somewhat of a ninja stealthily making your way through a cattail patch to be a successful pollen collector. If you go through a patch like a bull in a china shop, all the pollen will have been knocked off the spikes before you can get to it. One way to control the experience is to have a solid, functional pollen collector. The best one for the task has the following attributes: It is a solid container, white enough to reflect the heat of the sun, but clear enough so you can monitor pollen levels as they build up on the inside. It is long enough to receive at least a 10-inch pollen spike through a hole you cut in its side. It has a handle.

John Kallas in full mosquito gear gathering cattail pollen near Sandpoint, Idaho, 1979. The stalk has been bent over so the pollen-packed spike can be shaken, releasing the pollen inside the bag. Plastic bags are makeshift collection tools that will work if they are the only thing handy, but are inefficient and not very manageable. A specially designed cattail pollen collector is shown on the opposite page.

POLLENIN

If I understand it correctly, pollenin (sometimes referred to as sporopollenin) is a term given to the tough resistant outer coating of pollen. Pollen coats are made up of a specific kind of protein and lipid structure that is specifically suited for helping the pollen survive until it can rehydrate for the fertilization process. It's specific nutrients and digestibility have not been studied. If human digestive enzymes and gut microflora can break it down, it would make pollen a huge source of protein. Since gut microflora adjust to the diet, it might follow that the more pollen you eat regularly over time, the more they can break down pollen protein coats for absorption. Moist cooking may also make the pollenin more digestible.

Gallon jugs having all these attributes can be found in most supermarkets. You have to buy them for their contents (iced teas or juices), clean them out, and cut out a 2-inch hole opposite the handle. This extra hole (where you insert the cattail spike) is necessary because the area where the cap is serves as a receptacle for all the gathered pollen. The shape shown in the image here is not a milk jug, because the preferred shape is more tapered and has a larger handle than a milk jug.

You hold this contraption upside down (meaning its cap is facing downward); lift it high; and slowly, carefully, gently guide a pollen-filled cattail spike into its hole. Once the spike is inside, vigorously shake it until all its free pollen is released; then pull it out and go on to the next spike.

Keep track of the pollen level inside the collector. If you let it get too full, you will eventually begin losing pollen out of the side hole you made. Have another container nearby to periodically empty it into. On average, you should get about a teaspoon of pollen from each spike you shake.

If the day is windy, skip collecting. A windy day will knock all the loose pollen off before you can get to it. An alternative to gathering loose pollen is to gather spikes that are bloated and ready to release most of their pollen. Food dryer and vase methods covered next will show you how to extract pollen from the bloated spikes.

Take even more pollen home

Most of the spikes you've shaken will release even more pollen the next day if they have enough expanded material left on them. So if you take those spikes home you can potentially double your take. Here are two methods I've devised.

FOOD DRYER METHOD Place your harvested, already shaken-out spikes in a food dryer. As the spikes dry out they release pollen. Once dry, place the spikes in a sieve and shake out the pollen. This technique is less work than the vase method.

VASE METHOD Cut and harvest the stem, about 2 feet below the already shaken-out spike. Once home, make fresh cuts at the base of each stem and place them in water as you would flowers in a vase. They are, in fact, "flowers" in a vase. Make sure the spikes are spread out and not touching each other as you place them, or mold will develop, destroying it all. Place a sheet of plastic or newspaper underneath to catch any pollen that falls. After a day or two, the spikes will be packed with newly matured pollen. Carefully pull them out one at a time. Using the pollen collector, shake out the new pollen. Put them back in the water, allowing them to continue to mature, until they are exhausted of pollen. This gets you slightly more pollen than the food dryer technique, because the water feeding the stems allows the immature "pre-pollen" to continue maturing.

Beware of mold!

Anytime you harvest cattails, you must be concerned about mold. Cattails love to mold. If any of the spikes are touching each other in your vase, they will mold. If you stack the spikes and leave them on the counter overnight, they will mold. So the moral of the story is to dry them as soon as possible and, if they are not in a food dryer, at least spread them out in a dry place; making sure they are not touching each other!

Refining Cattail Pollen

The pollen comes with many impurities, mostly plant fiber, live bugs, and parts of leaves. So the first thing I do is to shake the pollen through a normal kitchen sieve. This removes most of the larger debris. In fact, the pollen is usable after this first filtering. But it is not pure until you do the following, for which you will need two things: a fine mesh coffee filter, particularly the gold kind, and a vibrating massager. A paper coffee filter will not work.

Above: Cattail flowers in a vase allow the pollen spikes to continue maturing in controlled conditions. Make sure to underlay this with a plastic sheet since pollen will fall as you remove each spike. After you have extracted all the removable pollen from the spikes, you can gather up the pollen that has fallen onto the plastic.

Tools I find useful for gathering and processing cattail pollen. Left to right: pollen collecting container, normal kitchen sieve, fine mesh coffee filter, pollen brush (paintbrush), and vibrating massager. The stronger the vibration, the better.

Vibrating coffee filter technique for refining cattail pollen. The vibrating massager shakes the filter with such vigor that the pollen pours right out of its minute holes, while the filter holds back any contaminants.

Pour the initially filtered pollen into the coffee filter. Hold the massager tightly against the filter. The rapid vibrating action allows the tiny pollen grains to pour out of the filter at a speed you could never do by shaking it yourself. The refined pollen is very pure, mustard yellow, and has a texture reminiscent of corn-starch. Don't sneeze into it! Use a brush to move the pollen from surfaces it sticks to, to where you want to put it.

At this point, the pollen is ready for use. Again, I emphasize the mold issue. If the pollen, refined or not, is not thoroughly dry, it will mold.

Storing Pollen

To maximize pollen quality, I dry the pollen thoroughly before any kind of storage. Once dried, store it in sealed containers in the freezer until you are ready to use it. If you want it to last forever, vacuum-seal the dried pollen in mason jars and store it in the freezer. Many of the vacuum-sealing appliances, known for sealing food in specially adapted bags, have mason jar attachments.

Drying cattail pollen in a food dryer. Cups are used to contain the pollen so it does not disperse or blow away when the dryer fan is turned on. Dryer spacers are used to increase the depth of the dryer compartment so the cups will fit. A top fits over this (not shown) before the food dryer is turned on. Use the lowest heat setting that the dryer allows, usually 95°F. Give it at least 4 hours.

Pollen as an Ingredient

Cattail pollen is delicious and has a wonderful aroma. Its unique flavor adds yellow color to foods if used strategically. The pollen can be eaten raw sprinkled on popcorn and fruit salads, or mixed into oatmeal, porridge, grits, rice, quinoa, and the like. It can be added to soups, stews, and sauces. It is best known for its use as a flour-like component of baked products.

When working with pollen, consider that it is hydrophobic (repels water) and gluten free and has a flavor that you do not want to mask or hide with other ingredients. Since it does not mix well with water, plan to mix it with other ingredients before adding the water. If you are going to bake with it, mix it well with other dry ingredients prior to adding wet ingredients.

As a gluten-free ingredient, pollen does not contribute to the rise you see in baked products that use yeast or other leaveners like baking powder.

I prefer whole wheat flour when baking for the clear nutritional benefits. However, when I make cattail baked goods in my workshops I always use white flour as an ingredient. White flour accomplishes two things; it allows both the yellow color and the unique flavor of the cattail pollen to shine, because it is not contributing much of its own flavor and color. I want my students' first experience with cattail pollen to be as clear and dynamic as possible. However, in my own everyday baking, I use whole wheat flour and can easily taste the pollen deliciousness. After your first experiences baking with pollen, I recommend transitioning to mixing the pollen with whole grains.

All of pollen's nutritional goodness can be digested and utilized by the human body except possibly its tough outer covering, the pollenin. Pollen is food for your gut microflora. At just less than 20 micrograms in size, raw pollen grains can enter the bloodstream undigested (Linskens, 1997). I have not been able to determine what it does in there, good or bad. I have heard no reports of problems.

Past cultures have eaten pollen, I eat it, my students eat it. I have seen no apparent problems, except a few students grew antennas and stingers after a couple of weeks, a persistent problem. Those symptoms subsided when they were fed royal jelly and are now normal functioning members of the entomological society. However, their dating life is still suffering.

Cattail pollen has not shown any significant allergic response (Durham, 1951). I have never experienced myself nor seen any reports of cattail pollen being a food or nasal allergen. None of my students with nasal allergies have ever reported a problem with cattail pollen. But, as with any new food, pay attention to your body when you gather or ingest it.

Below left: Cattail pollen pancakes. Below right: Elderberry flower pancakes made by students at the 2011 GingerRoot Wild Food Rendezvous. Along with the pancakes is Melody Ferris, photo courtesy of her sister and photographer Michelle Ferris.

Cooking and Serving Cattail Pollen

Cattail pollen is waterproof in its raw form. For any recipe you invent, the pollen will either remain as it is (for example, if you sprinkle it on popcorn, where butter or olive oil will allow it to stick), or will have to be mixed in with other ingredients in a way that allows it to incorporate, that is, not float to the surface or clump into water-resistant masses. To allow pollen to mix with water, you will have to selectively combine it with specific ingredients. The pollen will blend in with melted fats, oils, and emulsifiers like egg yolks, honey, and mayonnaise fairly quickly. It will even blend with more water-soluble substances if soaked long enough (like overnight in the fridge). Here are some recipes that use pollen.

Sunshine Pancakes

Makes 20 (4-inch) pancakes

INGREDIENTS

1 cup cattail pollen (see page 83)
2 cups all-purpose flour
6 tablespoons packed brown sugar
1 tablespoon baking powder
1 1/2 teaspoons salt
4 large eggs
1/2 cup safflower oil (any unflavored cooking oil will work)
1 tablespoon vanilla extract
2 cups milk, divided
Safflower oil, to grease the griddle

DIRECTIONS

Preheat a griddle over high heat.

In a large bowl, mix cattail pollen, flour, brown sugar, baking powder, and salt together until well blended.

In a second bowl, mix eggs, safflower oil, vanilla, and 1 1/2 cups milk until well blended.

Gradually add the wet ingredients to the dry, stirring gently. Add the remaining 1/2 cup of milk, a little at a time, until the mixture is thick and still has some dry spots. Stop adding milk when you've reached that point. Let the batter rest for about 5 minutes.

Reduce the griddle heat down to 350°F while the batter is resting. Grease the griddle with oil and ladle the batter on to create 4-inch pancakes. Spread the batter on the burner to gain an even thickness immediately after pouring it on. The pancakes should fry to a golden yellow-brown on both sides. When flipping, flip gently and DO NOT PRESS THEM FLAT. Never press pancakes of any kind flat. If you have done this in the past, it is time to get therapy.

Increase or decrease heat if the pancakes are cooking too slowly or too fast. If they cook too slowly, they will dry up. If they cook too fast, they will burn and be wet in the center. As you remove the cooked pancakes from the griddle, place in a 200°F oven no more than two pancakes deep until served. Cover with a lightly dampened towel so the pancakes won't dry out.

Sprinkle with powdered sugar and serve. Try eating without syrup first to fully enjoy the flavor.

Cattail Pollen–Banana Nut Whole Wheat Muffins

Makes 5 to 6 large muffins

These are great-tasting muffins. They won't rise as much as regular whole wheat muffins, but still have a nice consistency. Pollen gives these muffins a slight yellow glean.

INGREDIENTS

¾ cup cattail pollen (see pages 83 and 84)
¾ cup fresh whole wheat flour
1 teaspoon salt
2 teaspoons double-acting baking powder
2 tablespoons packed dark brown sugar
1 egg, room temperature
1 cup milk, room temperature
1½ tablespoons vegetable oil
½ cup finely chopped banana
½ cup sliced almonds

DIRECTIONS

Preheat oven to 400°F. Prepare a muffin tin by greasing the cups with any vegetable oil or butter.

In a large bowl, combine the cattail pollen, flour, salt, baking powder, and brown sugar until well blended. Set aside.

In a second bowl, lightly beat the egg. Add milk and oil, stirring until well blended. Gradually add the wet ingredients into the dry ingredients, being careful to not overstir. You want to see some unblended flour remaining, and the batter should be somewhat lumpy when you stop stirring. Gently fold in the banana and almonds. Again, don't overstir.

Fill each muffin tin cup about ⅔ full. Bake for 20 to 25 minutes.

Let muffins cool in the tin for 5 minutes before removing to a wire rack. Try not to eat them all at once!

From a wild food perspective, cattails are best known for their green immature male and female pollen spikes. Here are some spike recipes that really showcase these wild ingredients.

Cattail Spike Frittata

Serves 4

INGREDIENTS

4 large eggs
2 tablespoons water
2 tablespoons extra virgin olive oil
1 cup sliced red onion
$1/2$ cup sliced celery
1 cup sliced precooked mushrooms
1 cup shavings of boiled (for
    10 minutes) female and/or
    male spikes (see pages 77–79)
1 teaspoon finely chopped fresh
    rosemary
2 cloves garlic, minced
Salt, to taste
Pepper, to taste

DIRECTIONS

Preheat oven to 350°F.

In small bowl, whisk the eggs and water together until well blended. Set aside.

Pour olive oil in an ovenproof skillet and heat until shimmering. Add red onion, celery, and mushrooms. Stir-fry until the celery and onion begin to wilt. Stir in the cattail, rosemary, and garlic and continue cooking until they begin releasing their aromas.

Pour the eggs over the cooking vegetables and season with salt and pepper. Place the skillet in the oven and bake for 15 to 18 minutes, until eggs are set and lightly browned.

Cattail Guacamole

Makes about 1 cup

INGREDIENTS

> 1 cup boiled (for 10 minutes) female cattail spike shavings (see pages 78 and 79)
> 5 tablespoons extra virgin olive oil
> 2 tablespoons lime juice
> 1/4 teaspoon ground cumin
> 1 small clove garlic, minced
> 1/4 teaspoon salt
> 1/2 Roma tomato, chopped
> 2 tablespoons chopped red onion
> 1 tablespoon chopped fresh parsley
> Paprika, to taste
> Tortilla chips, for serving

DIRECTIONS

Place the cattail shavings in a food processor small enough to manage the amount of shavings (one that is too big will be inefficient), and add oil, lime juice, cumin, garlic, and salt. Process until the ingredients start flowing together. If they do not, add more olive oil in tiny amounts until they do. You can stop here and use this mixture for a spread for sandwiches or just on bread.

To finish the guacamole, stir in the tomato, red onion, and parsley; then add paprika to taste. Dip in your chips and enjoy.

Tip: Let the guacamole rest for an hour after making it (assuming you can wait), to allow the flavors to meld. Stir before serving since the olive oil will separate some from the other ingredients.

Soft Cattail Core Vanilla Pudding

Makes 3 (¹/₂ cup) servings

This is softer than store-bought varieties of pudding. At first I thought this was a failure of my recipe as it did not gel into a solid pudding unless I added more core flour. But as I've learned over and over, each wild food has unique properties. While this pudding does not fully set up and will pour out if you tilt the cup, it is thick on the spoon and in your mouth. It has all the properties of the core. The softness is a feature, not a fault.

INGREDIENTS

   3 tablespoons dried/powdered cattail rhizome core
      flour (see pages 66–71)
   ¹/₃ cup sugar
   ¹/₈ teaspoon salt
   2 cups whole milk
   1 teaspoon vanilla extract

DIRECTIONS

   Mix together: cattail core flour, sugar, and salt. Slowly add milk to the dry ingredients, stirring constantly.

   If you are using fully ground and sifted flour, proceed to making the pudding. If your flour is not fully ground,

let it set for 30 minutes in the fridge so the larger pieces can absorb more of the liquid.

Heat the pudding mixture in a nonstick saucepan over medium-high heat. Use a rubber or silicone spatula to constantly scrape all inner surfaces of the pan so gelling material can be cleared systematically over and over again. You do not want any part of the mixture to solidify where it contacts the pan. Turn the heat down a notch when the mix begins to boil; you just want a slow boil. Don't stop scraping.

Once it begins to thicken, stir in the vanilla and remove from the heat. Pour into three individual serving cups or ramekins. Eat while hot, or place in the refrigerator for a few hours to further set and then serve as a cold dessert. Some skin will form at the top while they are setting in the fridge. That is OK. If you cover them with plastic, like is recommended for most puddings to prevent a skin, much of it will stick to the plastic.

VARIATIONS

If you have plenty of cattail core flour, double the recipe and use a larger saucepan.

If you want a thicker pudding, add $1^1/2$ teaspoons more cattail core flour.

Serve as is, or top with whipped cream, maple syrup, caramel sauce, or fruit.

Sprinkle with cinnamon or confectioner's sugar.

To add a butterscotch-like flavor, use dark brown sugar as a substitution for white sugar.

Your imagination on further additions is unlimited. But note that the more additions you make, the more you will hide the underlying flavor of the cattail.

Chapter 10

FAMILY: Urticaceae
SPECIES: *Urtica dioica*

Stinging Nettle

An amazing food whose sting is a thing.

Young spring nettle plants, perfect for gathering.

STINGING NETTLE

Estimated Range

Official Species Name:
• *Urtica dioica* L.

Synonyms
• None

Common Names:
• Stinging nettle
• Tall nettle
• Slender nettle
• California nettle

Herbaceous perennial native to Europe but naturalized, widespread, and abundant in North America, Europe, Asia, and North Africa. It can tolerate a wide range of temperatures and thrives in moist soil.

Edible Parts:
• Young leafy stems
• Tender leaves
• Flower buds
• New leafy-stem tips on plants not gone to seed yet

It's a beautiful day. Dew is glistening on plants from the morning mist. The sun is out and you are enjoying the first warm days of spring. You wear shorts, a tank top, and squish your toes in the mud. Plants are emerging from the spring rains and warming temperatures. You wander through an open meadow, the edge of a field by a creek, and climb down an embankment, feeling the dew cooling your legs. Then, *Yeeowww*! Your legs are burning. No matter where you turn, the vicious sting is everywhere! You find a clearing hoping for relief. The sting persists. *Ahh*, spring.

The sting of nettles is a defining characteristic that is hard to ignore. This dubious distinction results in a lot of mythology and creative license. From a food perspective, because of their often-hyperbolic reputation (good and bad), nettles seem to play a prominent role even when it minor or peripheral. Here are a couple of examples:

You hear that Cornish Yarg, a semihard cow's milk cheese dating back to the thirteenth century, is made with nettles. Wow, nettle cheese. When I heard this, I thought, OK, I want to make this. However, nettles were not a flavoring ingredient or used to cause curdling; rather, the ripening cheese was just wrapped in its leaves. Is it serving to help flavor the rind or prevent it from spoiling in some way? Are you supposed to eat the rind? Did the nettles merely have a symbolic use—for instance, like protecting the cheese (using the stingers as a shield) from evil spirits? If it was a symbolic use, we've lost its meaning over time. The nettles are not a component of the cheese itself. So when you hear of nettle cheese, check the details.

There is a 6,000-year-old recipe for nettle "pudding." Upon further investigation, I found that this is really a selective name for a savory barley flour pudding. That pudding is a mixture of ingredients enclosed within a cloth bag that is immersed in a pot of simmering meat. The barley creates the thickening agent (the pudding), while the meat broth and the greens help flavor the pudding. Nettles,

continued

How you might first see nettles, when you look down after you are feeling the sting of walking through them with shorts.

sorrel, watercress, dandelion, and chives are the wild greens used. It would be better named "Wild Greens and Meat, Barley Pudding." Calling this "nettle pudding" seems out of proportion.

Medicinally and pharmacologically, nettles have been used to treat arthritis and rheumatism, to aid libido, and used as a general tonic, among other things. They are also being investigated as an antibiotic and for numerous phytochemicals. There is quite a mass of research on the topic, which is beyond the scope of this book. If you are interested in more details, the nutritional and therapeutic value of nettles is ongoing (Joshi, 2014, Said, 2015).

Long fibers of old nettle stems have been an important source of fiber craft. They are very strong and have been used throughout history to make clothing, twine, rope, fishing nets, and other things. These tough fibers are the main reason that old nettle stems are not used for food. This is not dietary fiber here, just nondigestible, stringy, stick-in-the-teeth fiber. Another useful trait is that a green dye can be extracted from nettle leaves. While interesting, both these topics are beyond the scope of this book.

From a plant protein perspective, nettles are a great food. They have been valued due to their high leaf protein. Proportionately, 100 grams of fresh nettle leafy greens has 2.7 g protein, 0.7 g digestible carbohydrate, and 0.1 g fat (USDA, 2019). If you add all that up it only comes to 3.5 percent of nettle's total fresh plant matter. High for greens but greens are not known for their calories, which protein, fat, and carbohydrate provide. If you concentrate those calories by drying and powdering the nettle, it can be a great nutrient and flavor source to add to soups, stews, etc. Like all plant material, nettle protein is not complete protein, but it still can be a great contribution to the overall diet.

The leaves are excellent sources of dietary fiber, omega-3 fatty acids, and calcium. In fact, nettles are the new greens-based champion of omega-3 fatty acids, having 3 to 6 times the amount of our last champion, purslane. Its raw greens apparently provide more omega-3 fatty acids than boiled greens. Both purslane and nettles are excellent sources of this wonderful nutrient.

Dwarf nettle (*Urtica urens*), a native of Eurasia also found in the United States, has high amounts of fiber, zinc, copper, manganese, and magnesium, as well as huge amounts of calcium and iron—more calcium and iron than any other vegetable analyzed to date. An amazing food. I have not had a chance to study this plant yet, but look forward to learning it. It's known for a much stronger sting than you would get from regular stinging nettle. I can't wait to experience that!

COMPLETE DIETARY PROTEIN

Has all the essential amino acids in proper proportion to allow your body to build its own protein. Miss any of them, and none of them will work. That is why vegans complement their protein. That is, they eat a diverse enough diet of plant material so that all the essential amino acids are present. In that diverse diet, any one missing amino acid in one plant is made up by that found in another.

Nettles offer great food if you can get past the sting. And that is easily done. But first, let's cover the plant through its life.

Knowing Nettles

To a novice, nettles are pretty common looking and difficult to identify because they have traits in common with many plants, including many of the mints. Many plants have a square stem, opposite green leaves, and are hairy. To me, the best identifying characteristics are the sting and the fat teeth (scalloped edges) of the leaf margins. I'll go into exactly how the plant does its stinging magic later in this chapter. Nettles grow either from seedlings or from rhizomes that support a population of plants year after year. In this case, think of the rhizomes as a network of underground stems running parallel to the surface. They survive winter and are the food source and base of new aboveground plants in the spring. We'll start by discussing the seedlings and go on from there. Seeds can germinate as soon as they fall off the plant if the conditions are right.

The cotyledons emerging from the seed are small and round, unlike the first true leaves that follow. The first leaves start out egg-shaped. As the plant gets older, leaves

DO NETTLES HAVE A SQUARE STEM?

Nettles have a squarish stem. It is definitely four-sided, but not a perfect square. Here is how the stem is designed.

Three nettle seedlings. Lower left: one just emerging with its two cotyledons. Lower right, one with two leaves above the cotyledons. Center: one with four leaves, the cotyledons are hidden below them. The scalloped edges are prominent on the center plant even at this early stage of growth. The scallops get increasingly pointed and curved up toward the end of the leaf as the plant matures.

A patch of young nettles, roughly 5 to 8 inches tall, growing from a network of underground rhizomes. Brown stalks of the previous year tower above the plants.

WHAT ARE STIPULES?

Leaves typically have three parts: a blade, a leaf stem, and stipules. Stipules come in pairs and are found at the base of the leaf stem (petiole), where the leaf stem attaches to the main stem or branch. Stipules may be clearly present, as in nettles, or absent in some plants. All are small relative to the leaf blade, and vary greatly in shape, from hairlike to leaflike. One theory is that the original purpose of stipules was to protect newly budding leaves as they emerged from the stem. As the leaf outgrows the stipules, they remain at the base of the leaves they protected. Since some of them are very distinctive, as with nettles and roses, I find them one of the best ways to positively identify some plants, sometimes even better than the leaves themselves.

elongate and come to a point. Tiny stinging hairs are everywhere on the leaves and stems.

If the plants are growing from preestablished rhizomes, they will grow quickly, with stems that are more stout than those from seedlings. A rhizome-based patch will also have remnants of last year's stalks. Those stalks will be light brown, from 4 to 7 feet tall, and still be standing, or in a mix of broken and reclining stalks. The harsher the winter they experienced, the more broken the stalks.

The visual cue of seeing young plants growing underneath last year's dead brown stems is a clue you've found nettles. The stems are four-sided, with variations on exactly how square they are. From the outside they may appear like four thin, round stems fused together to make a round-cornered four-sided stem. The illustration on page 97 shows the typical pattern.

As I've said, a novice might mistake nettles for mint, since their leaves, and how those leaves are arranged on the stem, can be similar. All plants like these with square stems and opposite leaves have an additional characteristic. Each set of opposite leaf pairs is arranged 90° differently than the opposite leaf pairs both above and below them. You could call it alternating opposites. Botanists call it a *decussate* leaf arrangement. To visualize it, consider one pair of opposite leaves sticking out to the left and right of the stem. The next pair up will be rotated 90°, now facing toward and

Left: Overhead view of an 8-inch-tall plant growing from rhizomes. This plant is at prime for gathering.

Below: Nettle leaf top view (left) and bottom view (right). The scalloped teeth along the margins point both outward and upward. There are three main veins arising from the base of the blade, which is typical of plants in the Urtica genus. Stipules are at the base of each leaf stem. They appear narrower here than on the younger plants shown at left since they fold upward later in the season.

At left are two views of the nettle's decussate leaf arrangement. That is, the pattern of alternating opposite leaves. These photos show two other features: small oval-shaped pointed stipules on both sides of each leaf base and stinging hairs throughout.
Left, top: The upper 4 inches of a young 6-inch-tall plant.
Left, bottom: The upper 8 inches of a 4-foot-tall plant prior to flowering.

away from you. The third pair up above that will again be to the sides, and on and on. You can see this arrangement in the lower two photographs on page 99.

Nettle leaves change as the plant becomes more mature. The younger plants' leaves are more heart-shaped and have stipules that are rounded, almost resembling tiny greenish-white flower petals. The older plants' leaves are an elongated egg shape (lanceolate) and have slightly longer stipules that look thinner because they are folded lengthwise.

What About That Sting?

Although historical literature praises the nettle for its food value and other practical uses, modern health pamphlets typically label it a poisonous plant. Poisonous plant books consider it a dermatoxin, and hiking guidebooks consider it a nuisance to avoid. Nettle is often covered alongside poison ivy and poison oak in educational pamphlets that warn you to keep away. I am a little more loving and accepting of this spirited plant.

Nettle leaves and stems are covered with specialized stinging hairs called trichomes. Trichomes are interspersed with regular, tiny nonstinging hairs. Nettle trichomes are larger than its regular hairs and are designed to sting you. Think of the trichomes as miniature hypodermic needles.

How do nettles sting you? When the tip of this trichome hits the skin, the blunt end shears off, creating an extremely sharp beveled tip similar to a hypodermic needle. Shearing allows two things to happen simultaneously: the sharp end pierces the skin and the trichome's reservoir of fluid gets forcefully injected under the skin. Hundreds of these trichomes may be piercing/injecting a victim at any one moment of contact.

Nettle trichomes inject specialized plant cytoplasm where it does not belong, under the skin. Normal plant acids are in the cytoplasm, like ascorbic acid, citric acid, malic acid, and some formic acid. The nettle fluid also contains histamine, acetylcholine, and 5-hydroxytrypamine.

TRICHOMES

Trichomes are outgrowths or appendages growing from part of the outer skin of some organisms. Nettle hypodermics are only one kind of trichome. For instance, there are long trichomes tipped with a bead of fluid on the carnivorous sundew plant. That fluid is an insect attractant, contains a digestive agent, and is sticky to trap and digest its victims. *Drosera capensis* (Cape sundew) trichomes are shown here. Photo courtesy of Alberto Garcia (Trebol-a) from Wikipedia Commons.

At the concentrations found in nettles, all these chemicals on the surface of our skin or in our digestive tract would be harmless. But put them where they do not belong, under the skin, and they sting. You may experience anything from a mild sting to major pain. It could be annoying for 20 minutes to a couple of days. Some redness and welting of the skin occurs in some people, and in rare cases, certain individuals might experience a serious allergic reaction from nettle proteins. But except for some pain, the sting is mostly harmless for most people. I have never personally known or heard of anyone going into anaphylaxis or dying from the sting. Believe it or not, understanding how nettles sting will give you more options in how to use them for food. We'll cover this more in our discussion of use and processing.

As nettle plants mature, they get tall and lanky, depending on moisture and sunlight. I've seen some up

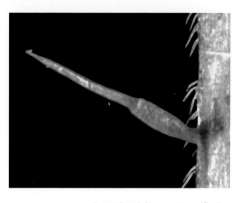

A nettle trichome magnified (25x). Each trichome is a single cell (up to 3mm long) in the shape of a fluid-filled needlelike shaft. The base of the trichome's fluid reservoir is surrounded by other cells creating an inward pressure. The shaft and the tip are composed mostly of silica, making them stiff enough to pierce skin.

A dense patch of older nettles, about 5 feet tall.

Above: The upper 6 inches of a 4-foot nettle plant that is just beginning to reveal its flower buds.

Above: A fully mature male nettle plant in reproductive mode. Leaves are longer and narrower in older plants than in young ones.

Below: Male nettle flower buds. They branch out from where the leaf stem meets the main stem. A couple of the buds have opened into flowers here. Each flower has four stamens spreading out.

Right: Female nettle flowers have a furry appearance. Like the male flowers, their stems arise where the leaves meet the main stem.

to 7 feet tall in the wild. Flower buds emerge from the leaf nodes on upper parts of the plant. Nettles are divided into male and female plants.

Cystoliths

Older nettle leaves and stems contain tiny structures called cystoliths. If you read the wild food literature, you get warnings not to eat older plants or these cystoliths will irritate your urinary tract. I ignore the warnings for three reasons. First, the danger is made up by authors who don't know the difference between plant structures and kidney stone formation. They hear "liths" meaning "stones" and their mind wanders to a totally unrelated area, kidney stones. There is no evidence for these claims. Second, the older leaves and stems are very fibrous and you would not eat them anyway. Third, nettle cystoliths are tiny packets of calcium carbonate. You know . . . like over-the-counter antacids which

Female nettle plant seed clusters, late in the season after the leaves have fallen.

are thousands of times bigger than any cystoliths. I have seen no evidence that they will harm your urinary tract as many wild food sources blindly repeat. Unless nettle cystoliths can survive the harsh acid conditions of the digestive tract, and be absorbed whole, I don't know how they could wander through your bloodstream, through your liver and kidneys, and make it to your urinary tract. In fact, stinging nettle has been used as an anti-inflammatory, antibacterial agent and to *treat* urinary tract disorders (Joshi, 2014). There is no evidence that nettle cystoliths are a problem and it does not make sense that they would be.

Nettle look-alikes

Lots of plants can look like stinging nettle, though after studying this chapter, your chance of confusing them will be reduced greatly. Once you've gathered and eaten it, you will easily recognize nettle from a distance. As I've said, many aromatic mint species with leaves the size of nettles can resemble them, but instead of being stung, you will smell the sweet scent of mint, so I will not cover them here. There are two other nettles in North America: heartleaf nettle (*Urtica chamaedryoides*) and dwarf or dog nettle (*Urtica urens*), not as widespread and much lower-growing plants, mostly found in the southeastern United States. I do not have any experience with them. Both apparently have stinging trichomes, with dwarf nettle having the strongest sting of the three *Urticas*.

There are two other plants in the nettle family (Urticaceae) that are not mints but confuse some people: clearweed and woodnettle. They are clearly different from stinging nettle, but are mentioned in the literature often, so I will briefly describe them here. Based on their lack of historical cultural food use, I do not consider either of these plants edible. Other authors differ on this. I have not found any information about toxicity, but that does not mean something is edible.

Clearweed

Pilea pumila

Clearweed is lower-growing than stinging nettle, typically 6 to 24 inches tall at maturity. Range is restricted to eastern woodlands. There is no sting. Clearweed has three main things in common with stinging nettle: decussate leaf arrangement, three main veins on the leaf

Above: Mature clearweed, showing leaves, leaf arrangement, and flower buds. Note the decussate arrangement of the leaves, similar to nettle.

Below: Mature clearweed showing branched flower clusters arising from the stem where the leaf stem meets the stem. Photo courtesy of Peter M. Dziuk. MinnesotaWildflowers.info

blade, and scalloped teeth. What differs is that it does not sting, the young stems are weaker and somewhat translucent, and the main veins point back up toward the tip. The leaves are shiny and have a rubbery feel to them. It is taprooted like a carrot while nettles grow from rhizomes. Clearweed has no verifiable cultural food use. Fernald (1943) mentions that they "may be edible," based on an edible relative found in the tropics. However, plants in the same genus can be radically different in their chemical makeup and toxicity. So making assumptions about edibility is problematic.

Woodnettle

Laportea canadensis

Also known as Canadian woodnettle and Canada lettuce. The greatest difference is that woodnettle has alternate leaves, while nettle and clearweed have opposite/decussate leaves. Its stem zigzags from leaf to leaf, whereas nettle and clearweed are quite straight. Leaf veins on woodnettle are in a treelike (pinnate) arrangement, characterized by one main vein down the center of the leaf blade with tributary veins branching off from it. In contrast, nettle and clearweed have three main veins arising from the base of the blade. The woodnettle plant has prominent stingers, which can lead people to wrongly assume it is stinging nettle.

Above: A patch of woodnettle. The leaves are larger, broader, and more spread out than stinging nettle. Leaves grow alternately on the branches. Photo courtesy of Peter M. Dziuk.

This plant is native to North America. I could find no records of native peoples eating it. François Couplan (1998) referenced an 1800s naturalist who reported: "The young shoots and leaves are edible as cooked greens and in soups." But by whom? A new use? Sam Thayer (2006) has eaten the young shoots and greens saying they are delicious and edible. I still have questions about this plant's safety pending further study on my part.

Right: A woodnettle plant showing female flowers stems (top) where the seeds will develop, and male flower stems below. During seed development, the female stem branching gets quite elaborate. Photo Courtesy of © Steve R. Turner.

Harvesting Nettles

I collect nettles bare-handed, because while real, the sting is an ignorable annoyance to me. Once I collected it this way for about a half hour and the result was amazing. It felt like my hands were vibrating with pulsations. Like there were reverberations when I tapped them.

Nettle sting is accepted in many cultures. In fact, many old-world therapists stung people on purpose to treat things like arthritis. The key to collecting bare-handed is to just ignore the sting and go on with whatever you are doing. Sometimes the sting lasts for half an hour; sometimes, if I try hard enough, I can still feel it the next day. But that is me. You can test your ability to tolerate the sting by collecting bare-handed on purpose and then moving on to do some chore that requires your attention: Bushwhack up a hillside, climb a tree, go for a jog, clean your toilet, bungee jump, do your taxes, etc. Observe if the sting disappears into the background while your brain is occupied with other things.

For some, the pain is great, burning, and intolerable. For them, gloves are necessary. Keep in mind that being stung on the tender skin of a bare leg is not the same as being stung on the pads of your hands. If you work with your hands at all, you will have built up thicker skin there that reacts less to the stingers than your legs do. No matter how careful you are, if you work with nettles a lot, gathering, chopping, processing, etc., you will get stung on occasion. The back of my hand is where nettles sting me the most.

Young leafy nettle stems

New plants emerging in the spring, or later in response to mowing, are rapid-growing and tender. Most of the upper 6 inches of an 8-inch nettle plant will be tender enough to eat. Since growing conditions vary, the snap test is the best judge of tenderness. Anything above where the stem snaps cleanly (without tugging), should be tender enough to eat.

As the plants get taller, the snappable location of the growing point of the stem will get shorter and shorter, until only the very end can be plucked away.

Nettle leaves

The leaves remain tender a short way down the stem below the point where the stem has gotten tough. So while the stem is tender from the snap point on upward, leaves can be harvested just below that. The younger the plant, the farther down you can gather the leaves, usually around 6 inches below where the stem is tough. If the plant is already producing flower buds, you might only be able to get the very tip of the plant, if that. Around flowering time, it is very difficult to get any useful leaves. They become too papery.

For some people, lifting the leaves at the tip of the stem upward seems to allow them to gather nettles bare-handed without much sting. Pull up and pinch off the tip as shown.

Nettle flower buds

When the flower buds are light greenish-yellow, almost white, and mostly closed, they are tender enough to gather and use. Snap off whole clusters of flower buds. Once the flowers are pollinated, they become impractical to use due to the fibrousness of the supporting flower stem.

Serving Nettles

Raw nettles

Stinging nettles are perfectly edible, nutritious, and delicious raw. Of course, you can juice or puree them—which shreds and disables the stingers. But what if you just want to eat the fresh greens as greens? The answer is to serve them with other foods and position them wisely. Nettle stingers need to pierce the skin of your hands, tongue, or oral cavity in order to do their damage. Deny access or disable, break, or mash the stingers and you are good to go. To do this, sandwich them within other foods that will mash the surface of the nettle leaves.

If you make a sandwich, you can just replace lettuce with nettle leaves. Positioning them wisely is important

Fresh nettle leaves used in place of lettuce in a sandwich. The pressure of the surrounding matter smashes/disarms the stingers. There was no sting in eating this sandwich.

here. Make sure all the leaves are internal to the sandwich, not sticking out the sides. The layers of bread and other sandwich internals serve to mash the needles, releasing their juices harmlessly into the sandwich. You do not have to mash the sandwich for this to happen—just build it. Then, when you bite and chew, that completely disables the needles, allowing you to enjoy the sandwich unharmed. The only things getting stung are the tomato slices and cheese inside the sandwich. Their screams of pain will be muffled by the bread.

You might get stung mildly if you accidently let any leaf parts roam to the outsides as you would with lettuce. This is not lettuce. If you want to handle the leaves directly, you can reduce their stinging capacity by placing them in a towel after washing and rolling them around a bit. That will break many, but not all, of the stingers.

Nettle pesto is quite different from basil pesto. Not only is the flavor different, but nettles have different properties that you have to adapt to. If you just replace nettles for basil in a standard basil pesto recipe, the results will be disappointing. The final product will be fairly dry. Much of the oil will leak out or will not absorb into the greens during the blending process. Made this way it does not

mix well with things like spaghetti. After experimenting I came to the conclusion that I had to do something about the dryness. The problem was nettle greens were somewhat lipophobic—that is, they were rejecting the olive oil that basil binds to in basil pesto. So I had to come up with a way to make everything moister. My solution was avocado and water. Avocado is an emulsifier. It allows water to mix with oil. The resultant pesto is a little thicker than the fairly liquidy ones you see illustrated all the time, but the flavor is marvelous—the best nettle pesto I've ever eaten. My recipe is on the next page. I hope you enjoy it too.

Most nettle pesto recipes you see have you boiling the greens first. This is likely to be because people are afraid of the stingers. As you know from this chapter, nettles can be eaten raw if you manage the stingers. Your food processor totally destroys them. Boiling is not only unnecessary, overcooking changes the quality and nutrition of the pesto. Since ignorance and fear drive many people who are on the periphery of wild foods, you will find gobs of

Vegetable mini tortilla wraps made with fresh stinging nettle leaves. The pressure of the surrounding food matter smashes/disarms the stingers. These were made using flour tortillas, fresh nettle leaves, carrots, sweet red peppers, jicama, shallots, and tzatziki sauce. They were wrapped tight and sliced for easy handling.

recipes telling you to boil the nettles first. Don't fall for it. Go with fresh ingredients here unless you purposefully want the cooked product.

John's Nettle-Avocado Pesto

Makes about 12 ounces or 10 servings

INGREDIENTS

$1/2$ cup pecan halves

1 cup extra virgin olive oil

2 cloves garlic

$1/3$ cup mashed avocado

$1/3$ cup water, or the water from canned or freshly boiled mushrooms, or water from previously boiled nettles

2 cups tightly packed fresh nettle leaves and tender tops

1 cup finely grated Parmesan cheese

$1/2$ teaspoon kosher salt, or more to taste

DIRECTIONS

Use protective gloves at your own discretion for this and all nettle recipes.

In a small skillet, toast the pecans over medium heat for about 10 minutes, flipping and stirring occasionally until they turn a shade darker and start giving off a wonderful aroma.

Pulse the pecans in a food processor until they are finely ground. Add the oil, garlic, avocado, and water, then pulse the mix until the garlic is finely chopped.

Roughly chop the nettles into pieces, then add them. Pulse several times, stop, use a spatula to scrape the sides of the food processor bowl, and repeat until the pesto is the consistency you desire.

Pour the pesto into a bowl, add the Parmesan and salt, and stir. The pesto will be very dry at first, but keep stirring. It is ready to eat when everything moistens.

VARIATIONS AND TIPS

For a lighter pesto, use half the cheese.

If you like a moister pesto, add an extra tablespoon of oil and/or water early on in the recipe. You can add them later, but the oil will not blend as well.

To keep the pesto green (it will turn brown with exposure to oxygen) boil the greens for a minute, and drain well before you blend them. Add some lemon juice to taste at the end.

To store the pesto in a plastic container, pour a little olive oil over the top. To store in a zip-top bag, press all the air out of it or vacuum-seal it. In either case, it can be refrigerated for 3 to 5 days, or frozen for a year. The sooner you do this after making, the more green the pesto will retain.

Nettle avocado pesto, served on pasta, garnished with roasted red pepper, mint leaves, and field mustard flowers.

Cooking nettles

All cooking methods disarm the hypodermic stingers once they reach boiling temperature. That heat pops open the capsule holding the fluid at the base of the trichome, so there is no pressure left to inject it anywhere. Nettle trichomes, however, have a second issue. They are stiff. So even though the fluid can no longer be injected, if you under boil or just steam nettles, you can still feel the trichomes as stiff hairs. No sting, just some mildly annoying coarseness. This is only a concern if you are eating the nettles as a stand-alone cooked green. This is not an issue if the nettle greens are lost in the mass of a larger dish.

Steaming does not soften the stingers since it does not agitate them like boiling. Try this experiment when you are familiarizing yourself with nettles. Boil one batch for 5 minutes and steam one batch for 5 minutes. Make sure the water is boiling before adding the greens in each set. Sample the difference. This experiment is a good basis for building understanding when you invent your own recipes.

If you manage trichome stiffness well, in both leaves and stems, nettles work much like cooked spinach. So any spinach recipe will work. Even just wilting the greens in a sauté pan with a little virgin olive oil is amazing.

Nettle leaves, tender young stems, and flower bud clusters boiled for about 6 minutes, served with extra virgin olive oil and lemon juice. Delicious. Young leafy plants were available during flowering of older plants because I found a nearby patch that had been mowed weeks earlier, allowing new, still tender plants to emerge from the rhizomes.

Chapter 11

FAMILY: Malvaceae
SPECIES: *Althaea officinalis*

Marsh Mallow

This plant lives up to its name in more ways than one.

The upper 4 feet of a fully mature 9-foot-tall marsh mallow plant in flower and seed development. This is as tall as you'll ever see it. In the wild this would have bent over from its top-heavy weight, leaving secondary branches to grow upward. This one in my backyard was tied to a stake, so it did not fall over.

Estimated Range

Official Species Name:
- *Althaea officinalis* L.

Synonyms:
- *Althaea sublobata* Stokes
- *Althaea taurinensis* DC.
- *Malva officinalis* (L.)
  K. F. Schimp. & Spenn.

Common Names:
- Marsh mallow
- Marshmallow
- Guimauve officinale
  (French)

A taprooted perennial that grows tall and produces tough, hair-covered leaves. It loves moisture and is quite tolerant of salty marshes.

Edible Parts:
- Young shoots
- Young leaves
- Immature fruits
  (mallow peas)
- Taproots and their
  branchings

MARSH MALLOW

The name of this plant brings back memories of childhood. The joys of eating this soft, spongy melt-in-your-mouth confection got even greater when they were roasted over a campfire into a golden-brown mass of goodness. S'mores, pinwheel cookies, and moon pies, all containing marshmallow, chocolate, and some graham cracker–like material, became my favorite sweets in my youth. Then there are the Rice Krispies Treats, which have no chocolate, just toasted rice glued together with marshmallow. And, of course, just eating marshmallows plain, right out of the bag was a treat until about half the bag was gone, making the joy oh so fleeting.

You'd think I'd be dead by now, eating all that sugar in my youth. But I survived and now lead a much more nutritious life as an adult. Other than the obvious inability to write well or find a wife, I experienced no important long-term harm.

All of my childhood experiences were about the modern Jet-Puffed marshmallow, made from cornstarch, gelatin, sugar, and other non–marsh mallow constituents. The original marshmallow confection was, indeed, made using the marsh mallow root. The history on it is somewhat vague, but here is a short summary based on some marvelous research by Helena Nichols (2020a, 2020b, 2020c).

- Thousands of years ago, the ancient Egyptians mixed the dried, pulverized mallow root with water, honey, and possibly nuts and seeds to make a sweet confection.
- Around the end of the 1700s and through the 1800s, the French confectioners made *Pâte de guimauve*. It was a combination of marsh mallow root, egg whites, and sugar. The mixture was whipped into a meringue and dried for sale. The marshmallow provided a soft chewiness instead of the dry, crumbly mess that resulted when the egg-white alone meringue dried.

Sometimes rosewater or orange blossom water was added for flavor and variety.

- In the 1800s some of the marshmallow in the recipe was replaced with gum arabic. Marshmallow has a flavor that some loved and others did not. Gum arabic was flavorless and provided the same gooeyness.
- In the late 1800s, two things happened: First, marsh mallow root was totally phased out once Charles Knox's gelatin replaced both it and gum arabic as the dual thickeners. Gelatin is less expensive, flavorless, and still used today. Second, a process called the "starch mogul system" allowed the creamy mixture to be poured into cornstarch lined molds that would not stick to the gooey material, making production much easier. Like the original confection, these new marshmallows were mostly handmade and sold by confectioners. In 1895 Joseph Demerath founded the Rochester Marshmallow Company using that starch mogul system.
- The 1927 book *Tramping and Trailing with the Girl Scouts* gave the first-ever recipe for s'mores.
- In 1948, Alex Doumak invented the extrusion process necessary for forming the familiar, consistent shape of today's marshmallows on a massive scale.
- In 1958, Kraft introduced more air into the mixture, making the soft Jet-Puffed marshmallows. This airy form, and a marshmallow cream, are now made by all manufacturers of this confection. The ingredients of campfire marshmallows are listed as, in order of largest quantity first: sugar in the form of corn syrup, sugar (cane sugar), cornstarch, gelatin, water, dextrose (sugar), and flavors. There are no eggs, gum arabic, or marsh mallow root in them.

OK, enough about the confection and my musings about the past; let's talk about the plant itself.

MARSHMALLOW TREATS

S'mores are hot roasted (typically over an open campfire or in a fireplace) marshmallows placed on a section of Hershey's chocolate, then sandwiched between two segments of graham cracker. Pinwheel cookies are marshmallows on a thin gram cake covered in a shell of chocolate. Moon pies have the same components as pinwheels, just a different shape. Rice Krispies Treats are Rice Krispies folded into softened marshmallow, sometimes with added butter, and pressed flat into a oiled casserole dish. Once the mix solidifies, it is cut into bars for eating.

The marsh mallow plant originated around the Mediterranean and western Asia, but is now widespread throughout Europe and North America. Initially spread to promote both food and medicinal uses, its use as a food has waned over the last one hundred years due to the world's greater reliance on modern food markets. It is now almost exclusively spread by escape from cultivation from medicinal herb farms around the world. This plant thrives in very moist habitats including salt marshes. The Latin name *Althaea* comes from the Greek word for *healer*. *Officinalis* typically refers to plant preparations sold in herbal apothecaries of the past.

Most of the focus on marsh mallow root over time is due to its medicinal applications related to its mucilage. Mallow mucilage is widely known for its emollient and anti-inflammatory properties and is supportive of mucosal linings. Recent studies have shown it is supportive of the immune system. Edible mucilage, in general, is also known for its digestive and blood sugar-lowering properties (Al-Snafi, 2013, Ali Shah, 2011).

Due to the focus on medicinal preparations, and not food, complete nutrient data is lacking on this plant. There is a lot of work now on the plant's mucilage and phytochemicals, which is great, but out of the scope of this book. The mucilage is good for us, since it gives us a lot of food possibilities that we'll cover later in the chapter. The most mucilage is in the roots, less in the seeds and flowers, with some in the leaves and the least in the stems. The mature seeds have both mucilage and over 9 percent fat by weight. Both these things add to its properties and savoriness.

What's in a Name?

Let's say that you are the bigwig that names all the plants. You're knee-deep wading through some marshland. You discover a new mallow plant and you debate with yourself, what should I name this mallow that grows in a marsh? It's a tough decision, but you say to yourself, maybe I'll call this a marsh mallow? The rest of us think that is a good choice.

OK, other than, yes, this is an obvious and appropriate name, my goal is to draw you to something that will help you understand this chapter. I am directing you to the difference between marsh mallow and its contraction marshmallow.

Marsh mallow refers to the plant. Marshmallow refers to the sweet confection made from it. This is how I will refer to them in this chapter and anytime I mention them anywhere. Some people call them both marshmallow. If I used the compound word marshmallow for both the plant and the confection, how would you know which one I was referring to? I'd have to elaborate on every use of the word. So if you are wondering which one I am referring to, just look for that space in between.

If you have Volume 1 of this book series, I covered common mallow (*Malva neglecta*). It is a cousin that is much more commonly found than marsh mallow (*Althaea officinalis*). I invented a way to make what I call mallow-mallows out of the immature fruits (mallow peas) of common mallow and first reported about it in my *Wild Food Adventurer Newsletter* (Kallas, 2005b). This is because the immature fruits have some of the same kind of mucilage as the marsh mallow. That means you will see some commonalities and differences for the uses of these two cousins. Read on to find out just what those differences are.

Knowing Marsh Mallow

The marsh mallow plant grows both from seed and from the previous year's taproots. Seeds are spread by dropping from the plant to grow near their parents, or are tracked off by passing wildlife. They also float off to new locations if the plant is growing in a flood plain.

At germination the leaf-like cotyledons are egg-shaped, roughly a half-inch long, and blunt-tipped, with smooth margins. Three veins arise from their base. The first leaves are either egg-shaped or rounded, with lots of teeth

IMMATURE SEEDS

For common mallow in Volume 1 of this book series and marsh mallow here, I refer to immature fruits and mature fruits. Immature fruits are fruits in development that are used in many of my recipes. They are greenish-white, softer than mature fruits and not yet capable of germination. Mature fruits are hard, tan, and its seeds are capable of generating new plants. You could say the same thing about fresh peas and beans. They are immature seeds that are tender to eat.

Marsh mallow seedlings. The one on the left shows the cotyledons. The one on the right is about an inch tall showing the first true leaf.

Young leaves on a marsh mallow plant growing from seed. The youngest leaves can be absolutely round, but most will be egg-shaped, like the ones here. This plant is about 9 inches tall and almost 7 inches left to right.

along their margins. The leaf veins are both palmate and pinnate: palmate in that several veins radiate out from the base; pinnate in that each palmate vein produces tributaries, like the branches of a tree.

After the leaves multiply and enlarge, you see up to seven palmate veins arising from the base, and all of them have pinnate branches after that. The younger leaves can be round to egg-shaped. The plant grows a stem right from the start with leaves in an alternate arrangement. All these leaves have toothed margins that show some lobes coinciding with the tips of the veins. Some leaves will develop enough leaf blade to be forced to start buckling/folding along the veins, but many will remain flat.

The upper and lower sides of leaves, stems, sepals, and seeds are covered with a dense blanket of hair. Flower petals, roots, and cotyledons are hairless.

Plants growing directly from taproots emerge earlier and grow more rapidly than those from seedlings. Multiple new shoots arise from each major root, looking sort of like

There is a related plant, *Althaea armeniaca*, that is also known as marsh mallow. Originally from Russia, Iran, and Armenia, it is so rare in the US that you will never find it, though it is sold as an ornamental in the US. In case you start doing research on our plant I do not want you to confuse the two. One big difference is that its leaves are deeply divided. Otherwise, I do not know anything about it. Photo courtesy of Dana Holubová, PhD and the Botanical Photogallery

Above: Leaf variation in a young marsh mallow plant. Note both the palmate and pinnate venation and lobe formation fully actualized on the right. Leaf blades vary in length in this photo, from 1 inch, on the left, to 3 inches on the right.

Below: New marsh mallow shoots arising from overwintering taproots. Last year's old dead stems are persistent and remain intact unless a harsh winter tears them down. The shoots can grow up to 7 inches tall before leafing out.

reddish or purplish pencil asparagus, but thinner than pencil asparagus.

If shoots are shaded by underbrush, they will grow taller before leafing out. If the shoots are exposed to direct sunlight as they emerge, they will leaf out earlier.

In the wild, these plants grow 5 to 7 feet tall before the upper part's weight forces them to fall over unless they are supported by surrounding plants. When the main stems are lying on their sides, their branches grow upward from there. This means that when you find them late in the season, all crowded together, it can be quite a mess to move through the plants. A mature plant produces great quantities of leaves, flowers, and fruit (mallow peas).

Marsh mallow flowers are often over an inch in diameter, white petaled, and beautiful. Occasionally you'll find ones that have a pinkish hue, and many take on that hue as the petals get old. These flowers are similar to those of the common mallow, except much larger. They are also similar to hibiscus flowers. What they all have in common is five petals, a single pistil sticking out the center, and lots of stamens. Like other mallows, the stamens together can look like a

Bottom right: Marsh mallow plants arising from overwintering taproots. I removed last year's old dead stems to reduce visual confusion in this shot. Note rounder leaves at the base and more pointy-lobed leaves near the top. The tallest plants in this photo are about 14 inches tall.

miniature thermonuclear cloud exploding out the center of the flower. Five green sepals alternate with the white petals. The flowers cluster at the base of the upper leaves, and not all bloom at the same time.

Once the flowers are pollinated, they form a round of immature seed capsules that loosely resembles a tiny cheese round. Only it is greenish-white and not cheese. The common mallow (*Malva neglecta*) is sometimes called *cheeseweed* due to the resemblance of the shape of its fruit to a cheese round. I prefer the term *mallow peas* for all immature mallow fruits, since they are about the size of large sweet peas flattened along one plane. Of course, they are not in the pea family, nor are they in pods. *Mallow pea* is the best name I could come up for a small vegetable of this shape without calling it cheese-something or "tractor tire" shaped. At this stage mallow peas are small green vegetable-like packs of immature seed capsules with seeds inside. If you can come up with a better name for them let me know before I lose more sleep over it.

The greenish-white mallow peas, over time, turn tan-brown, harden, and dry out. In late summer the structures holding them on the plant also dry out and begin deteriorating. So by the time fall weather beats away at them, they begin to drop from the plant either whole or disassembling into individual seeds.

By the second year of growth, each plant will have developed some substantial root material. Typically, there will be a main root that branches quite a bit. Depending on the age, the top of the root can get to about $1\frac{1}{2}$ inches in diameter and reach down about 14 inches into the soil. Many adventitious (side) roots will grow down or out from the upper part of the root. If it is a multiyear root, more side roots spreads out to support new shoot growth. Root color ranges from tan to off-white with a slight yellow hue. The skin is always a darker hue than the internal meat.

MALLOW PEAS

Fruit in the plant world can be many things. The fruit of mallows are the seed rounds they make (more on this later). I call them *mallow peas*. Society normally considers fruit to be something sweet and juicy like an orange or apple. Mallow peas are more like a mildly sweet vegetable.

Above: Marsh mallow flower. These are typically over an inch in diameter.

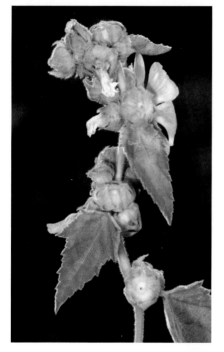

Above: A fully mature mallow plant with flowers and fruit development. This plant is over 8 feet tall. In my yard, I had to tie this one up to a tall stake to keep it from falling over. We've been dating ever since.

Above: Immature green fruits and small upper leaves of the marsh mallow. As the fruits mature, they will turn tan-brown and dry out.

Right: Freshly dug marsh mallow roots from a single plant.

Unlike the normal roots of the other mallows, marsh mallow roots are filled with mucilage-producing cells. If the root is broken or cut, you will be able to feel the mucilage. And, as we will see, this is a great feature for playing with in the kitchen.

Gathering and Edibility

Mucilage is everywhere in this plant, just waiting to show itself. While eating parts raw, you can sense a mild, pleasant mucilaginous mouthfeel; once boiled, this feature blossoms. Okra pods do the same thing. Okra, marsh mallow, common mallow, and hollyhocks are all in the same plant family, the *Malvaceae*. Most have some mucilage in one or more parts.

Too much mucilage at once is a disconcerting mouthfeel if you are not used to it. The mucilage is a fantastic ingredient for thickening soups, stews, gumbos, stir-fries, and sauces. It takes the wateriness out and adds substance or gravitas, if you will, to any dish. So proportion is the key word here for your eating pleasure. The goal is to use just enough of each cooked plant part in any dish to contribute just the right amount of thickener to make you happy.

Marsh mallow flowers as part of a salad. Other wild foods in this salad include everlasting pea flowers, borage leaves, wood sorrel leaves and pods, and field mustard greens.

Marsh mallow flowers

Marsh mallow flowers are sweet and delicious, great eaten fresh off the plant or used as a garnish on any dish or dessert. If you have enough of them, you can add them to any cooked dish, where they will lose their look, but add nutrition.

Mallowsparagus

The early spring mallow shoots, up to about 8 inches tall, can either be pried off the root or snipped with scissors. The lower part of these shoots is reminiscent of

Mallowsparagus—young shoots of marsh mallow, at 3 to 5 inches long here.

tender root material until they get tall and fibrous, turning into stalks.

The best shoots are gathered at ground level growing around previous year's stems. The only way you are going to find them in the underbrush is if you recognize the old dead stalks as you walk by or if you go back to an annual site that you know and love.

Like any plant that grows from last year's underground storage organs (roots), you can deplete their survival potential by constantly cutting new shoots from the same plants. Doing a single harvest each spring from each set of roots seems to work fine.

The shoots can be eaten as a fresh vegetable, steamed, or boiled like asparagus. Once cooked they get somewhat mucilaginous, but not intolerably so. With the right seasoning and sauces, they make a good asparagus-shaped vegetable. They have their own flavor. If you have enough of them, use in any asparagus recipe. The only thing you will have to train yourself about is understanding when they transition from chewable to being too tough.

Marsh mallow leaves

To gather the leaves, snip them at the base of the blade, leaving the tough leaf stem on the plant. Only choose the young, rapidly growing beautiful new leaves near the upper, faster-growing sections of the plant. Keep them cool and lightly moist until ready to use.

Chopped-up marsh mallow leaves used like lettuce in a sandwich.

Marsh mallow leaves are eaten regularly in the Mediterranean and Arab countries. There is no getting around the fact that the leaves are hairy and tough to chew whole. To eat fresh, counteract the toughness by chopping them into small pieces before adding to dishes as you would lettuce. Adding them to a salad, rather than eating a whole salad of marsh mallow leaves, also counteracts their hairiness.

Boiling tenderizes the leaves somewhat and brings on the mucilage. The mucilage is great for thickening things. Add the chopped leaves anywhere you would add spinach. They are great in mixed-green vegetable pies and anywhere they are incorporated into cooked vegetable dishes.

Mallow pea fruits

As I have said, my term for the immature seed rounds of mallows is *mallow peas*. The goal is to gather the peas while they are still in the green, vegetable-like stage. These fruits can be quite abundant on any one plant. They are easily plucked by just pulling. The green fruits are delicious and great to eat out of hand, more solid to chew than the common mallow peas I explored in volume 1 of this book series.

The immature fruits can be added fresh to salads or cooked in any dish

Mallow peas—Immature greenish-white seed rounds. Left: Mallow pea, sepals spread out. Right: Mallow pea, sepals removed. Most are just under 1 cm in diameter. These are larger then common mallow peas (*Malva neglecta*). Once they mature, turn light brown, and dry out, each segment (capsule) produces one small reddish-brown seed.

where they will add both flavor and mucilage. Again, great for thickening soups, stews, gumbos, stir-fries, and sauces.

The fruits, as well as the roots, can be made into meringue, marshmallow cream, or marshmallows. The recipe using the peas is exactly the same as for mallow-mallows covered in volume 1. Since the peas are larger in marsh mallow, it is a lot less work to gather than for common mallow.

If the fruits mature too long on the plant, they will turn light brown, dry out, and each segment will produce one small reddish-brown kidney-shaped seed.

Marsh mallow roots

The taproots are not like pulling up garden carrots, since they are typically not in one neat, easy piece. They are in multiple branches of multiple sizes spreading down and out from the central root. They are up to 18 inches long, so if you are in tough or rocky soil, there will be a lot of broken roots. While broken ends can be trimmed off during the cleaning process, small pieces make it more work to peel off the skin, if that is part of your processing goal.

While you can collect them any time of year, most people dig the roots in the fall after the aboveground plant dies or in spring before the shoots emerge, identifying the location by the old dead stalks.

Adjust your digging technique to soil conditions. If digging is tough, go for the big, easy-to-get pieces, and don't necessarily worry about the smaller branches. If digging is easy, go for it all. To reduce breakage, I dig a big hole next to the plant and then move in from the side. Once you've dug the initial hole, you get less breakage if you use a pick to carefully break the soil away from the roots. This can take a while.

Be careful not to include non-mallow roots that may come from adjacent plants. The best way to do that is to make sure roots you gather are all connected to the plant you are extracting. The good thing is that dandelion, for

Washed roots of about 20 early spring marsh mallow plants. Large taproots as well as many smaller branching roots are evident here. These roots are still attached to last year's dead stalks. The dead stalks are how you find the roots. You do not have to keep the stalks when gathering. They are here only to illustrate how they are attached. Clip them off at the gathering location so you only have to haul the roots. There are some new shoots on some of these plants at the top of the roots.

instance, or poison hemlock for that matter, both with tap-roots, will have obvious aboveground growth before marsh mallow emerges. So their greens or old stems will alert you to the fact that their roots are there too. Make note of all the adjacent plants prior to digging, so you will have fair warning of what you might find below. Poison hemlock is extensively covered later in this book. Dandelion taproots won't hurt you; they will just contribute a bitter flavor that you will not be expecting.

The roots will need cleaning to get the soil out of all the nooks and crannies. Clay soil is the worst to clean out. I line all of the roots up in my driveway and use the jet spray of my hose to remove most of the dirt. If the dirt is really stub-born, I soak all the roots for about an hour, then repeat the spray. Under most circumstances, that is all you need to get the roots clean. Dirt may be lodged where side roots emerge or where the main root branches. Cut those off to get better access to where dirt may be trapped. Cleaning straight cut-off pieces is easier than cleaning the whole root complex.

Sort through the roots, trim off dead or stringy parts, and separate by size. Root strands that are narrower in diameter have a higher skin-to-meat ratio. The skin has a mild vegetable flavor making its inclusion better for some things than others. Any size piece is good to eat as a veg-etable. The larger diameter pieces, $3/8$-inch and larger, are better if you want to peel them and/or use them for making marshmallow.

Test the larger roots for woodiness, beginning with the largest diameters, near the top of each root. Using a sharp kitchen knife, slice through the root about $1/4$ inch from the top. If you hit a core that is so hard you have to struggle to cut through, then try again another quarter-inch down. Keep repeating this farther down the root, until you can slice through cleanly without having to struggle or rock the knife. It should be around the same effort you would use to cut through a fresh carrot of the same size. Everything below that level is good for every use. You can also reclaim

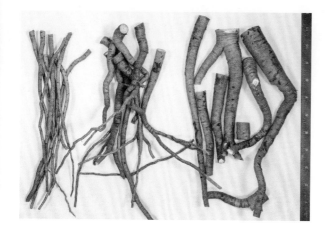

Left: Cleaned, trimmed, and sorted marsh mallow roots. All these roots are great for most vegetable uses. The larger ones on the right are easier to peel.

A cross section of the upper part of an older marsh mallow root. Older roots have more layers and tougher cores, particularly near the tops of the roots.

the area surrounding the woody core of the upper root. I would not quite call this a rind, but you can peel the outer part for use with your other usable root sections. Compost the woody upper core.

Roots larger than $^3/_8$-inch in diameter are substantial enough to peel efficiently. Use a standard potato peeler. There is nutrition in the skin, so the only reasons to peel the roots are for aesthetics and for a slightly less earthy flavor. Do you want a whiter end product or an earthier looking and tasting end product?

You can eat these roots raw, if tender enough. The mild flavor is its own, being a little sweet with a crispy texture. When cooked, the flavor is reminiscent of, but different than, potato. I like to chop them up. Chopping makes sure that when you bite into a core that is fairly solid, it is enjoyably chewable. Raw, the root material is interesting and not overpoweringly mucilaginous. Cooked, the mucilage is released, so your options must take advantage of that feature.

The roots do not work well as chunks in baked goods or foods like omelets. If you do this, you will find that every time your tongue encounters a chunk of the cooked root, you will get a hit of mucilage. That is quite a distracting mouthfeel.

Peeled and then chopped mallow root, ready for any use. That is an unpeeled root on the left.

Marsh Mallow Soup

Serves 5

While you could add marsh mallow root to any soup recipe, here is one of mine, in case you just want to see how it fits with other ingredients. Typically, I use 1 cup of mallow root for every 4 cups of liquid. The mallow adds both thickness and flavor to the soup. No need to peel the roots.

INGREDIENTS

1 cup chopped marsh mallow root
2³⁄₄ cups diced red onion
1¹⁄₂ cups chopped broccoli
1 cup sliced carrot
1 cup diced celery
1 cup diced red bell pepper
4 cups water
4 bouillon cubes (vegetable or meat flavored)
1 teaspoon ground ginger
¹⁄₂ teaspoon ground nutmeg
2 teaspoon curry powder
4 cloves garlic, minced
2 tablespoons olive oil

DIRECTIONS

Place marsh mallow root, red onion, broccoli, carrot, celery, and bell pepper in a 4-quart pot. Add water, bouillon, ginger, nutmeg, curry, garlic, and olive oil.

Bring to a rapid boil on high heat. Immediately turn the heat down so it's just enough to keep a slow boil.

Cook for 15 minutes or until the vegetables are tender. Serve hot.

Producing Marsh Mallow Confections

This is a huge amount of fun and a big hit for small and big kids alike. This is not a way to save money on marshmallows. The time, labor, ingredients, and electricity costs make this a labor of love, just like baking your own bread. Of course, you will probably be the only person in your state who is doing it, so that is pretty special. It is also a great way to teach kids about where their food comes from—which is true of any wild or garden food.

The recipes I am giving you are my own, invented for the modern person using a modern kitchen from fresh mallow peas or roots. Historically, marshmallows were made commercially by confectioners who used powdered marsh mallow root and added things like guar gum and flavored waters like those from rose and orange blossoms. My recipes do not require you to dry and powder anything or to find unusual ingredients. I have successfully made marshmallow-like products from the mallow peas of common mallow (*Malva neglecta*), marsh mallow (*Althaea officinalis*), and high mallow (*Malva sylvestris*). Ditto from the roots of marsh mallow. Roots of common mallow and high mallow do not have mucilage.

The mucopolysaccharides in the mallow are the foundation of these confections. They work in conjunction with protein in the egg whites to form a foam when whipped. Whipping causes tightly wrapped individual protein molecules to unwind and rebind to adjacent molecules. They form a network of molecules trapping air, sort of like gluten in bread making. Somehow the mucopolysaccharides in the mallow intertwine with the mucoproteins and albumin of the eggs to form a somewhat stable foam.

Preparing mallow whites from the peas

Marsh mallow peas are easy to gather relative to common mallow peas. They are twice as big, and high enough on the plant so you that don't have to bend over. You can fill an 8-ounce cup in a half an hour, faster if you are more efficient than I am or if you involve your whole family in the gathering process. Use the peas, sepals and all. I give you this process with the peas, since you may have easier access to them than you do to the roots. The peas make fine meringue and fat-free whipped cream, but the roots make superior marshmallows with a much more stable foam. What that means is that marshmallow from the fruits will weep/bleed out the mallow-white liquid if not served in a reasonable amount of time after making. Slight drying of the surface and refrigeration help all wild-derived marshmallow to last longer.

While I hate to repeat myself, the process for making mallow whites from marsh mallow fruits (mallow peas) is almost the same as what I wrote in my last book (Kallas, 2010). I am mostly repeating it here (yes, I hate myself), with minor modifications so you won't have to buy volume 1 of this series just for this recipe.

Preparing mallow whites from the fruits

To start out, you will need 1 cup of mallow peas and 3 cups of water. This will always be a 1 to 3 ratio whatever quantity you have to work with. Do not mash, rather press the peas into the cup to get an accurate measure.

Pour just the water into a pot that is tall and relatively narrow in diameter. The pot should be large enough to accommodate the volume of peas and water, with space above to boil. If the base is too wide, with such a little amount of boiling material, the water will evaporate too quickly and the contents will burn. If that happens, you will be quite unhappy and you will chastise yourself. Cover the pot and bring the water to a rapid boil on high heat.

Remove from the heat and take the cover off. Add the mallow peas. Insert a measuring device to determine the depth of the mallow-filled water. Remove the measure and mark the halfway point of that depth for later. Leaving the cover off, return the pot to the heat and boil gently until the total contents reduce by about half. Watch this carefully or the liquid will evaporate and your contents will burn.

As you watch the water boil, you'll know that it is thickening, because the speed at which the bubbles emerge will slow down. Once the depth is reduced by half, test the liquid for proper consistency, using the spoon test. Try to extract a spoonful of the liquid. If the liquid pours off the spoon like water, keep boiling. If it glops or slips off like it doesn't want to be in the spoon, you're done.

Pour the hot contents of the pot through a standard metal kitchen sieve, catching the mallow whites below. A light pressing of the remaining mallow peas is okay if you need more juice. Do not forcefully squeeze the cooked peas for juice or you will get more of a vegetable flavor and fragments of the peas in the juice.

Allow the mallow whites to cool to room temperature before using them in any of the following recipes. Set aside the spent/drained peas for later use as a side dish vegetable, or add them to other foods just as you would add peas. Now that you have mallow whites, you can whip them into mallow foam.

Based on my experiments working with the roots, there may be a nonboiling method to extract mucilage from the mallow peas. That will have to wait for future experiments.

Preparing mallow whites from the roots

Once you've dug the marsh mallow roots and cleaned them off well, you can use a vegetable peeler to peel the skin or you can leave it on. Keeping the peel on has two advantages: First, the root just under the peel has a higher concentration of mucilage than the core, allowing you to make a more stable product in less time. Second, it is less work if you don't have to peel all those many different-sized and -shaped roots.

MEASURING DEPTH

To measure the depth of the pre-boiled mallows in water and its halfway point: Use a washed wooden or metal ruler with millimeter markings. Measure the full depth, and then note the halfway point for checking later. Or dip a wooden chopstick in, note the depth, and mark the halfway point on the chopstick for checking the depth later.

Whisking the chopped mallow roots in water to extract the mucilage. You could also use an electric hand mixer on low speed.

Mallow whites draining from the whisked material. The whites are thick and gloppy, having a light tan hue to them.

Including the skin adds a barely perceptible vegetable flavor, a light tan hue, and tiny speckles of brown to the finished product. Only a persnickety person may notice the difference as everyone in sight is scarfing down the mallow cream, mallow meringue, and marshmallows. Either way, you end up with delicious marshmallowy goodness. An alternative to peeling is to use larger roots since they will have a much greater proportion of internal mallow meat to skin.

Extracting marsh mallow mucilage cannot be done effectively from whole roots. The mucilage-producing cells are trapped inside root cells. The goal is to expose those cells so their mucilage can migrate into the water you will be introducing in the next step. The finer you chop the root, the more cells are exposed, the more mucilage makes its way into the water. A perfect chop would make the pieces about the size of rice grains, but you do not have to go that far.

A food processor does a thorough job of chopping the roots into tiny pieces, allowing more of the mucilage cells to be exposed. However, if you have not peeled the roots, the food processor will have made some pieces so small that tiny particles of the brown skin will get through the sieve you use later. That is more a feature than a problem.

Once you have chopped up the mallow root, press it into a measuring cup to see the volume you've prepared. For extracting the mucilage, you want 1 part of root material to 2 parts of water. So if you've filled 1 cup (8 ounces) with chopped root, get a glass or stainless steel bowl and pour 16 ounces of water into it. Add the root material to the water and begin whisking. Whisk for 5 minutes or more. It gets tiring, but longer whisking gets more mucilage into the water.

As you whisk, you will notice the water starting to thicken and hold together. The more mucilage that moves into the water, the thicker the whisking will get. If you removed the skin, the mallow whites will be a light tan

Fresh marshmallow cream used to top a variety of fruit and sweet treats. Some of these treats are like open-faced s'mores. Maria's cookies or thin chocolate wafers are great cookie/cake bases upon which to create these treats. Make mini strawberry shortcake-like treats. The cream is decadent on soft, chewy chocolate chip cookies. Some of these treats are topped with borage flowers for fun.

color. If you left the skin on, they will be slightly darker. Don't fret about this, my friend; the finished product will still be white.

After 5 or more minutes have passed and your arm has lost all feeling, you can do one of two things. You could put the container, covered, into the fridge for a day or three, allowing more of the mucilage to seep into the liquid before you sieve the contents. To do this you must be a patient person and likely would have passed the *marshmallow test* as a child. You are more disciplined and responsible. More likely to have saved for retirement. You are kind to others.

This waiting period may be the key to foam stability and marshmallow perfection. More experiments need to be done to consistently produce the best marshmallows. But let's work with what we know now.

The second choice is to immediately pour this mixture, as is, through a sieve. This is where the fun begins. As the liquid passes through, you will see it glopping out the bottom of the sieve. Give it some time. If you chopped, you can just sit there and watch. If you used a food processor, you might have to use a spatula to stir the material, allowing the trapped mucilage to pass downward and out of the sieve.

You now have mallow whites. Since there are so many variables, I cannot guarantee how thick your mucilage will be. The bottom line is: the thicker it is, the more stable the marshmallows will be in the end.

THE STANFORD MARSHMALLOW TEST

This was a challenge given to children to study delayed gratification. If they could hold off on eating one marshmallow for a given period of time, they would be given two marshmallows as a later reward. The children who could delay gratification, were later in life found to be more disciplined and purposeful. They were seen as eventually being more successful at making decisions in their lives. These conclusions are now being contested.

Marshmallow Cream

Makes approximately 4 cups

This is my recipe, designed to fit with my general principle that any food named after a wild food should be primarily made up of that material. The main ingredients here are the whipables (4 parts mallow whites to 1 part egg white) and sugar. In contrast, in the **Pâte de Guimauve** recipe re-created by Nichols (2020b), there were 1,000 grams of gum arabic and 360 grams of egg whites for only 125 grams of mallow root. So that recipe for that early marshmallow was really mostly gum arabic and egg whites, just as today's store-bought marshmallow is mostly gelatin and corn syrup.

Whether you use mallow whites made from the fruits or the roots, the process of making marshmallow products is the same.

Marshmallow cream made from marsh mallow peas in a fruity dessert with raspberries and blueberries, topped with a marsh mallow flower.

INGREDIENTS

1 egg white

$^{1}/_{2}$ teaspoon cream of tartar, divided

$^{1}/_{2}$ cup mallow whites

$^{3}/_{4}$ cup sugar

$^{1}/_{2}$ teaspoon vanilla extract

$^{1}/_{4}$ teaspoon maple extract (optional)

DIRECTIONS

Use a large, clear glass bowl that could easily hold more than the amount of meringue you would find on a lemon meringue pie.

Using a hand beater at the second-highest speed setting, whip the egg white until it reaches the soft-peak stage. Note that a single egg is small, so you may have to tilt the bowl for the beater blades to incorporate air into the egg white. The more the blades interact with the white, the faster this will go.

Once the egg white has reached the soft-peak stage, sprinkle in about $^{1}/_{4}$ of the cream of tartar. Continue beating, now at full speed.

Once the egg white has foamed again to the soft-peak stage, begin adding the mallow whites in stages, about 1 ounce (2 tablespoons) at a time. Let each pour of the

You know you've reached marshmallow perfection when the foam is so thick and solid that it rides up and won't come off the beater blades. It only gets this good when the mallow whites have a certain high concentration of mucilage. You may not get there on the first try. Even if you can only achieve a thick foam, it will still work.

mallow fully incorporate into the whites before adding more. This is where a glass bowl comes in handy: you can see if the mallow liquid is accumulating at the bottom of the bowl. Don't let it accumulate. Keep whipping.

Gradually add ¼ of the cream of tartar after each addition of the mallow until you are out of the cream of tartar. Keep whipping. Don't stop.

Gradually begin adding the sugar as you are whipping, sprinkling in roughly 1 tablespoon at a time until it has all been added.

What you will begin to experience is a gradual thickening of the foam. The beater will begin to struggle slightly and may want to call the union to report you. But don't relent, it can do it.

Add the vanilla and maple extracts. Keep whipping.

The foam will begin mounding up, holding its shape. If the foam mounds up onto the blades and their stems, you've reached the pinnacle! The most stable foam possible and the best natural marshmallow that money cannot buy.

If you've been whipping for over 25 minutes and the foam has not mounded up on the blades but can form stable peaks in the bowl, you've reached a reasonably stable foam that will still hold up well. Good enough, you can stop there.

What you now have is marshmallow cream. You can use it as is like whipped cream, as a meringue on pies, to make meringue cookies, or pipette it for various uses. Use it to make s'mores, add it to fruit desserts, make strawberry shortcake, add it to hot cocoa, use it to top cookies, make cookie sandwiches, fold it into chocolate mousse, eat it over ice cream, or just eat it directly out of the bowl. You are limited only by your imagination.

Keep in mind that the egg whites in this are not cooked, providing potential risk of something nefarious eventually growing in the marshmallow products you are making. While it would be great to do a study on this, my guess is that the concentration of sugar and mucilage are so hydrophilic (water-loving), that they would starve any bacteria, or mold for that matter, of moisture. Organisms need moisture to grow. It is not unreasonable to conclude that marshmallow will dry out before it would go bad. I have never seen it go bad, but then again, once it's made, I, and everyone around me, are devouring it before it goes stale.

Marshmallows

Technically speaking, all of the products I've talked about so far are marshmallow. Marshmallow cream is the fresh material. Marshmallow meringue is the same material that is baked. Marshmallow in the form you buy in plastic bags is slightly dried and covered in cornstarch so that its surface is not sticky and the foam has a little more body and chew to it.

Making stand-alone marshmallows is a little tricky. All the marshmallow uses I've shown so far have been on another food, like a cookie, chocolate, or a pie, in the case of meringue. Freshly made marshmallow foam is like glue, so if you put it on another food that stickiness is a benefit since you are going to eat both foods together.

But what if you just want stand-alone marshmallows? Time, the right tools, and patience are required to get there. It is not for the faint of heart. You can do all the right things and your marshmallow may still refuse to release from the nonstick surface you put them on. I cover all this, in depth, in my first book with mallowmallow. Here is what you need if you choose to go the distance here:

- Really great marshmallow foam that is pretty stiff, like seen on the beater blades on page 135
- A food dryer
- A silicone nonstick baking sheet cut to fit into your food dryer
- Cornstarch
- Dry powdered flavorless fiber supplement (optional)

Stuff the marshmallow foam you whipped up into a zip-top bag. Remove as much air as you can and seal the bag shut. Cut a small hole in one corner. Pipe that foam onto your nonstick sheet in your food dryer. The dollops should look somewhat like chocolate kisses. Close up the food dryer and set the temperature at 110°F.

Now comes the tricky part. The length of the drying process depends on how much moisture is in your foam.

Mallowmallow from common mallow being piped onto a nonstick baking sheet cut to fit in a food dryer. Marshmallows are piped exactly the same way and look exactly the same as this.

Less moisture means they will be done earlier. More moisture and they can take up to four hours.

The difficulty is in achieving a dried base on each marshmallow. The upper part is easy and does not need much drying. It is where the mallow connects to the surface that has to dry enough to release the marshmallows. If they have not released, they will still be glued to the surface and you will be pulling and mashing while ineffectively trying to pick them up. They still taste great smashed, and you will have to eat all the ones you destroyed. It's a rule!

Start with an hour in the food dryer and gently prod one of the dollops. Use a cornstarch dusted finger or spoon handle end to see if you can gently pry it free. If it and others easily separate from the surface, they are done. If they are not close to done (still really glued), check in another hour, then another, then another. If you go over four hours in the food dryer, the pieces will start getting crispy instead of gooey—resulting in a hard meringue cookie.

Once they are ready to remove, dust their surface with cornstarch, pour some cornstarch into a zip-top bag, then drop in the marshmallows. Gently shake the bag around so that all the pieces are coated. That way they won't stick to each other.

Sift out the cornstarch, and you are done.

These marshmallows are ready to eat and best eaten fresh. They will store in the fridge in sealed containers for a few days.

TIPS

1. To facilitate the base of the marshmallows separating from the nonstick surface earlier, place a layer of dry powdered fiber supplement on the nonstick surface. It will absorb some of the moisture from the base and allow the marshmallow to come off earlier.

2. Make marshmallows with a smaller base. The marshmallows in the photograph have a wide base like chocolate kisses. It is harder for the circulating air in a food dryer to reach the bottom center of a wide base. That part has to dry to release from its surface. So if you can shape the marshmallows like narrow pillars instead of kisses, those bases will dry and release earlier.

3. Once you have your own system down with practice, you can predict more accurately how long to leave the food dryer on.

4. Pipe the marshmallow directly onto a thick bed of cornstarch in the food dryer. The only difference is that you will create a marshmallow rope rather than individual marshmallows. This solves the problem of individual pieces sticking to drying surfaces.

Recognizing how much extra work and time this is to make individual stand-alone marshmallows, it is much easier, and also cool, to put marshmallow on other foods. In fact, it's cooler.

Marshmallows are so much fun; I hope you get a chance to try this.

Chapter 12

Family: Phytolaccaceae
Species: *Phytolacca americana*

Pokeweed

Pokeweed festivals honor this delectable spring edible.

Mature pokeweed plant fruiting in summer, at about 7 feet tall.

Estimated Range

Official Species Name:
• *Phytolacca americana* L.

Synonyms
• None

Common Names:
• Pokeweed
• Inkberry
• Pokeberry
• Pigeonberry
• Poke

A taprooted perennial whose aboveground growth dies back every year. Native to the eastern United States, but now widespread and abundant in North America. A weedy plant that produces lots of seed-filled fruits and loves to spread. Not found in abundance in deserts, plains, and generally hot regions with low moisture and intense sunlight.

continued

POKEWEED

I typically start out explaining the marvelous virtues of a wild food. And pokeweed (poke) is generously virtuous. But since there is room for error here, I am going to begin by focusing on offering you a healthy respect for how you can go wrong. If you know how to go right, you will likely have a lifetime of great experiences with poke. Doing it right is not rocket science.

As popular as this wild food is, you typically do not find pokeweed covered in wild food guides. The simple reason is fear. Since there are many poisonings that occur, and sometimes confusing ones, wild food authors shy away from covering this plant. Understanding why people get poisoned will help you stay on the path to more fun culinary experiences. This is a great wild food. And while there are no guarantees in life about anything, knowledge is power.

The edible parts of pokeweed are poisonous raw. When processed properly, they are edible and delicious. There are far more deadly poisonous plants around, but due to ignorance of poke's cooking requirement, you will hear stories of poisonings and a lot of unjustified fear.

Most poisonings with pokeweed occur because of these three circumstances: eating any part of the root, which can be deadly; undercooking the shoots and greens; or being ignorant of the meaning of the name *poke sallet*. Poke sallet, sometimes called *poke salet*, is a cooked food. When people who don't know any better hear or read this, they think *poke salad*. In modern American culture a *salad* is mostly a side dish filled with fresh raw greens, eaten with some sort of dressing. Of course, there are fancy salads sometimes eaten as main dishes today that have almost any ingredient under the sun, including cooked items and meats. But most people still think of a salad as a side dish with fresh greens. Given that *salads* are eaten raw, people who don't know any better incorrectly assume that poke sallet is a raw dish. They then eat poke greens raw, resulting in the following symptoms: digestive upset, cramps, and often uncontrollable diarrhea. With proper cooking of pokeweed, most people will feel fine and happy, like me, after eating it.

The Really Poisonous Root

Toxins in the aboveground pokeweed growth can be rendered neutral during cooking, but those in the root cannot. The root is poisonous no matter how you process it. You cannot boil the toxins out of the root. *Do not eat the root, ever.*

Many writers of scholarly articles and government educational materials discussing toxicity of pokeweed are mostly referring to the root in their accounts. The worst symptoms and documented deaths are from the root, not the upper parts of the plant. Unfortunately, the writings are confusing, because both article titles and coverage often just refer to the pokeweed plant when discussing toxicity, not clearly distinguishing whether they are referring to the roots or the upper parts of the plant. Other writers are worried about the idiot factor, or are ignorant themselves about the edibility, so they scare the dickens out of you, out of an abundance of caution. Most people writing about pokeweed have never eaten it themselves, and/or are only repeating what they think they have learned from reading about it. And making matters worse, wild food authors are all over the place, giving vague recommendations about preparing/detoxifying poke.

Skin Rash

In the course of my research, I have handled poke leaves, stems, flowers, fruits, and roots, whenever it is in season, all my adult life. No problem. And if you watch people gathering it in online recordings, no one seems worried about skin rash. However, there are documented cases of a few unlucky individuals who can develop a rash when the plant contacts sensitive areas of the skin. So while the pads of your hands might be unaffected, the skin on your forearms might react. This is not the end of the world if you are one

Edible Parts:
• All parts are considered poisonous until boiled properly. Once boiled, new shoots, growing tips of leafy stems, leaves, and flowers are edible. Root crown and root are irretrievably poisonous. Berry juice is mostly used as a food dye; its edibility is debated.

WHAT IS A POISON?
A **poison** is anything that you ingest, touch, or breathe in that can cause anything from discomfort to death. Unfortunately, most people hear "poison," and think it always means a quick death. However, results of poisoning could just be nausea, a queasy stomach, or an undesired laxative effect.

MEDICINE IS NOT FOOD!
Don't be fooled into complacency by herbal remedies that include poke root. Most medicines are poisons prescribed in controlled amounts to accomplish a certain physiological result. And those who think more "natural" medicine is better have been poisoned by ingesting too much of herbal remedies containing poke root.

of the few affected. Just wear long sleeves and don't dance naked in a pokeweed patch. Wear gloves if you find you are supersensitive. You do not need to wear a hazmat suit when going into nature.

Pharmaceutical Potential

Poke has a number of beneficial chemicals that were initially thought of as cancer causing. They are called *mitogens*, and, in a lab, can speed up the growth of cells, initially making people think that they might be carcinogens. But how the body in real life uses these chemicals is only now being discovered. A mitogen can also promote healing. In addition, there is a whole slew of research suggesting that poke contains chemicals that may fend off HIV and be immunostimulatory (Wagner, 1985). You could write a whole book on pokeweed's pharmaceutical potential, but that is way beyond the scope of this book. I will concentrate on food here.

Color from Berries

The berry juice is an amazing pink/magenta color that has both food and nonfood possibilities. Apparently, the concentrated juice was used as an ink for writing and to color cheap wine, fruit pies, and any other food you wanted to look more pink. It has been used to dye fabric with mixed results, since it washes out easily. It has also been used to double solar cell energy-absorbing efficiency (Graf, 2010).

Esteemed Food from the Upper Plant

Poke is a cherished food in history. In the not-too-distant past, after a long, cold winter devoid of any fresh greens, people rejoiced as each important green food emerged in spring. These were a gift of nature. Greens provide life-saving nutrients and diversity to the diet. Pokeweed is one of those gifts. Even today, there are pokeweed festivals each spring throughout the southeastern United States.

Festivals happen in Arab, Alabama; Harlan, Kentucky; Gainesboro, Tennessee; Blanchard, Louisiana; and other places. Pokeweeds are not the first greens to pop up in spring, but they are an abundant, important green. Because of its big perennial roots that store lots of energy, pokeweed produces gobs of aboveground growth whose various parts can be eaten over months. The plant is the inspiration of the original 1968 song, "Poke Salad Annie," by Tony Joe White. Check recordings of it online. Poke was such a normal food that you could buy it canned. I will get into the details of processing to make this a delicious food later in this chapter.

The Allens company sold cooked poke greens in canned form to the general public. This product is no longer available.

Pokeweed as Invasive Enemy

Pokeweed is an amazingly vigorous plant that can grow in a variety of soils and sunlight. And it grows fast—from both seed and perennial taproots. That makes it great from a food-producing standpoint, but terrible for those who don't appreciate the food and whose goal is to manicure/tame nature. People target this plant for death for a variety of reasons. Many consider it too weedy and vigorous, wanting to reduce its numbers. When some hear that it is poisonous, they don't want it in their neighborhood. Of course, many people purchase poisonous indoor tropical house plants without knowing they are poisonous. This contradiction just shows how context is everything.

After a few years of root development, it is difficult to physically remove an unwanted pokeweed plant. You have to dig a big hole over a foot or more down, cutting out as much of the massive root and its side branches as you can. Discard the root in the trash, not a compost pile, otherwise it will start growing again. If you don't dig deep enough, lower remaining root fragments will survive, sending up new plants.

There are a few poke plants around my house that I manage carefully. I want as much plant diversity as possible for both eating and teaching, and poke is part of that. I

Pokeweed seedlings, the two on the left are cotyledons only. The one on the right has two real leaves with one remaining cotyledon. The center seedling is about an inch long from tip to tip.

First-year 20-inch-tall pokeweed plant. The green stem may or may not be covered by a thin reddish membrane.

prevent its spread by trimming off all the seed-filled fruits before they can drop in the fall. The seeds are very efficient at sprouting under almost any conditions. So I stop new plants before they begin. The few plants that I have produce gobs of food already. It's just enough for me.

Knowing Pokeweed

First-year plant

Pokeweed seeds love to germinate. They will germinate any time of the year with temperatures consistently above 50°F, once exposed to moisture. The embryonic root pierces rapidly downward, reaching depths where moisture is more likely retained, even when surface soil begins to dry. These roots know how to survive. That taproot is there to stay, even if you hack off the aboveground growth. The cotyledons, the first two embryonic leaflike structures that emerge from the seed, are teardrop shaped and pointed, more pointed than most cotyledons. Tip to base, they can range in size from $1/2$ inch to over an inch.

As the plant grows, true, egg-shaped leaves emerge from a fledgling stem. After a few weeks, the taproot begins to fatten. As more leaves form, they get longer and more pointed. In the plant's early stages, the leaves grow from 2 to 6 inches long. Leaf veins are pinnate, meaning they have a main vein running the length of each leaf, with branches coming off like a tree or feather. Veins continue branching toward the margins of the leaves. Veins are visible from the upper surface of the leaves, and they clearly protrude from the underside.

By the time the plant is 1 foot tall, the stem has thickened considerably to about an inch in diameter at the base and gradually tapering toward the top. That stem is mostly green with some reddish coloration. The red can be sparse or coloring whole areas. Once the stems reach diameters larger than $1/2$ inch, their centers become hollow. This is true of both the main stem and branches.

Leaves and stems are hairless and smooth. On larger stems a whitish bloom becomes apparent, more easily seen if you rub the stem—the rubbed area becomes slightly darker.

First-year plants are smaller at maturity than sequential year plants. Typically, first-year plants are 3 to 5 feet tall. Subsequent year plants can grow to 8 feet for more. The size depends on how large and deep the roots are. More years of growth yield larger roots, which produce larger plants. The aboveground plant dies away each winter, growing new shoots each spring. Poke can produce flowers and fruits in the first year.

Spotting pokeweed

Spring pokeweed shows itself by its previous year's stalks—stalks that prominently stick up above other plants. Once you know how they look, you can spot this plant from quite a distance. The old dead stalks can be over 8 feet tall, branching about halfway up. In a mild winter, they may still be standing. If they have been knocked down from harsh weather, they can be a mess of old stems splayed over their still-living taproots. The main stalks are typically an inch or greater in diameter all the way from their base to where branching begins. All branched stems are progressively thinner the farther they spread out from the main stem. Dead overwintering stems have irregular off-white, to yellowish, to gray scarred surfaces. By winter, all stalks have become brittle, are hollow, and easily crushed by hand.

Once you've found the old stalks it is time to look down at the ground for the root crowns that birthed them. Root crowns are the tops of taproots that typically stick up just above ground level. Every spring the crowns send up new stalks that live their seasonal life, then die in the fall. The roots and their crowns producing those temporary annual stalks last for years. The crowns grow bigger as the roots grow bigger.

After several years of growth root crowns can get quite large, sticking up several inches from the ground

Two pokeweed roots. The root grows fast. Left: A very young small aboveground plant is already producing a root the size of a thin carrot. Right: By the end of the first growing season, the root is almost 1.5 inches thick for most of the upper 8 inches of a 12-inch root . After several years this root can get as big as an arm, 3 feet deep, and branch in all directions.

Each year pokeweed sends up new stalks from perennial taproots. These two stalks have lived out their year, produced fruit, died in the fall, and represent what is left as they overwinter. Leaves and fruits have all dried up and fallen away revealing all the underlying branching. Harsh winter weather would easily knock these brittle stalks down. Each plant has one main stalk with branching starting 3 to 4 feet up from the base.

and expanding to more than 8 inches in diameter. The crowns are live material intermixed with what is left of the base of old dead stalks. The larger a crown, the more shoots are born. The shoots here are young aboveground plants. Shoots, in general, are new growths from established roots as compared to seedlings developing roots for the first time. The larger and older the crown, the more shoots emerge.

Early leaf behavior varies depending on the intensity of sunlight hitting the root crown. If the plant is out in the open getting lots of sunlight, the first leaves will splay outward. If growing in the shade, the first leaves will be more pressed against the fledgling stem. But soon all the leaves spread outward. Each shoot will become a separate stemmed plant. Since the root is feeding those new stems, they grow more rapidly than the first-year plant. Each stem on the same crown may grow at a slightly different rate, but will eventually top off at about the same height.

Poke plants grow rapidly, producing many large leaves on thick stems. Thick main stems are necessary to support the weight of leaves and upper stems.

Young leaves are elliptical in overall shape, gaining wider bases as they enlarge. While some leaves have nearly equal-sided bases, others have a different left and right shape, made clearer by the blade's indent on one side. As leaves grow older and larger, the indent is less obvious, making them more equal on both sides. Leaves (blade plus leaf stem) on adult plants can get quite large, from 12 to 18 inches long.

For a while the stems grow straight and produce axillary buds. But at some point, the upper part of the plant's

AXILLARY

Axillary is a location. Think of it as the upward-facing armpit (a location) between a leaf and the stem it is attached to. That location would be a leaf axil.

Axillary can also be the upward-facing armpit location between a main stem and a branch stem. That location would be a stem axil.

Buds that will grow into new leaves, stems, and flowers often originate from axillary locations.

A pokeweed root crown with new pokeweed shoots sprouting forth. This crown sits atop a large five-year-old taproot. Remnants of the old stalks are evident. This is the time that lovers of this plant celebrate. Shoots to the left are about 10 inches tall. The ones center-front range from 3 to 5 inches tall. All these shoots represent good rapid tender growth.

Several pokeweed stems vigorously growing from one taproot. The tallest plant here is about 30 inches tall.

INDENT   INDENT

Young pokeweed leaves of an 18- to 20-inch tall plant. These leaves are about 8 inches from top to bottom. Left: Upper side of the leaf is darker, with veins relatively flat, even with the overall surface. Right: Underside of the leaf is lighter, with veins, particularly the main one, that clearly stick up from the blade. Leaf veins are pinnate (treelike), continuing to branch toward the margins of the leaves.

Below: Pokeweed flowers in a raceme flower arrangement. These racemes range in length from a few inches to over a foot long.

Above: As the plant matures, the upper part of the stem branches outward instead of continuing on a straight trajectory. Compare this photograph to the one earlier of the two dead stalks, page 146. This plant is just over 6 feet tall and still growing. The main stem here is over an inch in diameter. You can see a flower stalk at the upper right. This plant will fill with flower stalks as it matures. New, younger leaves and stems grow out of the base of older leaves.

Right: Tiny pokeweed flower, showing five petal-like sepals, 10 stamens, and a green turban-shaped pistil. The sepals are often pure white, but can also be green- or red-tinted. There are no true petals here.

Right: Pokeweed fruits regularly ripen at different rates, even on the same raceme. Immature fruits are green. They turn almost black when fully ripe. The raceme on the right is about 9 inches long.

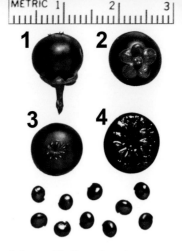

main stem branches/splits into four or so stems. This branching is staggered, meaning that they do not all branch from the same spot on the main stem This allows the plant to spread out in its upper canopy, giving it more sunlight to produce more growth.

Flowers are borne on delicate stems in a raceme arrangement. A raceme is a simple stem with tiny side stems (peduncles) along its length, tipped with flowers. A raceme does not branch. There could be anywhere from 30 to 100 flowers on one pokeweed raceme. Their stamens and petal-like sepals are white, with green protruding turban-shaped ovaries sitting above the sepals. There are no petals. Each flower on the raceme is small, about 1/4 inch in diameter. The sepals might have shades of green or pink to them.

All those ovaries within the pistils, once pollinated, mature into fruits. The fruits start out green, then get greenish-white, turning maroon and then almost black in color. The ripe berries are juicy, but they are mostly filled with seeds. The end of the berry has a pattern that looks like a circular exploding firework. Seeds typically spread in two ways: once the berries ripen, they drop to the ground; or birds come by and swallow them whole. The birds fly off and poop the seeds somewhere else, where they can spread.

After temperatures cool in the fall, the ripe fruits drop to the ground. The leaves turn reddish, shrivel, droop down, and fall off. The stem loses its green color, turns yellowish, then light brown, and becomes brittle. The stems are easily broken and slowly fall away during fall and winter's wind, rain, and snow. Sometimes all that remains in the following spring is the root crown sticking out of the ground. And the annual cycle continues.

Pokeweed fruits and seeds from all angles. 1. Side view showing fruit stem. 2. Underside showing reddened sepals and cut stem stub in center. 3. Fruit top showing circular fireworks pattern. 4. Cut in half, showing inside pulp and seeds. Bottom are the 10 seeds packed into each fruit.

Gathering and Edibility of Pokeweed

Pokeweed keeps on giving throughout its life span. The key is to find great-looking, fresh, rapidly growing aboveground parts in the first and subsequent years and pay attention to

Pokeweed fruits showing a close-up of the circular fireworks pattern. I have seen no other berry with this pattern and appearance. Note the smaller reddish immature fruits, still in development and the commonly red stem of the raceme.

the detail I given you here. And part of that detail is: **Never eat the root, make a tea out of it, boil it, fry it, or beat it with a stick.** None of that will make it edible. There is nothing you can do to the root to make it edible, so stop thinking that you are the genius that can do it. I say that to the beginner survival enthusiasts who seem to take these things on as a challenge: "Don't eat, eh? I'll show you." Be smart and spend your time learning about things you can actually eat. Note that the root crown is root.

Before I get into individual parts, let's discuss processing, because it is key to edibility. I am only referring to the nonfruit, aboveground tender parts of the plant here. Once you identify good tender material, the first thing you must do before anything else is a proper boiling. Tender, rapidly growing leaves and shoots are ready to boil as is, but certain tough parts of the stem must be peeled first. Once you've got your tender leaves and stems and peeled stem material, you can begin the boiling process. This boiling, when done right, makes the poke edible and delicious.

"A boiling" defined

While some variation exists in the literature, here is how I am defining a boiling. Start a pot of boiling water. Once rapidly boiling, insert the plant material, and bring the pot back to a full rolling boil. That full boil starts the timer for however long you want to boil it. Once done, discard the water. Then go on to any next step with the cooked greens. That next step could be a second boil just like the first, or it might be skipping that and incorporating the greens right into a dish.

Each boiling is designed to clear something out of the plant material, by leaching toxic substances out of the plant and moving them into the water and/or using the heat to denature, destroy, or make harmless any toxic substances. For some plants, a boiling might be done just to improve flavor; for instance, by removing bitter or bad-tasting substances from plant material. But for poke, the primary aim is to detoxify the plant material you are going to eat.

In order for a boiling to work properly, the volume of water must be big enough to allow the plant material you are cooking to roll around in the water. Do not stuff so much material in a pot that nothing can move around. If there is enough movement within the water, there is enough water to do its magic on the greens. So invest in big pots if you want to cook lots of greens at once.

If multiple boilings are necessary or desired, do not let the greens cool down between boilings. To assure this, start heating the second pot around the same time that you are heating the first pot. That way the second pot will be ready and you can just transfer the greens from one pot to the other that is already boiling.

Water takes a lot of energy to heat up. To maximize your efficiency, keep tight-fitting lids on the pots while heating—this traps in the heat. Once the greens are in, remove the lids and boil away.

What practitioners have done and said about cooking pokeweed

Here is what makes the preparation of pokeweed confusing. There is huge variation in reported preparation techniques. Practitioners (those who actually eat pokeweed) are often unclear in expressing exactly what they are doing and why. Their descriptions are often inadequate and they may not know why they are doing certain things. You know— the old "my parents did it this way, so that is how I do it" kind of practice.

Young shoots, peeled young shoots, young leaves, and peeled older stalks, may have different preparation requirements to manage toxicity, texture, and flavor. Due to all this confusion and reports of poisonings, some authors, in an effort to be overly cautious, recommend boiling the parts in three or four boils of water. Unfortunately, this is part of the zero-tolerance syndrome our country seems to be in these days. Since this plant is poisonous in the raw form, it brings the fear of god into the hearts of many who just

A Cooking Folktale

The ways people do things are not always based on effectiveness, efficiency, and factual knowledge. Some things are based in idiosyncratic patterns having nothing to do with the task at hand. That is why there are so many confusing ways people recommend to process pokeweed and other wild foods. To illustrate how things can happen, I am going to repeat the story about cooking a roast, handed down in Jewish storytelling. The story goes like this:

A newlywed is about to cook a big roast in the oven. She cuts off the end of the roast and drops it in the roasting pan. Her husband asks her why she is wasting the end of the roast. She replies that that is how you cook a roast, and that she learned it from her mother. As a result of her husband's question, she asks her mother what the point was of cutting off the end of the roast? Her mom replied, it was because the roasting pan we had was too small to fit the whole roast.

The moral to the story is to understand *why* you do things. For all the people in history that have cooked pokeweed, their individual circumstances and habits have created a variety of methods that made sense to them. What they learned from their parents, cooking equipment available, understanding of poke's toxicity, experiences or reports of poisonings they heard about, all contribute to one family's understanding of what to do. Unfortunately, these variable cooking procedures just add to the confusion and don't give us the *why*.

don't know plants anymore. The modern fear of plants and fear of being poisoned is overwhelming. The less-informed solution is to overcook, and then overcook some more. People brought up on these plants had no such fears. They did what needed to be done, given their own circumstances and traditions without thinking much about it.

Government and university publications that publish plant fact sheets are often simplistic and are typically written by people who have no real experience with the plant or understanding of cultural uses. They get their information from botanical sources and poisoning reports from the medical toxicology literature. Without real-world experience, and therefore, in ignorance, and with an abundance of caution, they either tell you to overcook the plant or just leave it alone as too dangerous. For novices who don't do their homework, leaving plants like this alone is not a bad idea. But for those who do their homework, pokeweed is a great wild food worthy of celebrating.

Your author and most others that teach about wild foods consider all "edible" parts on pokeweed poisonous until boiled properly. For context, remember that an edible part is defined as one that is properly prepared.

To confuse matters, a rare few authors believe that the peeled stems are safe to eat raw. Billy Joe Tatum offered the following optimistic interpretation of poke edibility. "The stalk, after peeling, the young shoots when they're 6 to 8 inches high, and the leaves, gathered before the flower head has formed, are all delectable and completely safe" (Tatum, 1976). However, all her recipes have at least one boiling, except for the peeled, breaded, and fried stalk. Both she and Gibbons (1962) have said that the peeled stem negates the need for parboiling. Both assume that the toxins are only in the skin of the stem. This may or may not be true. Or, at the minimum, this may not be true for everyone since some people may be more sensitive to tiny amounts of toxin than others.

Many practitioners have pointed to redness in the skin of poke as an indication of toxicity. Some say that if it is red, leave it alone. This may or may not be a folktale. I have always ignored the red scare since it never made a difference in the poke that I've eaten. Red pigmentation is often a result of sunlight's interaction with surface cells and may indeed indicate more of the toxin and other chemicals in the skin of poke. But in my experience, whether the skin is red or green, the boiling process leaches out and/or destroys the toxins from poke.

Boiling seems to be the main detoxification method for poke—not frying, grilling, steaming, or baking. Boiling, according to the accounts I've read, is done for one or more of three reasons: detoxification, tenderization, and in some second boilings letting added flavors soak into the greens.

For instance, after an initial boiling to detoxify, some authors have suggested simmering the greens for 45 minutes or more in a second change of water. That simmer is almost always to further tenderize and/or allow flavors of spices and oils to permeate the greens. That new water is not used for detoxification. It is, in fact, often used as part of the dish or its preparation, usually to create a sauce or produce a moist final product. Some have suggested that older (meaning tall plants) tender rapidly growing plant shoots and leaves require longer cooking to finish off whatever toxins remain.

Most practitioners do one of the following two options for most rapidly growing shoots and leaves:

- A 5- to 10-minute boil, drain, toss water; use.
  This seems to be the minimum prep for the early spring shoots
- A 5- to 10-minute boil, drain, toss water; boil a second time, then either drain and use, or add more things to the poke in its cooking water and use that.
  This second boil option is mostly used to tenderize older, tougher leaves and stems.

These boilings are intended to detoxify and remove the accompanying bitterness. After the cook follows one of these two boiling options, the poke is typically cooked in combination with other flavors and foods to make the intended finished dish. Flavorings typically added are butter or bacon grease, garlic, onions, spices, wine, meat or vegetable broth, salt, and pepper. The greens can be glazed with oil or butter, along with sugar, honey, or maple syrup. Foods added often are eggs, bacon, cream or cheese sauces, and for some reason, corn bread. The second cooking water is sometimes used to help create a broth. If you start a boil, but that cooking water becomes part of the dish and is not poured off, then it is not an additional *boil,* the way I am using the term.

I am ignoring any third or fourth boilings some writers recommend as unnecessary, excessive, and fear-based.

Tender rapidly growing parts do not require long cooking times. If you are using larger leaves and leaf stems, they will definitely get more tender and possibly less "reactive" with longer cooking. If you are someone who loves supersoft greens, go ahead and cook them till the cows come home.

In rare instances, some practitioners, in the course of making a cooked pokeweed dish, either do not boil the shoots at all (for instance, breading and frying raw poke), or use the single boil along with its cooking water as part of the final dish (Wigginton 1973, Kluger 1973, Brackett 1975, and Tatum, 1976). These kinds of experiments are for those willing to see what their bodies can tolerate. I do not recommend this since nausea, vomiting, and diarrhea are not fun.

So what does your author do?

As a proponent of less cooking, I want to know, what is the minimal cooking needed to detoxify tender young poke? Less cooking destroys fewer nutrients, keeps more flavor, and allows the already tender greens to have some body to them. In my experiments, **I have come to do a single 10-minute boiling of the tender, rapidly growing fresh leaves and shoots.** Once that is done, the greens are ready to use in any dish I want to include them in—as plain old cooked greens or within another dish. For some applications, you can add boiled, then drained greens. For others, you may want to drain, then blot them with a towel to take off all surface moisture, like before frying.

Varying from a 10-minute boil: What I recommend may not be enough cooking for everyone, since it is possible that some rare people are more sensitive to the toxins in poke than I am. If you want to be cautious on your first dining experience, boil them in two changes of water. Once you feel great about that, try only one boil. And there are some who might be able to tolerate as little as a 5-minute boil. That is not for everyone, so start out cautious and only reduce the time if you don't mind chancing more bathroom visits.

My Interpretation of the Toxicologic Literature

There are reports of people being poisoned by consuming pokeweed. Those reports fall into three categories:

1. Out of ignorance, victims did not cook or cooked inadequately, and the reports make sense.
2. Victims thought they did everything right but still got poisoned.
3. Something else caused the problem, but poke gets the blame because they don't have a better answer.

People who have never eaten poke are frightened by these reports and tend to reject it as a food out of fear. Here are some examples of reports of poisoning by pokeweed along with my analyses of what probably happened. Again, I do not fear it because, like other people who eat it, I know what I am doing and have had nothing but good experiences with it.

The greens

CAMP RUN-A-MUCK: In 1981 the Center for Disease Control (Callahan, 1981), reported an incident where 52 campers and counselors consumed a pokeweed salad made up of young leaves that had been boiled in two changes of water. Virtually everyone got sick. Four were hospitalized due to protracted vomiting and the resultant dehydration. They ruled out staphylococcus. Although no permanent ill effects were reported, this event raised the fear that two boilings were not enough. It gave the impression that pokeweed greens were unpredictable and therefore more dangerous than earlier thought.

My first read of this report disturbed me. How can this be? How can there be festivals and so much tradition, with people annually dining on this food, and yet after years of doing this safely, people got poisoned in this one incident after two boilings? I read the report several times. After my third read I began to have some questions, mostly about the report's completeness and accuracy. The problem with reports on plant poisonings by people who do not know the plant and its nuances is that the medical responders and the later analysts don't necessarily know what questions to ask. Here are my questions:

- Who did the actual gathering of the plant parts in this instance? The kids? Their counselors? The cook?
- How informed were the collectors about pokeweed's edibility and did they pay attention to its toxicity? Did everyone involved know exactly what they

were supposed to do and why? Since this plant was eventually served to them on a plate like a normal food, did that provide gatherers with a sense of indifference or lack of concern about the plant's toxicity? Did they all know about its toxicity?

- Did anyone carefully check the material after it was collected to verify what exactly was gathered?
- What actual plant material is being called *leaves*? Were they including the shoots, since they have leaves?
- Are the "leaves" gathered from the same poke plants each year, or were these new plants from a new area?
- Could some fresh raw poke leaves been accidently added to any fresh salad they were eating?

Here are some additional useful details: This camp had used the two-boilings method and had served this pokeweed cooked "salad" for years before this without incident. While diarrhea (mostly), nausea, and stomach queasiness are typical symptoms for eating undercooked pokeweed, additional symptoms reported were dizziness, headaches, and a burning in the stomach or mouth. Those are more symptoms of eating the root, not the greens. And after two boilings, assuming they were using the appropriate plant parts and had boiled them properly as represented, none of these symptoms *should have* occurred. So that raises the question: Was root material included in the boiled material? Boiling will not detoxify the root.

If this group was picking from the same perennial pokeweed plants they have been picking for years, that would rule out a new plant that was a genetic mutation that might enhance the toxicity in the greens with poisons resistant to cooking—like those found in the roots. If untrained people (kids or their counselors) were collecting the young shoots, could any of them have cut too low and included some root material? Could an ignorant participant collector, not understanding the toxicity of the root, have collected some on purpose, thinking it would add a crispy texture and some bulk to the cooked greens? And then be too embarrassed/afraid to admit it later when they learned that everyone got poisoned and it was their fault? Or perhaps inexperienced gatherers still do not know what they did.

My point is that while no one can be sure about the true facts of this now historical case, it is unlikely to me that properly boiled pokeweed was the problem here. There was something else going on. But this case, probably more than any other, is why so many nonconsumers of pokeweed and some wild food instructors recommend so many boilings. And as an instructor who offers workshops within which we cook up wild foods, I understand the need to protect students from unreasonable risk. It can be a career-ending event if all your students got sick and you could have prevented it.

It is always possible that there may be a few rare individuals that are more sensitive to the toxin you are destroying by boiling. But that would be an individual, not a group thing as in this story.

The berries

Most online sources of information only add to the confusion of pokeberry edibility—including medical sites and Wikipedia. The recommendations range from "avoid at all costs" to "they are harmless." It is always good to consider long-held concerns about the berries. There is often a grain of truth in cultural knowledge. However, some truths can begin from misunderstandings and be repeated enough to become cultural knowledge. There are widely held beliefs that pokeberries are poisonous. So let's look at reports of pokeberry ingestion.

I have seen reference to a mom who crushed enough berries to make a pokeberry juice. She fed it to her child, who later died. I cannot find an official account of this anywhere, or the recipe that was used, or when or where this happened, or if there could have been another cause of death. It could be true or could be a folktale. It is mentioned in Wikipedia but is missing a reference. This story should be viewed with skepticism, considering the lack of documentation, and the following reports.

POKEBERRY PANCAKES: In 1981 Boy Scouts and their leaders (six total) ate some pancakes with pokeberries in the batter. Nothing significant happened. Two had some minor diarrhea, and one had stomach cramps over a day later, possibly due to exercise. This would have totally gone unnoticed as normal, since variations in dietary patterns and sanitation during scouting outings often cause minor digestive changes. A control group would have been a good idea at the time, of other scouts who attended the same event but did not eat the pokeberry pancakes. What made a story out of this was that someone on the outside learned that pokeberries were involved and possibly dangerous, so they contacted the Kentucky Poison Center. Center staff then did a follow-up investigation and survey of all six pancake eaters. What they concluded was that there was no correlation between the number of pancakes eaten and the symptoms experienced. None required medical attention. The 17-year-old who ate the most pokeberries had no symptoms (Edwards, 1982). We cannot conclude that the berries were harmless from this report. But we could conclude that their impact could be anywhere from harmless to mild, certainly not serious or life-threatening.

WHAT'S HAPPENING TO CHILDREN IN KENTUCKY? In 1984 the Kentucky Regional Poison Center decided to keep track of all pokeberry ingestion reports to hospitals. Most of the children involved ranged from a year and three months to five years of age. Twenty-six percent were thought to have ingested 20 or more raw berries. Almost all were asymptomatic. The evaluation concluded that no patients required hospitalization, and "the ingestion of up to 20 pokeberries appears to be easily tolerated in small children. Symptoms are rare, mild and resolve rapidly" (Matyunas, 1985). The only cautionary tale I saw in this account is that parents often overestimate how many berries their children have eaten when they discover the red-faced tykes next to the plant. What clued me in to this is that after inducing vomiting in emergency rooms out of fear and caution, not due to symptoms, the vomit revealed berries in only two of 14 cases.

Before you decide from all this that pokeberries are perfectly edible, take into consideration that ingestion is a rare occurrence in these reports, not an everyday thing. And these are relatively small amounts of berries. So just because they are not a strong toxin does not mean they would be fine to eat like raspberries, particularly for growing bodies.

ANIMAL STUDIES OF THE BERRIES: Scientists tried to determine the lethality of pokeberries in adult mice as their physiology is a good model for ours. All berries were uncooked. They tested whole berries, the separated pulp, and the seeds. They found it extremely difficult to feed the mice enough to kill them, saying: "If human beings are equally as sensitive (or resistant) to pokeberry poisoning as were the mice used, it would take about 45 pounds of fresh berries to kill an average adult male." And "The acute oral lethal dose of pokeberries in mice was larger than the quantity that could be administered" (Ogzewalla, 1962). They looked at only lethality; they did not report on physiological changes, pain, and suffering from all the pokeberries. They found the seeds to be about twice as toxic as the pulp when ingested in huge amounts.

Scientists tried to determine the physiological and developmental implications of feeding raw pokeberries to rapidly growing infant turkeys. They found, "Growth rate was reduced with each increase in level of pokeberries." Death occurred in 38 percent of the rapidly growing chicks when pokeberries replaced 10 percent (dried weight) of their normal diet over a three-week period. Chicks experienced ataxia (stumbling, imbalance), enlarged and crooked joints, abdominal swelling, and gall bladder issues (Barnett, 1975). So when a significant portion of their diet was replaced with poke-berry, developing chicks showed signs of developmental abnormalities and, unlike the study with adult mice, significant numbers died.

Unpublished Experiences Eating Poke

The case of traveling diarrhea

One person tried to batter and fry the cut-up raw poke stem without boiling first and served it at a potluck. The outcome was not pretty for one of my colleagues who ate the undercooked, unboiled poke nested within the batter. He experienced uncontrollable, quick-onset diarrhea soon thereafter and his pants felt the brunt of it. Yeah, once it hit, while he was driving home, it was that quick and uncontrolled. He soiled his pants. He had no other symptoms (personal communication).

Roy Conley, June 25, 2019

This was posted in the comments section of the *University of California Weed Science Newsletter*. It is shown as written, including spelling and local ways of expression. This man evidently eats young spring, rapidly growing pokeweed shoots raw. Note that *pear boiled* likely means *parboiled*.

"I am 67 and have ate Poke Salad front I was a small child. My parents believed that needed to be pear boiled and then they would cook it scrambled with eggs. In contrast I found it growing in St Louis in Forest Park with a very heavy leaf mulch. I actually use an asparagus knife and cut Spears 6 to 8 in tall and cook them exactly like asparagus. They were wonderful. An addition I have taken young plants with very young leaves and put them in tall salads again with no problem. I routinely cut the plants back in the summer to promote new growth. This new growth I have never pear boiled and I have never had an issue. The first time I generally eat it in the spring it does act like a laxative. After that no issue. I am now growing it in pots in Alaska." (Comments Section: Oneto, 2018).

Some people like Roy may be able to tolerate some of the toxin in pokeweed without apparent issue. How to interpret this: Nature, genetics, and your unique physiology may react in different ways to the heat-sensitive toxins in poke. My guess is that most people will be able to enjoy poke with only that 5-minute rolling boil (parboil) that I suggest. That is how I prepare it and have never had a problem. However, nature is not here for our convenience and there are no guarantees in life. Some people cannot eat wheat, dairy, soy, shellfish, onions, or peanuts. You and your family will have to figure this out for yourselves. Also note a couple of other things from Roy's account. Roy indicates that his body adapts to the laxative effect. It is mild at first, but then normal. Second, if the poke is buried in deep leaf mulch, then it has less exposure to the sun and perhaps is less toxic prior to boiling. But keep this in perspective. Roy is an adult. Just because he showed no symptoms, it does not mean that underlying things are not happening to his body. And due to the turkey study mentioned earlier, it is certainly not right to assume that any raw part of poke is safe for developing bodies, even if they show no overt signs of damage. And remember, Roy's parents fed him cooked poke as a developing child, so his body was exposed to, and could adjust over time to, the harmless amounts of toxin that remained in the foods he ate.

What Does This Mean for You?

It is clear, from both scientific studies and reports of poisonings, that there are toxins in raw pokeweed. It is also clear that there is a long tradition of eating and enjoying properly cooked pokeweed shoots leaves and peeled stems. Assuming proper preparation, I have seen no restrictions made for growing children or pregnant women by regular consumers of this plant. It appears that some rare people can tolerate raw shoots and greens, but most cannot.

Given all this, it is my opinion that almost everyone properly boiling the *edible* parts of pokeweed will have a great experience right from the start. Your minimum preparation should start out with a 10-minute boil. If you are super cautious, do two 10-minute boils, if you are daring, do only a 5-minute boil. Always toss the water from the first boil. Once boiled, the sky is the limit with what you can do.

Keep in mind that trying any new food might result in a mild laxative effect that stops happening as your body adjusts with repeated exposure. You may need a laxative in your life. For perspective, dandelion greens can serve as a mild laxative. Neither plant has ever caused a laxative effect in me.

Gathering the Young Plant

As the plant grows from a seedling, you can harvest the whole aboveground leaves and stem up to about 8 inches from the ground. Cut clearly above the root so you do not accidentally include root material.

There may be some red on the stem. That is fine. Some of the wild food literature warns about avoiding poke with red stems. There is no evidence that red on the stems is worse than green stems if it is prepared properly. Almost all poke has red on the stems. My guess is that the few people that may be able to tolerate poke raw found that they cannot tolerate it if it is red. I am not going to test that on myself. I have regularly eaten both green- and red-stemmed boiled poke and there is no difference. Boil them and treat like spinach.

New Shoots of Spring

New shoots arising from the root crown of a multiyear root will have thicker stems than new plants growing directly from seed. That thicker stem makes this a more substantial food than the seedlings. Once the root crowns begin producing, these shoots can be plentiful. Every time you slice off a shoot, it stimulates the crown to send up more. Since this plant is so vigorous, it far outperforms asparagus in productivity. You can clip a lot away from this plant without harming or depleting the root. Always be careful to cut at least $1/2$ inch above where the shoot arises from

Whole young poke plants grown from seed. These leaves and upper stems can be boiled and eaten like spinach. **Cut off and discard all root material and stem up to where the first leaves branch off** before boiling and eating the upper plant. Even these baby roots are poisonous. Never, never, never eat the roots!

Left: Properly boiled poke, made from shoots like the ones below sprinkled with grated cheese while still hot, and seasoned with olive oil, salt, and pepper. Any sauce you pour over asparagus will work here. Boiling renders these more limp than boiled asparagus. This dish is garnished with an oxeye daisy flower.

the crown. Wash, boil, and use it in any way you would use asparagus. The raw shoots will hold their shape, but boiled, they go limp. So if you want them to be visually reminiscent of asparagus when serving, you have to carefully lay them out one by one.

The Stem

Once the plant stem grows above 8 inches, the lowest part, attached to the root, begins to get fibrous. This happens on all plants with a main stem. As the plant becomes more massive above, the stem has to become stronger and more rigid to support the upper weight. Otherwise, the plant would limp over. The cool thing is that all that fiber is limited to the rind. Rinds can be peeled, revealing a tender core.

As poke grows tall, the stem goes through two stages. At first, each stem grows straight, with only minor axillary growth. At around 3 to 5 feet tall, the upper stem diverges into multiple stems angling out to the sides, as shown earlier. During the first stage, most of the stem can be peeled, boiled, and eaten. This can be a significant amount of food. The stem is hollow, with bamboo-like segments throughout. The peel is thin and easily removed.

When processing the long peeled stems, I cut them specifically for cooking. First, I slice them into 7-inch-long segments so they will fit within the inside diameter of my boiling pot. Then, I cut them lengthwise so that all segmented parts of the core are exposed directly to water during the boiling process, helping to prevent undercooking. If I left them whole, air pockets between flanges along

Young poke shoots harvested from an established multiyear root. These were cut just above the root crown. The stems here started out thicker than plants grown from seed. Once boiled properly, these shoots can be treated just like cooked asparagus (see top photo) or spinach.

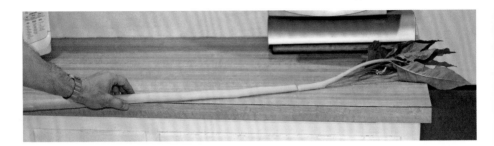

Above: A peeled young poke stem, about 40 inches long, with upper leaves still attached. All but the very base is tender enough to boil and eat.

Above: This shows where the peeled stem is likely to be tender depending on the maturity of the plant. Lighter green shows where the stem has been peeled. Left: The youngest plant just prior to the main stem branching out at the top. Center: This plant's upper branches have emerged. Right: The upper branches of this oldest plant have fully spread out and is producing flower bud racemes. For all three plants, the only part showing is where the peeled stem is tender enough to boil and eat. The younger plant on the left is still growing so it has the most tender peeled material. The middle-aged plant in the center only has a small part of the peeled main stem, with all the branching above, that is still tender. The oldest plant on the right has peeled stem tenderness limited to only the most terminal parts of the upper branches. All the fresh green rapidly growing leaves and uppermost stems on all of these are tender enough to boil and eat. Lower right is what the unpeeled stem looks like.

In preparation for boiling, stems are peeled, sliced into 7-inch lengths, and split lengthwise. This clearly shows the flanged core. Observe how thin the skin can be.

the stem might slow the cooking process. Once peeled and cut, these stems are ready for proper boiling. Once boiled, use them the way you would eat any tender vegetable, like cooked zucchini.

Once poke plants begin to branch at the top, the lower parts of the stem become too fibrous to eat, even after peeling. The new, rapidly growing upper branches will continue to be tender under the peel for a limited time—less and less so, up to the point when the tops are producing flowers. These stems will be narrower, but still great as a food. The best way to determine if the peeled stem is tender is to do a snap test. If the peeled stem snaps cleanly, it is tender. If it resists and bends but does not break, it is too tough.

Peeled, sliced, boiled for 5 minutes, and drained poke stems used as the green vegetable in an omelet. Include them as an additional vegetable in any omelet recipe.

The Leaves

Any fresh, rapidly growing, good-looking leafy material on pokeweed is fair game at almost any stage of growth. While the wild food literature seems to focus on the young shoots, much of the southeastern United States, where poke is eaten, also loves the leaves. The canned greens shown at the beginning of this chapter were leaves, not the young shoots. Culturally, the focus on the shoots may be because they are the first really appreciated food available of several on this plant. In addition, the fact that they are reminiscent

Right: The key to edibility for any poke leaves is good green vibrant color without yellowing and blotching. Fast growth promoted by large roots means that even many of the larger leaves are still relatively young, rapidly growing and good for cooking. Great looking leaves means great eating.

Perfectly edible (once boiled) upper growth tips (whole leafy stems like this). At any pokeweed height (even 6 to 7 feet tall) the leading leafy stems and new stems arising from leaf axils can be used. Test for tenderness by ease of cutting. If a scissors slices through the stem like it's butter, then the stem will be tender from there up. Boil this like any other part. Trim off any flower bud stalks before using. Avoid tips where flowers have opened.

of asparagus gives them some regard in the wild food literature. Asparagus seems to be the holy grail of wild foods, a highly prized wild food. Consequently, asparagus-like shoots of poke and other plants like Japanese knotweed seem to get more attention and acclaim.

I look for clean, unblemished, fully green leaves that look so good I could imagine them on a supermarket shelf. All rapidly growing leaves should fit this description. They are found at new growth points throughout the life of the plant. They could be from young plants, or leaves and stems from the leaf axils at the bases of older leaves. Just pluck off all the leaves you want. Always check the leaf stems for tenderness before using; you may want to remove them if they are too tough. Boil the leaves like all other

Salad rolls using pre-boiled poke leaves for wrapping. That is a peeled, boiled green poke stem resting on the open leaf with other vegetables. Consider including cheese, peppers, carrots, avocados, mushrooms, jicama, rice, fish, and other things in these poke wraps. Be adventurous and use boiled poke leaves in place of grape leaves for dolmathes (dolmas) with avgolemono sauce.

pokeweed parts. Then use them like any other cooked green: by themselves or in any dish in place of cooked spinach, kale, collards, or dandelions.

If you choose to include the leaf stems (petioles) of some of the larger foot-long leaves, longer boiling times will tenderize them somewhat.

Poke leaves can get pretty large and still be tender, which makes them great for making food wraps. Today many people are trying to find alternatives to bread for holding food together, in order to cut down on carbohydrates. Poke has a big enough leaf to provide a good experimental canvas for testing ideas. Just make sure you properly boil them prior to wrapping food in them.

Pokeweed greens. Boiled 10 minutes and seasoned with olive oil, balsamic vinegar, salt and pepper. Garnished with everlasting pea flowers. These greens could have been used in any way that cooked spinach is used. There are millions of recipes for that.

And Finally, the Fruits

All the things we traditionally think of as berries have three parts: skin, pulp, and seeds. As of this writing, I do not have enough confidence that the cooked pulp and skins of pokeweed berries are safe to eat in quantity as you would eat cooked blueberries or blackberries. Again, pokeweed seeds are considered poisonous raw or cooked.

For such a famous plant whose greens are eaten in massive quantities, it is telling that I have, to date, been unsuccessful in finding traditional recipes for its fruits. You'd think that recipes would have been handed down for generations, but I have not found them. Not in old recipe books or ethnobotanical reports. You only see sporadic users ingesting small amounts of the whole berries and declaring them okay because they did not suffer obvious consequences. I've ingested as many as 5 whole unchewed berries with no difficulty. It is possible that unchewed seeds pass undigested through the intestinal tract, but who is verifying that by examining their feces for such things? I have not.

I have seen some medicinal uses. For instance, one to three unchewed raw pokeberries swallowed whole have been used in adults and kids as a spring tonic. Animal studies, like the one I mentioned earlier, give us pause about potential harm to rapidly growing humans, particularly when the berries are raw. While boiling apparently removes the toxins in the vegetable matter, that process may not be transferable to the fruits or their seeds. Unlike the greens, you cannot pour off the cooking water with berries, since that "water" is the berry juice. If this was a slam dunk, there should be a long glowing history of use. There is not. So I am not recommending that the berries be used for food.

Here are some instances when the berries were used for food-*like* products along with my commentary to help further illustrate my doubts about berry edibility. Focus on the difference between how people labeled their foods vs what they actually produced.

Pokeberry Jelly?

Recently I viewed an online video (Georgia Gleaners: https://youtu.be/hJKBiLcxNbU) of a person making what she called *pokeberry jelly*. She used some sort of double-boiler juicing device to extract pokeberry juice, leaving the seeds and skin behind. I document her main ingredients by proportion here.

In order of greatest volume her jelly was:
9 parts sugar
4 parts apple juice
2 parts lemon juice
1 part extracted pokeberry juice
pectin

My analysis: If you add up the ingredients, this is really apple/lemon jelly colored by pokeberry juice. The actual amount of poke juice was roughly one-sixteenth the contents of this recipe. Once you spread this "pokeberry jelly" on toast, the actual number of cooked berries represented on that toast in terms of the juice extracted may only be two or three. As one does not typically eat a whole jar of jelly at one sitting, consumption is spread out. Contrast that with the number of berries you would imagine to find on a slice of pure pokeberry pie—if it was made like a traditional blueberry pie. When I see this real-world example, and from what I have read, it is not unreasonable to assume that most food products labeled as pokeberry, may be just colored by them. In other words, small amounts of pokeberry juice are primarily used in small quantities as a food dye.

Pokeberry Wine?

Here are Mrs. Carrie Dixon's pokeberry wine directions:

"Gather ripe pokeberries, wash, and place in a crock. Cover with cheesecloth and let set until it ferments. Strain off the juice and sweeten to taste" (Wigginton, 1973).

Evidently, you take a teaspoon of this "wine" whenever your rheumatism acts up. My point is, it is not what a normal human would call wine. It's a liquid used as a medicine that you use sparingly. This is the problem with cutesy names that people attribute to things they make. When people see *wine*, they assume there is another thing you can make with pokeberries.

Pokeberry Wine?

There is a historical record of pokeberry juice used to deepen the red of wines. Wine connoisseurs saw this as a cheat. And, if too much is used, the poke flavor is easily detected and the wine is ruined. These were not called pokeberry wine, but the wines were adulterated with small amounts of its juice for its magenta color.

Pokeberry Pie?

Government publications add confusing information about the berries that you can typically ignore. For instance, The North Carolina State extension service declares, "Cooked berries are safe for making pies" (https://plants.ces.ncsu .edu/plants/phytolacca-americana-var-rigida/ 1/15/2020). However, they offer no references or recipes likely because they do not have anyone on staff who really knows anything of detail. My guess is that poke was used to color an otherwise apple or peach pie and then called a pokeberry pie due to the striking magenta coloration.

You can see how all these food *sounding* uses can make people think that the berries are like regular edible berries. Ignorant sources reading the titles above, will blindly report that pokeberries are used to make, pies, jams, jellies, and wine. But there is no good evidence for any of that, and you now know better.

Chapter 13

Family: Asteraceae
Species: *Cirsium vulgare*

Bull Thistle

Rejects you on the outside, loves you on the inside.

Upper 6 inches of an adult bull thistle plant in flower. Only the upper petals are useful at this stage.

Estimated Range

Official Species Name:
• *Cirsium vulgare* (Savi) Ten.

Synonyms
• *Carduus lanceolatus* L.
• *Carduus vulgaris* Savi
• *Cirsium lanceolatum*
  (L.) Scop., non Hill
• *Cirsium lanceolatum*
  var. *hypoleucum* DC

Common Names:
• Bull thistle
• Common thistle
• Spear thistle

Herbaceous annual or biennial naturalized from Europe, North Africa, and Western Asia. Widespread and abundant in North America anywhere Europeans have disturbed native soils.

Edible Parts:
• Baby plants, roots prior to bolting, rapidly bolting peeled stems, and the colored parts of the petals.

BULL THISTLE

One of the homes I lived in had a big, unkempt backyard with mostly grass. One of the many invaded weeds was bull thistle. You could find a plant every few feet. Because of their needle-sharp leaf spines, it was a potential danger to anyone walking barefoot.

Within three years my yard thistles were extinct. I had eaten the roots of the new spring plants. They did not have a chance.

Bull thistle is a menace to many because the spines, often called its armor, are painful to interact with. You cannot grab the plant with bare hands without injury. If you want to remove it from your yard you need leather gloves. Sometimes the spines will pierce leather gloves and find their way through the seams of the stitching. Bleeding can occur.

I neglected studying this plant for its food in my early career because the spines made me think it was not so valuable. That it was more like what you would consider a "survival food." You would eat it as a last resort if there wasn't much else around. And you had those damn spines to contend with. But that was a mistake. Bull thistle is now a regular part of my diet.

Plants have many ways to protect themselves from herbivory (being eaten). They can evolve to generate toxins, they can develop armor (spines, thorns, spikes), or both. Many plants that are armored do not have to develop toxins, because the armor is so successful at keeping the herbivores away. All of the armored thistles I know in North America are nontoxic. Of course, there are many that I do not know. Some are better than others from a food perspective. The key is working around the spines to get to the food.

Bull thistle can be an annual or a biennial depending on when it germinates and how good growing conditions are. The trigger for going to seed in the first or second year is how much food is stored in the root. Once enough food packs into the root to support feeding a stalk and going to seed, the plants grows to its mature form. If there isn't enough food in the root, and/or other conditions aren't right, it will wait, overwinter, and produce that stalk in the next year. There is food at each stage of growth, you just need to know where to look.

Knowing Bull Thistle

Bull thistle seedlings are large, relative to other plants. The cotyledons (first leaflike structures emerging from a seed) can be ¹/₅- to ³/₄-inch long from tip to tip. They are slightly oblong and do not have any spines on the margins. All true leaves on thistles have spines on their margins with both spines and hairs on their surfaces. The seeds sprout in the early spring, or during fall rains after the mature plants have dropped their seeds.

From early on, all parts of this plant are covered with long hairs and spines. Spines appear at the tips of teeth on the leaf margins and along the stem. As the plant ages, the leaves get wavier along the margins. This waviness creates a three-dimensional motif, allowing the spines to stick up, down, and sideways. Leaves spread out in what's called a *basal rosette*. That is, they all span out from the root in a 360° pattern like the plants on this page.

While the leaves grow in number and size, the plant grows a taproot that is carrot-like, often branching, and

Bull thistle sprout and young plant. Both plants have the rounded cotyledons (first leaflike structures), but the right plant's cotyledons are double the size of the other. The larger plant here is about 3 inches wide tip to tip. Leaves have both spines and slender white hairs.

As the plant grows, leaf margins take on a wavier appearance. This plant is about 10 inches wide tip to tip.

Above left: Leaves enlarge and multiply as the plant gets older. This plant is about 30 inches in diameter, rapidly growing in the spring from overwintering roots. Overwintering is what makes this a second-year plant, a biennial.

Above right: Roots of a first-year bull thistle plant. These often have a main taproot with side roots branching off. Spines on the leaves are stabbing my hand as I hold this.

A mature bull thistle leaf. The leaf margins become deeply toothed sticking out to the sides, as well as folding up and down allowing the spines to stick in every direction, becoming three-dimensional as the leaves mature. Leaves and stems are covered with hairs and spines.

off-white. It varies in size from thinner than a pencil to as big as a commercial carrot. The number and size of the aboveground leaves are sometimes an indication of how big the taproot will be. The larger the aboveground plant (all leaves at this point), the larger the taproot is likely to be.

From a root development perspective, this is what I would consider phase 1. Where the leaves are in a basal rosette, spreading out in all directions and pumping energy from photosynthesis into the rapidly growing root. Phase 2 begins when the plant is transitioning into a stalk producer.

Formation of a flower stalk

In my experience, the plant is ready to send up a flowering stalk when three conditions are true. First, there is enough food stored in the root to support the growth of a stalk. Second, there are enough leaves to pump new energy into the growth of a stalk. And third, there is enough of the season left for the stalk to bear seeds before winter arrives.

Stalk formation coincides with the root transitioning to its phase 2. As the stalk begins to emerge from between the leaves, the root changes from growth and storage function to a support function to stabilize and anchor a forming stalk. At the same time, the core of the root transitions from being chewable to woody.

A stalk does not instantly bolt up from the root, the plant has to change. The first aboveground indicator that a stalk is about to form is the pointing of the leaves. If you see a cluster of smaller leaves around the center of the plant

Above: A transitioning bull thistle plant. Center leaves pointing upward here signifies that the plant has already transitioned to a second-year plant and is producing the beginnings of a flowering stem. You just don't see that stem yet.

Right: Bull thistle root rind peeled away from the woody core. Once the bull thistle transitions to a plant producing a flower stalk, the root's core becomes absolutely woody. The rind is still chewable if you get it early enough in the transition.

Above: A close-up of the branching stem showing the intimidating spines and white hairs. You can really hurt yourself handling this.

Above: A young bull thistle plant with developing flower stalk that bolted as soon as the plant woke up in the spring. You can see that it is already showing the beginning of branching where the leaves meet the stem. This stem is a about ¾ inch in diameter. This plant is about 18 inches tall. It will get much bigger and the stem will thicken as it more than triples in height.

Right: A healthy, thick bull thistle stalk growing in a patch of thistles. To simplify this photo, I've trimmed away leaves and secondary stems to reveal the main stalk. You will not find them trimmed in the wild—unless I've been there first. This stem is 1½ inches in diameter and about 2 feet tall with leaves reaching above that. This is a key stage of growth, which will provide an edible core once the stem is peeled. This plant is still growing— destined to be over 5 feet tall when mature.

Maturation of bull thistle flower heads. Left is a flower bud cluster, next is the bloomed flower head, next is the newly pollinated head, and right are the fully developed seeds being dispersed by wind.

starting to point upward, then a flower stalk is already forming on the root.

Bull thistle stalk development

The flower stalk starts out as a straight, unbranched shoot with leaves. As the stem gets taller, leaves reach out and upward from it. At about 18 inches, you can see the beginnings of branches at the leaf axils, the location where the leaves meet the stem.

A developing stalk from a bull thistle root can grow up to $1^{1}/_{2}$ inches in diameter. If it is struggling with competition or lack of moisture, it will be less than an inch wide. Growth is rapid during stalk development and the plant branches regularly. As the stem reaches maturity, the uppermost stems are thin and produce flower bud clusters. The buds are roundish to egg-shaped and green. They begin emerging about a month before the summer solstice and can continue through July in northern climates. When this bud cluster reaches a critical size, the typically hot-pink flower petals emerge from the tips. Once the flowers are pollinated, seed development begins. The flowers wither and are replaced by a fluffy structure that can carry the seeds away in the wind.

WHAT IS A FLOWER HEAD?

What appears to be a bull thistle flower is really a tight cluster of many flowers forming one big head of flowers. So bull thistle has a flower head, not a flower. The flowers are so tightly packed together, they give the appearance of being one big flower.

Canadian Thistle

Cirsium arvense

Edible look-alike

Canadian thistle is a much less valuable food plant than bull thistle. It is found in many of the same habitats, but its spread tends to outpace bull thistle. It can germinate in areas where bull thistle cannot get a foothold, thanks to its persistent and fast-growing rhizomes. You can pull the tops, but the plant continues to spread by rhizomes. It is the bane of many farmers and land managers. Pull it until the rhizomes are depleted of all their energy. And don't let it go to seed. Just don't!

I gave up on this plant long ago as a reasonable food. I have since learned that in most of Europe and northern North America it was used only in times of famine, as a last resort. If it is rapidly growing, you chop it enough, and boil it enough, you can make the youngest parts chewable and soften the spines. Very rapid growth is your only hope to be able to chew it, even after processing. The stems are much smaller and narrower than bull thistle. If you try to peel the rind off the stem, there is little left of the core to eat.

Below: Unlike bull thistle that has a taproot, Canadian thistle spreads by deep underground rhizomes. They are almost impossible to stop because the rhizomes spread 6 to 8 inches below the surface where no one wants to go down and dig.

Above: Young Canadian thistle plant, about 3 inches tall. Its stout leaves at this young stage indicate it is growing from an underground rhizome.

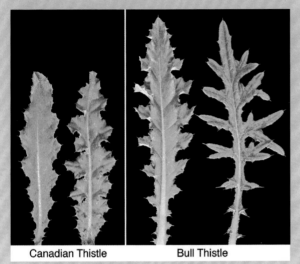

Canadian Thistle · Bull Thistle

Leaf comparison of Canadian thistle (left) and bull thistle (right). Canadian thistle has thinner, smaller, and apparently darker green leaves with hundreds of small sharp spines along its wavy margins. Bull thistle has larger, hairier leaves and longer, more menacing spines. Bull thistle leaves and stems have more and longer white hairs covering its surfaces, giving it a whiter appearance than Canadian thistle which has fewer hairs. The leaves of both species can range from relatively flat to highly fluted along the margins.

Left: Mature Canadian thistle plant in flower. Some of the branches have been removed to decrease the complexity of this picture. Notice the smaller leaves on these stems relative to the whole plant. These flowers produce tons of seeds every summer that are spread by the wind. Canadian thistle typically grows 3 to 4 feet tall. Bull thistle is typically 5 to 7 feet tall.

Right: Flower and bud heads of Canadian thistle.

Gathering and Edibility of Bull Thistle

Young sprouts

Each bull thistle plant produces thousands of seeds that love to germinate. They will germinate easily whether they are in the middle of an unkempt lawn or in recently disturbed soil. And they grow fast. When these plants are small, less than 3 inches in diameter, it is time to gather them. This will only work if they are in their rapid growth stage. They are well worth gathering if tons of seeds have germinated, giving you lots to choose from. Beware of small plants that are slow growing in dry conditions; they will be too tough and spiny, even at that small size.

Young bull thistle plants at the prime size for gathering.

Pluck these whole baby bull thistle plants from the soil, roots and all. Don't eat them raw, as the spines on the leaves will be sharp and cut you. Yes, even this young, the spines can be injurious. Boiling is the solution. Not steaming or frying, just boiling. Boiling for 5 minutes seems to soften the young spines into tenderness. That will not work with older plants where the woodiness of the spines is intractable. Just eat the whole root and leaves as one piece of food. Once boiled, they have the fine dual taste of both the roots and greens. Eat a mess of them as a boiled vegetable with vinegar and oil, do a stir-fry, or make some fancy dish featuring them. This is the only stage of growth where the spines will soften with cooking.

Once the leaves grow larger, they become an unrealistic food. Juicing may be another story. I have not tried this, since I am not a juicing person, but it seems that this would be a way to extract some use from the lovely (gruesome, menacing) larger leaves. I do not know of any substances in the older leaves that would be a problem to consume.

Sam Thayer (2006) recommends peeling the blades off the main vein of the beautiful rapidly growing leaves. You toss the spine-filled blade and eat that vein like you would celery. Even on larger leaves. You might want gloves for this.

First-season bull thistle root

Rapid spring or fall growth from seed produces quite a vigorous rosette of leaves. Again, the size and number of the leaves showing can sometimes be predictive of how big the taproot will be. A larger root is better than a smaller one. Unfortunately, sometimes, even with big aboveground growth, the roots might be small. I have no clue what causes this contrariness. Look for any plant between 1 to 3 feet in diameter whose leaves arch to the sides. You should be able to easily slice through a tender root. If you are struggling, it might be too late.

Remember, if the center leaves have begun growing upward, and you begin to see many fibrous side roots branching off the main taproot, the root will be woody. It transitions quickly. During the transition, the core of the root is, well, wood—too tough to do anything with. For a short period, the rind can be salvageable and worth it if it is thick enough. Just peel it off the core. The rind is more substantial if the root is large, too much fuss if it is small or too branched. Don't bother about any of this if the aboveground stem has reared its ugly head amongst the center leaves.

The tender root is delicious and can be eaten raw. Once cut, the raw pieces brown fast, which is unsightly to modern diners. Browning does not affect the flavor. To slow browning, I submerge a small cutting board in a basin filled with water and cut the root while it's in the water. Cut pieces are never exposed to the air. Then place the cut pieces in a small ice water bowl with a spritz

Bull thistle root from a plant that has not yet transitioned to a flowering stage. This is a good-size root. Often the root will branch much more than this, particularly if it is in rocky soil. This root is perfect for eating.

Shaved slices of bull thistle root on a salad looking like shaved almonds.

Boiled bull thistle roots, unpeeled and sliced into sections, seasoned with olive oil, salt, and pepper. Served over mixed steamed wild greens, and garnished with cherry tomatoes and wood sorrel.

of lemon juice, as you would for apples. A pinch of sugar also helps slow the browning process. Leave the root pieces in this water until you are ready to serve or cook them. If you are serving them fresh, don't cut them too far ahead of time. Browning gets worse over time no matter what you do. If you do not care about browning, or you want browning while cooking, don't go through all this fuss. But if you're trying to impress your kids with the fresh stuff—use the water technique!

Small rootlets and the end tip of the main root have a fibrous stringy core thread. So cut off any root or rootlet that is less than 3/16 inch in diameter.

One of my favorite ways to serve bull thistle roots fresh is like shaved almonds in various dishes. Assuming the root is thick enough, slice it thin and at an angle, not straight across. The cut pieces will look just like shaved almonds. The thin slicing vastly improves their tenderness, since you are cutting across whatever long root fibers are there. Thin slicing also makes it look like you have more root to spread around. Again, do this under water to reduce browning or you will lose the shaved almond effect.

When raw, the bull thistle root's flavor is reminiscent of carrot's freshness without the carrot flavor. That will not make sense until you try it. Life is complex, and we just have to experience some things to understand them. Cooked, the flavor is more akin to potato with a hint of artichoke. Any accoutrement like salt, garlic, butter, or olive oil will improve it. So cooked in any way, this is a potato-tasting food that, due to its shape, you would use in any way you would use and cook carrots or potatoes. I personally prefer boiled thistle root to steamed, both for flavor and texture. Test for yourself to see if you prefer steaming or a 5- or 10-minute boil.

Young stem cores of bull thistle

Once the energy in the root is adequate and the time of year is right, the bull thistle will send up a flower stalk. When that central/main stalk reaches 18 to 24 inches tall, before flower buds appear, its core supplies an excellent vegetable. Rapid growth and a thick stem mean that there will be more of the tender material within that stem. To harvest, first trim off the branches to make the stem easier to handle. Keep those branches. Cut the main stem about 9 to 12 inches below its tip.

Examine the cut side of the stem and observe how the core looks different from the rind. The core should be hollow unless the cut point is close to the ground. Insert a knife just inside the line where the rind meets the core, just enough so you have a grip on the rind; then pull away and down, just like peeling a cattail rhizome. If the stem is being nice to you, the rind will peel cleanly from the core. Your goal is to remove all the stringy material that makes up the rind.

Bull thistle stems trimmed of their branches. These were cut farther down toward the base than I am recommending to you, since I was experimenting with the peeling process when this photo was taken. These are almost 30 inches long. You only need to peel the upper 12 inches or so. The top plant shows thistle with all its branches. The middle two show unpeeled stalks whose branches have been removed. The Bottom two long stems have been peeled. The most tender cores are from the upper 9 to 12 inches of stem. That is all you want, not the long stems I am showing here. On the bottom left is an asparagus sprig for comparison. On the bottom right are two upper branches, one peeled, one not. Compost all the leafy material including that found at the tips of these stems.

Peeling away the rind from the core of bull thistle stem. Insert a knife just inside the rind and peel down. Remove as much of the fibrous rind as possible. Place the stem in iced or cold water immediately after peeling to prevent browning.

The rind is bitter, tough, and stringy. You want it gone. Most of the time, this process is a little messy. As you are peeling you will notice many stray fibers remaining. Use your knife to shave them off. Work quickly as the longer you take, the more brown develops on the stem. With time and practice, you can get pretty fast at this. Once all the stringiness has been removed, the stems are ready to use.

Test the lower part of the peeled core for fibrousness. Cut off any part that is too tough to chew. If there is a lot of tough material at the base, you've cut the stem too long. If it is all very tender, you might have been able to cut a longer piece from the live plant prior to peeling. You will get better at deciding that with experience. My guidance is general to get you started.

Put the peeled cores in iced or cold water right away to slow the browning process and allow them to crisp up. Cores will curl in the water toward any minor fibers that remain, giving a C-shaped appearance. You cannot get all the embedded fibers while peeling. This is not a problem; it is a feature. The peeled stems are now ready to eat fresh or cooked, as you would cook curly asparagus. The water from soaking will initially turn pink. If you soak them over time in a refrigerator, that water will turn brownish.

The freshly peeled stalks taste somewhat like zucchini. They are good used fresh in salads with other ingredients and dressings, cooked with other ingredients and spices, or sautéed like asparagus in olive oil and garlic. Everything is good with olive oil and garlic.

You can also peel the new young (rapidly growing) side branches. You can peel them fresh or try this: boil them vigorously, spines and all, for 10 minutes prior to peeling. Then pull off just the stingy spiny material. No rind removal is required. These are good to eat like asparagus. Sautéing in olive oil for 3 minutes results in a flavor hinting of zucchini and eggplant.

Above: Fresh bull thistle stem cores that have been crisped in cold water, ready to use in any dish, fresh or cooked.

Left: Bull thistle peeled stems that have been soaking in iced water and are ready to use raw or cooked. They curl as they soak up water.

Above: Roasted thistle peeled stems with salmon on a bed of nipplewort, with roasted sweet peppers and garnished with borage flowers.

Left: Upper rapidly growing branches of bull thistle can be peeled and used like the main stem. They are smaller but better tasting. The branch tip to the left has not been peeled yet. The two to the right are peeled. Don't include that end in the middle one, the spines are too sharp.

Flower petals

Bull thistle flowers, separated from their green encasement, showing both the silky fibrous white bases and the exposed pink tops. There are at least 18 flowers shown here, each having five pink petals.

Just harvest the tips of the flowers in the head, where all the color is, and use the trimmings fresh.

When blooming, the pink flower petals and stamens of bull thistle stick out of the end of their green flower head encasement. The lower parts of the flowers, which are hidden in the encasement, are white and fibrous. Only the fresh new pink flower tips are worth collecting. Don't pull them out; cut off the visible pink material with scissors. This material has a very mild fruity flavor, is colorful, dry, and a bit fibrous. Since all this trim is tiny, the dryness and fibrousness are lost in whatever food you are sprinkling it on. Which for me are toppings for salads and garnishes for almost anything. Use these colorful petal tips mostly for visual appeal and nutrition.

These pink flower tips look great spread over a salad or just about any food ready to serve. Second, scientists are finding that flowers, particularly the more colorful and aromatic ones, are rich in phytochemicals that are likely great for your diet. And, as I will repeat ad nauseam, the best overall diet is one that includes a great number of plant and animal species. So sprinkle them on a salad, on roasted asparagus, on sautéed shrimp, on sushi. There is no limit. You will never notice the fibrousness unless you stuff a handful of them raw into your mouth and try to chew. Spread them around and enjoy them as one more piece of your visual and nutritional world.

Chapter 14

FAMILY: Lamiaceae
SPECIES: *Lamium purpureum*

Purple Sweet Nettle

This sweet purple pagoda plant colorfully blankets many a yard and field.

Purple sweet nettle in flower, carpeting a grassy field.

Estimated Range

Official Species Name:
• *Lamium purpureum* L.

Synonyms
• None

Common Names:
• Purple deadnettle
• Purple sweet nettle*
• Red deadnettle
• Purple pagoda*
  *My names for this plant

Herbaceous weed naturalized from Europe. Widespread and abundant in North America, primarily where humans have invaded and where soil has been disturbed. Found often in unkempt lawns and fallow fields, intermixed with grasses and other wayside plants.

Edible Parts:
• Growing tips of leafy stems, leaves, buds, and flowers.

What's in a Name?

The most well-known name of this plant, *purple deadnettle*, is another one of those unfortunate acts of dismissal that many unappreciated plants undergo. The person who gave it this name apparently thought it looked like nettle (it doesn't really), but since it has no sting, they thought it should be referred to as a *dead* nettle. What a horrible name. *Purple* or *red* and *dead* makes it sound like a homicide scene. That is an anti-name, like *false dandelion*. Where is the imagination to come up with something unique that better fits its description and use as a food? (Lettuce does not sting, so should we call that *dead lettuce?*)

A much better name, particularly from a food perspective, is *purple sweet nettle* or *purple pagoda*. Let's face it, the older adult plant looks like a Japanese pagoda. And to be accurate, the flowers are typically lavender in color—what could be interpreted as a light purple. The leaves and stems are typically green with a reddish tinge to the upper leaves and lower stem. This plant is a mix of colors.

Throughout this chapter I am going to refer to this plant as *purple sweet nettle, dropping the dead concept*. In parts of this chapter, I will use the term *pagoda* to refer to the cluster of leaves at the top of the long flowering stems.

Knowing Purple Sweet Nettle

The first time you see this plant it will most likely be late winter or early spring in an old lawn or field with tall grass.

Ho Quoc Pagoda: Monastery and Buddhist temple in Vietnam. This temple houses a giant bell and a variety of Buddha statues. Pagodas take many shapes, but this one is reminiscent of the purple sweet nettle's overlapping and downward-tilting leaves.

It can outcompete other plants in cold weather and is considered a winter annual. Its two features, the overlapping pagoda-like leaves and the reddish coloration in the upper leaves, distinguish it from most other plants.

Purple sweet nettle in flower as you might first see it, in an open field, lawn, farmland, or your yard.

Purple sweet nettle seeds can germinate at any time of year, but require moisture and cold to moderate temperatures. Most germination occurs in spring and fall. Once germinated, the plant thrives in cold weather. It is an annual herb, in that it germinates and dies within a short period of time. To some it might seem like a perennial, because it can germinate at any time in the year with new moisture and temperatures ranging between 40 to 60°F.

The cotyledons are almost round. There is a whitish nub at the center of their blunt tip. The first leaves to emerge, and all that follow, are opposite each other.

Purple sweet nettle showing its first leaves overtopping the cotyledons.

Each plant can have several stems arising from fibrous roots. These fragile stems help support each other as they grow upward. Surrounding vegetation

Young purple sweet nettle plant about 2½ inches in diameter. Early young leaves are heart shaped and more defined than the roundish cotyledons.

Purple sweet nettle plants showing both young and more adult plant leaves. Leaves on the taller stems are more egg-shaped and pointed than the younger and lower leaves.

A typical purple sweet nettle plant, about 1 foot tall. The stem on the left—which has a long, unbranched segment leading to the pagoda—is the most common form I see.

The whole nettle plant is supported by square, hollow stems.

also helps support the plants. If they fall over, the side branches grow upward.

All stems are square, including the side branches. Everything is opposite on this plant. All lower stems arise opposite each other off the main stems. All leaves anywhere on the plant are opposite each other.

The tallest stems, capable of reaching up to 12 inches, do not have regularly spaced leaves or branching stems. There is typically a long stretch of stem leading to the terminal cluster (the pagoda) of leaves and flowers. This upper leafy stem is how the plant is most often recognized. Most people do not pay attention to the lower branches and leaves, because they are hidden by surrounding vegetation. Branching can occur anywhere on the tall stems, but it is mostly found at the lower parts of the stem.

Let's talk about the pagoda at the top of the stem. It is a work in progress, constantly growing additional leaves and flowers at the top. The pagoda starts out with only a few leaves. Top leaves are new and therefore smaller than the ones just below them. As the pagoda ages, those upper leaves will reach full size and be replaced by newer leaves above them. As this plant gets older, the number of overlapping leaves forming the pagoda will increase—making a taller pagoda with more "floors." The largest leaves can be 1 1/2 inches wide under great growing conditions. These pagoda leaves are more egg-shaped and pointed than the heart-shaped ones found at the base of the plant, or on younger plants.

The pagoda is where the flowers form sandwiched between the leaves. Purple sweet nettle mostly produces lavender-colored flowers, but they also can be white or bluish-purple. While there seem to be an endless parade of new flowers and leaves at the top of the plant, the lower flowers get pollinated and the petals fall off. This leaves the spiny sepals (together known as the *calyx*) menacingly hiding under the leaves. As the stem lengthens and new leaves form above, the rings of calyxes stack up along the stem. Each calyx protects maturing seeds. You have to pluck off leaves to see these underlying spiny structures.

The first few pagoda leaves at the top of one of its long, up-reaching stems. Newest leaves are at the top. Fully grown leaves can be seen below these flowers.

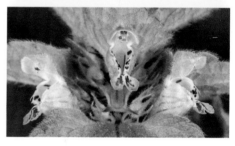

Above: Flowers arise in rings just above where each pair of leaves attaches to the stem. Petals are fused into an interesting mint-style set of united petals that look like a hippopotamus yawning. There are irregular hot-pink-colored spots that sometimes show up on the lavender-colored petals. The petals are hairy, particularly the top of the upper one. Sepals are green, stiff, and fused to each other at their bases.

Left: The typical look of an older pagoda, producing flowers at the top. Leaves hide the spiny calyxes. Right: Leaves have been cut away to reveal the calyxes stacked along the stem.

Above: A young cut-leaved purple sweetnettle plant prior to flowering.

Cut-Leaved Purple Sweet Nettle

Edible look-alike

Cut-leaved purple sweet nettle is a leaf-form variation of the same species as purple sweet nettle. It's designated as *Lamium purpureum* variety *incisum* and differs from regular purple sweet nettle in the way the lobes cut deeper into the leaf blades. It has the same overall form, including the long stem leading to the primary leaf cluster (pagoda) at the top. It is better tasting and fresher in mouthfeel than regular purple sweet nettle, but much less common.

Above: Cut-leaved purple sweet nettle has the overall look of purple sweet nettle, but its pagoda is more spaced out. The whole plant looks more dynamic due to the cuts in the leaves and the fact that its flowers stick up more prominently.

Above: These flowers look more like a yawning clam than a hippopotamus. This also gives a good view of the spiny calyxes (united sepals).

Right: Leaves of regular purple sweet nettle on left; cut-leaved variety on right. Upper side of leaves on the top, undersides of leaves on the bottom. The most obvious difference between these two are their leaf margins. Cut-leaved leaves have deeper cuts in their margins and the irregular teeth have little nubs at their points. Regular sweet nettle has short rounded teeth with dull points.

Gathering and Preparation of Purple Sweet Nettle

Use scissors to gather the upper parts of young preflowering plants. Keep them moist and cool until you can use them. I do not recommend uprooting them, since that introduces dirt into your bag, making later cleaning more difficult. Other than washing, these are ready to use fresh or cooked.

A young purple sweet nettle plant prior to flowering. This is an ideal young sprig for eating whole.

When you get home, you can put them in water as you would flowers in a vase, covered with a loose plastic bag. They will stay fresh in the fridge like that for up to a week. Just prior to serving, discard most of the stem, leaving just less than an inch of it attached to the overlapping leaves. I find that the still rapidly growing upper leafy stem areas (the whole pagoda) are best suited to boiling or steaming. They toughen up if you try to sauté them. Look for beautiful fresh leaves with no damage or discoloration.

Use the upper stem leaves (from the pagoda) in a salad if you free them from the stem. This is easily done with scissors, since the leaves are all lined up on each of four sides—that is just four carefully made snips. You could also use the very top of the pagoda, which has the most tender leaves and stem. What remains is the stem and texturally spiky calyxes, which are not great raw if old. The leaves can be used fresh in salads and sandwiches, or as a cooked green, steamed or boiled. Purple sweet nettle shrinks in size when cooked. So 5 cups of loosely packed fresh greens reduce down to about 1 cup cooked.

All the edible parts of a purple sweet nettle plant. This shows the pagoda's flowering leafy stem, surrounded by younger base and side parts. Tender parts are all edible in this raw form. The underlying calyxes need special consideration as they can get tough on older plants.

Trimming off most but not all of the stem material from young plants. Keep the tender leafy stems but not any of the main stems. New young side branches provide great tender material.

Trimming off the leaves from each side and the tip of purple sweet nettle. Since the leaves are all lined up, it is easy to clip a bunch at a time.

Raw purple sweet nettle is a mild-tasting green that is slightly dry. That dryness will not matter in most of the ways that you will be eating it. Boiling it adds moisture. Raw, add it to other things with more moisture. Most salads have vinegar, oil, tomatoes, cucumbers, and/or avocado, all adding plenty of moisture. Any sandwich will have moist ingredients. It is hard to add enough purple sweet nettle to make an overall dish too dry or chewy. I typically do not eat raw purple sweet nettle, or most vegetables for that matter, all by itself. These are greens to add variety and flavor to other things.

The spiny green calyxes soften up with boiling, so many of them can still be used. Some of the calyxes will be too old and tough to tenderize. You'll need to experiment to see exactly what to look for to determine what is tender enough to gather and what isn't.

Large rapidly growing leaves, those that look bright green and fresh, are going to be the most tender. Cold, late-winter and early spring days are when you will find purple sweet nettle at its best. In moderate climates that do not freeze, you can find it all winter.

However, these plants can suffer from lack of moisture and age quickly. Hot and dry conditions force already ger-minated purple sweet nettle to grow smaller overall, their leaves fold more tightly down the sides of the plant, and a whitish mold can cover the leaves. It will be obvious that they look frail, dry, and lacking in color. In this case, they are worthless as food.

Both regular and cut-leaved purple sweet nettle have the same uses and can be included in any recipe where variety is desired—which should be the goal of every nutritious diet.

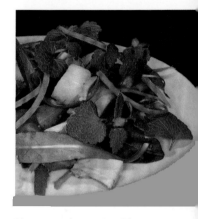

Young purple sweet nettle leaves in a wild late-winter salad. Ingredients include wild sweet fennel, wild chicory, little western bittercress, red leaf lettuce, avocado, small cubes of pineapple, carrot strings, and red pepper slices for color.

Purple sweet nettle greens. Boil or steam for 3 minutes, garnish with fresh purple sweet nettle flowers, and serve with your favorite dressing. It takes about 5 cups of loosely packed fresh greens to make one serving of cooked greens. Some of the stems with spiny calyxes can be included in the boiled greens and still be tender.

Sautéed Purple Sweet Nettle with an Omelet

Makes 2 servings

INGREDIENTS

4 eggs

Grated Swiss cheese, to taste

3 cups loose-packed purple sweet nettle leaves and tender leafy stems

Put aside a few fresh leafy stems for garnish

2 tablespoons olive oil

⅔ cup chopped onion

2 cloves garlic, minced

Salt and black pepper, to taste

Fruit of choice

DIRECTIONS

Make a four-egg omelet (from any recipe of your choice) and top with some cheese to melt while still hot.

For the greens topping, steam the purple sweet nettle for about 2 minutes and set aside.

Heat the oil in a skillet over medium heat. Once hot, add the onion and sauté until it begins to become translucent but not quite caramelized. Add the garlic and steamed sweet nettle. Sauté until the aroma of the garlic blossoms, remove from the heat, and serve with the omelet. Add salt and pepper to taste.

Garnish with fresh sweet nettle leaves and fruit.

Tart Plants

Plants in this section have a pleasant sour or acidic flavor. They are suitable for occasions where you want to add some mouthwatering character to a dish. Tart plants are often added to milder vegetables or complex dishes to add interest and nuance. Like the foundation plants, they can also cut the power of pungent and bitter greens, but they are not neutral like foundation plants. They are edible raw and cooked, but their best uses depend on what you are preparing. Tart greens and vegetables have the potential to greatly improve a dish by using just a little or to dramatically change the character of a dish by adding a lot. People will enjoy them as a flavor enhancer for other foods or eaten on their own.

Tart plants covered in volume 1 of this book series are:
- Curly dock (*Rumex crispus*)
- Broad-leaved dock (*Rumex obtusifolius*)
- Sheep sorrel (*Rumex acetosella*)
- Wood sorrel (*Oxalis stricta*)

In this volume of the Wild Food Adventure Series, there is only one plant fitting this category, Japanese knotweed. Most plants in the tart category happen to be either in the buckwheat (Polygonaceae) or the oxalis family (Oxalidaceae). Knotweed is in the buckwheat family, along with rhubarb, French sorrel, sheep sorrel, and the docks. The only sour vegetable you will typically find in the supermarket is rhubarb. French sorrel, eaten as a green, is sold in nurseries for planting in your garden. It is as close to the plant in this chapter, or those in volume 1, as you will get from a nonwild perspective.

Tart plants have their own characteristic flavors and textures. Fresh, they are excellent in combination salads, added to sandwiches, used as garnishes, in fruit products, and made into pestos and other greens-based sauces. If you are like me, you will enjoy salads with nothing but sour vegetables. Cooked, their flavors mellow, often giving the impression of foundation greens with a squirt of lemon juice. They go well with other vegetables, any kind of meat, and especially with fish.

Some books will give warnings about plants with oxalates poisoning sheep, cattle, or chickens. These accounts are real but do not apply to humans. First, these animals have different physiology and digestive processes than humans; they are less able to manage oxalate intake. Second, all animals poisoned were restricted to eating the mass of their total diet from days to weeks of very high oxalate plants. Imagine trying to eat about 8 pounds of spinach every day for a week as over 50 percent of your diet. Oxalates are relatively harmless in the context of a normally diverse human diet. See volume 1 of this book series for detailed coverage of oxalates.

Flavors offered by sour plants are an excellent addition to the gourmet's arsenal of tastes.

Chapter 15

Family: Polygonaceae
Species: *Fallopia japonica, Fallopia sachalinensis*

Japanese Knotweed

A delicious surprising food that offers more than you can imagine.

Branches of Sakhalin (giant) knotweed whose flower buds are just forming. Those leaf blades are over a foot long.

**Japanese Knotweed
Estimated Range**

Species Name:
• *Fallopia japonica*
  (Houtt.) Ronse Decr.

Synonyms for *Fallopia
japonica*, Japanese knotweed:
• *Polygonum cuspidatum*
  (Siebold & Zucc.)
• *Reynoutria japonica* Houtt.
• *Pleuropterus cuspidatus*
  (Siebold & Zucc.) Moldenke
• *Pleuropterus
  zuccarinii* Small
• *Polygonum zuccarinii* Small

Common Names for
Fallopia japonica:
• Japanese knotweed
• Japanese bamboo
• Mexican bamboo
• False bamboo

Edible Parts:
• Young shoots
• Peeled stems

JAPANESE KNOTWEED AND SAKHALIN KNOTWEED

What glorious plants these are. I respect their ability to thrive. They grow fast, spread easily, and provide great seasonal foods in abundance. Japanese knotweed and its kin, giant knotweed (Sakhalin knotweed) are beautiful plants, first spread around the globe as ornamentals. But many people are afraid of their proliferation—and for good reason, which I will get to. Japanese and Sakhalin knotweeds have exactly the same food uses, so I will refer to them interchangeably throughout this chapter. I am calling giant knotweed by its less common name, *Sakhalin*, because if I said, "*a giant knotweed patch*," am I referring to the plant or the giant patch? So Sakhalin it is.

Both plants originated in Asia, where they learned to grow as a pioneer species in volcanic rock and other challenging habitats. When growing under sidewalks or foundations, they can lift or break through concrete! My kind of plants. I love their spunk and vigor . . . unless it is my foundation they are piercing through.

And while it grows prolifically when unchecked, to single out knotweed for this cement busting thing seems unfair. It is another one of those, "run for your lives" moments. I know that plant-lifted concrete is not unique to knotweed. We have all seen normal neighborhood tree roots cause problems as they expand and grow underneath sidewalks.

Sakhalin knotweed growing in a colony of about 20 plants. They are all likely clones and/or are connected by rhizomes. This patch is about 8 feet tall and 16 feet wide.

And there are regulations about how close you can plant trees to foundations because the roots could bust through.

I have seen knotweed taking over fields having huge root crowns so big they resemble tree stumps. But I have not yet witnessed it destroying humanity. I trust that someone has seen it breaking through something, but those are cases were neglect (where no one is managing the land over long periods) has allowed this plant to grow unrestricted.

Japanese knotweed grows large clump-forming rhizomes (underground stems). Here are some amazing facts, assuming my reference is accurate (Traylor, 2018). Keep in mind that these facts are the extremes the plant is capable of, not what you will normally see. My notes are in parentheses.

1. The plant can survive up to 20 years in total darkness. (This may be from below lava flows where it was not burnt to a crisp, so it also has a reputation of surviving great heat. However, soil is a great insulator.)

Japanese knotweed rhizomes resemble the stems, except they are curved, branched, have a reddish hue, and fibrous roots. The red may be due to resveratrol or some other phytochemical they contain. Note the rounded mass or root crown on the left, giving rise to the two stems. The rhizome segment shown here is only about 14 inches wide—broken away from more rhizome material that shot out both left and right of this piece.

Sakhalin Knotweed Estimated Range

Species Name:
- *Fallopia sachalinensis* (F. Schmidt) Ronse Decr.

Synonyms for *Fallopia sachalinensis*, Giant knotweed:
- *Polygonum sachalinense* F. Schmidt ex Maxim.
- *Reynoutria sachalinensis* (F. Schmidt ex Maxim.) Nakai

Common Names for *Fallopia sachalinensis*:
- Giant knotweed
- Sakhalin knotweed

Edible Parts:
- Young shoots
- Peeled stems

Both species are taprooted perennials. Native to eastern Asia, but now widespread and abundant in North America. These weedy plants love the sun, spread by rhizomes and by live pieces that break off and grow new plants.

2. The rhizomes can grow up to 10 feet deep and 60 feet in all directions from the base of the plant. ("Can" is the operative word here. What it does is another story. Patches I've seen did not show this spreading power unless the ground was very moist all year long.)

3. Established roots can alter the foundations of homes, upend sidewalks, and grow through asphalt pavement. (So can other plants.)

4. Any part of the plant moved with soil in construction can cause spreading. (So can other plants.)

5. It only takes a piece the size of a pea to grow a new plant. (My guess is that this last statement is a laboratory experiment and not real life. It is more likely that you would need a whole segment of stalk for new plants to easily grow in nature. Plants can be grown from just a few cells in controlled laboratory conditions.)

Well . . . it looks like we found a new way to defeat Russian aggression around the world: Drop pea-sized pieces of this plant around their military bases. In 20 years, all their infrastructure will be destroyed. They won't know what hit 'em!

This is what I've personally seen about knotweed:

1. If new shoots are mowed regularly, like grass, before it can turn into Godzilla, it does not thrive. The rhizomes remain in the soil and will still spread. Mowing inhibits its growth, keeping the aboveground shoots small, but does not kill it.

2. If you harvest all the aboveground shoots for food, relentlessly each year, it does not thrive. Again, you are inhibiting its growth.

3. I have seen both Japanese and Sakhalin knotweed growing for years in one spot like a multiplant shrub rather than spreading out. Of course, I have

also enjoyed seeing it spread gradually. It seems to spread more easily in soft moist soil.

4. I have seen whole monoculture fields of this plant and have taken students to these spots, until the plants were discovered by authorities. Once the plants are discovered, the authorities come in with strong herbicides that turn the areas black for a while. If they keep on it and spray over several years, knotweed can be destroyed. One application will just slow it down and it will grow back less vigorously at first. After three years it will be back to its vigorous self.

5. Regarding whole fields of knotweed that I have seen: I never saw knotweed disturbing nearby sidewalks, driveways, or buildings. Perhaps I should have looked closer.

Young Japanese knotweed growing from an underground network of rhizomes in a regularly mowed area. The plants still spread, but are weak, thin, and cannot do any of the destructive things you hear about. If the mowing stops, then these plants have a strong foothold to grow like crazy.

Since there is a major effort to kill this plant, the first thing you should be looking for, if you want to gather it as food, is evidence that chemical spray has been used to kill it. If it has been sprayed in the current year, that should be obvious. The whole area will be blackened. If you find this, abandon that location as a food source. Evidence of less strong herbicides will show stems with an *S* curve. That is, the healthy plant, once sprayed, will droop down from the toxin, then recover, and begin growing upward again. So there will be a sideways "ℕ" curve in the stem. Even if this year's new shoots look great, examine last year's stalks and see if they look mangled, shrunken, or have sideways *S* curves. If all this looks great and it is a healthy stand, then go for it.

Better yet, if you have access to the landowner, ask if the area has been sprayed for anything. If they know that they have knotweed and do not care if it is there or that you are gathering it, then, great. If they want to destroy the crop, that is their choice. You might have done them a big favor by alerting them, while depriving yourself of this great food.

MANAGING KNOTWEEDS

While North Americans and Europeans view our knotweeds as unmanageable, the Japanese know the plant well and are not intimidated by it. They view it as a normal feature of both wild and inhabited areas. They have been harvesting and managing it for centuries (Michiko, 2016).

RESERATROL

Knotweed rhizomes contain the most active form of resveratrol, trans-resveratrol, a polyphenolic stilbene. That is more than most people need to know and will only get you perplexed stares if you share this at dinner parties.

That is what unconditional love is all about—doing the right thing even if you don't benefit. Please love your neighbor.

My second warning to you is don't spread knotweed accidentally. As I've said, under experimentally controlled conditions, even small pea-sized parts of this plant can grow new plants. In real life, my guess is that more of the plant is necessary, and conditions have to promote it. I potted a segment that had a node on both ends. Being like bamboo between the nodes, it was filled with moist air, helping to protect it from drying out. I figured this gave it the best chance to grow into a new plant. It died. Since I do not have a green thumb, this just was further evidence of my incompetence, but demonstrated that a lot of the fear-mongering is only directing your attention to the worst-possible scenarios.

Here is how to prevent knotweed's accidental spread: When you are harvesting the shoots and stems, discard as much of the unusable material as you can right back on top of the plants where you found them. If a piece grows there, it will just compete with itself. If you harvest by stream or lakeside, DO NOT allow any material to fall in the water and re-root elsewhere. And discard any unusable material uphill in the knotweed growth area so the parts will not be carried away by flooding. When processing this material at home, DO NOT throw any uncooked discarded remnants into the compost—throw them in the trash. Any cooked material will be dead (though I am surprised that "coming back from the dead" or "growing in your stomach" were not numbers 6 and 7 in the earlier list of horrors about this plant).

On the bright side, in addition to the great food, the rhizomes of this plant are a major commercial source of resveratrol, an antiaging phytochemical. Resveratrol might be in the edible shoots too, but that is not where they harvest it from. You might have heard of the other sources: red wine, red grape skins, purple grape juice, blueberries, cocoa, and even peanut butter. Resveratrol serves as an antioxidant, anti-inflammatory, improves immune function, and kills some cancer cells, among other things. But alas, we are not eating the rhizomes and I do not know how to extract the resveratrol. It is all the rage in Chinese herbal medicine.

These knotweeds do not have edible rhizomes as far as I can tell, though some people have reported them as edible. They may be confused with *Polygonatum odoratum* var. *japonicum* (also called *Polygonatum japonicum*), which had been reported by Tanaka (1976) to have edible roots. I have found no corroborative information showing either of our edible *Fallopias* having edible rhizomes. A synonym genus for our knotweeds is *Polygonatum*, and many Japanese plants are given the *japonica* or *japonicum* epithets, so given sloppy research skills of many wild food enthusiasts, it is possible that people put 1 + 2 together to get 4. Also, since resveratrol is found in Japanese knotweed rhizomes, and we associate that with something good to consume, that may also motivate people to imagine that the rhizomes are edible. Interestingly, I have found no reports of anyone eating them. **Don't eat them!**

I have found no historical or scientific records of people eating the leaves of our knotweeds, so I assume that they are not edible. It is interesting to note that rhubarb, which is in the same plant family as knotweed, has poisonous leaves, but edible leaf stalks. Our knotweeds have edible plant stalks, but not edible leaves.

Knowing Knotweed

Both knotweeds in this chapter grow vigorously from rhizomes and root crowns. I tried to grow them from seed but failed miserably. In fact, these plants are known for their erratic reproduction from seed. Some plants produce viable seeds; others do not. So I have no seedlings to show you.

Locations where knotweed grows are easy to spot at any time due to the remnants they leave. Another name for this plant is *false bamboo*, because it grows long, large bamboo-like stems, up to $1\frac{1}{2}$ inches in diameter. If you come

RHIZOMES
Are underground stems, not roots.

PHOTOSENSITIZING AGENT?
I hear warnings that Japanese knotweed is a photosensitizing agent, but have not been able to verify this. My students and I have been handling and eating this plant for years without incident. A photosensitizing plant typically has some juice on or in it that can cause a skin rash. For this to happen, the juice has to absorb into the skin and be activated by direct sunlight. The sun's photons interact with the cells that absorbed the juice, producing damage ranging from mild discoloration to painful severe skin damage similar to that caused by poison ivy. If you are exposed but stay out of the sun, you will not get a rash.

A Japanese knotweed patch showing the new green shoots arising out of layers of old dead stalks from previous years. The root crown of all these new shoots is buried below the old stalks.

SHOOT

A shoot, in botanical lingo, is just the beginning of a new stem. For instance, asparagus is a shoot. Once its leaves emerge and it begins taking on its adult form, it would be considered a young plant.

upon Japanese knotweed, you may be walking through a bamboo-like forest with dead, tan-colored previous year's stalks crunching underfoot. The crunching sound is unique and a delight to hear. You may find yourself crunching through them on purpose just to hear the sound.

Sometimes the old, fallen stalks are so thick and intertwined, covering irregularly shaped root crowns, that you can barely make your way through them. Fallen stalks can be anywhere from 5 to 12 inches thick above ground level. I have fallen many times while searching through this mass for the young shoots. The undignified falls are fun since you are cushioned by layers of stalks.

Japanese knotweed shoots emerging from an established root crown. This crown is about 6 inches tall and a foot wide at its base. You can see last year's old brown stems still attached.

Left, a single Sakhalin knotweed shoot emerging through a mass of old, dead recumbent stalks. It could be arising from a rhizome or from a small root crown hidden below all the dead stalks. What is visible is about 7 inches tall, but the whole shoot is actually over a foot tall if you dig down under the dead recumbent stalks and debris. Right, multiple Japanese knotweed stalks arising from a single root crown. The tallest in this photo is 10 inches.

Knotweed plants can emerge out of what looks like normal ground, through a mess of the old stalks, or from the top of a root crown. That crown can be 5 inches to two feet in diameter and over a foot tall. That is what I've seen—they could be bigger. Like a tree stump, only not a tree stump. If a thick shoot is emerging directly out of the ground, it is coming from an established rhizome that you cannot see. If the shoot coming up is thin, around a half inch or less in diameter, it is coming from a weak rhizome.

The larger the stump, the more food stored, so the plant can send up many new stalks. I've seen 15 coming from one crown. Most of those shoots probably don't make it, since, when young, they are tender morsels for herbivores to consume.

If the shoots are receiving a lot of direct sunlight, or they are coming from meager rhizomes, they begin leafing out early. If they are well shaded, coming from huge root crowns, or if the spring is mostly cloudy, the shoots will look more like fat asparagus before they open their leaves. Sakhalin knotweed leafs out earlier than Japanese knotweed. Otherwise, they both behave similarly, whether growing singly or en masse from a crown.

Healthy shoots are straight, show segments, and range in size from large asparagus to being almost an inch thick. There are many short segments in the young shoots. But as the plants grow, the segments between

Sakhalin knotweed stems growing straight, here reaching 36 inches (left and center) to 45 inches (on the right). These might all be arising from the same root crown. This also shows the whitish ocrea membrane growing from nodes and wrapping around the stem. At the upper growth point, the ocrea wraps around the whole top. Ocrea on the lower nodes has already dried up, browned, and mostly fallen away.

The upper 12 inches of a healthy, still growing Japanese knotweed stem nearing the 6-foot mark, showing marked zigzagging at the nodes. Below this (cropped out of the picture) is a long straight stem. Note how quickly the ocrea have dried up on these upper stems and are no longer covering new growth. Each node supports one leaf. Now that the plant is maturing, new branches are emerging from each node.

the nodes expand and enlarge to lengths reaching up to 10 inches long and over an inch in diameter. The nodes are solid plant material. The segments between them are hollow. Single leaves arise from each node in an alternating pattern.

All members of the buckwheat family, the Polyonaceae, and therefore all knotweeds (there are many) have a structure called an *ocrea (sometimes spelled ochrea).* This is typically a thin weak almost white membrane that surrounds new growth. On our knotweeds that membrane totally covers new growth and all node locations. As the plant matures, the ocrea shrivels, turns brown, and tears away or falls off. One would think that they serve a protective function, either to shield the fragile new growths from the sun, to keep in moisture, or have a chemistry that prevents predation. They are too weak and delicate to serve as a shield to physical damage.

The zig and the zag

Rapid growth on healthy plants results in stalks that grow straight up to a point. Straight stalks are important from a food perspective as we will see later. As the plants grow tall, the upper and now branching stems begin zigzagging at the nodes. The ones growing from substantial rhizomes or root crowns grow straight, up to about 4 or, if you are lucky, 5 feet before beginning to zigzag. Mature knot-weeds can grow up to 9 feet tall (Japanese) or 12 feet tall (Sakhalin). Locations with more moisture promote taller, more vigorous straight growth. Lots of branching occurs in the upper parts of mature plants.

Weak plants growing from seed, where the rhizomes have been depleted, or where soil moisture is lacking will zigzag almost from the start. They will be smaller, thinner plants, generally not reaching over 6 feet tall. Refer back to the mowed area picture (page 203) at the beginning of this chapter to see short, thin zigzaggy stems.

Differences between our two knotweeds are mostly a matter of size. Japanese knotweed is the shorter of our two plants with smaller leaves and stems of a smaller diameter. And that stem often has a lot of reddish speckles to it. Sakhalin knotweed is larger, with larger leaves, and a stem that can be up to 1 1/2 inches in diameter. There is less red on the stems, but as with Japanese knotweed, the nodes can have a rust color.

Japanese knotweed leaves can be up to 7 inches wide, and they have a flattened leaf-blade base. The leaves are roughly triangular. Sakhalin knotweed leaves can be up to double that size, and the leaf-base is more rounded, giving it an almost as wide as tall, rounded egg-shape. Both have gently pointed tips.

Japanese knotweed leaves and stem (left) compared to Sakhalin knotweed (right). Also shown is the cross section of each stem. The Japanese knotweed stem is of smaller diameter, but it has a thicker wall than Sakhalin's. This makes the volume of solid stem material roughly the same for each inch of stem material harvested.

Japanese knotweed male flowers arise from the same nodes as the leaves in the upper regions of the plant. Note the zigzag in the upper stem. Male flowers are upright, white, and found in clusters.

Knotweeds have separate male and female plants. The flowers on male Japanese knotweeds are small and white and grow in upright clusters on the upper branches. The female flowers (not pictured here) recline somewhat and are greenish-white. Sakhalin has more flexibility. Some plants are male, some are female, and some are both. One thing complicating life is that Japanese and Sakhalin knotweeds can interbreed, so hybrids end up with averaged features. This is not a problem from a food perspective, but it is a problem for finicky taxonomists.

The seeds that develop from pollinated female flowers are encased in a three-winged papery structure called an *achene*. The achenes start out a light green color, turning tan or reddish tan as they dry out and the black seed inside matures.

Gathering and Edibility

Parts of importance

Throughout my coverage of knotweed, I am going to use the following terms to define its edibility and to describe the contents of recipes. It is all about stem material.

Japanese knotweed male flowers.

BF STEMS: Defined as *big, fat, juicy, and rapidly growing straight shoots or stems*. Or just *Big Fat Stems,* with the caveat that along with being big and fat, they are rapidly growing and straight to about 5 feet tall. *Straight* means no zigzagging on the stem. I prefer the fat stems, those that are $^3/_4$ to $1^1/_8$ inches in diameter at the base. Not pencil-thin stems but as fat as you can find them. Big fat stems grow faster and straighter than thin ones. Faster growth means more mass to collect with less effort and more tender material within to eat. If you want to learn about thin, branching, zigzaggy stems, you will need to find another author.

You may find Japanese and Sakhalin knotweeds at any stage of development from an inch to more than 10 feet

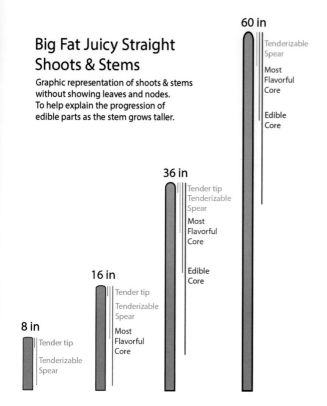

Big Fat Juicy Straight Shoots & Stems

Graphic representation of shoots & stems without showing leaves and nodes. To help explain the progression of edible parts as the stem grows taller.

60 in
Tenderizable Spear
Most Flavorful Core
Edible Core

36 in
Tender tip
Tenderizable Spear
Most Flavorful Core
Edible Core

16 in
Tender tip
Tenderizable Spear
Most Flavorful Core

8 in
Tender tip
Tenderizable Spear

tall. For the parts I am referring to, you want the young rapidly growing plants of spring. The good stuff can be found from late March through early May, depending on how early spring is where you live. All the terms here refer to distance from the tip or growth point of the BF Stem, no matter how tall the plant is.

Determining the edible parts on growing stems is an art as much as it is a science. Environmental conditions cause variability in the estimates I am giving here.

TENDER TIP: This is the top 3 inches of any BF Stem that is 30 inches or less. This part is typically tender, needs no peeling, and can be eaten raw or cooked.

TENDERIZABLE SPEAR: This is the top 6 to 10 inches of any BF Stem that is 60 inches or less in height. Also called a *shoot* or a *spear*. This spear includes the tender tip. At rapid growth stages it is possible that this part of the uppermost stem is tender enough to steam and eat without peeling. The upper three inches are always tender. As the plant gradually gets taller, the length of the tenderizable spear gradually gets shorter. Below this tenderizable area, everything requires peeling. Since this is tenderizable, you can use the peel for savory vegetable applications, and the sweet core for sweet-vegetable or fruit-simulating applications.

MOST FLAVORFUL CORE: This is the top 16 inches of any BF Stem. While you can peel and eat parts of the core of any BF stemmed knotweed up to about 5 feet, the top 16 inches are the most tender, have the thickest cores, and the most concentrated flavor. The tender tips and tenderizable spears are within this 16-inch segment. Except for the very top of this section, peeling is necessary to remove the fibrous skin.

EDIBLE CORE: This is the top 30 inches of any BF Stem that is 5 feet tall or less. Good for peeling to use the core. The upper 16 of this 30 inches will have the most flavor, but all can be used for food. Further down the stem, the core gets more and more fibrous and flavorless.

OUT TO PASTURE: These are plants that are over 5 feet tall with zigzaggy upper branches. The whole plant is too fibrous, even peeled, to be very beneficial. Don't get me wrong, there is always new branching and you might be able to find some peelable tender growth somewhere. But this is mostly just fibrous material.

Seedlings of Japanese knotweed are a rare thing. This plant does not typically reproduce by seed. I have not yet seen one in the wild so I do not know exactly when they germinate. Knowing this seedling may be useful to someone so I am showing it here. I am putting all of my focus on the plants that arise from knotweed rhizomes.

Japanese knotweed seedling. The cotyledons are long and narrow. The first true leaves are egg-shaped and pointed. The leaves (on the left and right) somewhat resemble the cotyledons of pokeweed. Like the much larger shoots of this plant, the tiny stem here has segments with leaves occurring at each node. Photo courtesy of the Ohio State University OARDC Weed Lab Image Archive.

Left: The perfect young Japanese knotweed shoot, about 4 inches tall. Right: Perfect Sakhalin knotweed shoot at 4 inches tall. Both are totally tender and delicious. The three top inches of each here represents the "tender tip." This does not need to be peeled and can be used fresh or cooked. The shoot on the left was partially buried under old debris so, having almost no sunlight, it is a lighter green in color. That, combined with the even whiter ocrea, make it a delight to behold.

Knotweed shoots arising from rhizomes

The young shoots can be found in the spring amongst the old, tan, long, bamboo-like 1-inch-diameter dead stalks. Some dead stalks will be upright, still attached to their root crown source, but most others from several years past will be lying on the ground. Since the old, fallen stalks create a substructure, a loose network of material to wade through, you have to search down below the surface to find the newest baby stalks. To me, this is very much like mushroom hunting—where you search and search for that slightest bit of mushroom sticking out from under the leaves. Then, once you find one, your eye and brain begin to see them everywhere. Here you are searching for green, white, and shades of red underneath the old loose material.

Young, freshly picked Japanese knotweed shoots. The tenderizable spears.

Do your best to pull aside and reach down through the old stalks as far as you can to the base of the new asparagus-like shoots. Cut 1 inch above the base. Use a scissors or knife. DO NOT pull or you will crush the tender shoot, making it harder to peel, and you will have a slimy hand. And who wants a slimy hand? If you cut too low, there will be a reddishness to the base of the shoot, signifying you got part of the root, and it will be fibrous.

Asparagus shoot on the left; Japanese knotweed shoot on the right. Asparagus is solid, with alternating bracts. The knotweed has hollow chambers separated by nodes. Ocrea arise from the nodes and surround the stem just above the nodes. Leaves arise alternately from the edges of the nodes.

The young shoots

Most people do not know whether they are picking Japanese or Sakhalin knotweed shoots, and often call everything "Japanese knotweed." In fact, I used to do that when I was a novice. But that is okay. There are only minor differences in structure. Food uses are the same for both species, so it does not matter what you are calling the plant.

If the knotweed shoots are growing out in the open without the old stalks, that means either a new stand is beginning or someone is managing the land, mowing, clearing things away, and possibly treating the knotweed as an ornamental.

What you collect depends on what you want to do. For instance, you can locate BF Stems that are 4 to 16 inches long and just gather the upper 3 inches at the top—the "tender tips." Treat them as a fresh vegetable. No peeling necessary. You can use these chopped up into dishes or put into stir-fries, small leaves and all. If you go to taller, older plants, the usable part at the top gets smaller.

You can gather any BF Stem up to 16 inches long, peel the whole thing, and use it fresh like a sweet/sour celery. Or you can gather plants up to 5 feet tall to process the full upper 30 inches of "edible core."

Whatever you collect, keep the fresh stems spray-misted (moist), cool, and protected from sunlight until you are ready to use them. When home, place them in bags in the refrigerator. If you have no refrigeration available, place them in water, as you would flowers. Be forewarned that they will continue to grow in water, which will cause them to fiber up over time. So don't let them sit there unattended for days.

The easiest cooked dish you can make from the "tenderizable spears," thin or fat, is what I call Knotweed Pâté.

Left: Upper leafy "tender tips" of the taller BF Stems. These are tender fresh, no peeling required. More typically cooked in some way than eaten fresh.

Right: This is the closest I could come to cooked asparagus in appearance with knotweed. These were peeled and steamed for 1 minute, not enough to cook all the way through. Flavor and texture were totally different than asparagus. You can see the chambers in between the nodes collapsing. These are creamy, delicious, and melt in your mouth, but have no body. I could barely get them on the plate without having them fall apart. These are better served as Knotweed Pâté or used in some other knotweed-appropriate dish.

Above: Knotweed Pâté. There is no liver or fat in this pâté, just knotweed. This is what happens when you steam Japanese knotweed tenderizable spears with the skin on for 5 minutes. These are soft, super tender, and creamy. Add olive oil and salt for a treat by itself, or use this as an ingredient in a million other foods requiring moist, creamy, lemony vegetables.

You just steam the spears for 5 minutes and literally pour them into a bowl. A little olive oil and salt and you are all set. Cooked knotweed is quite creamy in its mouthfeel. No real cream, no real fat, but a creamy mouthfeel.

Since the fresh shoot is reminiscent of asparagus in appearance, people think you can substitute it for asparagus in any recipe. You cannot. Don't even think about it. Okay, maybe you could if I dared you. But you will not like the results.

Knotweed is often presented like asparagus in photographs by many wild food enthusiasts. In fact, the earlier photo of me (page 213) holding the shoots in my hand is iconic. This will not be the last time you see that kind of image in the wild food literature. But you'll never see knotweed served like cooked asparagus in a photo except here, for illustrative purposes. I would never prepare them like cooked asparagus for myself.

Young knotweed "tenderizable spears" have 4 properties that distinguish them from asparagus.

- First, the outer skin of knotweed has a mild foulness to it that blends with the inner sweetness to make a fine vegetable. Once steamed, the foulness disappears.
- Second, the shoots do not hold their shape when cooked, but the skin needs to be cooked to become tender. Yep, it's an impossible situation. The only way to be able to chew the skin is to steam it for 5 minutes. This causes the shoot to go flaccid—something no one should ever see. It just does not hold its shape and gets so tender it falls apart. If you try to roast the "tenderizable spears," they will go flaccid by the time there is a nice browning going on. But you can view this as a feature, like I do with the Knotweed Pâté.
- Third, knotweed has a wonderful lemony flavor that asparagus does not have. So you can use it like rhubarb leaf stalks to make fruit-like foods. The

vegetable flavor in the skin, however, interferes with its uses as a fruit-like product. If you are using the shoots as a sweet vegetable or a fruit-like product, then use a potato peeler to remove the thin skin.

- Fourth, knotweed turns from a strong green to a greenish yellow with cooking, just like sheep and wood sorrels. The yellowish color turns some people off. Each plant however should be appreciated for whatever its attributes present.

The moral to the story is that knotweed is not asparagus and you should not try to make it such. On the other hand, asparagus is not knotweed, which has its own virtues—different virtues.

Peel knotweed to reveal its inner sweet, fresh flavor. To peel knotweed, use a very sharp, solid, preferably serrated horseshoe peeler. I find that they work better because you can get a more controlled peel. They can easily dig into the skin to grab it without exerting a lot of downward pressure. Flexible blades on cheap peelers tend to crush the stems, rather than dig in, when you press down.

Keeping the general principles in mind that I covered, let's look at practical food uses. You can eat the peeled shoots of the "Flavorful Core" raw in fruit and vegetable salads, smoothies, sliced lengthwise and added to

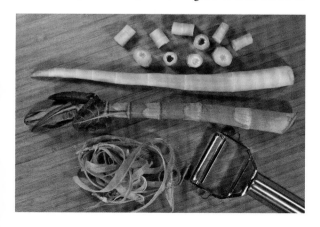

Peeling knotweed separates the sweet shoot from its not-sweet skin. The pieces at the top show that these peeled stems are hollow, except for where the nodes were. A good-quality solid serrated horseshoe peeler is shown. Horseshoe peelers seem to work better for me than the straight peelers due to better control.

Raw peeled sliced knotweed shoots served as a snack or to dip in something delicious. They are sweet and crisp with a mild lemony flavor. You can make these from any part of the stalk, though the upper 2 feet has the most flavor.

sandwiches, and, among other things, served as vegetables to dip in sauces at a party. I personally love the peeled shoots raw if I am just eating it out of hand, as you would munch on celery or on a rhubarb stalk. There is a mild, sweet taste reminiscent of green apples.

Unpeeled or peeled sliced "tenderizable spears" can be added to stir-fries and other foods when the last foods are added, a couple of minutes before taking off the heat. Take the food off the heat when knotweed pieces take on a moist appearance. If you cook knotweed long enough, it will collapse. Of course, you may want it to collapse. But if you want it to retain any body, only cook it a couple of minutes.

Japanese knotweed stir-fry, including sliced "tenderizable knotweed spears," sliced tawny daylily shoots, mushrooms, carrots, sweet red pepper, and broccoli.

Cream of Knotweed Soup

Makes 4 to 5 servings

This is an excellent soup that takes advantage of the creamy properties of knotweed. It is only simulating real cream or butter, as neither are part of this recipe. It's smooth, creamy, lemony, and will impress the most finicky of eaters. This is a thick, rich soup with not a lot of water. If you like more watery soup, you have my sympathies.

INGREDIENTS

1 large red onion, minced (any color of onion will do)
3 tablespoons extra virgin olive oil, divided
2 cloves garlic, minced
3 cups water
3 1/2 bouillon cubes, or more to taste
1 pound fresh knotweed "tenderizable spears" with skin on
(about 5 cups), cut into half-inch pieces
1 (10-ounce) jar chopped mushrooms, with liquid
1 1/2 teaspoons ginger powder
Sprigs of parsley or wild carrot, to taste
Salt and pepper, to taste

DIRECTIONS

In a large skillet, sauté onion in 1 tablespoon olive oil until soft. Add garlic and continue cooking for a couple of minutes, until the garlic aroma blooms.

Pour water into a 2-quart pot, add the sautéed onion, bouillon, knotweed, remaining olive oil, mushrooms with liquid, and ginger powder. Over medium heat, bring to a gentle boil and cook for 10 minutes.

Serve hot with parsley or wild carrot sprigs and season with salt and pepper, if needed.

Knotweed spaghetti noodles. Noodles here are the peeled skin of the "tenderizable spears," served with spaghetti sauce, Parmesan cheese, and garnished with young wild carrot leaves. If you get carried away and include the stalk below the tenderizable area, you will be spitting out fiber. Boiling or steaming the peeled knotweed skin for 5 to 10 minutes should do the trick. Just as with spaghetti, taste for tenderness while still in the pot, so you will know if you have to cook it longer.

Knotweed stir-fry using the "tender tips." Mix them in any stir-fry only a couple of minutes before removing from the heat.

Using the peel

You can add the "tenderizable spear" peel to dishes that will be cooked more than 5 minutes. They must be cooked to become tender, otherwise you will be spitting out fiber at your dinner party.

The tender tips

The small leaves on "tender tips" are fine to eat and have a mild spinach flavor. They are the only leaves I could find that had a cultural use. I would not eat leaves other than those on the tips of the upper shoots and would eat none of those down the stalk, no matter how big or small. All cultures who ate this plant discarded all the leaves except those at the tip.

The "tender tips" are totally chewable and can be collected for use in any dish you would add broccoli, cauliflower, Brussels sprouts, or bok choy to. If cooked, it will add a mild lemon flavor and a creamy mouthfeel.

They are a great vegetable that can be chopped up into salads, placed in sandwiches, or cooked lightly. While you can make pâté out of them, their leafiness and edibility raw give them many other possibilities that are only limited by your imagination. I've seen them battered and

fried, but you will not find any battered and fried recipes in my books.

Working with taller stalks

BF Stems anywhere from 4 inches to 5 feet tall can be collected by using scissors or a knife to cut them free. You will only be able to use the upper 30 inches of the taller 60-inch straight stems, so just take what you can use. During the plant's straight growth, the outer skin, although somewhat resistant, is still easy to cut through with good strong scissors.

Knotweed take from a foraging excursion. Plant material here ranges from 8-inch shoots to 38-inch stalks. This was 22 pounds of raw material.

Since you are taking a significant mass of each plant, the material is more resistant to dehydration than loose leaves of many other forageables. But in keeping with good foraging practice, it is good to wrap your take in big white plastic bags and keep it cool until you're ready to process it. This means keeping the stalks out of the sun, as you should all plant material. With large pieces like this, people sometimes make the mistake of putting their take into the back of a hot car with the sun's rays cooking the contents through the windows as they drive for an hour to get home. If you don't have plastic bags, use moistened white blankets if you can. Keeping the stalks moist is another good reason to carry a spray mister with you everywhere you go.

Taller stalks will have a fibrous skin that has to be removed. The farther from the growth tip, the thicker that skin is.

If you select BF Stems ranging from 16 to 30 inches in length, you can use a potato peeler to carefully remove the fibrous skin. This can give you a substantial amount of food. Peeling takes some practice and experience to get it right.

While some people prefer peeling the 30-inch or shorter stalks like bananas, I find that it does not work

ANTS LOVE KNOTWEED

These plants have a higher concentration of sugar in their stalks than most plants have. This attracts ants, which either feed off sugars that the plant exudes or bite into the plant to feed. Sometimes you bring these ants home with you. Hosing these stalks down does a pretty good job of driving off the ants.

A mix of peeled knotweed shoots up to 20 inches long, cut into shorter lengths (3 to 8 inches long) to make peeling more manageable.

well. Too much fiber is left behind, requiring you to use a potato peeler anyway. Just use a potato peeler from the start. It takes practice to peel them efficiently. You want to remove all of the fibrous skin, but none of the underlying meat of the core.

Taller plants

The skin of 3- to 6-foot BF Stems, near their base, becomes almost woody. Since these stalks are more mature than the early shoots and the shorter stalks, their skin is filled with thick fiber. The unfortunate thing is that the fiber is not in a distinct layer. The very outside is fairly solid, with fiber most solid at the skin and gradually becoming less so near the core of the stem. When I say "core" I just mean the meaty material that is closer to the hollow center. This gradual change in fibrousness is maddening, since it makes separating the sweet, edible, tender core of the stems from the fibrous rind extremely difficult.

I have done experiments using a spoon and other devices to try to scrape the edible core away from the rind. You do this by slicing the stem lengthwise, so the inside is facing you, and scraping down with a very round-tipped spoon. Unfortunately, you invariably scrape a lot of the transitional areas with a mix of fibrous and inner tender material. The fibrous chew that results is most obvious in the raw state. So I have found little use for this scraping method. If only there were distinct layers of fibrous and tender material.

Steaming makes the separation of the tender material easy. So using the "edible core," I devised a system to extract the core meat of the upper 30 inches of BF Stems up to 6 feet tall. For all cooking applications when you are just prepping knotweed for core extraction, you want to steam it. That will preserve the most flavor and nutrients.

Boiling leaches a lot of the flavor into the cooking water. Great if you want a soup base using both the water and cooked cores, but not so good if you want flavorful

Pre-steamed (green) and post-steamed (greenish-yellow) halved segments of knotweed.

knotweed core material. Boiling does not make sense over-all, since you still have to pull out the segments to scrape them, just to put them back again. It is easier to steam everything.

I find my widest (not wildest) pot, usually just under 10 inches in diameter, and put my metal steamer basket in it. Then I cut my knotweed stalks into 9-inch segments, which will just fit into the pot, and slice them lengthwise. I steam the segments for 5 minutes and lay them out to cool. At this point the scraping method is easy and just removes the tender material, the sweet core, leaving behind the fibrous rind. I use a tablespoon for the scraping process.

As you scrape the steamed stalks, discard the whitish nodes. They are tough to chew.

If you are steaming a lot of stalks, the steaming broth is concentrated enough to make a fine soup stock with a spir-ited lemony flavor. Used as a cold drink, the steaming water has hints of asparagus with a pleasant lemony tang to it.

That core material you've scraped can now be used in any savory or sweet recipe you can imagine. It is pulpy and reminiscent of jam. Here are some recipes I came up with, starting with the savory option and then on to the sweet ones.

Scraping the sweet core from steamed knotweed segments using a wide round tablespoon. On the right you can see the whitish nodes I've removed, since I do not use them.

Knocamole

Makes approximately 1½ cups
This is a fine dip to make for the fun of it and is remarkably like guacamole.

1½ cups chopped knotweed cores from peeled "tenderizable spears" (see page 217)

1 ounce cream cheese

¼ teaspoon salt

¾ cup chopped tomato meat (no seeds or watery pulp)

¼ cup finely chopped red onion

DIRECTIONS

Put the knotweed into a food processor, adding cream cheese and salt. Pulse until smooth.

Transfer to a bowl, add tomato and onion, and gently fold into the knotweed mixture.

The knocamole is ready to use.

Use as a dip for tortilla chips, broccoli, cattail celery, or any other thing you can imagine. Add to tacos, burritos, burgers, sandwiches, and other dishes as a condiment.

Notes: Since I added no thickeners, there will be some separation of liquid, which you can stir back in. Lemon or lime juice added to normal guacamole is not necessary here, since the knotweed has its own acids and does not discolor to any discernible extent.

Zesty Knotweed Sauce

Makes approximately 1 cup

Here is a zippy-flavored sauce that blends the flavors of knotweed and lime so beautifully that you do not know where the knotweed flavor ends and the lime flavor begins. Great for adding to things as you would add fruit: for swirling into yogurt; as a topping on ice cream, pudding, or custard; as a top layer on a cheesecake; or use your imagination. The sweet and sour flavor of knotweed cores is enhanced by lime, so consider that in other recipes.

INGREDIENTS

1 cup steamed knotweed core scrapings (see page 223)
3 tablespoons sugar
2 tablespoons lime juice
1 teaspoon finely chopped lime zest

DIRECTIONS

Mix the knotweed, sugar, lime juice, and lime zest together and pour into a saucepan. Over medium-low heat, bring the mixture to a simmer for about 1 minute, stirring constantly. (You do not want to brown the sauce at all. The point of heating it is to help all the ingredients blend well while slightly reducing the moisture content.) Remove from heat.

Either leave it as it is or place in a blender to homogenize the small pieces into a smooth sauce. It can be used either hot or cold. If you prefer a cool sauce, chill in the refrigerator until ready to use.

Note: For a more subtle flavor that highlights the knotweed, just use $1/2$ of the lime zest and no lime juice.

Knotweed Meringue Pie

Makes 1 (9-inch) pie or fills 6 to 8 custard cups

This pie is akin to a lemon or lime pie usually associated with meringue. In fact, if you want to top this with meringue, you will have all the egg whites you need from this recipe. No need for me to repeat a basic meringue recipe—you can look that up or use your favorite recipe. Or if you don't want to make pie, forget the crust, forget the meringue, and just pour this cooked mixture into custard cups for a fantastic knotweed treat. I did not make the meringue for this photo since I was experimenting, had two baking projects going on at the same time, and could not manage adding meringue before it cooled. But since I had some marsh mallow root, marshmallow cream handy (see page 134), I just used that.

INGREDIENTS

2 cups chopped knotweed (see directions)
1 (9-inch) prebaked piecrust
4 large egg yolks (you can use the whites for meringue)
1 1/4 cups sugar
3 tablespoons cornstarch
1/2 teaspoon ground ginger
1/8 teaspoon salt
1 tablespoon finely chopped lime zest (zest from 2 limes)
3 tablespoons unsalted butter, melted

DIRECTIONS

To make the purée: Peel lots of "tenderizable spears," (see page 217). Chop into 1/2-inch pieces until you have about 6 cups. Steam the pieces for 6 minutes. Liquefy them in a blender. Do not add water. 6 cups of fresh peeled, chopped knotweed makes about 2 cups of purée, which you can use for this and other recipes. Some few half-inch fibers will remain, because peeling is not an exact science, but you will not notice them when eating. Blending concentrates the knotweed for more flavor.

Preheat the oven to 325°F if you plan on making the meringue topping.

Have a fully baked pie shell ready to go, and a piecrust protector shield so the crust doesn't dry out and brown. A pie shield is not necessary if you cover the crust with meringue.

To prepare the knotweed curd for the pie: Pour the knotweed purée into a large mixing bowl. In a separate bowl, whisk the egg yolks until well blended, and then whisk them into the purée.

One at a time add in the sugar, cornstarch, ginger, salt, lime zest, and butter, whisking as you are adding.

If you are going to use meringue to top the pie, make it now and set it aside. Once the meringue is made:

Pour the knotweed mixture into a 10- or 12-inch saucepan over medium heat. Using a silicone or rubber spatula, continually and systematically scrape the liquid from all surfaces of the pan so none of it has a chance to sit in one place and cook. You want the liquid to thicken, not solidify. The liquid will bubble some and gradually thicken to the point where when you scrape along the bottom, it no longer fills in right away.

Pour the thickened curd into the piecrust. You are done and can just let it cool for eating, unless you want to top it with meringue, which you should have ready at this point.

So if you want to top the pie, spread the meringue over the whole top while the curd is still hot (no dillydallying), making sure you connect the meringue to the crust on all sides. Overtop the fluted edges of the crust to make sure the meringue is adhering strongly to the inside of the edges. If you don't, the meringue will shrink and float in the center of the pie, so when you cut it, it will slide around, sticking to your knife more than the pie, and your whole day will be ruined. Since the crust is prebaked, it does not need to cook more. And it might burn if you expose it.

Put the pie in the oven and bake 20 minutes or until lightly browned. Let cool and eat, or refrigerate for a few days if you have the discipline or just enjoy torturing yourself.

Knotweed Custard Pie

Makes 1 (9-inch) pie plus extra custard or 2 (8-inch) pies

This is a pumpkin-style pie with its own unique flavor and color. If you overcook it, it will go past forming a custard, the eggs will congeal, and it will begin weeping. If you undercook it, it will just be a creamy hot dish. The photo here shows an undercooked pie that does not hold its shape. If only making one pie, pour the extra filling into ramekins for smaller treats, but don't leave them in the oven as long as the pie. Take them out when a toothpick inserted in the middle comes out clean.

INGREDIENTS

1 egg yolk for each piecrust

$^1/_2$ teaspoon salt, plus more for egg yolks

1 (9-inch) prepared piecrust dough or 2 (8-inch) piecrusts (if you are a gambler)

2 cups knotweed purée (see page 226)

2 large eggs

$^3/_4$ cup milk

$^3/_4$ cup heavy cream

$^3/_4$ cup sugar

2 tablespoons cornstarch

1 teaspoon ground ginger

1 teaspoon finely chopped lemon or lime zest

DIRECTIONS

Preheat the oven to 425°F.

Whip up 1 yolk with a pinch of salt for each piecrust. Brush the yolk on the bottom and sides of the crust where the filling will touch. Put aside.

To make the custard, pour the knotweed purée into a large mixing bowl. In a separate bowl, whisk the eggs until well blended; then whisk them into the purée.

Add the milk, cream, sugar, cornstarch, ginger, and zest one at a time into the puree, whisking all along. Pour the mixture into the prepared crust.

Place on the middle oven rack and bake at 425°F for 15 minutes. Reduce the temperature to 350°F. Bake for 20 minutes and pull the rack out briefly to place the edge protector on the fluted area to prevent burning. Push the rack back in oven and continue baking for 25 or so minutes until done. You know it is done when a toothpick inserted in the center comes out clean, without filling sticking to it. The custard's structure should be set (semisolid) on the margins while the center is still slightly jiggly.

Let the pie cool to room temperature; then place in the refrigerator for a few hours to chill. Eat before anyone else discovers these pies, or refrigerate them in sealed containers to eat within the next couple of days.

Euell Gibbons's Classic Knotweed Pie

Makes 1 (9-inch) pie

This is the classic knotweed pie recipe that almost every advanced forager I know has tried. It was first published in *Stalking the Wild Asparagus* by Euell Gibbons in 1962. These are the limited directions he gave to make his filling. This dessert is sort of a mix between what one would expect in something like a rhubarb pie commingled with a custard pie. He used a vegetable oil piecrust, which you can look up if you want. Or use any piecrust. Gibbons also dictated both a bottom and top crust. Of the three pie recipes in this section of the book, I prefer them in this order: Knotweed Meringue Pie, by far; Knotweed Custard Pie; and Gibbon's Knotweed Pie. You may have different preferences. The beautifully crafted Gibbons pie in the photograph here was made by Michelle Illuminato at my 2013 Native Shores Wild Food Rendezvous.

INGREDIENTS

$1\frac{1}{2}$ cups sugar

$\frac{1}{4}$ cup flour

$\frac{3}{4}$ teaspoon grated (Gibbons) or ground (most people) nutmeg

3 eggs

4 cups peeled and chopped knotweed stalks

Prepared piecrust dough for a 9-inch double-crust pie, top crust optional

DIRECTIONS

Preheat the oven to 400°F.

In medium bowl, blend together sugar, flour, and nutmeg. Set aside.

In a large bowl, beat the eggs. Then gradually blend the dry ingredients into the eggs. Stir in the knotweed stalks.

Pour the filling into the prepared uncooked bottom piecrust and add the top crust, if using.

Place the pie in the oven and bake for 50 minutes. This timing assumes you've put a top crust on the pie, so timing would be less if you did not use a top crust. Cool before serving.

Pungent or Peppery Plants

The plants in this chapter have mildly pungent and/or peppery and/or acrid flavors. These are greens and vegetables that are suitable for occasions where you want to add some character to the dish you are making. Vegetables with these flavors are often added to milder ones (the Foundation Plants) or complex dishes to add interest and nuance. They are edible raw and cooked, but their best uses depend on your flavor goals for whatever you are preparing. They have the potential to greatly improve a dish if you use just the right amount to suit your taste sensibilities. At certain stages of growth, some of these vegetables are mild enough that you might even be able to make a whole dish with them alone, but many people will prefer to use them as a flavor enhancer for other foods.

Pungent or peppery plants covered in volume 1 of this book series are:

- Field mustard (*Brassica rapa*)
- Wintercress (*Barbarea vulgaris*)
- Upland cress (*Barbarea verna*)
- Garlic mustard (*Alliaria petiolata*)
- Shepherd's purse (*Capsella bursa-pastoris*)

All of the plants covered in the Pungent section of volume 1 and one plant here, wild radish, are in the mustard family. Mustards are known for their pepperiness and pungency. In the typical American diet, most people are exposed to mustards as a condiment. Those yellow and fancy brown condiments are made from the seeds of certain mustards. One variety of mustard greens (typically *Brassica juncea*) is what you find in the stores.

Mustard greens, in general, can be nutritional powerhouses packed with nutrients and phytochemicals. Garlic mustard, covered in volume 1, for instance, is one of the most nutritious leafy greens ever analyzed, according to our nutrient charts. Mustards have many phytochemicals in common including glucosinolates sinigrin, progoitrin, goitrin, and glucobrassicin; indoles; and isothiocyanates. These compounds are thought to fight cancer and heart disease through a variety of mechanisms.

Not all mustard family plants or their parts taste alike. Each has its own characteristic flavor and texture. When fresh, some are excellent in combination salads, added to sandwiches, used as garnishes, and made into pesto or other greens-based sauces. Cooked, their flavors vary tremendously—some remaining pungent, others transforming into foundation flavors.

The plants covered here in Pungent or Peppery Plants include daylily and wild radish. Daylily is in the aloe family (*Xanthorrhoeaceae*), though it is often mistakenly thought to be in the lily family (*Liliaceae*). It has much in common with lilies and has *lily* in the name, so the confusion is understandable.

Wild radish (*Raphanus raphanistrum*), closely related to domesticated radish, is in the mustard family (*Brassicaceae*). *Raphanus sativus*, which became, through domestication, our cultivated radish, is also known as "wild radish." All versions of this can be found alongside our other wild radish. Pungent or Peppery Plants are an excellent addition to the gourmet's arsenal of tastes.

Chapter 16

FAMILY: Xanthorrhoeaceae
SPECIES: *Hemerocallis fulva*

Tawny Daylily

The biggest flowers you might ever eat in the wild.

Tawny daylilies in flower among their sword-shaped leaves. Each flower opens for only a day. Many plants grow in clusters due to underground propagation.

Estimated Range

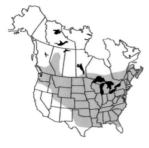

Official Species Name:
• *Hemerocallis fulva* (L.) L.

Synonyms:
• None, but thousands of showy ornamentals of the same species are described as variations and subspecies.

Common Names:
• Tawny daylily
• Orange daylily

An herbaceous plant native to Asia, escaped and naturalized. Widespread over Europe and North America in yards, old fields, ditches, and stream sides. Typically introduced into regions as ornamental plantings, then spread widely.

Edible Parts:
• Young leaf bases
• Buds
• Tepals (sepals plus petals)
• Tubers

continued

TAWNY DAYLILY

Tawny daylilies are amazing plants. They are prolific, growing pretty much everywhere people are: in yards, old fields, farmland, near stream banks, and maybe even out your front door. They produce copious amounts of food all year long and have some of the biggest edible flowers I know of. They are not without issues, which I will get to later.

All daylilies, including tawny ones, originated in Asia, where several species have been cultivated and eaten for thousands of years. They are grown on a massive scale to be sold in markets all over the world. Most Asian markets in the United States and Europe sell dried daylily buds. Although multiple parts of the plant are eaten, the buds are the primary commercial focus since dried, they are available for use all year. Fresh parts, like the open flowers and tender stems, are fleeting, making them more seasonal. The tubers are eaten, but not as widely as the other parts. As Europeans opened trade routes to China, daylilies were spread as ornamentals, not typically used for food—first throughout Europe, then to the rest of the world. Now they are widespread across North America.

According to Arlow Stout (1933), one of the foremost American authorities on daylilies, the buds (primarily), flowers, and newly shriveled flowers were dried, packaged into bundles, and distributed widely to markets. These were eaten by pretty much everyone in Asia, reconstituted in soups, stir-fries, and a variety of other dishes. Fresh flowers and buds were also eaten locally in season. Today, dried daylily buds are sold in Asian markets as "dried lily flowers." The exact species harvested is not indicated on the packages.

Daylilies are known for their single-day blossoms. At dawn, one or sometimes two of the largest buds on a flower stem begin transforming, fully opening before noon and staying open all day. Some time after dusk on the same day, they close up—never to open again. They open for one day and that is it. By the next morning, the previous day's flowers have shriveled into thin clusters of flower parts. Most daylilies produce no seed.

Above: Tawny daylily flower stalk showing all stages of the flowering cycle: balloon-shaped flower buds at different stages of development: the day's fully open flower (about 3½ to 4 inches across); yesterday's shriveling flower (upper right); and receptacles (bases) of previous flowers that have already shriveled and fallen away, lower on the stem. One or two flowers per flower stalk may open at once on any particular day. Flowers continue to open each day until all buds are spent. Each flower lives for a day: opening in the morning, and dying by night.

Poisonous Parts:
• Possibly the ovary on rare daylily mutants

Above: Dried daylily buds are sold in Asian markets in the US and Europe as "Dried Lily Flowers." The species is not indicated on any of the different brands I found for sale. From various sources I have heard that it could be any one of these: *Hemerocallis fulva*, *Hemerocallis citrina*, *Hemerocallis esculenta*, or *Hemerocallis minor*. One dried lily flower package I found was actually not *Hemerocallis* at all, but from the *Lilium* genus. You can tell if it is a *Lilium* by both the look of the dried material and by the State of California cancer warning on US packaging. If there is a cancer warning, it is not daylily.

I have not found any credible sources of nutrient analyses done on fresh parts of this plant. All we have was reported by Stout on the chemical analysis of the dried "flowers" purchased in a Peking, China, market in 1929 (1933). It is likely that these were the dried buds, not dried flowers or shriveled flowers. Dried buds almost certainly have different nutritional profiles than dried flowers.

Plants are mostly water. So an analysis of fresh materials finds mostly water with relatively small amounts of nutrients—what you see in most nutrient tables. Dried materials include just the solids, so a nutrient analysis of them would show higher percentages by weight. What Stout reported on the dried flower parts was 11.42% protein, 2.77% fat, 10.44%, carbohydrate, 8.48% crude fiber, and 5.35% ash (Stout, 1933). On two commercial packages I purchased, the nutrient data listed were so varied that I don't trust them enough to report them to you. Nutrients in general maximize at flower opening, then decline rapidly as flowers shrivel (Rodriguez-Enriquez, 2013). Flowers have incredible potential for being nutrient and phytochemical powerhouses due to their chemical complexities: strong colors and aromatic chemicals used for insect attraction. Researchers analyzed the edible flowers of 12 plant species (not including *Hemerocallis*) and found them to be high in minerals (Otakar, 2012). This raises the question: Are all open pre-pollination flowers at their peak in minerals and other nutrients over earlier and later stages? Daylilies apparently have a lot of potential as strong antioxidants (Que, 2007). *Hemerocallis* flowers and buds are worth more study for their nutrient and phytochemical potential.

The mass of research on medicinal and toxic aspects of daylilies is being done in China, and that research is in Chinese. So if you are interested in pursuing this further, abstracts and summaries of that work translated into English, rather than whole articles, are mostly what you will find. In the modern literature, the toxicity information you hear is a nonspecific mess. What you do get are generalizations from literature on farm animals grazing on daylily. They do not distinguish exactly which part of the plant is being referred to, and lump all *Hemerocallis* species together in discussions to further confuse the issue.

Referring to daylilies, or the *Hemerocallis* genus, as if they all represent just one species becomes a real problem when referring to toxic compounds like hemerocallin. Hemerocallin is found in the "roots" of some species and not others. According to Wang (1989), the "roots," of *Hemerocallis citrina* and two varieties of *Hemerocallis fulva* did not contain the toxin hemerocallin to any measurable degree. I am assuming he is referring to its tubers when he says "roots," since that is what people would eat. Underground parts of daylily are rhizomes, tubers, and roots. So although two varieties of *Hemerocallis fulva*

Belowground parts of daylily are not all root material. Rhizomes and tubers are stem material. Rhizomes transport food to and from the tuber. The tuber stores food and is capable of producing new plants from those stores. Roots bring nutrients and water from the soil, into the plant.

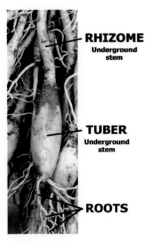

RHIZOME
Underground stem

TUBER
Underground stem

ROOTS

cannot represent all tawny daylilies, this information is consistent with the lack of reported poisonings associated with daylily consumption in North America.

Here is what Wang wrote: "The roots of *Hemerocallis* species (daylilies) ingested by goats, sheep, and cattle, and used for the treatment of schistosomiasis (snail fever) in humans, have caused fatalities in the People's Republic of China. *H. thunbergii, H. esculenta, H. altissima, H. lilio-asphodelus,* and *H. minor* are toxic." Note that *Hemerocallis fulva* is not in this list of plants with tuber problems. And none of this refers to the flower buds, flowers, or growing stems of the species listed.

Yellow daylilies *Hemerocallis altissima* and *Hemerocallis lilioasphodelus* (sometimes known as *Hemerocallis flava*), due to hemerocallin in their "roots," can cause dilation of the pupils, blindness, paralysis, inflammation, difficulty urinating, and even death in goats, rabbits, and mice. So my recommendation is that you, mice, goats, and rabbits stay away from underground parts of yellow daylilies. I have not found any references documenting these specific symptoms in humans, and I have found no records in the toxicology literature of human poisoning from tawny daylily roots in the Americas. There may be no record because people are not eating yellow flowered daylily roots of these odd species. **For safety reasons, I recommend you stay away from tubers of yellow daylilies that you might find in peoples' gardens. Even if they are a yellow variant of *Hemerocallis fulva*, you should probably leave it alone to prevent accidental poisonings from *altissima* and *lilioasphodelus*.**

Knowing Tawny Daylily

The classic version of tawny daylily is easily recognized . . . well, sort of. You will probably first see it in early summer when its flowers are blooming like big orange trumpets. They are showy and grow in dense patches. But as an ornamental, the plant has been selected for so many variations in flower

Above: Young daylily shoots emerging in midwinter (February) in Portland, Oregon. The plant in this photograph is about 5 inches left to right, tip to tip, and about 5 inches tall. Observe how the leaf blades are creased along the center and folded upward.

Above: Young shoots 5 to 10 inches tall emerging from a patch of underground tubers. Thick patches develop over time, crowding out other plants.

Left: Young daylily shoots; the tallest in this photograph is 10 inches. Leaves all originate at the base and tightly wrap around each other, giving the false impression that there is a stem.

Above left: By early spring, leaves are growing in dense clusters—mostly hanging down like these, sometimes a little more upright. Above right: A close-up of the base shows how the daylily leaves overlap each other, similar to iris (see Cattail chapter, page 56), but not flattened like iris.

color, shape, and size—thousands, in fact—that knowing exactly which plant you are working with will be difficult. The American Hemerocallis Society's Online Daylily Registry (http://www.daylilies.org/DaylilyDB/) lists over 70,000 cultivars, of which most are likely *Hemerocallis* cultivars, a subset of which look like the original. Fortunately, the original parent plants were spread across the globe and took root before most of the cultivars became available.

In the early spring you will see patches of young green shoots emerging in force almost before any other plants. They will come up through the snow as long as temperatures do not go too far below freezing. These plants grow fast since they are fed by starch-filled underground tubers from last year's growth. Leaves tightly overlap each other at the base of the plant. This overlapping gives the look of a short fat stem, when it is really just made up of clustered leaves tightly wrapped around each other in a left/right opposing arrangement. True flowering stems develop later. On the ones I've seen, water beads off, as if they were waterproof.

Late in spring reproductive stalks emerge, topped with what resembles the beak of a bird.

As the plant continues to grow, the leaves lengthen considerably. They can range from 12 to 30 inches long. The leaves are swordlike, pointed, and hairless and have a crease down the center. They mostly arch downward when they reach a certain length, due to their own weight. All but a few very short stem leaves arise directly from the ground.

In mid-spring, the plant starts sending up a flower stalk, which easily overtops the leaves. Stems can reach 30 to 60 inches tall. By late spring the top of the stalk branches, with each branch producing five to nine flower buds. The buds mature at varying rates, so each branch only allows one or two open flowers at a time. Buds are hot dog-shaped, ranging from $1\frac{1}{2}$ to 3 inches long. Sepals serve as the outer layer of the buds, with the petals lying underneath.

Daylilies can be confused with "true" lilies—those of the *Lilium* genus. That is primarily because both have

Tawny daylily flower parts, showing the three wider, more delicate and textured petals alternating with narrower, slightly more rigid and uniform-shaped sepals. The petals and sepals considered together are called tepals. This is the delicious "Flasher" variety of tawny daylily.

Old daylily stem, showing the remaining round-tipped nubs left over after the flowers have fallen away.

flowers with parts in threes (three sepals, three petals, six stamens), whose sepals look like petals. So instead of seeing just three showy petals, it looks like you are seeing six showy petals. When referring to petals and sepals together, they can be referred to as *tepals*. In daylily, if you look closely, you can clearly see the difference between the petals and sepals. The petals are more delicate, textured, wavy, and wider than the sepals. The sepals are relatively more sturdy, less textured, less wavy, and narrower. These distinctions sometimes make a difference in food applications—which I will get to later.

Tawny daylily tepals are typically variations on orange, sometimes reddish-orange, with a central ray of orangey-yellow that widens at the base. There are six long, upwardly curved stamens with large shoe-shaped anthers at their tips. The long female pistil is also curved upward, but separates itself from the stamens.

A patch of daylilies can produce hundreds of flowers over the course of a month, since stems mature at different rates and flowers on those stems mature at different rates. So by late summer you see lots of empty stems standing up over dense patches of the arching leaves.

This is the time that the plant's purpose changes from putting energy into all parts of the plant to pumping energy into the underground tubers for the next generation of plants. Tubers are continuously formed all year long, but the plant focuses all its energies into tuber growth after the flowers have finished.

Most tawny daylilies are sterile, producing no viable seed. Reproduction occurs primarily from continuous propagation of the underground tubers.

I have been working under the assumption that the original tawny daylily plants have flowers with narrower petals, more resembling the sepals than the petals of the showy varieties. Those are the kinds I see in the older stands around homes that are over one hundred years old. But without doing genetic testing, I do not know how anyone can tell the difference between the original daylilies and some of the first crop of variants. Many of the new ornamentals are obviously different from the originals.

On the following page are some modern ornamental variants of *Hemerocallis, all* created by selective breeding to serve gardeners and landscapers who want variety. Some people assume all these varieties have the same edibility. I am dubious about that, particularly since they are not all *Hemerocallis fulva.*

Since it is impossible to tell exactly which variety of daylily you have, I personally try to stick to ones that look like the tawny daylilies shown at the beginning of this chapter, not the variants. To me, anything that looks like a standard tawny daylily, I consider a potential edible. And while others have said all daylilies are edible, that would be a wishful thinking assumption with potentially unpredictable consequences.

Several uprooted daylily plants mid-spring, after significant leaf growth but before flower stalks have grown. This shows rhizomes leading to tubers.

Gathering and Edibility of Tawny Daylily

All parts of the daylily plant have a peppery flavor. If you eat them by themselves, they leave a strong aftertaste that I find disagreeable, but you might like. Mix them with other

Here are just a few variations on *Hemerocallis*. The last two are "Flasher" and "Aquire the Fire." I don't know what the others are. If you want to see even more forms, visit the American Hemerocallis Society website: http://www. daylilies.org/ahs_dictionary/ flower_forms.html

foods to add character and enhance overall flavor. Any disagreeability disappears.

Bases of young shoots

Until you know this plant well or know you are gathering from a patch you saw flower in the previous year, I would not collect young, preflowering pseudo-stems made of tightly wrapped leaf bases. If you are certain of your

Left: Young shoot of tightly compressed daylily leaf bases, clasping each other. Right: the sliced bases of a slightly older and bigger shoots, ready to stir-fry, along with some lower, tender parts of leaves.

identification, any part of the young, aboveground plant near the base that is chewable is usable like celery. The young shoot's tightly compressed leaves are tender at their base, because that is where they are still growing. The farther you go up each leaf, the more fibrous that leaf is. If you slice across the base, the overlapping leaves hold together, making them great additions to salads, stir-fries, and soups.

Flower buds

The buds are easily gathered and snap cleanly from their receptacles. Unless you are going for a certain size, always collect the largest one or two per plant, leaving the rest to grow for later harvest. The largest are the ones that will most likely open the next day. This selective gathering can supply you from a moderate patch for a whole month. The buds can be 2 to 3 inches long. Serve fresh, sauté quickly (less than a minute), steam, or boil them for about 2 minutes. They are delicate and easily destroyed if treated roughly. I recommend that everyone cut off and discard the handle, or lower part of the bud, about an $1/8$ inch above where it connects to the tepals.

Fresh daylily buds in hand. The upper part is made up of sepals enclosing the petals. The lower greener part is what I call the handle—which encloses the ovary of the plant. The ovary should be discarded, or left on the plate if you are biting off the fresh bud above it.

Buds cooked differently have different appearances. Left: buds pan-seared for about 30 seconds on both sides. Center: Steamed 30 seconds. Right: Boiled 30 seconds.

Why Cut Off the Base of the Buds?

Here is some history behind a problem with eating the ovary area at the base of each bud. This is an edited version of a story I wrote for the June 2000 *Wild Food Adventurer* newsletter, based on events that occurred around 1996 (Kallas, 2000).

I had been eating daylily flowers and buds without incident for about five years before I heard a thirdhand report that there was a potential problem. The story went something like this: A group of Ann Arbor, Michigan, students and their teacher had become ill after eating a meal that included tawny daylily. And that the instructor was, as a result, frightened away from teaching about wild foods.

Having had so much success with the plant myself, I noted the information, but assumed that something else was probably at fault for the illness suffered by those students. I did not pursue it further at that time.

Ten years later, in late June of 1996, I had my friend Susan over for a wild food dinner. We actually ate what you see on the plate here.

This included a fresh tawny daylily flower and buds that I had gathered from my yard. There are about 60 or so of these densely-grouped

Susan and I each ate this plateful of wild foods for dinner. It included one fresh daylily flower, about six daylily buds, boiled cattail spikes, a fresh wild salad, steamed wild greens, and shell pasta with wild clam sauce.

plants growing in a bed along the west side of the house. And I had eaten the buds and flowers before on several occasions—either raw, steamed, or boiled.

It was a fine wild meal that we enjoyed at around 7:15 p.m. that evening. Soon, within a half hour, we were both feeling nauseous, on the verge of upchucking. And there was a certain queasy sensitivity to the stomach. These feelings were tenacious and strong. I hate nausea.

At around 8:30 p.m. we drank some fresh ginger tea in an attempt to reduce the nausea. The tea did not help.

I was horrified and embarrassed to have fed a good friend a wild food meal with such an outcome. I was so sure of myself and my knowledge as a wild food instructor—how could this happen? The Ann Arbor story I had heard 10 years earlier suddenly hit me with a vengeance. You never know when thirdhand information will be true.

Warning: Gory details follow in the name of science—please shield your eyes while you read the rest of this . . .

At 9:10 p.m., I experienced a cathartic watery evacuation of my bowels. This left me feeling somewhat better, but still perceptibly nauseous. Susan, at about 10 p.m., had a very soft diarrhea event, after which she felt much better. No symptoms lingered in either of us the next day.

This experience prompted me to do some more in-depth research. Interestingly enough, of the over 200 books on edible, medicinal, and poisonous plants I reviewed, none mentioned the Ann Arbor event, nausea, or illness associated with tawny daylily flowers or buds.

At most, two books mentioned the possibility of tawny daylily having a laxative effect if eaten in quantity. The amount that I ate was six buds and a fresh flower—is that a large quantity?

Since the nausea event, I've eaten buds and flowers, both cooked and raw, four or five times, from the same group of plants lining the west side of my house, with no ill effect.

This could mean one of two things: Either there was one or more poisonous daylily plants lost somewhere in the mass of edible daylilies—and that it is just a matter of time before I again eat from the poisonous one. Or all 60 daylily plants shift between edible and toxic depending on some age or environmental condition.

The original toxic event—now 50 years ago

Soon after the unfortunate dinner, I called the botany department at the University of Michigan, Ann Arbor, to see if anyone had heard of the original event. I had the privilege to eventually connect with Florence Wagner, the University of Michigan botanist, who had that original frightening experience with tawny daylily.

She was teaching high school teachers about edible wild plants in a two-day continuing education class. This was some time in the late '60s or early '70s at the University of Michigan, Dearborn, campus.

On the second day, the class cooked a wild lunch that included, among other foods, sautéed tawny daylily buds.

The class ended soon after the meal and everyone went on their way. Within two hours most of the luncheon participants had developed one or more of the following symptoms: nausea, vomiting, and diarrhea. One person's symptoms were so severe, he was taken to a hospital.

This was horrifying for Florence, who had eaten tawny daylily many times before with no ill effect. She recalled to me that the late Edgar T. Wherry, PhD, a University of Pennsylvania botanist, had warned her of a potential problem with the buds. But, like in my case, the warning went unheeded due to past successful experiences with the plant.

Florence's husband, Herb Wagner, also a University of Michigan botanist, saw the same teacher's group for a different class about two days later. Florence had Herb administer a questionnaire about what they had eaten and how they felt after the wild food luncheon. Everyone who had eaten the daylily buds experienced the disturbing symptomology. The data from Florence's questionnaire pinpointed daylilies as the most likely source of the problem. Following this event, chemical analyses were done on the daylily buds in an attempt to determine the toxic agent. No particular component could be identified.

Both edible and poisonous?!

Back in 1998, I talked to Herb about his wife's experience. According to Herb, daylilies may be chemodenes, that is, plants of the same species, but whose chemistry differs. There is no way to tell these two variants apart by looks alone. This is probably why some daylilies are edible and some poisonous. Since tawny daylily can reproduce asexually by its underground tubers, large colonies (genetically identical clones) of the poisonous variety can arise from a single plant.

It is possible that some time in history, the seeds of these toxic daylilies (from either propagating nurseries, or by wild distribution) got spread all over North America and now grow alongside and inter-mixed with the safe nontoxic variety. There is no way to tell them apart by appearance or flavor.

Cooking does not reduce the problem. So how is this food widely eaten in Asia without the risk of poisoning people?

Here is an update to the potential cause and solution. Stout (1933) reported the following about the Chinese tradition of eating daylily. Again, when he says "flowers" here, he means buds. This is evidently a common way to refer to the buds:

> In culinary uses the flowers of daylilies are employed chiefly in soups, in various meat dishes, and with noodles. **In preparation the basal end of the dried flowers, consisting of the ovary, is removed** and the rest is cut into several segments. Enough water is added to the quantity desired to ensure complete soaking, which soon makes the parts become soft, pliable, and somewhat gelatinous. In this condition the material is added to soups that are already cooked, and when the whole is brought to a boil again, a matter of a few minutes, the dish is ready to be served. To various dishes of meats and noodles the soaked flowers are added during the final stages of cooking, or the flowers may be cooked separately for a few minutes and added as a garnish—somewhat as mushrooms are often employed.

Stout does not explain and probably does not know why the ovary is removed and discarded by the Chinese. It was just done this way, probably for centuries. The ovary is perfectly chewable and has the same flavor as the rest of the bud, so why remove it? This example shows the value of examining traditional methods of preparations for plants. It is possible that the ovary is where this sometime toxin exists. Remove the ovary, and you likely eliminate the chance of a problem. That way, whole populations can eat the buds and flowers without incident.

Of course, I am speculating here and cannot guarantee that cutting off the ovaries will solve the problem. But the logic to its reality is compelling. So I am recommending that if you eat daylily flowers or buds, remove the ovary area.

Tepals (petals and sepals)

The daylily flowers are easily plucked from their receptacles. They are delicate but stand up to careful handling. If you want to transport them, use an open container lined with a soft towel. You can gently pile them about two deep with only a little breakage. Lightly spray-mist them. Do not soak them! Put them in the fridge in closed zip-top bags with plenty of trapped air so they don't get crushed. You can store more in a smaller space if you just include the tepals. They can last there well for up to three days. Note that refrigeration prevents them from shriveling, allowing them to last two days longer than they would on the plant.

WHEN TO HARVEST THE TEPALS IN ORDER TO HAVE THEIR BEAUTY AND EAT THEM TOO: In cities all over the planet there are homeowners who have tawny daylily in their yards or fallow fields. If I just asked them if I could pluck their beautiful flowers and cart them off for my purposes, they would say no. Instead, I educate them about the daylily name and that every bloom they see today will be closed in the night, never to open again. I ask if I can come by at dusk, to collect today's flowers that will wilt before morning. To that they say yes. And they are pleased to see that their patch looks perfectly full of flowers the next day as that day's buds open. And if it is a big enough patch, and/or I can collect from there several days in a row, providing me with enough flowers, I make daylily preserves. I follow up by giving the homeowners a jar of those preserves as a thank-you gift. If you do this, you make friends for life.

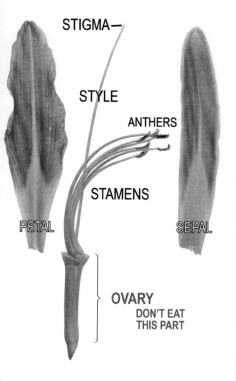

STIGMA—

STYLE

ANTHERS

STAMENS

PETAL

SEPAL

OVARY
DON'T EAT
THIS PART

Left: Parts of the daylily flower highlighting the ovary. I recommend you do not eat the ovary. Daylily flowers have six tepals made up of three petals and three sepals. There are six stamens which have anthers on their tips. The anthers release the pollen. The pistil (female part of the flower) has three parts: a sticky tip called a stigma, a long neck called the style, and an ovary at the base where the seeds develop. The ovary is below the tepals.

Daylily tepals as a decorative salad ingredient.

Sepals in water, strictly as decoration. Petals will deteriorate in water; sepals will hold up.

Spring rolls made with "Flasher" variety tawny daylily. Ingredients include daylily tepals, sweet red peppers, mozzarella cheese, avocado, and lettuce, wrapped in rice paper.

Tepals are best used fresh if your goal is to retain their color and body for more visual and textural impact. They will also add nutrition, flavor, and body to cooked dishes melting into a thin membranous material without their bright color. Tepals can also be used as a garnish on any dish.

These are huge flowers, which makes them a little awkward to eat whole. In fact, given our discussion about the ovaries, what you should mostly just be eating are the tepals. Of course the stamens and top part of the pistil are edible too. To harvest, grab the tip of each tepal and peel them off one at a time like you would a banana.

From a flavor perspective, I find daylily flowers and buds serve me best when added to other foods to improve complexity and character. By themselves, their pepperiness is a little strong—they leave a strong aftertaste. Eaten alone, fresh flowers can leave you with bad breath. Yes, you heard me, bad breath. Eat a bunch of tepals and go to a party. Watch your personal space increase dramatically. Cooking and eating with other things seem to negate that problem. Boiling the buds or flowers for 2 to 3 minutes moderates the pepperiness, providing a flavor reminiscent of spinach. While the edible parts of this plant are mildly sweet, the tepals have the mildest pepperiness.

Daylily juice

You can get overwhelmed with flowers from a daylily patch. A patch can produce hundreds of tepals a day. One thing you can do with them is make daylily juice. Once the juice is made you have the potential to make/invent many food products. To make the juice you will need to gather lots of tepals. Again, don't use the other flower parts. It takes about six large flowers for enough tepals to make a cup of chopped tepals. The example I show you is from the "Flasher" variety of tawny daylily. The more aromatic the flowers, the more flavorful the juice.

For every cup of chopped tepals you'll need a cup of water. To make the juice, bring the water to a full boil. Stir in the chopped tepals, bring the water back to a full boil, then reduce the heat to low, allowing a slow boil for about 2 minutes. Remove from the heat and let steep for 5 minutes. Pour into sanitized canning jars. Let cool and store them in the fridge until the juice is all used up. If you want to preserve it for longer, storing it on unrefrigerated shelves, you should use a pressure canner to prevent botulism from forming. Since this is a low-acid juice, only pressure canning can bring the temperature to the higher temperatures required to kill all microorganisms.

Canned daylily juice and the filtered-out tepals. It took 7 cups of tepals and 7 cups of water to make 8 cups of juice and 1 cup of filtered out cooked tepals.

Although you can filter out the cooked tepal material before canning, I prefer to leave tepals in to yield a more whole product. The resultant juice will be some shade of the original tepal colors. If you filter out the cooked tepals, they are mild tasting, with no real pepperiness. They can be added as is or blended and added to soups and sauces at your discretion. Use the juice to make things like daylily jam or daylily curd.

Daylily jam on toast. This could also be used as a topping for ice cream.

Daylily Jam

This is a fine, flavorful jam that can be used like any other jam. This is a half recipe in case you don't have access to a lot of flowers. Expand the recipe proportionately if you want to make more.

INGREDIENTS

 1 cup water
 1 cup chopped tawny daylily tepals
 1 cup sugar
 $1/8$ cup lemon juice
 $1/2$ package MCP Pectin (about $1\,1/2$ ounces)

DIRECTIONS

 Prepare and sterilize canning jars.
 In a saucepan over medium heat, bring water to a full boil. Add chopped tepals, cover, and simmer for 5 minutes.
 Stir in lemon juice and sugar; then bring to full rolling boil. Add pectin, stir until well mixed, and return to a full rolling boil for exactly 2 minutes.
 Pour hot into sterilized canning jars.

Daylily Meringue Pie

The curd created here can be used to make daylily meringue pie, or you can just serve the curd as its own treat by pouring it into ramekins. This recipe is just enough to make 1 (8-inch) pie.

INGREDIENTS

$1/3$ cup cornstarch

$2 1/2$ cups daylily juice, divided
(see page 250)

2 tablespoons fresh lemon juice

1 tablespoon lemon zest

2 tablespoons unsalted butter, cut into cubes

1 cup sugar

$1/8$ tablespoon salt

2 egg yolks

Daylily-mallow meringue pie. High mallow peas (*Malva sylvestris*) were used to make the meringue. High mallow's flowers and mallow peas are garnishing the plate. You could make the meringue with marsh mallow, or common mallow peas as well.

DIRECTIONS

Thoroughly mix cornstarch into 1 cup cold or room temperature daylily juice; set aside.

In a small bowl, combine lemon juice, zest, and butter; mix well and set aside.

In a mixing bowl, combine sugar, salt, egg yolks, and remaining $1 1/2$ cups daylily juice. Mix well so the yolks are all blended into the mixture. Pour into a saucepan over medium heat. As it warms up, stir in the daylily juice/cornstarch mixture.

Stir in the lemon and butter mixture, bring to a simmer, not a boil, and use a spatula to patiently scrape the curd along the pan bottom to prevent it from sticking and browning. Cook for 1 more minute, continuing to scrape.

Once the mixture thickens, it is ready to be poured into whatever you are making—a precooked pie shell or custard dishes. Depending on how you want to serve the curd, you can eat it warm, or let it cool. As it cools, it firms up.

For the meringue, follow any egg-based meringue recipe, the marshmallow meringue recipe from this book, or the mallow meringue recipe from page 119 in volume 1 of this book series.

The tubers

Daylily tubers are available all year long and have a wonderfully fresh clean flavor. If they have different qualities at different times of year, I cannot tell you because I do not have enough experience with them beyond spring. Most of the time when I find daylilies, they are on someone's property. It is easy to get permission to collect flowers, given the right context, but not so easy to ask people to let you dig up their land. And you have to have a shovel with you if you are out in the field. The tubers are a regular feature at events like the North Carolina Wild Food Weekend (http://wildfoodadventures.com/workshop/north-carolina -wild-food-weekend/).

My recommendation is to stick as closely to the original tawny daylily as possible to avoid potential genetic variation that might be harmful to humans. It should look exactly like or closely resemble the plant in this chapter. And even then, I cannot guarantee there will not be problems. So start out cautiously when eating from any particular patch.

The tubers are fairly easy to dig up with a shovel. Just loosen the soil around the plant and pull upward. If there is not too much clay, the rhizomes are strong enough to hold onto their tubers as you pull upward. Choose the tubers that are robust and solid.

If you are going to eat the tubers raw, discard the roots and rhizome as both are too fibrous to include. Between the rhizome and tuber, there is an obvious point at which to slice the tuber off. There is no clear spot for the roots. Don't just pry the roots off, cut off about $1/8$ inch of the very base of the tuber where all the roots come off. That area is particularly fibrous. At this point the tubers may be used fresh and added to various dishes. They are best sliced into thin pieces like watercress. The skin is very thin, but tough; it adds a slight chewiness. If the tubers are sliced into thin pieces, the chewiness disappears.

The rhizome above the tuber becomes conditionally chewable if boiled or steamed for 15 minutes or more. The skin, as is, is still too tough to chew. To make it tolerably chewable, slice the rhizome into $\frac{1}{8}$-inch pieces after boiling. If you cannot slice easily through it, you have to cook it longer. Since these slices are tiny, they can be added to soups and stews, or randomly sprinkled in to almost anything. They taste just like the tubers with a tiny more pepperiness, like you find in the upper parts of the plant.

A warning on the rhizomes: Just because you can make them chewable by cooking and slicing does not mean they are good for you. I have found no traditional references to anyone eating the rhizome. That could be because they are too much hassle to include, that you have a much easier and great-tasting piece (the tuber) right next to it outshining it, or it causes some immediate or long-term problems. We don't know. Just because I've figured out how to make them useful and I did not have any immediate symptoms, does not mean they are safe to eat over time.

Daylily tubers being washed off with a hose at the 2001 North Carolina Wild Food Weekend. They were served to everyone there in various dishes.

Cleaned daylily tubers, free from their rhizomes and roots. Ready to use.

Removing the skin from the tuber: Once you boil or steam the tubers for 15 minutes and slice off each end (removing the rhizome and roots), the skin sometimes slides right off with just a little effort. This leaves you with a delicious cooked skinless tuber with no chewiness whatsoever. You could then season these with thyme, olive oil, and vinegar and eat them as a side dish. Don't overdo it the first few times you eat them.

My limited experience with the tubers along with meager available cultural information tells me to experiment more and eat the tubers in moderation in the meantime. The literature is clear that the Chinese and Japanese used the tubers of this and a few other species of the Hemerocallis genus (Tanaka, 1976) but don't go nearly into enough detail. When I eat a bunch of them by themselves on an empty stomach, they seem to work as a mild laxative. Mixing them with other things seems to stop that effect. Raw dandelion leaves might have the same laxative effect for you. Daylily tubers work great as thin slices in a salad, in a stir-fry, or bite-size (one tuber cut into four pieces or more) slices in a soup. The delicious and abundant tubers make this a worthy subject for more study.

Chapter 17

FAMILY: Brassicaceae
SPECIES: *Raphanus raphanistrum* and *Raphanus sativus*

Wild Radish

A wild relative of radish that provides a continuous source of leaves.

Thousands of white-flowered wild radish plants overtaking a farmland field.

WILD RADISH—TWO SPECIES

Estimated Range

Official Species Names:
- *Raphanus raphanistrum* L.
- *Raphanus sativus* L.

Synonyms:
- *Raphanus fugax* C. Presl
- *Raphanus microcarpus* (Lange) Willk.
- *Raphanus sylvestris* Lam.
- *Raphanistrum arvense* (All.) Mérat
- *Raphanistrum fugax* (C. Presl) Nyman
- *Raphanistrum innocuum* Moench
- *Raphanistrum lampsana* Gaertner
- *Raphanistrum raphanistrum* (L.) Karsten
- *Raphanistrum segetum* Baumg.
- *Raphanistrum silvestre* Asch.
- *Rapistrum arvense* All.
- *Brassica heleniana* Burch. ex Loudon
- *Crucifera raphanistrum* E. H. L. Krause

continued

There are two "wild" radishes: *Raphanus sativus*, from which domesticated radish was derived, and *Raphanus raphanistrum*, a close relative. The domesticated radish is known for its typically red enlarged upper taproot. What you often see in the stores are round bright red radishes, sold separately or in bunches attached to their greens. But different varieties can be more white-skinned and have elongated edible taproots. "Radish" is the name of the plant, but can also just refer to the root as a food. The original *Raphanus sativus* has a fleshy taproot, but is it not cute, red, and round.

Raphanus raphanistrum is less well known. Its primary difference from the wild *R. sativus* is that there is no desirable root to consume. There are additional minor differences, but from a wild food perspective, the upper parts of the two species can be used almost interchangeably. In this chapter I focus on *raphanistrum*, even though they are both be found in the wild. Domesticated radish escapes from cultivated fields and can also grow wild.

Both wild radishes are extremely successful plants—meaning that they produce huge amounts of viable seeds that just love to grow in a variety of soils. They particularly love disturbed soils, like garden beds, farmland, and building sites. They also love to interbreed. So, while you can find pure domesticated and pure wild radish growing, you also find a mystifying mass of mixtures. I bring this up to warn you that if you try to key out or identify which you have found, it may be annoyingly confusing. If you find a plant with no hair and pink or white flowers, it is likely a *R. sativus*. But if you find a plant covered with raspy hairs and pink or white flowers it could be either *R. sativus* or *R. raphanistrum*. Finding a nice red radish at the base of the plant will mean you have a domesticated radish, but over generations of growing wild, it may lose that feature and revert back to a plain whitish root, like the wild one.

From here on, I will be referring to both species and everything in between as *wild radish*, distinguishing the two only when it is important to do so.

You have probably seen wild radishes as you've driven by or visited farmland, either before the farmer has planted in the spring or concurrent with the early rapid growth stage of any well-watered crop. Tall flowering wild radishes rapidly grow and overtop whatever crop has been planted. One here, one there—no real pattern to it. It could be five to hundreds of plants popping up in any particular field.

Wild radish is very annoying to farmers because it competes with their crops for nutrients and water as a weed. It is not as bad as green amaranth for interfering with crop growth, but farmers would rather have neither.

They are higher than our top domesticated greens in calcium, iron, and zinc.

Knowing Wild Radish

Once wild radish seeds are in the soil, they can survive for years—germinating near the surface when adequate moisture is present. If you know the seasonal high-moisture times of your own area, that will be when these plants germinate. They can germinate in watered garden beds any time of year it is above 45°F.

Wild radish seeds germinate like crazy whenever the soil is disturbed. They are vigorous growers all the way through seed development to maturity. Upon germination you can often see hundreds, if not thousands, of the easily recognizable cotyledons blanketing the soil. Before the first true leaves develop, the cotyledons have a very distinct look of two hearts facing each other on tiny stems. If the ground has been tilled, these will be obviously blanketing the ground. If there are established plants blocking your view of the soil, spotting them requires you to bend the overtopping plants to the side to see the ground. After germination, they grow a few delicate hairy simple leaves on a short, delicate stem. The stem begins to elongate early in this plant's life, allowing it to reach the sun earlier than competing plants.

The leaves start out with various shapes ranging from having no lobes to more and more as the plant gets older.

- *Durandea unilocularis* Delarbre
- *Sinapis raphanistrum* (L.) Gueldenst. ex Ledeb.

Common Names:
- Radish
- Wild radish
- Garden radish
- Cultivated radish
- Jointed charlock

A taprooted annual/biennial.

Edible Parts:
- Young shoots
- Leaves
- Bud clusters
- Flowers

Wild radish seedling with the heart-shaped cotyledons seen in many mustard family plants, and its first two true leaves. It's about an inch across from left to right. Insert shows earlier when just the cotyledons have emerged.

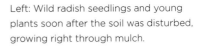

Left: Wild radish seedlings and young plants soon after the soil was disturbed, growing right through mulch.

Above: The large basal rosette of leaves develops just before the plant sends up a tall stalk. Each leaf here is about 7 inches long. The surrounding leaves have been darkened to highlight a single basal rosette.

Above: Young wild radish plants, so densely growing that they are covering the soil. Leaves here are about 5 to 6 inches long. Tender and perfect for harvesting.

Different leaf shapes you will see on wild radish. When the plants are first developing, you will see mostly the three shapes at the lower left at about 2 to 3 inches long, including the stems. But as the plants get more vigorous, you will see the whole bottom row of shapes. The largest leaf on the right will predominate just before and as the stem begins its rapid growth. Largest multi-lobed leaves can be 6 to 12 inches long. Every one of the leaf types in this image can be seen on a tall-stemmed mature flowering plant—the tiniest leaves at the top of the stem, the larger leaves near the base, with other sizes and shapes in between.

First, you will see a single blade, then a tiny pair of lobes will arise from the leaf stem under the main leaf blade. The lobes will increase in number and size as the plant continues to produce leaves. Once they reach a critical stage, just before the flower stalk develops, the leaves will be fully lobed along its full length of about 7 inches.

On all the wild radish leaves in my area, there appear to be reddish glands at the tips of each tooth on the leaf blades. They are red and associated with raspy hairs. They are tiny. If your eyes are sharp, you can see them without a hand lens. While mostly red, they can tend toward tan or gray-green. Since this feature has not been mentioned in botanical literature, I question my sanity. It just may be a feature not really noticed before, or an unusual variety found in my locale. But here, just seeing this feature is a sure sign that you have wild radish.

A close-up of the margin of the terminal lobe, showing the reddish glands at the tips of each tooth.

After the basal rosette has fully formed, the flower stalk begins growing upward, lifting some of the basal leaves onto the stem and creating new leaves. Stem leaves have many shapes that systematically change as you go up the plant. Most have a large terminal lobe with varying numbers of mostly paired smaller lobes. At the top of the stem near the flowers, leaves are so reduced in size that they no longer have lobes.

In the surrounding images, you can see leaf variations. Refer back to the original 7-inch fully developed basal leaf to compare and contrast how the leaves up the stem are different.

Radish is a weak-stemmed plant, particularly if growing in soft, fertile soil. It can grow upright or easily fall over, making its branches grow upward from the ground level. If it is growing among other plants, it can use them for support and climb around in a messy sort of way.

Radish can grow upright to a couple of feet if the soil is hard or rocky. I have seen many individual plants at the Oregon coast growing upright in rocky brackish (salty) soil.

Above: A young 10-inch-tall wild radish plant.

Right: The upper 20 inches of a 30-inch-tall plant. Flower buds at top, yellow flowers just below that, and seedpod development just below that. Note the clear leaf shape differences from top to bottom of the stem.

Left: An 18-inch-tall radish plant with flower buds at the top. Note the clear leaf shape differences from top to bottom of the stem.

Above right: Wild radish flower bud clusters above three open flowers. Buds are covered with unopened, sometimes spiky sepals. They separate slightly, cracking open as the petals emerge.

Flower parts

Wild radish flower buds are green and have few to many spikes sticking out of their upper half. The bud's outer covering is the flower's sepals, tightly closed along their seams. The top of the bud opens, allowing the petals to grow up and surpass the sepals. The sepals separate to loosely flank the base of the petals.

Wild radish flowers are distinctive. All flower parts begin/are attached at the bottom of the whole flower structure. Sepals, petals, pistil, and anthers are all attached at the base, adjacent to, and just inside where the sepals are attached. Narrow petals originate at the bottom of the flower and are hidden under the spiked green sepals. As the flower matures, the petals overtop the sepals and flare outward at a 90° angle. What you typically see of the flower petals is only their upper half. The unique shape of this flower helps distinguish wild radishes from other mustard family plants.

Like all mustard family plants, wild radish flowers have four sepals, four petals, and six stamens. Of the six stamens, four are long, two are short.

Like all mustard family plants, wild radish flowers have four separate petals. The visible parts of the petals, viewed from the top, are in the shape of a cross that is narrow at the center, then flaring out like paddles. Veins are prominent. Wild radish plants come in any one of three colors: pale yellow, purple tinged, and white with a slight tint of green. *Raphanus raphanistrum* can be any of these three, while *Raphanus sativus* can only be white or purple. That is a factoid that you can ignore since it mostly does not matter which of the two species it is from for an eating perspective, and there is so much hybridizing that the color could be a mix of the two species. The key to identifying wild radish is the shape of the overall structure of the flower: a vertical lower half loosely flanked by vertical sepals, and a horizontal upper half characterized by four veined, paddle-shaped petals, which can be any of three colors. Each individual plant will only have one of the three colors.

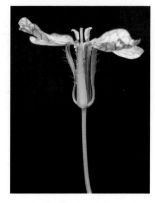

Wild radish flower, side view. Spiked sepals hide the lower, vertical parts of the petals, stamens, and pistil.

Wild radish flower petals can be any one of these three colors. These flowers are roughly ¾ inch in diameter.

Seedpods

Seedpods of wild radish are like pea pods, cylindrical with a rounded bottom and a tapered top. *Raphanus raphanistrum* has a longer pod with more seeds (mostly 4 to 8, up to 12), all about the same size, while *Raphanus sativus* has a shorter pod with fewer seeds (mostly two to three, up to five), which get smaller toward the tip. Both have a tapered tip. The *Raphanus raphanistrum* pod looks like it has been vacuum-sealed when it matures and dries out, with its pod tightly wrapped around its seeds—pretty cool! You'll know it when you see it. But again, there is so much interbreeding that pod variations make it hard to distinguish one wild radish species from the other.

Below: A green seedpod from *Raphanus sativus* (left) and *Raphanus raphanistrum* (right). The pods on the center plant (*Raphanus raphanistrum*) are very early in development.

The twisted lower stem

I have seen a distinct curve in almost all wild radish stems just above the root. It might be a simple bend or it could be just like a short corkscrew. I have seen bends in the lower stems of other plants

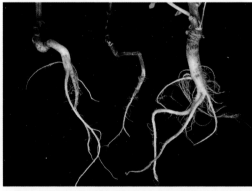

Above: Three different kinds of bends in the stem above wild radish root. The root begins where you see fibers coming out the sides. The bendy parts above that are the stem.

like garlic mustard (*Alliaria petiolata*), but nothing this extreme. I don't know how universal this feature is on wild radish, since I have not seen it mentioned as a distinguishing feature in the botanical texts. But it is true for all the wild radish plants around me.

Gathering and Edibility of Wild Radish

The leaves
Harvest only the rapidly growing leaves at any stage of growth. Plenty of moisture in the soil, and cool temperatures between 35°F and 50°F stimulate rapid growth of both new seedlings and existing plants. Choose the most perfect, healthy-looking leaves. Any will do on baby plants; upper leaves are better on older plants. Take each whole leaf for later processing.

Wild radish stem can bend to almost a corkscrew shape.

Keep them moist until ready to use. Wild radish, like most other mustards, will dry out quickly and limp out. If the leaves have wilted some, soak them in cold water for 20 minutes and they will come back to crisp.

Evaluate their quality for flavor, texture, and raspiness. Taste them and feel their raspiness. There is a mild mustard-leaf flavor with a slight pungency and bite. Each characteristic can vary somewhat. Even the best leaves range from tender to tough, soft-haired to raspy-haired, and sweet to mildly bitter. Plan on variability. Test the leaves before you put them in things to decide your best applications.

Because of the hairs, serving a whole salad of wild radish leaves would work as a dare to the intrepid, and would lead to rejection by normal people looking for a nice meal. For the most part, serving fresh wild radish greens should be done within something. For instance, the mild mustard flavor would work well as about ⅙ of a salad, or as the greens in a sandwich. The raspier the leaves, the more you want to chop and/or manage them in fresh dishes. Cooking softens the raspiness.

Fresh young leaves from new plants, ranging from 3 to 8 inches long. Always check for fibrous stems using the squeegee method. Squeegeed material of these very young leaves does not need to be chopped.

Larger rapidly growing leaves: Squeegee the tender blade material off the tough leaf stem.

Squeegeed leaf parts (left), chopped and ready for use on right.

To get the most out of wild radish leaves, particularly ones 8 to 12 inches long on older plants, squeegee the leaf stem of all tender material. Squeegee by grabbing the base of the leaf stem (petiole), wrapping your fingers around that stem, and stripping off the tender material by pulling. Tender leaflets and the upper leaf blade will break away from the fibrous lower part of the main vein. Discard the tough part of the leaf stems. What you keep can then be used in a variety of ways. Squeegeeing can take some skill. It gets easier with practice.

My recommendation is to chop up the squeegeed parts into roughly $1/2$-inch pieces. This both reduces any toughness and spreads out the hairs' raspiness so the chew is nice and the sting of the hairs is minimized or nonexistent. Now you can put these pieces into salads, sandwiches, and other places you would put spinach or lettuce. Sandwiches and wraps work better to cut the raspiness since the hairs are sticking into other food components, not into your oral cavity.

For cooked greens, just boil the squeegeed, chopped greens for 5 minutes. The result is quite mild in flavor, nonraspy, and delicious. Cooking it longer will tenderize it even more. It can then be used in any application that would work with cooked spinach. Top with just salt and pepper or add your favorite dressing.

If you are going to cook the greens in a casserole or lasagna, put them in fresh. To put on pizza, wilt them in a little olive oil first. The oil prevents them from burning.

Buds, flowers, pods, and roots

Wild radish buds and flowers are edible but very delicate. They will not hold up to much processing.

They are best used fresh. The flower and bud clusters at the tips of stems look great on a salad and can be added to sandwiches for color, flavor, and nutrition. To gather them, use an open container and gently snip the stems so they drop into the container. Don't stack them too high or they will get tangled and difficult to separate for an attractive presentation. If you don't care how they look, just mangle them into a bag. Flower parts have nutritional characteristics that are different from other parts of plants. Like all these plants and their parts, great diversity makes great nutrition. The more species and their parts you can add to your diet, the better your long-term health and longevity.

You can also eat the seedpods, but the window of opportunity is too short on each stem to make them practical for gathering in quantity. They are best reserved for snacking on right off the plant.

The roots are mostly just fibrous on *Raphanus raphanistrum*; however, in some of the crosses with *R. sativus*, you can find thicker roots, which can be grated using a cheese grater and added to dishes, giving a radish-root flavor.

Once wild radish gets established in an area, it can provide a plentiful, consistent source of tasty greens, flowers, and buds.

Very young or squeegeed wild radish leaves used in several applications. Cooked greens (upper left), in a salad (center), and in pita sandwiches. The only thing old enough to be squeegeed here is the single larger leaf on the lower left. Flowers are in the salad. There are also calendula flowers and petals in this picture. Yes, you can eat them too.

Bitter Plants

This introduction is designed to help you understand and manage bitter qualities in the plants that follow. It would be unfortunate if you skipped these plants just because you might not be a fan of this class of flavors. The benefits you will gain in flavor, dietary variety, and nutrition are worth it.

I'm defining the bitter plants here as ones that produce foods, that in the *raw unadorned form*, range from mildly to strongly bitter to most people. These are greens and vegetables that are suitable for occasions where you want to add some character to the dish you are making, or you just love bitter. Bitter plants are often paired with milder plants (foundation plants) or complex dishes to add interest and nuance. They are edible raw and cooked, but their best uses depend on your flavor goals for whatever you are preparing. They have the potential to greatly improve a dish if you use just the right amount or to destroy it if you add so much that it overpowers everything else. Most people will prefer to use them as flavor enhancers for other foods or to cook them in ways to produce more moderate flavors.

Bitter plants covered in volume 1 of this book series are:
- Dandelion (*Taraxacum officinale*)
- Cat's ear (*Hypochaeris radicata*)
- Sow thistle (*Sonchus oleraceus*)
- Spiny sow thistle (*Sonchus asper*)
- Nipplewort (*Lapsana communis*)

NOT ALL ASTERS ARE BITTER

While many members of the Aster family contain plants with bitter parts, many are not—including oxeye daisy (*Leucanthemum vulgare*) and salsify (*Tragopogon* spp.). To be covered in volume 3. So while there are tendencies, bitterness is not always defined by plant families.

Bitter plants can come from any plant family. In volume 1 of this book series, all of the plants in the bitter section come from the aster family. Chicory, also in the aster family, is covered in this book alongside of broad-leaved plantain from the plantain family. They both range from mild to moderately bitter depending on growing conditions. Flavors offered by bitter parts of plants are an excellent addition to the gourmet's arsenal of tastes.

Perceived Bitterness— Understanding Bitter

Historically, while many peoples ate bitter plant parts, they typically did not eat them raw and unadorned in their full bitter glory. In American culture prior to World War II, people ate far more bitter plants than today, but ate them cooked and/or combined with other foods. They were part of larger dishes that contained proteins, fats, and carbohydrates from a variety of plant and animal sources: sour, sweet, pungent, and umami flavors from other plants; as well as herbs, spices, salt, and whatever else they had. All these things moderate any harshness that bitters bring.

Plants differ, people differ

Taste is more complex than many people think. Most people I talk to classify foods as bitter or not, or they give a simple scale of intensity. I often give a scale from 0 to 10 to start discussions but know that it is not the whole story. In reality, there are thousands of bitter-flavored chemicals in plants, and our taste buds probably have hundreds of ways of sensing those chemicals. Since each of us has a unique array of taste buds, that explains why different people can disagree on whether a food is bitter or not. Some people can taste certain bitters in certain foods while others may taste something different in that same food.

For some people certain bitter flavors go to the pleasure center of the brain, for others to the torture center, and for others, they go nowhere at all because they might not have the taste buds to sense a particular bitter.

Then, of course, some of us are trained through cultural traditions and repeated exposure to like certain flavors. If you were fed raw dandelions as a child, then you would be more likely to have developed a tolerance for their bitterness and some taste connections to your brain's pleasure centers. But people trying them for the first time as an adult do not have this advantage. If you are determined, as an adult, to eat dandelions for philosophical, health, or machismo reasons, you will probably tolerate more bitterness with time and practice. Your body adjusts somewhat. Mine has. Here are ways to manage bitterness so you can enjoy more of your food.

Managing Bitterness

1. Gather bitter plant parts at their prime

The biggest mistake novices make is just consuming whatever plant part they find whenever they find it and expecting great results. If you gather plant parts at their prime, you will experience better flavor and texture, and you'll have an easier time managing what bitterness they have. Know your plants and their edible parts at their prime and much more enjoyable eating will be possible.

2. Turn bitter plant parts into a flavoring

Spearing a forkful of mixed greens in a salad is one thing. Spearing a forkful of nothing but bitter greens can be a horrible experience. One way to take the intensity out of leaves is to chop them into shreds and distribute them throughout a mixed salad or some other food.

Your chopping is doing two things here: first, you are making small pieces, and second, you are diluting their intensity by mixing them with other foods. Instead of a slap-in-the-face hit of bitterness, this adds a mild bitter bite within a more complex medley of flavors.

When I make a salad, bitter greens and vegetables are typically mixed with milder ones to dilute the bitterness. The intensity of bitterness of the parts I use will determine the degree of dilution I try to achieve. Really bitter greens may only make up a sixth of a mixed salad, but mildly bitter greens could be as much as a third of a salad. The goal is not to get rid of the flavor but to use it to its best advantage.

A very effective way to dilute bitter foods is to combine them with foods rich in protein, fat, and/or carbohydrates—the macronutrients. Cooking bitter vegetables with meat, dressing a salad with oil or fatty fruits like avocado, or cooking bitters with pasta or potatoes are excellent ways to dilute bitterness. These macronutrients provide calories that mild greens alone do not. Those calories can absorb a lot of bitter flavor.

3. Mask or transform the bitterness

Fat is the main ingredient for doing this. This is why many of the old-timers (like Euell Gibbons) poured hot bacon grease over their dandelions. Aside from the dilution factor that added fat provides, fat can mute and/or even change the flavor of different bitters. Fat flavored with bitters it has absorbed can provide a melded flavor that is often better than each one tasted separately. Fat may also coat the tongue, serving as a sort of shield or mask for taste bud receptors, reducing their exposure to the harshest forms of bitterness. My fat of choice is cold-pressed extra virgin olive oil.

4. Engage all your taste buds

Diluting bitter greens with mild greens helps to soften bitterness. But if you want to maximize the proportion of bitters to other foods in your dish, then engage more of your taste buds. If bitter taste buds are the only sensory organs firing signals to your brain, then that is all your brain will focus on. If you engage sweet, sour, salty, and umami taste buds, the brain hears a symphony rather than one note. Fruity vinaigrettes add sweet and sour to a salad. Smoked salmon shreds add smoked, salmon, umami, and salt flavors as well as protein to dilute the bitterness. Bitterness, while still there, would only be one of many sensations competing for your brain's attention.

5. Cooking

There are thousands (millions? billions?) of different bitter or just unpleasant substances in the plant kingdom. Each has different physical and chemical properties. They all react differently to the processing techniques we throw at them. Some bitters are volatile and will evaporate with heat in the escaping steam. Bitters in other plants will remain and break down into non-bitter substances. Others leach into the cooking water. And some are just persistent, unaffected by heat. Dry heating and boiling will not universally remove bitterness. You have to customize your behavior to what the plant demands.

Cooking of any kind will destroy a small proportion of nutrients while making others more available. Should you worry about this? No. If you are worried that your body is going to go into fits of deprivation over a 5 percent loss of some nutrients that are cooked out, then eat 5 percent more of the cooked material.

When I cook, my goal is to minimize loss and maximize flavor and texture. So I cook things as little as necessary to make a delectable food.

6. Leaching

Just as fat-soluble bitters are absorbed in fat that you might add to a dish, water-soluble substances are absorbed in water. In both these cases, the process of extraction is called *leaching*. Water-soluble bitters may leach out of a plant and into any surrounding water. Fat-soluble bitters may leach out of a plant and into any surrounding oil. Leaching can happen in cold water but is more effective under two conditions: first, if the greens are cut into small pieces, then there are more open areas for the bitterness to escape; second, the heat and agitation caused by boiling water speeds up the removal process. The greater the volume of liquid to the mass of greens, the more bitterness escapes into the water. With some greens, leaching is not useful, because they lose all their flavor. Your goal is to manage bitterness, not destroy all flavor. Many bitter wild greens, including dandelions, reveal a wonderfully rich flavor after being leached properly.

Nature is NOT Here for Our Convenience

No matter how much you know, how much you plan, and how good you are at selecting plant parts at their prime, nature can still throw you a curveball. A ripe berry on a particular plant might be more bitter than another plant of the same species growing right next to it. Same species, same part, but their flavor is different. Bitterness in plant parts varies in nature by both genetics and growing conditions. That is because nature is not here for our convenience. It gives us whatever it does at that moment in time.

Since you will gather at different times during the season from a variety of locations that experienced a variety of growing conditions, the degree and tenacity of bitterness may vary, even if you know what you are doing. So your job is to taste things before you commit them to recipes, particularly if you are planning to share your food with others. Ask yourself, "Is this the manageable bitterness I expect from this plant, or is it beyond the scope of use?" Following a recipe using a bad ingredient only gets you a bad result.

Bitter vegetables tend to be more powerful than other vegetables

In my experience, the plant parts in this section, particularly when eaten raw, can initially result in a more laxative effect than vegetables that are not bitter. This makes sense, because some of the bitters that may be beneficial in small amounts tend to be mildly toxic in large amounts. Sesquiterpenes and terpenes are two such classes of chemicals. Your intestines have to decide what to absorb and

NUTRIENT
Is a substance that is essential for growth, maintenance, and normal functioning of the human body. For a substance to earn the label of nutrient, scientists have to establish the exact physiological biochemical mechanism by which it enables growth, maintenance, and normal body function.

PHYTONUTRIENT VS PHYTOCHEMICAL
While vitamin C (ascorbic acid) derived from plants is legitimately a phytonutrient, we don't know enough about many of the other plant chemicals that are in the news today to classify them as such. Just because a substance has been discovered that may have potential for some human benefit, it has not earned the right to be called a phyto"nutrient" until we know exactly how it works. So it is appropriate to call potentially beneficial chemicals in plants, phytochemicals, not phytonutrients, until we fully understand the exact mechanism of the benefit.

what not to absorb, your liver has to metabolize these substances, and your kidneys have to excrete them. So the first few times that you eat a bitter wild green, you may have softer stools than normal. Some people may need that—you know who you are. Your body will adjust gradually as you eat these vegetables more and more. This is not something to worry about. Just be aware that softer stools are a normal thing when you are new to any plant.

Nutrition

Bitter greens and vegetables tend to be great carriers of phytochemicals (improperly labeled phytonutrients, mostly by supplements manufacturers), of which sesquiterpenes and terpenes are members. There are many reports these days about substances in plants that may have protective effects against cancer, heart disease, and some of the effects of aging. This is promising stuff. And while the bitter greens certainly have their share of phytochemicals, it is clear that the non-bitter greens and just about all other plants do too. If you want great, health-promoting phytochemicals, go ahead and eat bitter vegetables, but also eat non-bitter vegetables, fruits, nuts, seeds, and legumes. One of the nutritional benefits of wild foods is that they increase the variety of the plant part of the diet and, hence, the variety of phytochemicals in the diet.

The bitter greens and vegetables that follow add a wonderful contribution to the overall diet. You can make the best use of them by making them as delicious as you can using techniques described above. Experiment and improvise with chicory and plantain that you will read about here. Appreciate wild greens for whatever they bring to the table, and use them to your advantage, bitter or not.

Chapter 18

FAMILY: Asteraceae
SPECIES: *Cichorium intybus*

Wild Chicory

Chicory, most known for its roots, is best as a spring green.

Chicory in flower growing along an untended roadside along with grass
and other weeds. These are the easily recognized adult plants.

Estimated Range

Official Species Name:
- *Cichorium intybus* L.

Synonyms:
- *Cichorium intybus* var. *foliosum* Hegi
- *Cichorium intybus* var. *sativum* (Bisch.) Janch.

Common Names:
- Chicory
- French endive
- Succory
- Chickory
- Blue sailors
- Ragged sailors
- Coffeeweed
- Horseweed

A taprooted perennial that grows a stem and makes beautiful blue flowers.

Edible Parts:
- Leaves
- Young shoots
- Peeled stem
- Roots

WILD CHICORY

I remember rejecting chicory as a green early in my wild food career. I had learned that it was bitter, so did what I typically did back then, I boiled the hell out of it. That, after all, is how you reduced bitterness in all things wild if you are a novice. Even after lots of boiling, it was still way too bitter for me as a plain cooked green, so I abandoned it. About 15 years ago, when I both had more experience with wild foods and developed an open-mindedness about flavors, I began working with it again. I had matured from "I don't like this" to "How can I like this?" This is how any wild food enthusiast should think.

I discovered that the leaves are manageably bitter early in the season during rapid growth, and that it plays well with other foods. Who'd a thunk it? Previously, when I had no clue about what I was doing, I was trying it in the hot summer when it gets very bitter. So now it is one of many mildly bitter foods I enjoy eating without having to suffer through any harshness. If you love bitter, of course, there is something for you to enjoy here. If you get it at the appropriate stage of growth, it is only mildly bitter. And depending on how you use it, you won't sense any bitterness at all.

Chicory is everywhere in the United States after migrating here and around the world from the Mediterranean. Once it gets established in old fields and waste areas it multiplies over time. The long thin taproots, which can reach more than 3 feet down, protect it from drought or long dry seasons. It can survive while more water-dependent plants die off. It seems to like full sun and hard soils containing gravel or clay. It can also thrive in rich soil. It is a very versatile plant.

The root of this plant is the original source of chicory coffee, typically added to extend coffee, but also used on its own. The roots are harvested, oven dried, roasted, ground, and then leached for their flavor, just as you would dandelion roots or coffee beans. The root has many of the flavor components of the leaves that transform after roasting. In addition, the root is made up of about

20 percent inulin, a nondigestible carbohydrate. Inulin has about $1/10$th the sweetness of sugar. Chicory root is found in many herbal teas.

You can find cultivated varieties of chicory in supermarkets or as seed. *Cichorium intybus* var. *foliosum* is Belgian endive or puntarelle. Radicchios are *Cichorium intybus* without any formal scientific varietal names. Radicchio forms include Perseo, Bel Fiore, Giorgione, Indigo, Leonardo, Fiero, and Virtus. All of these varieties have vastly different appearances from wild chicory. Their nutritional profiles may also be quite different.

Wild chicory greens are high in vitamin E, fiber, iron, and magnesium, and are comparable to dandelion in food uses. Chicory is also confused for dandelion when the leaves are at their prime. So mistaking one for the other will give you great nutrition either way.

Knowing Chicory

Unless you are cultivating it, chicory is found growing among a dense crowd of plants. It is difficult to find the young seedlings without combing through the leaves of surrounding plants. It is best to select areas where you can see remnants of last year's chicory stems. Seeds can germinate in the spring or fall when rains moisten the soil.

Seedlings superficially resemble dandelion seedlings except that chicory has hairs on the underside of the main leaf vein. The cotyledons are lance-shaped. Many of the sprouts do not make it, since they get shaded out by their own species or others.

Early in their life, the young leaves show just a hint of the older ones in shape and design. At this stage, the lobes are nonexistent or represented by small points/ teeth along the margins. As the plant gets older and spring progresses, most of the leaves develop deep lobes. Shape and design varies a lot, both on a particular plant and between different plants, just like its relative, the dandelion.

WILD CHICORY?

Since the name "chicory" is used often referring to supermarket varieties of the species *Cichorium intybus*, I have referred to the plant covered in this chapter as "wild chicory." But in wild food circles, you just say "chicory." They are not readily confused since the domesticated chicories are more specifically referred to as endives, radicchio, and other names. So in the domesticated world, chicories refer to a class of bitter greens; in the wild, it is just one plant, *Cichorium intybus*.

Chicory sprout about ½ inch left to right. The beginning of the lobes, that you will see in older leaves, show up early as small teeth.

First year of growth (left): Young chicory plant, growing from seed. No lobes yet on this young plant, just teeth along the margins. Plants initially grow from seed and lay down a taproot which overwinters.

Second year of growth (right): A new young plant emerges from that over-wintered taproot. This plant will grow a flowering stalk by summer. The now larger, longer taproot will overwinter again.

Below: Side-by-side growth of chicory (left) and dandelion (right) in early spring. Both these plants are likely growing from three-year-old taproots. Multiple new plants are growing from each root. The older the root, the more rapid the leaf growth and the more shoots come up per root.

Left: Chicory leaves, showing some of the leaf shape variations you might see. The four variations on the left are what you will mostly see on the first leaves that emerge in the spring. Any of these shapes can be found at the base of older plants. Any one chicory plant will have similar-shaped leaves.

Plants growing from seed will be a light green and delicate, like young lettuce plants. If they germinate early enough they will produce a flowering stalk. Late germinators will overwinter before producing a stalk.

You can often find preestablished chicory by searching for last year's old dead stems. If you've just experienced a hard winter with snow and storms, many of the old stems will have broken away. If you can find them, that is where the new plant(s) will emerge. We'll cover the look of the stem later in this chapter.

Second- or third-year chicory plants produce leaves that are thicker, a couple of shades deeper green, and more physically solid than plants growing from seed. Like dandelions, the leaf shape on chicory varies greatly among different chicory plants. In late spring, as stems begin to grow, chicory leaves begin showing variation. One whole plant's leaves will be barely toothed along the margins, while another whole plant's leaves will be deeply lobed.

Identifying chicory by its leaves seems impossible at first. How do you possibly identify this plant by the leaves if they vary so much? These plants could be dandelions, cat's ear, hedge mustard, hawkweed, or a million other plants. There are four revealing characteristics to look for.

The first is a twist to the leaves. What I mean is, imagine a long flat leaf. Grab each end with your left and right hands. Roll one end. This twists the leaf into a helix. Since chicory does this on its own, you do not have to go through all the hard labor of twisting leaves yourself. Sometimes the twist is barely noticeable, sometimes it is obvious.

The second is abundant hair on the underside main vein of the leaf. That would make it different from dandelion, which typically has no obvious hair. And while chicory has short hairs all over its leaves, its appearance ranges from obvious, as the

Third year of growth: A chicory plant arising from a previous year's taproot, overtopped by the previous year's dead stems. More often than not, multiple plants arise from one chicory root crown.

Chicory leaves on multiple upright stems. Most chicory leaves twist into a helix along their lengths.

Chicory leaves have hairs all over. However, the density of hairs on the underside leaf vein is most prominent. This shows the lower 3 inches of a 12-inch leaf. It is curved so you don't see the cut base.

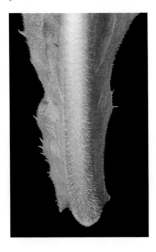

ARE DANDELIONS HAIRLESS?

While dandelion typically has no obvious hairs, I have recently found some that are quite hairy. But that is the exception, not the rule. The lessons here are that nature is not here for our convenience, and you should always use multiple characters to help you identify any plant.

thick hairs of cat's ear (*Hypochaeris radicata*), to difficult to see without close inspection. Leaf upper sides typically have fewer and less obvious hairs than the undersides.

Third, look for last year's old dead brown stems associated with the leaves of new plants. They are light brown and about 1/8 inch in diameter, with remnants of flower parts scattered sparingly along the stem. These could be complete old tall flower stems or could just appear as short brown stem stubs arising from the same root crown the leaves are growing from. The old stalks demonstrate that chicory is in the area. If there is one chicory growing in a field, there are likely lots more.

Fourth, while the basal leaf bases have a leaf stem that attaches to the plant in a way similar to dandelion leaves, once the stem develops, the chicory leaf bases either clasp partially or wrap all the way around the stem. The leaf bases flare out at the wrapping point, rather than taper to meet the stem, like the young pre-stem basal leaves.

In late spring the plants bolt, with leaves that grow up the stem clustered at first near the base, but spread out as the stem lengthens. Once chicory bolts, it is strikingly different from both dandelion and cat's ear. Dandelion has no obvious stem. The stem of cat's ear is thin, branching, almost leafless, and terminates in small, dandelion-like flowers. Chicory is much taller than both, with fully formed leaves making their way up the stem.

Chicory leaves in the upper stems tend toward to smaller and smaller leaves as the plant matures. Near the top of the plant—really the upper half—the leaves get very small and bract-like, almost disappearing. Each bract subtends or cradles each pair of flower buds.

Flower buds are found in pairs at periodic points on otherwise bare stems. Typically there is one large and one small. The larger bud opens first, and several days later, when the second bud reaches its appropriate size, it opens. Flowers bloom in the early morning and close before 2:00 p.m. There is only a small percent of the

Above: Chicory leaves that arise directly from the main stem do not have a leaf stem. The blades not only attach directly to the stem, they have lobes that wrap around that stem. That is, they clasp the stem. You can also see some of the leaf twisting here. To just show the leaf bases clearly, I snipped off the new branch shoots that were originating where the leaf attaches to the main stem.

Above: This is a healthy, robust chicory plant bolting. The stem is quite thick due to great growing conditions (Good moisture and soil). As usual, you can also see the leaves twisting slightly. This plant is about 18 inches tall. The stem is about $5/8$ inch in diameter near the base. Not all stems will be this fat. This is the stage at which chicsparagus (covered later) is available.

Above: Chicory leafy stems as they mature. From left: Stems start out with many overlapping leaves all the way to the top. As they grow taller, leaves begin to spread out and reduce in size. Finally, at right, just before stem branching and flower production, leaves reduce drastically in size, making the stem a more prominent feature.

Right: A fully mature, flowering chicory plant about 40 inches tall. The lower part of the plant is populated by leaves. About halfway up the stem, the leaves reduce in size drastically. The upper part of the plant is almost all stem with tiny scale-like leaves adjacent to buds and blue flowers.

Right: An upper branch showing one open flower and several places where flower buds arise in pairs on the stem. Each bud pair is subtended by leafy bracts. You can see bud pairs just above and below the open flower. There is typically one large and one small bud. The largest in each bud pair is the one that opens first. The second could open several days later when it grows big enough.

Left: Flowers are a beautiful pale blue with amazing darker blue stamens, and almost white pollen. Look closely when you find these flowers in real life for a visual treat.

I dug a hole around a chicory root and did not reach the bottom at 2 feet. This is a lot of work for 1 thin root.

flowers open at any point in time. As chicory grows new bud-covered stems, chicory can produce flowers for weeks.

The chicory root is what makes this plant a perennial. Although the aboveground growth dies over the winter, the root can last for years, growing new leaves as each new spring begins. From seed, the root grows fast, diving deep into the ground. After one year of growth, the root can reach over 2 feet downward. The first year is the freshest growth, likely the best for food uses and coffee. During that first year there is little branching and not a lot of fibrous roots coming off of it. After the first year, the root expands, branches somewhat, particularly near the top, begins to turn woody, and produces more hairy roots along its length.

I have not had time to work with the roots. Making chicory root coffee is a bit of work. The roots used to make chicory root coffee are long thin roots at their prime, roughly about $1/2$ inch to $5/8$ inch in diameter. To collect any great mass, many deep individual holes in typically hard ground would have to be dug.

If you are going to try this, I suggest finding a plant in the fall. Seek out chicory that has not sent up a stem, which is a sign it has grown from seed. Make a diagonal cut through the soil using a long-bladed shovel, slicing through the root as deep as you can. You end up with about 7 to 9 inches of upper root, leaving the lower part in the ground. That way you will not have to dig a huge hole for each root. Then extract that root from the shovelful of dirt. Go to the next plant and repeat this until you have collected enough to do something with.

Clean off all the dirt, slice the roots lengthwise, and then slice those into $1/2$-inch pieces. If they are woody, they are too old.

Chicory Coffee Experiment

If I were to try to make chicory coffee, this would be my first experiment: Put the roots in the oven, spread out on a baking pan at 200°F for about an hour to dry them out; then turn the heat up to 350°F. Watch them carefully, stirring on occasion, since there are many variables that could shift in that time, and the roots can burn from one minute to the next. If they burn, you have charcoal—not the best flavor. When they get brown and crunchy, not tough and hard, they are ready for storing as is or grinding. Grind and steep like coffee. I repeat, I have not done this yet myself, I am just suggesting this as my first experiment. I challenge you to beat me to this and send me your successful recipe. It might take a few tries to get it right.

Gathering and Preparation of Chicory

The main foods on chicory are the leaves, stems, flowers, and roots. In late winter and early spring, depending on where you live, the new rapid leaf growth of the basal

Collect chicory leaves by snipping just below ground level across the upper root to take the whole bunch at once; or use scissors to collect individual leaves.

rosettes is when chicory leaves are at their prime for gathering. Gatherable leaves can be up to a foot long, with several plants clustered over the same root. The key to flavor and relative tenderness is recent rapid growth from lots of moisture in the soil.

Either snip the leaves individually, or take them in clusters by cutting the root just below where all the leaves connect at ground level. Cutting them individually allows you to select the best-looking leaves right off the bat, but takes more time in the field. Snipping them at the tip of the root brings all the leaves above that root in one piece and allows you to grab more in the field quickly. Doing that requires more cleaning and separating out of the good leaves later. Sometimes it is easier to do both. When cleaning the collected leaves, I discard the root tip and the lowest part of the leaf stems, keeping only the most beautiful leaf blades.

These leaves from established roots are hearty and just slightly chewy. Tender enough to chew raw but right on the verge of being too chewy. They are about a 2 out of 10 on the bitterness scale for me. That low bitter level means they can be very useful in a variety of ways.

The more mature the plant, when it is growing a stem, the more bitter the greens will be, even when rapidly growing. As long as the greens look great on really healthy stemmed plants, you can still gather them. Just be prepared to manage the additional bitterness. Slow-growing leaves in a dry summer can go up to a 9 on the bitterness scale.

Later in the season, new plants will be growing from seed. Either in the spring, underneath the older plants, or in the fall, when the new rains begin. Those leaves will be more tender and delicate than those growing from established roots. You can use them more like delicate lettuce in your everyday meals. They will still have a low amount of bitterness.

To me, the best use of chicory leaves is as a fresh green to add flavor and nutrition to dishes. I would never eat a salad of just chicory greens. That would be both too bitter and too hairy. Chicory's best use is as a flavoring mixed into dishes with several ingredients. If the leaves are young enough and small enough, add them whole to salads. Mixed foods mute and transform any bitterness.

Chicory salad with whole but small leaves. Other ingredients are purple sweet nettle, red peppers, carrots, avocado, and pineapple to complement the mild bitter flavor.

Early spring leaves, 4 to 12 inches long, are mildly bitter and full flavored. They are somewhat chewy. To reduce the chewiness, chop them into quarter-inch strips before adding them raw to fresh dishes like salads or throwing them into dishes you are going to cook.

Adding sweet fresh or dried fruits like raisins or starch like beans to salads with sliced chicory greens provides great flavor and complements the bitterness.

Since I am not a bitter fan, I sprinkle them into salads as one of many ingredients. They add an interesting bite to the salad without being unpleasant to me. You might love their flavor and want to include more. Look up recipes for domesticated chicory for additional ideas. Just keep in mind that domesticated chicory does not come in individual leaves, it comes as a big, almost solid head. So while

A salad of sliced chicory greens, apples, raspberries, and red beans. Add your favorite dressing. Delicious.

In a sandwich that has protein, fat, and carbohydrates like bread, sliced meat, cheese, and avocado, chicory leaves provide a nice, flavorful addition with no perceptible bitterness.

Lightly boiled (2 to 4 minutes) chicory greens on an open-faced sandwich garnished with wild strawberry flowers.

you may be able to roast a large head, you could not do that to individual leaves.

Fresh or boiled, chicory leaves also work well added to sandwiches and wraps. The boiled greens by themselves might be of interest to you with a little added balsamic vinegar, olive oil, and salt.

Preparing the chicory greens

To boil the greens, first chop them up into about 1-inch pieces so they can fully engage with the boiling water. Bring a pot of water to a rapid boil and place in the greens for 3 to 5 minutes. If you have young, rapidly growing material, the bitterness will reduce to nothing over that time. By 8 minutes, they will almost melt in your mouth. I have found steaming not conducive to reducing bitterness. But if you love chicory's bitter, that might be a good route for you to go. Boiling older, slow-growing leaves or leaves that have reached their end size won't work so well to reduce their bitterness.

In casseroles, lasagnas, stews, and soups, use chicory leaves as you would use spinach. But pay attention to the amount you add, since the flavor is stronger than spinach. Experimenting is the key, and the fun of it. Just don't serve a first-time experiment at a potluck.

Chicosparagus

The young rapidly growing chicory stem provides a welcome addition to the other foods of chicory. After the basal rosette stage where leaves are all growing at ground level directly off an established root, chicory sends up one or more rapidly growing stems. Early in their growth they can be fat and juicy if there is enough moisture in the soil and substance to the root. Less fat if conditions are dry or you are in long-term drought conditions.

The key to getting the most from the stem is that you gather it when all the chicory is early in the bolting process. Desirable stems are straight, thick, have plenty of large leaves growing out of them, and the growth tip of the stem is covered with leaves.

If you wait until later in the season, all the stems, short and tall will begin to thin out. I will define *later* as two weeks after the first stems you see reach 18 inches in height. As they grow taller and thinner they provide less food for the amount of peeling you will be doing. The key for all of these is to get them before any branching, smaller leaves appear, or flowering stems elongate above the rest of the plant. Once the upper stems thin out and begin producing tiny leaves, they are way past prime gathering material.

Use your scissors to cut the stem for collecting. Start cutting lower than 12 inches down and work your way up the stem to get the feel for when your scissors (must be sharp) can easily slice through the stem. Any struggle when snipping means too much fibrousness has formed in the stem, so snip higher. Typically, the upper 6 to 10 inches of stem will be the most tender once peeled. It takes practice to learn the exact kind of resistance to cutting you need to feel for.

These stems offer us two foods: The peeled stems and the leaves that were on it. Both the leaves and the fibrous, inedible stem rinds will be bitter. Use the leaves as described earlier in the chapter. These stem leaves can be more tender than those from the basal rosette. But often are more bitter. They can be managed as is, or boiled to reduce the bitterness.

Peeled chicory stems and their leaf tips. The peeled rind and stem leaves are not in the picture. Peeled stems have no bitterness. The uppermost parts of the stem cannot be peeled, so retain a mild bitterness. They are tender. That part of the peel can be left on. The peeled stems with tender cores in this image ranged from exceptionally long (about 16 inches) since they were growing in optimal garden bed conditions with no competition, to about 6 inches long. Usable cores in the wild will typically range from 6 to 10 inches long.

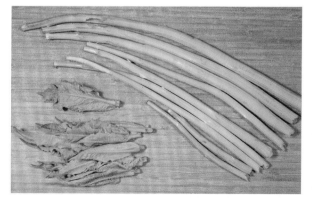

Steamed chicosparagus spears (center), boiled chopped upper stem leaves and leafy tips (upper right), and boiled unpeeled stem tips (lower left). Garnished with calendula flowers.

The peeled stem (all leaves and bitter rind removed) can be eaten fresh or treated like asparagus. These are hollow stems. Peel the stem like you would any other; by grabbing into the stem bottom-side up and peeling it down to its tip—like you would a banana. Sometimes this is very easy and sometimes it is difficult. Sometimes you have to keep going back to peel individual strands of fiber that you can see. When the rind is completely removed, the hollow core is crispy and delicious with little or no hint of bitterness. As you peel your way down to the stem tip, it is so tender, there is no fiber to peel, so don't even try. Leave that part of the peel on.

That last upper 2 or 4 inches near the tip is tender enough to chew without peeling. It will be mildly bitter and should be treated with that in mind. If you like its bitter, eat it fresh as is like a snack, and/or add it to things.

Peeled chicory stems can be eaten fresh like celery, so chop it into salads, dip it in peanut butter, or fill it with spiced cream cheese and slice it into small snacks or hors d'oeuvres. You can also add it to stir-fries, soups, stews, and alongside other roasted vegetables.

Chapter 19

FAMILY: Plantaginaceae
SPECIES: *Plantago major*

Plantain

This medicinal plant is generous in its food offerings.

Plantain's lush leaves showing immature greens as well as immature fruiting stalks.

Estimated Range

Official Species Name:
- *Plantago major* L.

Synonyms:
- *Plantago asiatica*
- *Plantago halophila*

Common Names:
- Plantain
- Common plantain
- Great plantain
- Broadleaf plantain
- Buckhorn plantain
- Rippleseed plantain
- White man's foot

An annual herb that goes to seed so quickly on first-year plants that it could be mistaken for a perennial. Native to Eurasia, it is now widespread and abundant in North America and the rest of the world, particularly in temperate areas. A weedy plant that enjoys soft to hard soils and foot-trafficked

continued

PLANTAIN

Plantain, now found all over the world, is believed to have originated in Eurasia. Its introduction to the Americas came with the settlers. It became known as "white man's foot," since when it appeared in a particular area, native peoples knew that white men had passed that way. Don't confuse this plantain (genus *Plantago*) with the supermarket plantain (genus *Musa*), which looks like a banana. You won't find banana plantains growing wild in your yard. Let me know if you do. No self-respecting monkey would eat *Plantago*. *Planta*, in Latin, refers to the sole of the foot.

Plantain grows anywhere that is managed by humans: farms, orchards, grasslands, roadsides, forest trails, around neighborhoods, in fallow fields, and in your yard. It prefers full sun, but can grow in partially shaded areas. It is considered a weed by most who kill it to maintain their yards in perfect grass monocultures. It tolerates compacted soils that range from poor to rich in quality. It can go from germination to producing seed within 6 weeks. That is fast. Flower and seed production can go on for over 3 months. That is a long time. The seeds typically like to overwinter in the soil at least once before germinating. So be patient if you spread the seed in your yard, you might have to wait a year to see it.

Plantain is mostly known for the medicinal uses of its leaves. In fact, aside from dandelion, it is one of the first plants most budding herbalists learn about, particularly for topical treatments like poultices. Predictably, almost every medicinal plant book mentions plantain edibility but skips any details. Then they go on to give a million herbal uses and offer many platitudes regarding plantain. This is hot stuff in the herbological world and well deserved. I will leave the medicinal stuff to that world and stick to edibility here. The medicinal uses do not interfere with the food uses.

From a "food is medicine" standpoint, the leaves have potential benefits independent of the fiber they provide: immune system support, antiulcer, antidiarrheal, antioxidant, etc. But as a food guy, I suggest you let these beneficial things work in the background, as all good vegetable matter does, when you eat them as normal foods in a diverse diet.

Plantain leaves are rich in fiber, beta-carotene, calcium, iron, and zinc—with more iron and zinc than any of the top cultivated greens.

If you eat the seeds, there are potential benefits: Aside from the amazing fiber provided, they are anti-inflammatory and anti-fatigue, among other things (Nazarizadeh, 2013). I have not noticed any anti-fatigue effects, since I'm too driven to notice fatigue in myself. Perhaps all the wild foods I eat are anti-fatigue.

Both the leaves and seeds add diversity to the diet as well as fiber and mucilage. The mucilage in the seeds, as with other mucilage-containing plants, is likely to promote healthy digestion and bowel movements in the same manner as psyllium fiber.

areas. It produces lots of seed-filled capsules. It grows anywhere that humans have inhabited and "tamed."

Edible Parts:
• Young leaves
• Immature green seed capsules
• Mature seeds
• Seed capsules

Knowing Plantain

Plantain grows new plants from seed. These seeds are tiny, just over a millimeter in length, and very light, so they are easily blown by the wind—once they break free from their capsules. Emerging cotyledons (first two embryonic

Above: A plantain seedling, about ¾ inch from left to right. The cotyledons are pointing up and down in this shot. They are dwarfed by three larger leaves. Compare to seedlings in the photo at left.

Young plantain plants at different stages of growth.

Two plantain plants growing so close together, they could be mistaken for a single plant. As plantains grow, they produce more leaves that overlap, all radiating out from their central stem.

leaves to emerge from the seed) are narrow, oblong to lance-shaped, and do not have the prominent veins of the more rounded plant leaves. The cotyledons are the first pair of leaflike material to emerge from the seed. The regular paddle-shaped leaves emerge soon after.

As you can see in the photographs, young leaves are fairly similar, mostly paddle- or elliptical in shape, arising off a thick leaf stem. Some are smooth, some appear quite wrinkled, and some have wavy margins. All leaves arise from a main stem that is so short, you cannot see it without close inspection. The leaf bases totally obscure the stem. What you see is called a *basal rosette* of leaves. All the leaves spread out from a single central point, just above ground level. Later in the season, many leaves arise from the stem, overlapping each other. Plantain leaves are covered with tiny short hairs.

Plantain has large veins that run from the base toward the tip, with the center ones more prominent. Small young leaves only have three veins. The largest leaves typically have seven veins. They stick out on the underside of the leaf blades. Veins on the upper side appear narrow, sinking in slightly from the surface of the blade. Veins on the underside of leaves pull down, away from the blade.

The center vein is always most prominent, with side veins reducing slightly in diameter as you look further to the sides of the leaf. The leaves are covered with inconspicuous hairs that seem to blend in with the leaf. They are easily seen if you look closely. While most leaves are smaller than this, large plantain leaves can get up to 8 inches long (including leaf stem) and about 5 inches wide. Blade margins can be flat to curled. The undersides are slightly paler than the upper sides.

Above: Plantain leaf blade showing veins. Top left: Upper side of leaf. Top center and right: underside of leaf showing raised veins. Note the wavy margins and more wrinkled appearance than the previous leaves.

Left: Plantain leaf veins are famous in the plant world for their elasticity. Carefully pull the leaf apart and the veins stretch across the gap. Other plants do this trick, but are not as well known for it. This stringy vein elasticity makes the leaves fibrous to chew.

A young plantain showing its roots.

Some plantain leaves have smooth blades; others look more corrugated, like this. Chalk it up to natural variation.

Plantain has fibrous roots that partially obscure a short taproot. Unlike dandelions, these are easily uprooted without leaving anything behind.

Blackseed plantain (*Plantago rugelii*) is an edible close relative of broad-leaved plantain. It can be used in the same ways and is primarily distinguished by red along the leaf stem.

Narrowleaf plantain (*Plantago lanceolata*), another close relative, is mostly known for its use as a tea. This plant has much narrower leaves.

Flower and seed spikes of plantain

Plantain spike development and appearance, with close-ups. On the left is the full range of spike development. A = Flower bud spikes. B = Flower spike releasing pollen. C = Immature green seed capsule spike. D = Mature brown seed capsule spike. Enlarged images of B, C, and D are to the right.

Plantain seed spikes arise from the base of the plant, just like the leaves. They typically are 8 to 12 inches long. A single plant can have numerous spikes. Often plants are clustered together, appearing to be one plant with many spikes arising from them all.

The spikes start out with light green flower buds tightly packed together. Eventually, the flowers blossom. Once pollinated, seed capsules emerge that are green in early development. The capsules are containers that hold

A B C D   **Flower Spike**   **Immature Seed Capsules**   **Mature Seed Capsules**

the tiny seeds of the plant. Once the capsules turn brown, the mature seeds can rattle around within.

The last two stages shown in the photo on page 294 are the ones most useful for food: the immature green seed capsules as a vegetable, the mature brown ones as a grain and source of fiber. In appearance, individual mature brown seed capsules are reminiscent of tiny acorns, but are hollow inside except for the seeds. Each capsule can contain several to many seeds. The seeds are dispersed when the upper part of the capsule pops or breaks off its base. The seed capsules can pop off with age, harsh weather, by being stepped on, or if you process them for food.

Plantain seed capsules alongside the seeds that rattle around inside.

Broadleaf, blackseed, and narrowleaf plantains are closely related to their cousins that produces psyllium (*Plantago ovata* and *Plantago psyllium*). Psyllium is a fiber supplement that people take to support softer stools and more regular bowel movements. Psyllium-based supplements are made from the seed coat of their tiny seeds. The seed coat has indigestible, water-soluble fiber in the form of mucopolysaccharides, which absorb and tenaciously hold on to moisture (Vandebroek, 2011). The simple term for them, when combined with water, is *mucilage*. Mucilage is a sticky, goopy, slimy, gelatinous substance.

Many seeds in nature have similar kinds of mucilage. Seeds of *Plantago*, *Mallow*, *Althaea* (marsh mallow), and *Salvia* (chia) genera all have similar kinds of water-loving mucilage. This water-binding capability helps assure the seeds have water to help in their germination and early development. For humans, mucilage (a soluble fiber) is also great for digestion, moving food efficiently through the digestive tract, and binding toxins for excretion (Nazarizadeh, 2013). Aside from these typical attributes, the mucilage in Plantago is useful to disperse seeds, since when wet, they stick to animals, feathers, shoes, tires, and other things that can move them to different locations (Sagar, 1964).

Water tenaciously adheres to *Plantago major* seeds because of microscopic strands of mucopolysaccharides in the seed coat.

Narrowleaf plantain
Plantago lanceolata

Narrowleaf plantain, also called English plantain, looks very different from broadleaf plantain. Both plants are extremely common, and sometimes confused regarding food and medicine.

I have not done an in-depth study of narrowleaf plantain, but here is what I know. The leaves of this plant are mostly used for tea, likely because they are so tough. This is a tough, bitter plant. Here are some identifying photographs to help you distinguish this from broadleaf plantain.

Above: You typically see narrowleaf plantain when it is in flower. Many flower stems arise from the base of the plant. At the top of the stem is a small hot dog–shaped flower spike. The spike is made up of a tightly packed cluster of individual flowers. At flower maturity, there is a ring of anthers radiating out somewhere along its length giving it a halo-like appearance. Flower stalks range from a foot to 18 inches tall. This picture shows the most typical shape of the fully grown leaves which are long and narrow.

Left: Narrowleaf plantain seedlings. The largest on the right is just under ⅝ inch tall and has two leaves. Cotyledons are long and thin.

Left: Close-up of the narrowleaf plantain flower spikes at different stages of maturity. The lower left spike is all unopened buds. Upper right the spike is just starting to mature. These spikes mature from the bottom upward. So you see the stamens just beginning to emerge. In the middle, the brown lower third of the spike has been pollinated as stamens emerge higher and higher on the spike.

Young leaves on narrowleaf plantain at about 3 inches in diameter. Leaves are typically much narrower than this, but sometimes they are this wide.

Gathering and Edibility

Plantain leaves

Just like many other plants, the utility of plantain leaves is determined by their appearance. Leaves from 2 to 6 inches long can be good—depending on how fresh, green, obviously well-hydrated and undamaged they look. Rapid growth is the key to all these attributes.

Fresh young plantain leaves ready for use as fresh or cooked greens. Larger leaves, up to about 6 inches long, can be used, but the larger they are, the more of an issue the stringy veins are.

The leaves have many useful and satisfying applications, as long as you manage three things to your personal satisfaction. First, they run from plain-tasting to mildly bitter. You don't know until you have gathered them where they are in that range. Second, they are generally a tough leaf to chew in the raw. Third, they have several stringy veins running the length of the leaf. But before you run screaming out the door, you can manage all three issues to enjoy them in fine dishes you prepare.

The bitterness is always a personal thing. Some people like the bitterness of plantain. Even if you're a bitter hater, mixing these greens with other foods, protein, fat, carbohydrates, other vegetables, adding sauces, etc., helps them to fit right in to your *enjoyables* category. I just would not make a salad out of this alone. To eat fresh, I add it to complex salads, sandwiches, and other lettuce-type applications for the additional diversity it adds to my diet, in both nutrients and phytochemicals.

Plantain leaf is no miner's lettuce or chickweed in texture, both of which are very tender. It is mildly tough overall, and has those dang fibrous veins. To make them less chewy, you can do three things. Keep the leaf blade, but discard the leaf stem (petiole). It contains the toughest of the veins. For most uses, I recommend chopping the leaf blades finely across the veins. This makes the veins very short, as seen on the sandwich plate. Once cut into narrow strips, these greens can be served fresh on sandwiches, in salads, cooked as greens, or cooked in dishes like vegetable pies, omelets, etc., as you would spinach. Used in these

Right: Young, freshly chopped plantain greens in a sandwich, next to those same greens boiled for 10 minutes on the left. To show what the chopped leafy material used in each looked like, there is some placed in the front of the plate. This would work fine in any sandwich. The cooked greens are greatly enhanced with olive oil and balsamic vinegar, though any favorite sauce will do. The cooked greens are garnished with a couple of high mallow flowers. The sandwich is garnished with an oxeye daisy flower.

Below: These are dolmathes (dolmas) my friend Rebecca Peck made at the 2016 GingerRoot Wild Food Rendezvous, using plantain leaves to hold the contents. Within the wraps were green amaranth, wild spinach, wild mint, oxeye daisy greens, sheep sorrel, wild rice, garlic, olive oil, and salt. The leaves and all the internal ingredients were cooked prior to assembly. They were garnished with wild everlasting pea flowers.

applications, the flavor is mild, pleasant, and lettuce-like. You would not eat it fresh all by itself for the flavor.

If you can find large enough leaves, you can use them to wrap other foods in, as you would use grape leaves. For this to work, you would cut off the leaf stems (petioles) and boil the blades for 20 minutes. This will tenderize the veins just enough to be able to hold the contents and be nicely chewable.

If you are going to make Greek-style food wraps, they should be served hot or cold with avgolemono sauce. It is a must, you have no choice.

If you don't, I'll have my grandmother pester you, and she is deceased.

John's Avgolemono Sauce (Egg-Lemon Sauce)

Makes about 1 cup sauce

This is my version of a classic Greek lemon sauce that is good to use with many foods including dolmathes (dolmas), soups, meats, and cooked vegetables. Of course, since it is my recipe, it is no longer classic, just good, in my opinion. No wild foods are harmed in this recipe.

INGREDIENTS

2 eggs, room temperature
$1/2$ cup hot vegetable or chicken bouillon
$1/4$ cup lemon juice
1 teaspoon finely chopped lemon zest (optional for a punch of flavor)
$1/2$ teaspoon water

DIRECTIONS

Separate eggs, breaking the yolks in a small bowl and placing the whites into a separate 4-cup glass bowl; set aside.

Place the hot bouillon into a bowl and slowly pour the broken yolks into it, stirring rapidly as you go, until it is all incorporated. Pour in the lemon juice and add lemon zest, if using. Mix well and set aside.

Add the water to the egg whites and beat on medium speed with a hand mixer until at the soft peak stage. While continuing to blend on low, very slowly and gradually pour in the still-warm bouillon-and-lemon mixture.

As soon as it is blended, it is ready to use as a lemony sauce on any food. If it sits for a while or has been stored in the fridge, stir just before use to distribute the foam, which will be floating on top. Pour over cold or warmed dolmathes.

Leda Meredith's Plantago Leaf Chips

Serves 2 to 3

This recipe was first published in Leda's blog (Meredith, 2015).

My friend Leda Meredith came up with a recipe for Plantago Leaf Chips. They are eaten like potato chips that are flavored to your liking. What makes this work is that baking makes the leaves and veins so crispy that they are no longer tough and chewy. They just crush in your mouth like chips, but with much less mass (they are only as thick as a dried leaf) and only the calories that you find in the flavorings and olive oil you add before baking. Since plantain leaves are rather bland, you will most likely enjoy them with your favorite flavorings. Use your imagination and your pantry to find chili powder, cumin, pepper steak flavoring, and lemon pepper seasoning, or just use fancy flavored popcorn salt. Start with Leda's suggestion here and experiment. Multiply the recipe if you have lots of leaves.

Photo courtesy of Leda Meredith.

INGREDIENTS

24 large leaves of any *Plantago* (plantain) species

2 teaspoons olive oil

¼ teaspoon salt

½ teaspoon seasoning (garlic powder, nutritional yeast, half the quantity of cayenne, za'atar, or any of your favorite spice blends)

DIRECTIONS

Preheat the oven to 250°F.

Wash the plantain leaves and dry them well in a salad spinner or by rolling them up in a clean dish towel.

In a large bowl, toss the leaves with the oil until each is well coated. Spread the leaves in a single layer on baking sheets. Depending on the amount of the leaves you gathered, you may need more than one baking sheet.

Sprinkle the leaves with the salt and seasoning. Bake until crisp but not burnt, which may take anywhere from 10 to 20 minutes, depending on the size of the leaves. Remember that they will continue to crisp up a bit as they cool, just as cookies do after you take them out of the oven. If you aren't sure if they're done, err on the side of underdone. Take them out, let them cool for just a minute, and if they're not crunchy enough, put them back in the oven.

Once they are completely cooled, you can store the chips in an airtight container for several weeks. If the container is not airtight, the chips may absorb some humidity from the air and lose their crispness. Not a problem: simply put them back into a 250°F oven for 3 to 5 minutes.

Plantain seed capsule spikes

The light green developing immature seed stalk (the left stalk of A on page 294) is short and narrow in its bud form with only small bumps along its length prior to flowering. The stalks are bitter, somewhat astringent, and quite unpleasant in the raw form. If you like bitter, you might enjoy them. They are quite tender since they are still growing. The most reasonable use would be to add them chopped into other foods where bitter can be used as a feature. No reasonable amount of boiling reduces that bitterness. Dice them nicely to add them to salads and other dishes.

After the flowers have been pollinated, the almost-mature green plantain seed spikes (stalk C on page 294) have great potential as a food and fiber source. If you are in an area with lots of plantain plants, you can continue to harvest them over weeks as new spikes are formed.

These immature green seed capsules can be eaten as a vegetable. While the capsules are green, the seeds inside have not totally matured yet, and the capsule holding the seeds is crunchy. The best green spikes have big fat capsules that are bright green. Ignore spikes with small undeveloped capsules—they are not worth the effort.

The best way to eat them fresh is to use your four front teeth. Here's how. Open wide, insert the upper part (the tip) of the spike as far into your mouth as possible without stimulating the gag reflex, gently clamp your four

A collection of immature green plantain seed spikes at their peak for eating as a vegetable.

front teeth, trapping the spike in the middle gap. Pull the spike out through the center gap in your teeth to strip the capsules off the spike. Chew, swallow, repeat. You'll enjoy a nice crunchy flavor, sort of corn-like. The fibrous naked central stalk remains. Practice makes perfect. If you mistakenly strip them with the bottom of the spike pointed into your mouth, a bunch of stringy material attached to the bottom of each capsule will end up in your chew.

These green spikes are also good as hors d'oeuvres—just have some kind of dip to accompany them. Extra virgin olive oil, melted butter, and hummus are fine flavorings to dip them in. Since the spikes are long, guests may need a warning, and extra napkins, for all the dip dripping on their party clothes. Or you can cut the spikes in half to make it less comedic. Get fancy with dip options if you want.

Cooking the green spikes results in a variety of features. Boiling, steaming, and stir-frying yield different results. If you boil the spikes for about 5 minutes, they retain their color, becoming soft, tender, and slightly mucilaginous. They get even softer with further boiling. Unfortunately, the longer you boil them, the harder it is to strip the capsules from the stem using your teeth. They sort of just smash and slide rather than break off. Longer boiling also results in a yellowish-green color change. Given the cooking complications, I prefer to either eat them raw, or just parboil for a minute or two at the most so they don't get too soft.

Dry brown plantain seed capsules

These have great potential. In fact, I would not be surprised if the capsules became a cultivated food for their fiber. The capsules are containers that hold the plant's seeds. They are arranged on the fruiting spikes in such a way that they are easily removed. I simply squeegee the stem for a mix of seeds and dry capsules.

According to my rough calculations, by volume, the fruiting bodies (seed plus capsule) are 22 percent seed and 78 percent capsule. Because the seeds are heavier than the capsules, they make up 65 percent of the weight. And while the seeds are heavier than the capsule material (chaff), they are still so light that they are difficult to separate. So I include the chaff when I am using the fruiting bodies in baked products. The chaff is fiber and perfectly consumable.

So you say you want pure seed, eh? You can remove chaff from seeds by a variety of processes. You can use sifters that let things through of a specific size; you can place the material in a long narrow jar and shake it so all the lighter chaff floats to the top; you can use a fan to blow the lighter chaff off the seed; and there are more ways. Unfortunately, when the seeds are as light as plantain, it can take a while and a combination of steps to get mostly seed, if that is what you want. In general, the more any seed differs from chaff in size and weight, the easier it is to separate them.

PLANTAIN SEEDS ARE DIFFICULT TO GRIND WITH NORMAL KITCHEN EQUIPMENT: For certain applications like smoothies, or to thicken soups, stews, or confections, you need to grind plantain, or any seeds for that matter, all the way down to flour. Otherwise, the seeds can provide an annoying mouthfeel. Baked goods are much more compatible with solid seeds. Due to the mucoproteins in the seed shells, this is an excellent fiber source, so you probably should just add them to baked goods rather than making whole foods out of just plantain seeds.

It is difficult to fully grind plantain seeds into flour without specialized equipment. I can get partially there by placing the seeds and capsules in a food processor or blender. But the contents are so light that they reach a point where they stop grinding and just float around in the vortex above the blades. Until I find a good way to grind them, I just use this partial food processor grind of the squeegeed material.

A collection of mature brown plantain seed spikes at their peak for eating like a grain.

Squeegee the capsules off the stem. The capsules' attachment to the stem is brittle and breaks easily, making their removal a joy.

Lemony Plantago-Seed Muffins

Makes 12 medium muffins

These muffins have a delightfully lemony flavor (not due to the plantain), and the extra virgin olive oil adds a deep richness to these sweet babies. Plantain seeds and capsules, ground fine enough so that the capsule and seed pieces are around the same size, add flavor, texture, fiber, and whatever nutrients they have to the flour.

INGREDIENTS

¾ cup sugar, plus more for sprinkling
3 tablespoons finely chopped fresh lemon zest
3 ounces (⅜ cup) dry measure ground brown
   plantain seed capsules
2 cups all-purpose flour
2 teaspoons baking powder
¼ teaspoon baking soda
¼ teaspoon salt
6 tablespoons extra virgin olive oil
6 tablespoons fresh lemon juice
2 large eggs
¼ cup fat-free milk
½ cup fat-free plain Greek yogurt

DIRECTIONS

Preheat the oven to 375°F. Place paper cupcake liners in a 12-cup muffin tin.

In a large bowl, combine the sugar and the lemon zest, mixing thoroughly until it looks like yellow sugar. Add the plantain seed grind, flour, baking powder, baking soda, and salt, and thoroughly combine.

In a separate bowl, add the olive oil, lemon juice, eggs, milk, and yogurt, whisking until well blended.

Pour the wet ingredients into the dry and slowly mix with a spatula. The mixture will seem really dry, but that is okay. Mix slowly and gently, and stop while you can still see some unmixed dry flour evenly spread in the batter. Over-stirring will result in rubbery, not tender, muffins.

Evenly distribute the batter into the muffin tin cups. Sprinkle a pinch of sugar on the top of each. Bake for about 20 minutes or until you can stick a toothpick into a muffin and it comes out clean. Let cool for a few minutes. They are amazing warm just as they are, or with a little butter on them.

Distinctive and Sweet Plants

These are plants that are either known for or have amazing flavor or aromatic features that help define the plant. They do more to tickle the senses in a distinctively sweet or floral way than other plants. If not for this category, most would all be placed in the Foundation Plants category.

To be clear, all the flavor categories in this book are somewhat arbitrary. Most species have different edible parts that offer different flavors and textures. Leaves, flowers, roots, and fruits on one plant may offer four different flavors. I choose to make executive decisions about which category to put them in with the hope that the categories will give you some guidance on their attributes and use. In a sense, any of the edible plants I cover in my books have unique flavors and aromas worthy of delight, depending on your sensibilities. Here are some examples of some plants having multiple flavors.

Although nettles and pokeweed have their own unique and delightful flavors, they are in the Foundation category because they are within the array of greens, with what most would classify as "greens" flavors. Roots of some plants have a basic starchy potato flavor, but unless that is all they are known for, other parts of those plants may shine over them. The Foundation Plants are often known for their greens, although their roots or other parts, like flowers and stems, may have other tones to their flavors (like bitter, sour, pungent, or floral).

Plants that could be in this section, but are not, include cattail. Cattail pollen has a unique sweet aroma and flavor. Cattail immature pollen spikes have a flavor and aroma reminiscent of corn. But the rest of the plant is quite normal flavored, so I've designated it as part of the Foundation Plants category. You could easily include

Japanese knotweed in this section, but that offers a mildly sour flavor, so it fits in the Tart Plants section.

Wild carrot is known for its distinctive carrot-flavored root. It also has wonderfully aromatic flower heads that smell totally different from the root. The stem has a normal green flavor. Fennel is also known for its distinctive anise flavor, with an extra punch of that flavor emanating from its blossoming flowers. Both wild carrot and sweet fennel are included in this section, along with everlasting pea—which has a distinct sweet pea flavor.

Chapter 20

FAMILY: Fabaceae
SPECIES: *Lathyrus latifolius*

Everlasting Pea

Food good enough to serve as a floral arrangement.

Everlasting pea vines in flower, blanketing a field and rising up over a fence.

EVERLASTING PEA

Estimated Range

Official Species Name:
• *Lathyrus latifolius* L.

Synonyms
• *Lathyrus latifolius*
  var. *splendens*
Common Names:
• Everlasting pea
• Perennial pea
• Wild sweet pea
• Everlasting peavine
• Perennial peavine
• Perennial sweetpea

A herbaceous perennial
climbing vine.

Edible Parts:
• Young shoots
• Flower buds
• Flowers
• Seeds

This is one of my favorite wild foods, and I look forward to eating it every year when it comes into season. It is widespread, abundant, beautiful, delicious, and provides food for several months in any year. This is an easily recognizable pea family member with large pea-shaped flowers and peapods. We make good use of this plant every year in our annual GingerRoot Wild Food Rendezvous. In fact, it is a big hit with participants. Since the flowers are beautiful, big, decorative, and delicious, they were found in at least half of the dishes at our wild food feasts.

Many members of the *Lathyrus* genus have been eaten all over the world and have been singled out for being able to survive both floods and drought. They are nitrogen fixers that improve the soil, can serve as green manure, and are a cover crop for agricultural plants (Alemán, 2003). They provide nutritious seeds that are used as a vegetable or grain, and they have tasty greens and flowers. These are all attributes that provide a good resource in adapting to climate change. Many other plants will not survive increasingly chaotic weather, but *Lathyrus* species can. Efforts are underway to crossbreed different varieties of *Lathyrus* for future cultivation on a massive scale (Singh, 2013).

Everlasting pea, while native to Asia, Europe, and the Mediterranean, is now widespread across North America. It has the distinct advantage of being recognizable from a distance, so it's easy to find. There are several plants with big pink flowers including foxglove (*Digitalis purpurea*) that might fool you at first, from a distance, only because of the flower color. But once you know everlasting pea, it looks like no other plant.

There are Lathyrus species, not covered here, native to North America whose various parts were, and may still be, consumed by first peoples (Moerman, 2010). They include beach pea (*Lathyrus japonicus*), Pacific pea (*Lathyrus vestitus*), grassleaf peavine (*Lathyrus graminifolius*), cream peavine (*Lathyrus ochroleucus*), slenderstem peavine (*Lathyrus palustris*), and manystem peavine (*Lathyrus polymorphus*). While there will be some overlap, exact edibility of these species should not be assumed from the edibility of everlasting pea covered here. Each has their own story of use, which I have not studied yet. Also, these native species are regional, none are as widespread as everlasting pea, so not as easily found. If you live close by to one of these other species, study it and get back to me about your experiences.

If you do any in-depth research on wild sweet pea plants, you will hear about *lathyrism*. Lathyrism is a disease associated with certain members of the lathyrus genus when they are eaten under very unusual conditions you will never experience. It does not seem to be of concern to normal, healthy individuals with a normally diverse diet. For those interested in learning more about this, I will cover it in depth later in this chapter.

Participant Eva Walls munching down on fresh pea flowers during the 2019 GingerRoot Wild Food Rendezvous.

Knowing Everlasting Pea

Everlasting pea can grow from seed or from already established underground rhizomes. The only difference between the two is that seedling plants start out thinner and grow more slowly than ones feeding off the rhizomes.

Seeds germinate in well-drained areas with full sun where the soil has been disturbed enough to sink them into the earth up to $1\frac{1}{2}$ inches deep. After a few years, established rhizomes promote enough aboveground growth to provide a ground cover. In fact, plants in the *Lathyrus* genus are valued for their ability to stop erosion and cover the ground enough to shade out and inhibit the growth of invasive plants.

Everlasting pea plants grow from perennial taproots. Having found some spring shoots, I dug down for the first time to examine them. Given the aboveground growth, I assumed I would find something pencil-sized running just below the surface. At some point I sliced through what I thought was a soft tree root, about 2 inches in diameter. I looked around and the closest tree was quite a distance. The more I dug, the more of this thick root material was

Three everlasting pea seedlings at different stages of growth. The shortest here is ½ inch tall and the tallest is 2 inches tall.

John Kallas in 2021, holding massive underground taproots of three everlasting pea plants intertwined and spreading out. They grew sideways and not down due to hitting a layer of rocks they could not penetrate.

A young spring everlasting pea shoot growing from a perennial taproot. The characteristic leaves and stems are not yet evident at this early stage of growth. This shoot is about 6 inches tall.

in the way. Then it struck me . . . Wow! This was not a tree root; it was the root of the everlasting pea.

The more I dug, the more massive the root. Minute by minute I was revealing more and more of these big roots. I began to realize that everlasting pea was a delicate herbaceous vine aboveground growing from massive storage organs below. No wonder this thing survives drought and gobs of competition from other plants and can even grow over Himalayan blackberry. The root directly below the plant I was digging was about 2 inches in diameter; I cut it off at about 2 yards. Who knows how long it continued? The area I dug the roots from was filled with large rocks and debris bricks, causing the rapid turn sideways that made the roots look like they were doing the splits.

After the plant reaches about a foot in height, the leaves, alternating on the stem, fully spread out and show their shape. Leaflet parts are tightly wrapped around each other early in growth, then spread out widely when reaching full size. Everlasting pea and a few other members of the *Lathyrus* genus have a unique leaf that has several striking characteristics.

- The leaf is trifoliate—meaning it has three leaflets. But not just any leaflets. The two leaflets off to the sides are lance-shaped with parallel veins. The center leaflet has evolved into a branching tendril that does the climbing for the plant. These tendrils are long, thin, and react to touch. If they touch anything, they try to wrap around it. This wrapping action is too slow to be seen with the naked eye. But plants, fencing, and other things they wrap around are not moving fast or at all themselves, so this form of climbing is very successful.

- Leaf stems look like plant stems. All the plant stems are winged. All the leaf stems are winged. Winged here means that the round stems have a membrane that flairs out on either side. Visualize this by imagining an airplane with wings that spanned the whole plane from tip to tail instead of just sticking out the center. You have a round center lined by wings. Since they look the same, the first time you examine this plant, you may be confused about where the plant stem ends and the leaf stem begins.

- At the base of the leaf stem are two very prominent stipules growing off to the sides. Stipules on many species are small and insignificant. On everlasting pea, they are relatively large and resemble small leaflets.

The main stems, like the leaf stems, have wings along their length. This is a characteristic shared by *Lathyrus sylvestris*, its closest relative, and *Lathyrus sativus*, which we will refer to later, and a few other members of the genus. The main stem wings are indistinguishable from the leaf stem wings, except for their location: the main stem supports all the leaves; each leaf stem supports its three leaflets. The stems have no tendrils. Tendrils are only found at the tips of the leaves. It is the leaves, not the stems, that do all the climbing for this vine.

Everlasting pea is a trailing vine that climbs whatever it can find to climb. When these plants are growing densely, they climb each other. They will not climb flat walls as much as they will lean against them. Then other plants

A mature everlasting pea leaf on its stem. I graphically darkened the plant stem and adjacent flower stem so you could see, without confusion, what this unique leaf looks like. At top is the tendril (a modified leaflet), center are the two regular leaflets, flaring out to the sides. Below them is the winged leaf stem. At the very base are the stipules that sandwich the leaf stem base. This leaf arises from the main stem. The leaf's stipules wrap partially around the plant stem.

Right: Everlasting pea stem running from lower right to upper left. Two leaves and two flower stalks are emerging from that stem. The plant stem is clearly winged, as are the leaf stems arising from it.

Below: Everlasting pea stems, climbing over themselves as they expand outward. This stage is in spring before the flower stalks appear.

Below: Everlasting pea, leafy stem growth tip variation. The left image shows several stipules protecting several developing leaves nested at the tip waiting to emerge. This is the stage of fastest growth. Midseason (center), the developing leaves are emerging more slowly and not so nested. The image at right shows an emerging flower stem just to the right of the emerging leaf. There is a flower stem associated with each leaf on the older stems.

Early season shoot   **Midseason shoot**   **Late season shoot**

will climb those leaning plants. To climb, the everlasting pea requires things its leaf tendrils can easily wrap around. Tendrils can wrap around most plant stems, wire fencing, and anything roughly ⅜ inch in diameter and smaller.

Stems grow very fast in the early spring. All the new, tender growth is at the tip of each expanding stem. These tips change in appearance over time since they are doing different things as the season progresses. In the early spring, growth is so rapid that the tips constantly have several layers of gestational leaves nested inside each other. Stipules flank each side of a developing leaves before each emerges and expands to its full size and shape, greatly overtopping the stipules at their base. Leaves are constantly being replaced at the tip by new, tightly wrapped leaves that will expand out next. And the cycle continues. This description of growth will make more sense when you examine the plant in real life.

Once the stem expands, you see maturing leaves distributed along it every 3 to 5 inches of its length. Leaves alternate on the stem. Due to the complex nature of the leaf shape and the winged stems, it is difficult to understand where the stem ends and the leaves begin. But you should know now if you've been following along.

Flower stalks appear in late spring and continue forming into the summer. Each stalk grows upward from where each leaf meets the stem on the newer upper parts of the stem. Flower stalks range from 5 to 14 inches long, growing vertically, straight up toward the sky, no matter what the orientation of the stem is. Each stalk generates from 4 to 10 flowers. Fat buds precede the flowers. Flower buds can be up to an inch long. Flowers are often over an inch wide and are pink to light purple. Some strains can be pure white. All are just quite beautiful. Flower stalks with

Everlasting pea stem showing three mature leaves alternating off the stem. New leafy stem material is emerging off the tip. This is before flower development.

Everlasting pea showing its growth tip on the left, bud development in the center, and full flowering stems on the right. Flower stalks are about 12 inches tall on the right. Flower stalks emerge opposite leaves along the stem.

longer stems are great for putting into a vase on your dinner table for show, to eat, or both.

The less common *Lathyrus sativus*, referred to later regarding lathyrism, has only a single blue flower per stalk.

By the time flower stalks appear, the lower, older leaves and stem of the plant are browning and shriveling. In fact, sometimes the lower stems are so shriveled and brown, you'd think the upper part of the plant would die. But somehow it is still supplying the upper plant with enough water and nutrients to thrive.

Flowers ripen from the lower part of the stalk first, gradually blooming up the stem until all the buds have opened. As the lower flowers age, likely after being pollinated, petals quickly transform to a pale blue. Soon after that, the peapods begin to grow from their base and the petals shrivel off.

Mature peapods can be greater than 4 inches long. They start out a dull green, transitioning to a dull yellow, then soon after turn light tan. They start out tough when green, becoming dry and brittle once they tan. The peas inside are green while the pod is green. Once the pod has transitioned to tannish-brown, the peas dry out, brown and harden.

When fully mature, brown and dry, the pods violently split open along their seams, either by touch, crashing against

Everlasting pea flowers and upper buds at the end of a long flower stalk.

each other in the wind, or naturally on their own. The result is that the seeds get spread by ejection into the surrounding area. If you are near when it's happening, it sounds like a small twig snapping. Each now-split pod remains on the plant, beautifully twisted, as two connected helixes.

Gathering and Preparation of Everlasting Pea

Throughout history, the most prized part of the *Lathyrus* genus has been the peas, mostly for protein and calorie reasons in subsistence cultures. But in today's world, my favorite parts are the new growth tips and the flowers.

The new growth tips are good to eat from early spring until you start seeing pod development. They are more substantial and gourmet prior to and in early flowering. They get smaller and a little less sweet on older plants. Size and shape differences can be seen back on page 312.

This is a wild fast food—you can eat them raw right off the plant. Just snap the end off and munch. With a little practice, you will be able to judge exactly where on the stem you should snap to get the most material. If you have to tug and pull, you've reached down into the older, more fibrous stem. You should be able to snap off the top 3 inches (earlier in the season), down to about 2 inches (later in the season) of delicious, usable material.

If you are planning on saving your findings for later, use scissors and cut farther down the stem. Place these cuttings into white bags (cloth or plastic). If the stems are long enough, put them cut-side down into a glass jar with about an inch of water. Keep them misted with water and out of the sun to prevent wilting and overheating. Jarred stems in water should be loosely covered in a plastic bag when placed in the fridge, and are best used within five days—the sooner, the better.

The tender tops may have a non-tender hitchhiker—an almost fully formed young leaf. With practice, you will be able to both identify and separate out the still-developing

Top: Green pods with fresh green peas inside.
Bottom: Two fully mature pods that have split open along their seams, ejected their seeds, and curled into helixes. Each pod separates into two helix halves.

Everlasting pea salad with slices of peeled Japanese knotweed stem, black olives, Swiss chard, and feta cheese. Everlasting peas shoots can be added to any fruit or vegetable salad.

Everlasting pea's leafy stem growth tips in cold water to keep them fresh. The tender upper halves of what you see here, must be snapped off for use. The tougher, lower part of the stems can be chopped finely for use such as lettuce, blended in smoothies or composted as too fibrous to eat. Putting the stems in water like this, and covering with a loose plastic bag is how I would keep the tips fresh in the fridge. They are best used in two days, but can last in there for a week.

leaves clinging to the side of the new growth tips. They look like they are part of the growth tip, but are now older and fibrous, so discard those leaves unless you don't mind the chew. You can identify them, since their tendrils are much longer than the new tips and all the leaf parts are easily distinguishable once you pull that leaf off during trimming. Note that all fully opened mature leaves on this plant are too fibrous to eat. So don't do it! They will just be a culinary disappointment.

These growth tips are fantastic added to any dish where you would use fresh spinach or snow peas. They have a sweet, fresh, mild pea flavor. Delicious! Use them in salads and sandwiches. Dip them in sauces at parties. Add them last minute to a stir-fry so they are barely cooked. And while they are fantastic cooked, they are so good raw it is a shame to cook them. Virtually everyone loves them. Even those afraid to eat wild foods will become new converts if you feed them these tips.

Flower parts of everlasting pea

As I have stated many times, if a whole aboveground plant is edible (aside from fibrous parts), anything you can chew is fair game. There is no history of root use for this plant that I could find, so we must assume it is inedible. But the upper plant is a different story. When the flower stalks are first developing, before the buds are formed, the whole stalk can be tender enough to eat. Once you've found the flowers, search for younger and younger bud stalks. For the youngest, much of the stalk itself will be tender and edible. Collect the edible part by tugging farther and farther up the stalk until it snaps cleanly away. That is what you can eat. You can cook these like asparagus. Once the buds reach their full size before blooming, their stalks will be too fibrous to chew.

You can eat the buds raw as a snack or add them anywhere you would add fresh peas to a dish. They have a mild pea flavor. They are mostly a raw food since heat destroys much of their color, texture, and flavor. To collect, clip the flower stem down near the base then transport and refrigerate them as you would the growth tips. When ready to use, squeegee the buds off the stem with your hands.

The flowers themselves are amazing. Their flavor, texture, and beauty are unbeatable. If there were awards for great overall wild foods, this would be one of the winners. The flowers are another wild fast food. Snack on them in the field if you want. Collect, refrigerate, and process the flowers just as you would the buds. When you are ready to use them, just pull them off the stem and add them fresh to anything. They decorate everything. You will get *ooohs*

Everlasting pea flowers and wild spinach in water containers, ready for transport in the back of an SUV. They should be kept out of the sun, in a cool place, and misted until ready to use.

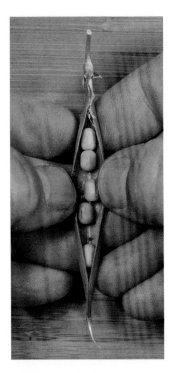

A wild salad I made for participants at the GingerRoot Wild Food Rendezvous in 2014. Contents included everlasting pea, oxeye daisy leaves and flowers, wild spinach, green amaranth, sheep sorrel, and a few other wild foods. This is a 16-inch bowl that fed about 25 people.

Splitting open a plump green pod by sticking thumbnails into its seams. These peas are smaller than store-bought sweet peas.

and *aaahs* just by placing them on a dessert or a drink, or as a garnish. Cover your salad with them to add color, flavor, and nutrition. Or go for broke and make a whole salad out of just the flowers.

The everlasting pea seeds

Harvest the pods when they are plump and green before they transition from green to yellow. Seeds are at their prime when their pods are plump and green. If you can, pick in the early morning after a cool night.

Stick your thumbnails in the seam to pry the pod open after slicing it with a razor blade. Scoop the seeds out. Depending on how well pollination went, there can be three to 10 peas per pod. Eat them fresh, as you would sweet peas. Although pleasant and reminiscent of domesticated sweet peas, they are not as sweet and tender. But they are the best *wild* peas you will find. I love them. The pods themselves are too tough to chew.

Like regular sweet peas, they are best when used just after picking. The longer they sit in the pods, the more the sweetness turns starchy. You can slow the transition to starch by removing the peas from their pods and plunging them in ice water for 10 minutes as soon as you get home. Drain them and put them in a plastic bag and into the fridge. Try to use within 24 hours for the sweetest experience. They will last almost a week in the fridge, but are best cooked or mixed with other foods after that first 24 hours.

You can also cook these fresh green peas like domesticated ones, eating them with a little olive oil and salt or adding them to other dishes.

You can still harvest the fresh peas when the pods are turning yellow, but they will be less sweet and more tough to chew. Sprinkle the fresh peas into salads, dips, and sandwiches, and eat them out of hand. Kids will love them because they are easy to collect, fun to open, cute, tiny, and great to eat.

They should be perfectly safe to eat in the context of any well-rounded diet. If rapidly growing children are going to eat them in large quantities over time (like in a food jag), boil them first in an open pot for 10 minutes and discard the cooking water. Boiling has been shown to destroy the already harmless (within the context of a healthy overall diverse diet) nonprotein amino acids.

If you wait until the pods are tan and dry, the peas will be rock hard, but are good for later boiling like other

Everlasting peas and crumbled cauliflower (boiled together for 5 minutes, red pepper and grated carrot (roasted together in extra virgin olive oil), all garnished with a flower. The small peas make the flower look huge in this photograph.

Fully mature, dried-in-the-pod everlasting peas. They are hard. Some of the peas will have holes in them from the pea weevil (*Bruchis affinis*) whose larval stage loves this pea as much as you will. This does not affect the edibility of the peas. The insect is very neat and leaves a clean hole.

FOOD JAG

A food jag is when a child will just eat one food over an extended period of time. Meal after meal, day after day.

dry peas, or for grinding into flour. Harvest the dry, hard brown seeds after the pods have gone fully dry and brittle. This is the way most cultures gathered the seeds. They would boil and then dry them for storage. When they were ready to use them, people would grind these high-protein peas into flour to add to other foods or to extend their wheat flour in bread making.

In areas of the world where people are at subsistence level, you use every resource. The peas were an extra protein and energy source. I haven't found any processing or detailed information on exactly how North American indigenous people consumed the seeds of our native *Lathyrus* species, just that they ate them. I have never worked with the dried brown peas myself, so have no experience to report to you.

WHAT ARE THE LIMITS OF EATING EVERLASTING PEA: From the research I've done, I cannot see any problem with eating any parts of this plant in moderation, in the context of a normal, healthy diverse diet. In fact, it is likely safer than dandelion greens for humans of any age.

There is an unlikely possibility that large amounts (like in food jags) of the unboiled peas (green or brown) eaten often might interfere, in temporary ways, with growth and development in rapidly growing bodies. From a perspective of an overabundance of caution, I would not make baby food out of the peas, or allow kids to engage in a food jag with the peas. Note that this is all about excess in a non-diverse diet, and even there, I am hesitant to mention this due to a lack of evidence that any negative experience will happen.

I have no concerns for any other parts of the plant, which are completely wholesome within a normally diverse diet, at any age.

What follows is an in-depth discussion of lathyrism if you are interested.

Lathyrism

As you read this, I want you to hold these three concepts to be true at the same time:

1. Seeds (peas) of certain members of the *Lathyrus* genus are known for a couple of *starvation-enabled* maladies collectively referred to as *lathyrism*. This is a serious disease with serious consequences, caused by circumstances so specific that you will never experience them.

2. My understanding is that the peas of virtually every member of this genus are not toxic if eaten by healthy people, in normal amounts, as one would eat any vegetable as a part of a complete, wholesome diet.

3. Aside from the peas and sprouted seeds, there is no known toxicity to aboveground parts of any of the *Lathyrus* species. Vegetative parts, buds, and flowers have never resulted in any toxicity.

In most of the following discussion, I am referring to grass pea (*Lathyrus sativus*), not everlasting pea. Everlasting pea (*Lathyrus latifolius*) will come up to make some comparisons where useful. Grass pea is the primary cause of lathyrism in humans. Everlasting peas has not been shown to cause lathyrism in humans.

Cultures all over the world eat members of this genus as a regular part of their diverse diet with no apparent toxic effects. In fact, grass pea, the most notorious member of the *Lathyrus* genus, is/has been a major protein and energy source for over 100 million people in drought-prone areas of Asia and Africa (Das, 2021). However, eating the peas of certain members of this genus, like grass pea, can cause neurological disorders under extremely specific dietary circumstances that you will likely never experience. The following has to be true in order for grass pea (*Lathyrus sativus*) and a few related species to cause the neurological problems of most concern—stiffness, then paralysis of the lower extremities. For the disease to show itself, both of these have to be true:

1. Long-term starvation (2 to 6 months) serious enough to cause physical maladies or even death on its own. Your body would be wasting away and you would start to look like a walking skeleton. This is a starvation characterized by protein malnutrition. That is, not consuming enough of the essential amino acids in the right proportions to support growth, development, or even maintenance in the human body. Protein is made up of amino acids. Essential amino acids are ones we need in our diet to survive.

2. Eating grass peas or closely related peas as 20 percent or more of total calories in this starvation diet for 2 to 6 months.

These are conditions you will never experience since it is unlikely you will ever be that starving while eating lots of grass peas over several months. Think about it. Any toxin that requires these specific draconian circumstances to show any symptoms is pretty weak.

There are the two types of lathyrism, both caused by nonprotein amino acids in *Lathyrus* genus seeds and seedlings (Borrows, 2013, Cheeke, 1998, Cooper, 1984, Deshpande, 2002). Neurolathyrism is seen in humans in subsistence areas during severe, long-term drought and famine. Osteolathyrism, a different disorder, has been demonstrated in the laboratory in experimental animals.

Neurolathyrism

Plants with peas known for causing neurolathyrism are *Lathyrus sativus*, and to a lesser degree, *Lathyrus cicera*, *Lathyrus ochrus*, and *Lathyrus clymenum*. The main toxic components, nonprotein amino acids, are mostly destroyed by boiling or roasting the seeds. Cultures that eat these plants know to do this. These wild peas are a normal part of their diverse diet.

However, in severe, long-term drought conditions, food, water, and firewood are scarce in subsistence cultures. So the unboiled seeds are ground into flour to be baked using what little firewood is available. Over months of severe drought, famine, protein malnutrition, and nonprotein amino acids gumming up the works, neurolathyrism develops. It is also speculated that a lack of methionine and cysteine, our two essential sulfur-based amino acids, also enable the nonprotein amino acids to cause their problems.

"Neurolathyrism affects adults more than children, and younger men more than older men and women" (Cooper, 1984). It most impacts men between the ages of 20 and 30 (Cheeke, 1998). "The gender proportions were 87.1% in males, 12.9% in females, 90% of both sexes were less than 30 years of age at time of onset" (Borrows, 2013).

Protective effects of a well-rounded diet

How can cultures that eat these species as a normal part of their regular diet do so without experiencing any of the toxic effects? In a normal well-rounded diet, where the *Lathyrus* peas are only a small part of the total, the good amino acids consumed from a variety of dietary protein sources outnumber, outcompete, and are *likely* preferred by the body's physiology over the bad ones. So the outnumbered bad ones end up getting passed by, ignored, and processed/broken down into energy instead of doing any damage.

Even if a few of the phony amino acids happen to do mischief after a single meal, rapid replacement and repair *likely* occur due to the body's ability to heal itself. I use the word "likely" because, while we don't actually know if human physiology "prefers" or "repairs" molecular level phenomena related to lathyrites, it is an assumption I am making since no observable instance of lathyrism has been documented in humans in the context of a healthy diet and, since the body's ability to repair itself, in general, is a well-established phenomenon.

How does everlasting pea fit into this story?

Don't confuse *Lathyrus latifolius* (everlasting pea) covered in this chapter, with *Lathyrus sativus* (grass pea). As far as I could find, everlasting pea has never been documented to have caused lathyrism or any other malady in humans. Everlasting pea seeds do contain some nonprotein amino acids. They are different than the ones in grass pea.

Since everlasting pea seeds contains some, but different, nonprotein amino acids, scientists have conducted animal experiments to see if they could find some effect. They have. If you force-feed farm animals (horses are particularly susceptible) large quantities of *Lathyrus latifolius*, they can develop osteolathyrism. Osteolathyrism is characterized by defective synthesis of cartilage and connective tissue over time. This results in skeletal deformities during growth and development of young foals. A foal is baby horse under a year old. It can also cause poor formation of collagen and elastin in blood capillaries. Osteolathyrism may have more impact on early development than neurolathyrism. But again, osteolathyrism has never been documented in humans, independent from neurolathyrism and high quantities in an unbalanced diet have to be eaten for it to express itself in farm animals.

EVERLASTING VERSUS GRASS PEA FLOWERS
Everlasting pea has three to 10 pink or white flowers on each flower stalk. Grass pea has a single blue flower on each flower stalk.

We don't know if boiling or roasting destroys everlasting pea's non-protein amino acids since no one has done those experiments. Of course, it is probably not necessary given a well-rounded diet and lack of any evidence of harm.

Toxins are not all bad

Many people misunderstand and overrate the *potential* toxicity of plant components. If you believe that any quantity of a human-labeled toxin under any circumstance is bad for you, you are wrong and would never be able to eat anything. Toxins live in the context of a complex world. Things that are toxic to one animal may be perfectly safe for another animal. Within a wholesome diet, some toxins consumed in tiny amounts are beneficial. Vitamin A is perfectly good and an essential nutrient, but in too high a quantity, it can be poisonous. Phytochemicals are great examples of this: tannins, flavones, triterpenoids, steroids, saponins, and alkaloids, for instance, are poisonous to humans in large amounts, yet are antioxidants, serving as antiaging and anticancer agents, as well as providing protection from cardiovascular disease, diabetes, and some neurodegenerative diseases, when consumed in tiny amounts within a diverse diet. You can conclude from this that just because a plant is associated with a toxin does not mean that the particular toxin is toxic to you. It just means that under certain unusual circumstances it might be.

All this talk of nonprotein amino acids has to do with seeds. Shoots and flowers, on the other hand, are parts containing little protein or calories of any kind. So even if they have nonprotein amino acids, they would only have a tiny fraction of what the seeds have. I personally eat the shoots, buds, and flowers often when they are in season. Occasionally, for the fun of it, I eat the peas.

Theoretically, osteolathyrism from eating everlasting peas could happen in modern society. You might be susceptible if you were severely malnourished, like someone with an advanced case of anorexia or some other wasting disease, or if you had chronic protein deficiency. And if 20 percent or more of your total calories came from everlasting peas over weeks or months, osteolathyrism might rear its ugly head. For a healthy person on a wholesome regular diverse diet, everlasting pea seeds are likely safe and nutritious. The delicious shoots, buds, and flowers are likely as safe as lettuce.

Chapter 21

FAMILY: Apiaceae
SPECIES: *Foeniculum vulgare*

Wild Sweet Fennel

*A big, feathery, fernlike carrier of sensational
sweet taste, aroma, and tender crunch.*

Upper stems of fennel showing young rapidly growing leaves, prior to flower development.

Estimated Range

Official Species Name:
• *Foeniculum vulgare* Mill.

Synonyms:
• *Foeniculum foeniculum*
  (L.) Karst.

Common Names:
• Wild sweet fennel
• Sweet fennel
• Finocchio

A taprooted perennial
native to the Mediterranean
that is now widespread
throughout Europe, northern
Africa, Eurasia, and all the
colonized countries.

Edible Parts:
• Rapidly growing
  peeled stems
• Young emerging leaves
• Emerging buds
• Flower tops
• Seeds

WILD SWEET FENNEL

Growing up, I hated black licorice. Horrible-tasting stuff. Made your teeth black if I remember correctly. Great to chew beforehand if you wanted to impress a date with your darkened teeth. Obviously, enough people liked it to make it commercially successful. But that was licorice candy, made up of sugar and starches, dyed black, and flavored with natural chemicals from the root of the licorice plant, *Glycyrrhiza glabra*, a legume. While I have not even seen this god-awful candy for decades, the thought of edible plants having a licorice or anise flavor, and there are several, made me assume that I would not enjoy their flavor.

Then I tasted the leaves of sweet cicely (*Osmorhiza berteroi*) in our Pacific Northwest forests and was pleasantly surprised. Its mild licorice flavor was fantastic, refreshing, and delightful. Not long after that I tasted wild sweet fennel, finding a similar pleasant flavor. It makes me wonder what natural licorice root tastes like without all the sugar, starch, and dye.

Complicating our everyday exposure to these kinds of flavors is that anise seed is now used in place of licorice root, since the taste is so similar. I've had licorice tea that was, in fact, flavored with star anise, having zero licorice root. Read your labels.

Evidently there is something called convergent evolution, where different plants, even ones from different plant families, evolve independently to produce chemicals so similar that you'd think they were related. Wild sweet fennel has its own version of this flavor, and it's great. To distinguish it from the black licorice candy flavor and texture, I am generally referring to this as green licorice. It is fresh, sweet, and delicious.

Which fennel am I talking about here? Apparently, there are many varieties you can come across, all derived from our wild type. The two you are most likely to encounter in your everyday life are our wild type, which I cover in this chapter, and the bulb type, which you can purchase in most supermarket produce departments. If you buy garden

Edible bulb from domesticated bulb fennel, *Foeniculum vulgare* var *azoricum*. Our wild variety does not have a bulb.

seed for planting, it is the bulb variety. Most fennel recipes you look up are based on the fennel bulb. The bulb does not exist in our wild variety. So don't look for a bulb.

Fennel seed that you buy as a spice is *Foeniculum vulgare* var. *dulce*. There are also purple- and bronze-colored ornamental varieties, mostly grown for show, though I am sure you could eat them just like our green wild type. The neighbors, however, might be upset to see you eating their ornamentals.

Fennel seed is well known, a commonly available spice, and is used in many conventional recipes. It is used both for food and in herbal remedies. It has many general health benefits (like many foods), and is considered great for digestion and a variety of other things (Badgujar, 2014 and Sadeghpour, 2015). Warnings you might come across about fennel are related to seed consumption or use of medicinal extracts of the seeds. Eating excessive amounts of seeds over time may alter your female hormone levels. For some people that is a benefit; for others, it is a problem. The fennel seed you buy as a spice is likely just good for healthy people when used in regular recipes calling for it.

Recipes intended for the fennel bulb will not work without modification for our wild type. The closest thing we have to the bulb is the peeled stem. You will need several peeled stems to take the place of one fennel bulb.

ARE FENNEL SEEDS A RISK FOR WOMEN WITH HORMONE ISSUES?

Fennel seed extracts may increase levels of estrogen, progesterone, and prolactin (Sadeghpour, 2015). For hormone-sensitive individuals, such as those with breast, uterine, or ovarian cancers; endometriosis; or uterine fibroids, your physician might warn you about the use of fennel seed to be on the safe side. I have not seen warnings about the vegetative or flower parts of this plant. Fennel vegetation in the context of a normal diverse diet should be safe. But I suppose anything is possible if your body is compromised enough.

Information about using wild fennel as food in the popular literature is limited to *suggestions* and *theories* of novices. If you followed their advice, mostly on using the leaves, you would likely reject it as a food or just use it as a novelty sprinkle on other foods.

Fennel, particularly the seeds, is used to spice things up. Here are some examples: alcoholic beverages like absinthe, ouzo, and akvavit; toothpaste, candies, and breath fresheners; and many foods, including meats, flavored sauces, sausages and fish, breads and pastries, pickles and vinegars.

Fennel and dill are closely related. Their leaves and stems are similar enough to cause some confusion in identification. Simply crushing and smelling the leaves will instantly reveal which you have in front of you. Fennel is much more likely to be found in the wild in persistent patches, since the taproots send up new plants each year. Dill must grow from seed each year, which puts a bigger burden on germination.

Knowing Wild Sweet Fennel

Fennel grows easily from both seed and perennial roots. The seed lasts for years in the soil and can germinate with only a little moisture and 60-degree weather. The seedling loosely resembles carrot, poppy, and other seedlings that

Fennel seedling, showing both cotyledons and the first true leaf, about 1½ inches tall here.

Young fennel plants growing from seed. Height ranges from 3 inches on the left to 7 inches on the right. For perspective, there are two leaves on the left, three leaves on the center plant, and two on the one on the right. Leaflets on those leaves are more needlelike than wild carrot or poison hemlock.

have deeply divided adult leaves. Its two cotyledons are long and narrow. The deeply divided and needlelike leaflets of the first new leaves give a clue as to what is to come with more mature leaves.

It grows so easily it is considered a noxious weed in many states. These plants grow fast and begin feathering out early in life. The leaves are compound, with many needlelike leaflets. The larger the leaves, the more leaflets.

These young plants develop a taproot, a stalk, many leaves, flower heads (umbels), and will produce seed in the first year.

You are more likely to see perennial plants growing year after year from established taproots than to see seedlings thrive under all the shade.

Dead, 7-foot-tall wild fennel stems from a cluster of live taproots. New plants will emerge from those taproots in the next growing season.

If you venture into a field with fennel in it during the winter or early spring, you should see the old stalks clustered together, reminiscent of a dead shrub. They are topped by whatever umbel skeletons survived the winter. These old stalks are quite stiff and brittle. They can range from 7 to over 9 feet tall.

Since the roots are stout and filled with overwintered stored energy, they have the power to send up thick stalks and leaves in early spring. Several stalks up to an inch in diameter will arise from each root. Many roots are often clustered below many stalks, making it hard to know when you have one plant or many producing the shrublike stalks. The leaves alternate on the stems. The stems are green with a cyan tint, have a whitish bloom, no hairs, and are hollow. If you rub or handle the stem, that area will be slightly darker, because you've removed the bloom.

Wild fennel leaves are unique for a variety of reasons. The first and easiest aspect is that, like the rest of the plant, they smell like sweet

Young wild fennel plants bolting from strong perennial roots.

Wild fennel leaves emerge from the stem as tight feathery clusters of needlelike leaves. I call these young leaf blades pom-poms (the four leaves on the left). As the leaf grows, the leaflets begin branching and spreading out. Although the leaflets are needlelike, the leaf blade they make up eventually becomes triangular in shape. You don't see that triangular shape on the rightmost leaf blades in this photo, because I curved the lower branches upward to fit leaves closer together. I did not want them to overlap. These are all young, still expanding and growing leaf blades, ranging from 4 inches at the left to 8 inches on the right. Mature leaf blades can be 16 inches long at maturity.

licorice, particularly when bruised. And they taste like mild green licorice.

New, emerging leaves are feathery, very soft to the touch, and contain hundreds of tightly clustered needle-shaped leaflets on small branching leaflet stems. New leaves look like a green, feathery, elongated pom-pom. As they grow, the leaf blades (all the leaflets and leaflet stems together) expand, branch, and rebranch until you have a large feathery triangular leaf.

The pom-poms are typically 2 to 5 inches long before leaflets branch out. A full-grown leaf blade is typically 10 to 12 inches long but can grow larger. That size does not include the leaf stem. Fennel leaves of all sizes are soft to the touch.

Let me be clear about two distinct parts of the plant: the plant stem versus the leaf. The plant stem is the main stem that supports all the leaves that grow on it. The plant stem branches as it gets older to support more leaves and to spread them out for photosynthesis.

The leaf stem, also known as a petiole by botanists, grows from the plant stem and supports its own leaf blade.

A leaf is made up of a petiole plus its leaf blade. If a plant has a compound leaf, like fennel, the leaf blade is represented by all the leaflets viewed together as a whole. And in this case, there is a lot of branching that occurs within the leaf blade to support all those leaflets. The overall shape of a fennel leaf blade is triangular.

As I've said, the petiole is the lower part of the leaf. It is the support structure that connects the leaf blade to the plant stem. The petiole on fennel is pretty specialized. When the leaf is young, the leaf stem so tightly clasps the plant stem that it just looks like it is part of that stem, giving the illusion that the plant stem is thicker than it is. The leaf stem clasps on so tightly, it is difficult to pry off. Since you don't see the leaf stem as separate from the main stem, the blade above the leaf stem appears to be coming almost directly out of the plant stem.

As the plant matures, the lowest older petioles release their grip on the plant stem and angle away from it. The blades at the ends of the released petioles now extend farther away from the stalk, allowing them to reach more sunlight.

The importance of the clasping petioles becomes apparent during processing of the plant stems and leaf blades.

Although fennel initially produces a straight stalk, it will branch many times as it gets older.

Plants growing near each other, in the same habitat, grow fairly uniformly in height. When growing from multiple taproot clusters, they can look like one big feathery shrub. The stalks are hollow, except at the leaf nodes (where leaves emerge from the stem), with structural fiber in the outer skin. The inner core of the young hollow rapidly growing stalks is tender, but that toughens up as the stem gets older.

The plants reproduce easily in fallow fields. The seed gets dispersed and you can end up with a fennel forest.

The stems start out thick in younger plants; upper stems thin out and start branching as the plants grow taller. Flower buds emerge along with and in place of new leaves on the upper parts of branches. If individual plants are

Plant stem of wild fennel showing two leaves. An upper leaf with the petiole still clasping the stem. The lower leaf's petiole has released its hold on the stem and angles the whole leaf (petiole plus blade) outward, allowing more sunlight to reach it. All fennel petioles will eventually release their clasp from the stem, bending outward as the plant matures. The petioles are greener on new plants under a foot tall, and become more yellow as the plant gets taller. This picture shows about 2 feet of plant stem.

Left: A cluster of wild fennel clones at almost 5 feet tall, looking like a feathery shrub. The plant will grow much taller than this by the time it is producing flowers.

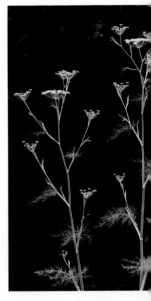

Above: Fennel flower umbels on mature plants.

Above: Close-up of fennel buds and flowers. Anthers sticking up indicate flowers that are blooming. Each umbellette hosts 12 to 24 individual flowers.

Above: One fennel umbel topped with 31 mini-umbels (umbellettes).

growing out in the open, flowers will emerge at the tips of lower as well as upper branches. If plants are growing in clonal clusters, partially shading each other out, flowers will mostly appear on upper parts of the plant.

Leaves on upper, older stems are markedly smaller than ones lower on the plant.

This plant is in the same family as carrot and, like it, has an umbel flower structure. It's actually a compound umbel, also like carrot: lots of mini-umbels (umbellettes) growing on the tips of the main umbel. Note that an umbel is not a flower, it is a flower cluster in a particular pattern. There is one flower at the end of each mini-umbel stem. There are 12 to 24 flowers on a single mini-umbel, with roughly 18 to 30 mini-umbels per umbel. That means one umbel can have over 700 flowers, which turn into that many dry seed-containing fruits.

Fennel umbels are flat-topped or slightly rounded. Flowers are yellow-petaled and tiny. The flowers have both male and female parts, and can self-fertilize; however, the anthers produce pollen before the pistils (female parts) are receptive. This favors cross-pollination and fennel population diversity. The flowers are most aromatic when the petals are bright yellow and the anthers are producing pollen. The bees go nuts flying from umbel to umbel when these flowers are at their peak.

Wild Sweet Fennel: Gathering, Processing, and Food

Before the flowering stage, all gathering of fennel is based on rapidly growing stems. Stems support three edible parts: stem cores, pom-poms, and young leaf blades. Again, there is no bulb on wild sweet fennel.

The young plants, at about a foot or two tall, will have the thickest stalks. Thickness is desirable for people harvesting fennel, since it leaves more core after the peeling is done. At this young stage, leaf petioles clasp the stem along their whole length and are almost the same color as

Wild fennel stalk collection containers. This is the most efficient way I've found to preserve stalk freshness during collection and transport. Here I have 3 plastic pitchers half-filled with water inside a 5-gallon bucket. This system is easier to manage than just throwing all the stems in the 5-gallon bucket. You can bring this system out to the field when you know what you are going to collect ahead of time. Of course, at the minimum, you can just carry the stalks in your arms with no buckets or bags. Collected here are the upper 2 feet of plants 3 to 5 feet tall.

the stem. The added girth of the petiole gives the illusion that the thick stem is even thicker than it is. Plants under 2 feet tall have the most edible material under the peel. Edible portions reducing in diameter as the plants grow taller. You can get productive amounts of edible stem material in plants up to about 5 feet.

My favorite way to harvest, other than peeling and eating stalks directly, is to use gallon-size water containers (plastic pitchers) inside 5-gallon buckets. The buckets have handles that make carrying all this plant matter much easier. The water containers both hold water and lessen tangling of the leaves. You can also use the containers to separate the stalks by thickness, if you want, for later processing. Multiple containers have the added advantage of providing receptacles for other plants you might find along the way. This system also reduces weight, since the water is only in the internal containers and does not fill the whole bucket. Of course, you can stuff all your stalks in one big 5-gallon bucket without the inserts, but I prefer multiple containers for the organization and gathering options they provide.

As the plants grow taller, up to about 5 feet, you want to gather just the upper three sections, roughly defined as the upper three petiole coverings. This also corresponds to just above the third visible node from the top. Although you can gather below that, the flavor and texture decline below that point. In fact, the most flavor and most tender texture can be found in the upper two segments. The third-lowest section is still good, but is less consistent in quality and harder to peel.

The best collecting is from rapidly growing upper stems of plants up to 4 feet tall. By the time the plant exceeds 5 feet, the stems are thinning out, branching, and fibering up, making them less beneficial to peel. Which translates to more work for less food. If you are in rough, very dry regions, only shorter plants will be as useful.

Harvest fennel stems by cutting them just above the third visible node. If you try to cut through the node, it will be tough, harder to peel later, and will be less likely to take up water, assuming you put the stems in water. The cut end will reveal its hollow stem. If you have big sharp scissors and you cannot cut through the stem easily, that is a sign that you are dealing with a stem that is too tough to eat. Gradually cut higher and higher up the stem until the scissors slices through without too much resistance. This assumes you do not have dull scissors.

Only the uppermost still-expanding leaves are tender enough to use, so discard all the lower, fully mature (full-size) leaves at the collection site.

Once they are harvested, you have different options with different parts of the stem and its uppermost leaves. Starting on the next page, refer to the first labeled photograph with letters A, B, C, etc., for the following explanation. The stem on the left is what I bring in from the wild; the one on the right has been peeled of all but the top petioles. The second labeled illustration on page 338 will have corresponding parts.

To collect the edible portions of a wild fennel stalk that is 5 feet or shorter, snip just above the third node down. This gives you about 20-plus inches of stem, assuming you have healthy, rapidly growing plants.

A. Pom-pom leaf blades are tender in the raw form. Remove and discard their petioles as they will be fibrous even at that young stage. Snack on the pom-poms while you are foraging or bring them home. When placing them in foods, you should strategically decide how a 4-inch leaf blade will behave. For instance, if you put whole pom-poms in a sandwich, each bite may drag the whole thing out, leaving it hanging out of your mouth. While this will be very entertaining to toddlers, it will be the opposite of romantic to that important date you are trying to impress with your wild food prowess. It might even pull out that

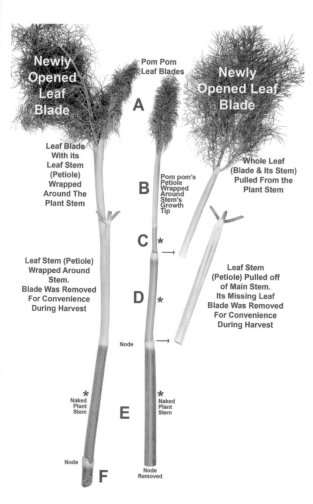

Newly Opened Leaf Blade

Pom Pom Leaf Blades

A

Newly Opened Leaf Blade

Leaf Blade With its Leaf Stem (Petiole) Wrapped Around The Plant Stem

Pom pom's Petiole Wrapped Around Stem's Growth Tip

B

Whole Leaf (Blade & Its Stem) Pulled From the Plant Stem

C *
→

Leaf Stem (Petiole) Wrapped Around Stem. Blade Was Removed For Convenience During Harvest

D *

Leaf Stem (Petiole) Pulled off of Main Stem. Its Missing Leaf Blade Was Removed For Convenience During Harvest

Node

→

* Naked Plant Stem

E

* Naked Plant Stem

Node

F

Node Removed

The edible parts of wild fennel stems, defined by location. Details are in the surrounding text.

tomato slice, which will end up on your lap.

The logical thing is to chop up the pom-poms into smaller pieces before adding them raw to things you are going to eat. This includes sandwiches as well as fruit and vegetable salads. Finely chop them if they are going into sauces, condiments, and spreads. The amount you add will depend on how much you enjoy the mild green licorice flavor.

Also in this illustration are the larger top leaf blades, former pom-poms that have expanded through growth. I call these *newly opened leaf blades*. They are arise just below the pom-poms on the stem. They are still young and expanding, about half the size they will be when fully mature. Leaves below this first expanded one will be older and less and less tender. Their quality will vary. From a chewability standpoint, only use the upper-most newly opened leaf blades, as shown in this illustration.

This uppermost newly opened leaf blade is not tender in its raw form, though if you chop it finely enough, you can sprinkle it in things for flavor. But the pom-poms are better for that. Even finely chopped first-blade leaflets will become annoying if you flood a food with them. At worst, it will be like chewing licorice-flavored clippings from a lawn mower. It's best to use the newly opened leaf blades as a cooked green. In fact, it is a great-tasting cooked green. Take a bunch of these leaf blades, roughly chop them into bite-size pieces, and boil them for 20 minutes. It takes that long to fully tenderize them. Then you can use them like cooked spinach. They will lose the fennel flavor in the process, but still taste like an excellent normal foundational cooked green. You can then use the excellent broth for soups or other purposes.

B. Below the pom-pom is the pom-pom's leaf stem, wrapped around the growth tip of the plant. That growth tip includes the next tiny pom-pom. That is all tender, edible raw, and can be used like green licorice–flavored celery. Just make sure the petiole wrapping around the growth tip has been removed.

C. The stem below the growth tip is also tender, edible raw, and can be used like green licorice–flavored celery.

D. This segment's skin is too fibrous to eat as is. Luckily, it is easily peeled like a banana. To peel it, stick your fingernail in the segment's end and pull down. That will remove the skin, leaving the tender, edible, and delicious core.

E. This segment is a little trickier to peel. As with Japanese knotweed, the fibers of the skin infiltrate the core somewhat, making peeling like a banana quite hit-and-miss. Sometimes it works like a charm, sometimes it is hopeless. Often, particularly with the taller stems, you likely have to peel this segment with a potato peeler. Examine these segments once peeled and do some snap tests to see if you removed all the fibers. Sometimes you cannot. Chopping this part into small pieces can mitigate any of the minor fibrousness that remains.

F. This segment below E is not worth pursuing. It is fibrous and the flavor is minimal.

The nodes that give rise to each leaf stem below C are typically too hard and tough to use in normal eating.

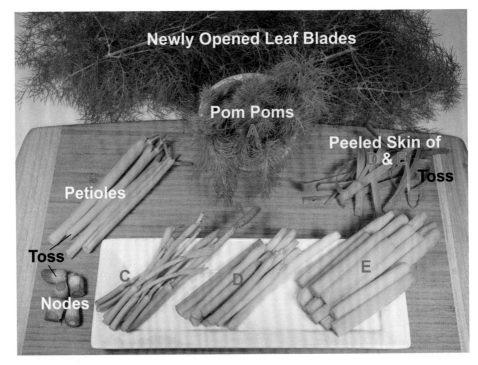

Newly Opened Leaf Blades

Pom Poms
A

Peeled Skin of
D & E

Toss

Petioles

Toss

Nodes

C

D

E

Here are edible parts of the wild fennel stem separated into peeled stems, pom-poms, and leaf blades. Also shown are parts to toss or compost. The letters correspond to the ones on page 336. **C** shows the growth tips revealed after peeling the petioles that were attached to the pom-poms at the tip of each plant. You can see that there are younger still developing pom-poms underneath. There are always new pom-poms growing to replace older pom-poms. Unpeeled **C** and the peeled **D** stem segments here are tender enough to eat as is. Peeled **E**'s have to be checked to make sure all the fiber on its outer surface has been removed.

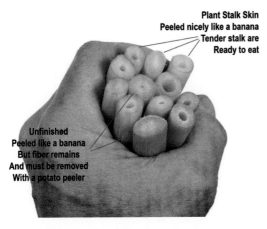

Plant Stalk Skin
Peeled nicely like a banana
Tender stalk are
Ready to eat

Unfinished
Peeled like a banana
But fiber remains
And must be removed
With a potato peeler

Peeled stems of segment **E**, showing how some skin fiber is difficult to remove. A potato peeler will be employed to finish the peeling process for some of these.

But you could probably juice or blend all of these parts, including the upper petioles and nodes, in a powerful machine.

All the edible parts have that marvelous green-licorice aroma and flavor. Long cooking and particularly boiling greatly reduce the licorice flavor, making wild fennel good as any conventional green. If you want to preserve the green-licorice flavor, do less cooking.

Fennel and Quinoa Salad

Makes 2 hearty servings

This is one of my favorite salads having a variety of flavors and textures. I mention alternative ingredients so you can do whatever is: less work, your preference, less expensive, or more available to you. Prepare quinoa and almonds before making the main recipe.

INGREDIENTS

1 cup cooked red or white quinoa

2 cups plus 2 tablespoons water

1 bouillon cube of choice

1 cup toasted or raw almond slivers

6 (4-inch) fennel pom-poms pulled into bite-size pieces (pictured), or chop them up for more even distribution

1 cup cherry tomatoes

1 (2-inch) section of a large cucumber, partially peeled to reduce some skin and cut into small quarters

$1/3$ cup thinly sliced shallot or red onion

$1/3$ cup sweetened dried cranberries or regular raisins

$1/2$ cup chopped and loosely packed fresh young lemon balm or mint leaves

Salt, to taste

Extra virgin olive oil, to taste

Fresh lemon juice, to taste

On the cutting board, there is a whole pom-pom on the left plus one pulled apart into six smaller pieces on the right. Whole pom-poms are too big for a single forkful of food. Smaller pieces work better in salads and sandwiches.

DIRECTIONS

Make the quinoa first.

1 cup dried quinoa makes about 3 cups cooked, which is more than you need for this recipe. I usually make the whole amount and use the additional 2 cups for other things, or just multiply the other ingredients in this recipe by three if I have six people I want to feed. To make the quinoa: Pour the quinoa, water, and bouillon into a 2-quart saucepan. Bring to a rapid boil, covered, over high heat. Let it boil for 1 minute. Turn off the heat and let rest while you prepare other ingredients. Once all the water is absorbed, reserve 1 cup of the finished quinoa for the recipe.

To toast the almonds, place in a large skillet over medium heat and stir or flip them regularly until golden brown. Don't let them burn by multitasking. Set aside until needed.

This salad is composed in layers so that the pom-poms don't cluster together. So into a mixing bowl, throw in a few pom-poms, some of the quinoa, and then add almonds.

Throw in a few more pom-poms with some more quinoa, and add the tomatoes.

Continue this layering in of pom-poms, adding the cucumber, shallot or onion, cranberries or raisins, and lemon balm or mint.

Using another mixing bowl, gently tumble all the ingredients from one bowl to the other until well mixed.

Add salt, olive oil, and lemon juice, and then tumble the salad again to evenly disperse these additions. Scoop into serving bowls and eat.

The flowers

In the marketplace of food, our fennel plant provides vegetative edible parts in the form of peeled stems and young developing leaves. From the reproductive perspective, it provides edible flowers, "pollen," and dry fruits. That pollen part is misleading, which I will get into soon.

Flower flavor intensity depends on finding them when their petals are at their brightest yellow color, and when the anthers are poking out above them. Anthers are what produce the pollen. They stick up above the flowers like

Peeled fennel stems, sliced for a salad. You could just as easily have added some chopped pom-poms.

Newly opened leaf blades of wild fennel, boiled for 20 minutes and drained. Eaten as greens along with some quinoa, cooked mushrooms, and roasted red sweet peppers. Served with salt, pepper, and olive oil. No recipe, I just threw this together.

Collected wild fennel flower stems in water. The only parts I'm interested in here are the flowers, since most of the other parts are too fibrous. Gathering them in these water pitchers keeps them fresh until use.

Martian antennas. Yes, real Martian antennas. It is a thing. Look it up.

Fennel flowers open over weeks. Each plant will have many umbels at different stages of flowering. Most of the flowers on an individual umbel will mature at the same time. But only a proportion of the umbels on a particular plant will be maturing at the same time. This allows you to come back several times to pick those umbels that are mature at each visit.

If your primary goal, like mine, is to gather the flowers at the peak of flavor, you should look for the bright yellow flower heads. Gather the flower heads by cutting about 10 inches down their support stem like you would long stem roses, and put them directly in water. Once you are home you can process them further.

While you could just gather the flower heads (umbels without their supporting stems) in the field, you will soon find that inefficient, time-consuming, and difficult to manage. So unless you are camping or hiking and want to add the flowers directly to your pancakes—bring the whole flower stalks home. Either use the flowers right away, or store the flower stems in the fridge, in the water containers, for use the next day. Any plants you have in water, in the fridge, should have a plastic bag over them to prevent them from drying out.

If you do not use them right away and leave them out in that water at room temperature, they will keep maturing and go past their prime. The petals will dry, shrivel, and fall off. The fridge slows development down a lot, which gives you a little more time. A day or two.

When you are examining flower status in the field, it pays to know where exactly they are in their developmental progression. As the flowers mature into seeds, flavors and texture change. Note that while my favorite flower flavor is when the reproductive parts are at the most attractive to pollinators (bright yellow petals with anthers out), your preference may be different from mine. In the comparison

BUDS FLOWERS FRUIT DEVELOPMENT MATURE DRY FRUIT

photograph, the sequence goes from the far left, representing the unopened buds, to the far right, where the mature fruits have dried. In the following descriptions, when I say "flavorful," that means having the greatest sweetness and floral licorice flavor.

The unopened buds are flavorful and quite useful as is, if that is all you have. They are not as flavorful as the opened flowers but still good. Again, the flowers are at their peak when the petals have expanded, and when the anthers have unraveled and are sticking up like antennas. The flavor is amazing. Once the flowers are pollinated, the petals and anthers (male parts) fall off gradually as the ovaries (female parts) start to enlarge. Ovary flavor is different from petal flavor. As seed development ensues, complex licorice flavors develop. Some bitterness and pungency blend with the licorice flavor as the ovaries fatten and turn into fruits.

If you like commercial fennel seed (see sidebar), you'll also enjoy wild dried sweet fennel fruits. And while the flavor is slightly different from the commercial, you can use them in the same ways.

Progression of wild fennel umbellettes, from flower buds to dried fruits containing seeds. Individual umbellettes have been separated out from their full umbels to show this developmental progression.

FENNEL FRUIT VERSUS SEED

The dried fruit of fennel it commonly mislabeled as fennel seed. That is how it is sold in the stores. What you see above are technically dried fennel fruits with seeds inside.

Fennel petals

When I first heard of fennel pollen, I thought, OK, I can figure out how to collect it, since I am familiar with when the plant is in flower. And I had seen pictures of what I thought were people brushing the pollen off the flower heads. I tried brushing the pollen off myself and made a

Brushing off fennel flower petals, stamens, and pollen. What is left behind on the umbellettes are the pistils and flower stems.

Close-up of brushed off fennel petals with lesser amounts of stamens and pollen. This is what is mistakenly called fennel pollen.

Cutting off the mini-umbels of fennel for use in different dishes.

discovery. What is called *fennel pollen* is actually mostly fennel flower petals with just a little pollen. Since the petals are so small and yellow, they have been passed off as pollen. I don't think this is malicious mislabeling; I think it just looked like pollen, so people called it that. Regardless of name, this is some delicious stuff.

The flavor of the petals at their prime is a fantastic feature of this plant. It is unique, powerful, sweet, and versatile. There are two ways to harvest them. You can use the brush-off or the snip-off method. The brush-off method involves using your hand to brush off the petals, stamens, and incidental pollen. This leaves the pistils (female parts that produce seeds) behind. Fennel petals are ready to use at this point.

The other method requires scissors and has you snipping off the umbellettes, which are then used whole to flavor things. If you include none of the main umbel stem, the umbellettes are quite tender. Since they carry all of the flavor of the flowers at their peak, they are great for flavoring dishes, adding to salads, and using as a garnish.

There are fennel "pollen" recipes on the internet for you to play with using the brushing technique I just mentioned, and you certainly can try those. The recipes in this chapter use the umbellettes and are fantastic as is. I have not seen recipes for umbellettes, labeled as such in any reference materials or on the internet. Both the petals or whole umbellettes give excellent results. You decide what you want to use as your flower ingredients.

John's Fennel Blossom Soup

Serves 4 to 6

I adapted this from a recipe by Jerry Traunfeld from his cookbook, *The Herbal Kitchen: Cooking with Fragrance and Flavor*, for use with wild sweet fennel stalks rather than store-bought fennel bulbs. Fennel stalks are fibrous, inedible, and don't benefit by peeling by the time the flowers are produced, so you will need to use previously frozen fennel stalks or buy fennel bulbs to make this soup.

INGREDIENTS

3 cups chopped wild fennel stalks, thawed from frozen, or fennel bulbs

2 cups sliced leek, tender white part only (about 1 large leek)

2 tablespoons extra virgin olive oil

4 cups vegetable broth

4 teaspoons finely chopped fresh fennel umbellettes in flower

Salt and pepper, to taste

Some umbellettes for garnish

DIRECTIONS

In a large saucepan, sauté the leeks in the olive oil until softened. Stir in the fennel stalks and cook for about 2 minutes, then add the broth. Turn down the heat and simmer, covered, for 30 minutes.

Stir in the chopped fennel umbellettes and season with salt and pepper. Immediately purée the soup in the pan using an immersion blender, or, working in batches, use a regular blender, being careful not to burn yourself.

Serve hot, or as a cold soup. Let's face it, it's good no matter what the temperature. Sprinkle on some fresh umbellettes as a garnish and enjoy.

Fennel Tzatziki (Greek Yogurt and Cucumber Sauce)

Makes 2 1/2 cups

This is a sauce usually made with dill, but it is even better with wild fennel. It is typically used as a dip for vegetables, like mayonnaise in sandwiches, or for flavoring meats, and its most famous use is in gyro food wraps. My version of this sauce can be used in the same ways.

INGREDIENTS

1/2 large cucumber, grated

1/2 tablespoon table salt

1 cup plain 1% milk fat Greek yogurt (it's thicker than regular yogurt and needs to be)

1/4 teaspoon kosher salt

2 tablespoons packed fresh fennel petals or umbellettes

1/4 cup sour cream

5 teaspoons lemon juice

1/2 tablespoon extra virgin olive oil

3/4 teaspoon minced garlic

Pinch of freshly ground black pepper

Extra umbellettes for garnish

DIRECTIONS

Place the grated cucumber in a colander over a bowl and sprinkle with the table salt to draw out its water. Let this sit in the fridge for 3 hours; then squeeze the excess liquid out of the cucumber with your hands.

In a mixing bowl, combine the cucumber with the yogurt, kosher salt, fennel, sour cream, lemon juice, olive oil, garlic, and pepper; stir well. Taste this and decide if you want to add more salt. Refrigerate for at least 2 hours before serving to allow the flavors to blend. Use chilled or at room temperature as a spread or sauce to improve foods. Garnish with fennel umbellettes.

Chapter 22

FAMILY: Apiaceae
SPECIES: *Daucus carota*

Wild Carrot

Wild carrot provides foods you can't get in a supermarket. It's not just for bunny rabbits.

Wild carrot in flower, showing clearly how abundant it is.

WILD CARROT

Wild carrot is one of the most abundant plants in North America. It is the source, or original heirloom, of the domesticated carrot. Wild carrot is an annual and a biennial. If the seed germinates in the spring, the plant can reach maturity in the same year, thus an annual. If it germinates late in the year, it will overwinter before producing flowers and new seed, thus a biennial. The key conditions needed for carrot to go to flower in the same year that it germinates are enough energy stored in the root, and enough nutrients and water in the soil to support stem and flower growth completion before the pollination season is over.

Estimated Range

Official Species Name:
• *Daucus carota* L.

Synonyms:
• none

Common Names:
• Wild carrot
• Bird's nest
• Queen Anne's lace

Herbaceous weed naturalized from Europe. Widespread and abundant in North America, primarily where humans have invaded and where soil has been disturbed and abandoned.

Edible Parts:
• Core of immature stem
• Growing tips of leafy stems
• Baby leaves
• Buds
• Flowers
• Root

The wild carrot and domesticated carrot share the same scientific species name, *Daucus carota*. More specifically, wild carrot is *Daucus carota* subsp. (subspecies) *carota*, and domesticated carrot is *Daucus carota* subsp. *sativus*. While these plants share some recognizable features, they are not the same. The wild carrot root differs from the domesticated carrot in three important ways. First, the wild carrot root is off-white or cream colored, not orange. Second, the wild carrot root tends to be tough and fibrous, not crispy. Third, the root size of the wild carrot ranges from $1/10$ to $1/2$ (under perfect growing conditions) of the size of the average domesticated carrot. Wild carrot is what existed before farmers, over the centuries, selected for size, color, and texture that brought us the modern carrot.

The biggest concern about harvesting and eating wild carrot at the young basal rosette or carrot-top stage is that, to the unknowing, it resembles poison hemlock (*Conium maculatum*), the second-most poisonous plant in North America. Anyone ignorant of the differences should not eat wild carrot, since a mistake could be deadly. I emphasize here that I have never heard of a case of poisoning of someone who knows the two can be mistaken for each other. They are too scared to guess and should be. There should be no guessing here.

The differences between young wild carrot and young poison hemlock are so clear and obvious that, once known, the identifier can have great confidence knowing which is which. Of course, sloppiness, poor judgment, haste, enthusiasm, and inattention to detail can lead to errors. In this chapter, I'll attempt to make those differences absolutely clear. It will be up to you to study those differences enough to have clarity.

Nutrient Values of Wild Carrot

The historical literature almost always focuses on and writes about domesticated carrots. So most of the information, including nutrient analysis, is on domesticated, not wild carrot. The strong orange color is a result of centuries of selection and crossbreeding by farmers. That color is caused by high amounts of beta-carotene, a precursor of vitamin A. Since wild carrot is off-white, it is clear that nutrient values should not be used interchangeably for the two. According to one study (Baranski, 2011), orange domesticated carrots have 30 times the carotenoids of white domesticated carrots. Wild carrots are likely more like the white domesticated carrots (yes, these exist) when it comes to beta-carotene. Unfortunately, some of the wild food lay literature uses the domesticated values for orange carrots to represent the wild ones. So wild carrot nutrient values are typically wrong when people report them.

I have not used carrot seed as a food or spice. Domesticated carrot seeds have been used as a morning-after contraceptive, an aphrodisiac, and for many other medicinal uses (Duke, 1985). The efficacy and safety of all these uses for humans is out of my expertise, but it is enough for me to leave these raspy covered seeds alone.

Knowing Wild Carrot

Seedlings of carrot are quite different than most you will come across. The cotyledons (first two leaflike structures) that emerge from the seed are tiny and thin. The first true leaf is quite dissected into irregular parts. It is reminiscent

Wild carrot seedlings. Tiny seedling (lower left), has two tiny, just emerging cotyledons. Seedling with emerging leaves (center), at about 1 inch tall. It has two older, longer cotyledons and two leaves. A dry fruit containing seeds is at lower right.

Below: Clusters of wild carrot plants growing amongst dandelions, clover, and sow thistle in an open field.

of poppy seedlings. Each leaf that follows is a more and more complex leaf of many dissected leaflets.

As the leaves grow larger and longer, many more leaflets emerge along the main leaf stems. Leaf-stem hairs become apparent as early as the first or second leaves. Leaf stems range in color from fully green to some with red. If there is red, it tends to concentrate at leaf bases, giving over to green around where the leaflets emerge. When red is apparent, it is not spotted or irregular, it is a smooth gradation.

You can find wild carrot as individual plants, or as clusters in open fields. Since carrot produces many dry spiky fruits per flower head, those fruits drop in great quantities, so many plants can develop.

Above left: Young, 7-inch-tall wild carrot plant, showing hairs and leaflets on six developing leaves. Many carrots have no red at all, but this one is starkly red at the leaf bases. Above right: A carrot spreading out more than growing upright, due to growing conditions. These are both at the "carrot-top" stage, more generally referred to as a basal rosette of leaves.

Once there is enough energy in the roots and the spring gets warmer, carrots bolt—that is, they send up a relatively straight stalk. Like the leaf stems, this plant stalk has hairs and may or may not have some reddishness. If reddishness exists, it is smooth and not spotted or irregular. Once these stems reach 12 to 18 inches tall, branches begin emerging from the nodes where the older leaves meet the stem.

Branches begin to emerge and elongate right around the time that some flower buds begin to

Right: A 14-inch-tall wild carrot stalk prior to branching. The stalk is covered with hairs and has some red coloration. Leaves arise from nodes with new branches just forming in their leaf axils.

Below: Wild carrot leaf variation. The top three elongated leaves are more typical of young plants and the lower parts of flowering carrot plants. The bottom three triangular leaves are more typical of the upper parts of mature plants. The leaflets on the upper left leaf look the most like poison hemlock. Poison hemlock, however, has a more triangular leaf.

Right: A more than 3-foot-tall wild carrot plant with flowers at various stages of maturity. Leaves are smaller at upper parts of the plant and contain fewer leaflets than the mature older leaves below.

Wild carrot flower head development. Above left: Early umbel development, starting with bracts wrapped around the many emerging flower buds, to the first opening of the concave early flower head. Pink highlights are not unusual in the pre-flowering buds. Above right: Fully mature either flat or convex flower head. Flower petals fall off as the ovaries are pollinated, again creating a concave, less white head. As seeds mature, the head curls up, creating that "bird's nest" look. Note that all six of these stems have hairs and all the flower heads (umbels) are cradled underneath by a set of elaborate bracts.

develop. Various stages of flower development occur simultaneously on the same plant. Older parts of the plant can have fully mature flowers while younger parts of the plant are still in bud. Upper leaves often are smaller, with fewer leaflets.

The carrot flower is not just a flower, it is gobs of flowers united in one big flower head. The shape of the head of the flowers as they are arranged here is called an umbel. What makes it an umbel is that all the flower stems arise from one spot and radiate upward and outward like spokes. And, furthermore, the carrot flower is a compound umbel, since at the tip of each flower stem is another mini-umbel or umbellette, leading to each individual flower within the head.

There are two unique characteristics of carrot umbels. Most important are the bracts that cradle the flower head. All flower heads I know of have bracts, but these are as distinctive as you can get. They explode outward at the base of the head before the flowers emerge, and they persist below the head through all its stages. The bracts are narrow modified leaves that branch into three parts; then the center branch branches again into three. For comparison, poison hemlock has tiny triangular scalelike bracts.

Another unique feature can be found on most but not all carrot flower heads is a single dark purple flower in the center of all the creamy-white flowers. It may appear black from a distance and, as tiny as it is, has

Above: A wild carrot's flower head is called an umbel. More specifically, it is a compound umbel due to the umbellette at the tip of each of the umbel's spokes. Each umbellette supports a bunch of tiny individual flowers. This wild carrot flower head displays a common single dark flower in the center. A darker central flower is on many but not all carrot umbels.

Above: Close-up of a dark purple wild carrot flower in the center of a flower head. It is about ⅛ inch in diameter. Regular white flowers surround it.

more flamboyant petals than the white flowers. The powers that be have theorized that the contrast of that one flower within all the white provides a decoy for local flies. As they zoom by, they glance down onto the flower and imagine they are seeing one of their friends doing something fun. They don't want to miss the party so they land to join the festivities. In doing so, they help to pollinate the carrot's flowers.

Pollinated wild carrot flowers lose their white petals and the flower head begins to transform. The outer umbel stems increase in length and curve upward and inward. As fruit maturation develops, the seed head takes on the appearance of a bird's nest, and many botanists call it that.

These dry fruits are light brown and covered with many raspy spines. This structure is more likely to attach to some passing animal than a spineless fruit. This helps spread the tiny seeds that are inside.

A close-up of an umbellette supporting mature wild carrot fruits. These are ready to fall off or attach to passing animals.

Poison Hemlock Complicates Life

Poison hemlock has killed many people over the ages—mostly because it is mistaken for wild carrot. The look and the flavors of wild carrot and poison hemlock, *when young*, are similar enough to fool, then kill, the unknowing. So become a knower. Poison hemlock is covered for important side-by-side comparisons in this chapter, and later as a stand-alone chapter in the Poisonous Plants section.

I affectionately refer to people not seriously studying wild foods as *civilians*, versus those of us in the trenches who are buying books, researching, and investigating the potential of edible wild plants. We know the importance of detail. The devil and the angels are in the detail. Civilians are people who don't take classes, do research, or study books on wild foods. Some might own books because they see themselves as outdoorsy, but never look at them. Many have preconceived notions and impressions of how the plant world works. Historically, most poisonings from poison hemlock happen to civilians.

Leaf Blade Comparison

WILD CARROT LEAF BLADES

Standard shape of leaf blade: long, like a spear head. Consider all the leaflets together as the blade. While this is the standard shape, carrot has a lot of variation so some leaves might be more triangular.

POISON HEMLOCK LEAF BLADES

Standard shape of leaf blade: triangular. Leaflet stems are often long. Poison hemlock leaves do not vary much from this overall triangular leaf blade shape

Although it is good to know their differences throughout the life spans of carrot and hemlock, it is vitally important to know the differences while these plants are in the carrot-top stage. Once stalks and flowers develop, these plants are much easier to distinguish, making them less of a risk. Most people who do not know what they are doing are even more clueless about the adult plants since neither looks like the carrot-top stage of carrot. Since these are ignored, there is less chance of poisoning from an adult plant.

Young plants with carrot-like tops are the problem stage. If you walk up and see a bunch of feathery leaves sticking out of the ground that look like carrot tops, slow down, curb your enthusiasm, and put on your thinking cap. You have some work to do to keep yourself safe. You have to positively determine what plant you have in front of you. No guessing, no assuming, you must be confident in your identification.

CARROT-TOP STAGE

The carrot-top stage is what you see when you go to the supermarket to buy a bunch of carrots, and the leafy tops are still attached. In the wild this is known as a basal rosette of leaves. You see aboveground leaves radiating out from their hidden root below. At this stage, no flower stalk has formed yet. This stage is illustrated by the photos at the bottom of pages 350 (carrot) and 377 (hemlock).

Leaf Stem Comparison

WILD CARROT

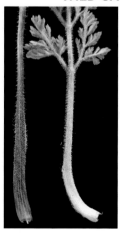

Wild carrot leaf stems are hairy. The hair is sometimes sparse and sometimes dense. Examine plants carefully from top to bottom if you don't see it at first. Leaf stem color: Mostly green or greenish yellow. When red is present, it is smooth and regular, not in spots. Odor of cut stem is a mild, typical green-plant smell, not strong like the carrot root.

POISON HEMLOCK

Poison hemlock leaf stems have no hair. Leaf stem color: Mostly green. When red is present, it is spotty and uneven. Look closely as those speckles of color can range from strong (left) to barely visible (right). Cut leaf stem odor is unusual and even unpleasantly fetid for most people. Just interesting and different for others, but not a typical 'green' aroma. For less than 10 percent, the smell is unbearable. Leaves and stems do not smell like carrot root.

Here is how a poisoning might occur

A civilian thinks they see carrot growing in the wild from the familiar-looking leafy tops. They've never investigated wild carrot before, but think they recognize it. Excited to find some free food and proud of themselves for recognizing it, they dig it up and smell the root. The root is not orange, but has a sweet carrot-family aroma and pleasant flavor. This is just enough information to make them feel confident in their identification. The lack of orange color (the root is off-white) does not deter them, since the sweet aroma has already intrigued them. Besides, they've already convinced themselves they've found a wild treasure. They take it home or to their campsite, cook it up, usually with other things, and happily eat the root. Most people die within hours after that.

The comparison photographs beginning on page 354 do not cover all the possible variations of each plant that you might come across. Use these comparisons as a point of reference, a starting point to examine many plants until you are confident you can get past the natural variation that exists. Never eat carrot until you are 100 percent sure you can identify it, and you

Leaflet Comparison — These are just the upper parts of larger leaves

WILD CARROT

Wild carrot leaflets can vary a lot. Their tips often look like the claws on long paws of a wolf and are generally pointed. Carrot leaves can be hairy, particularly along the underside of the main veins (not shown here). Leaflets are spread out with more gaps or space separating them than the hemlock.

POISON HEMLOCK

Poison hemlock leaflets near their tips together look like miniature trees arranged on larger trees. The tips of the leaflets are rounded. There are no hairs.

Carrot can sometimes look more like this hemlock, but the hemlock will not look like the leaflets to the left.

are 100 percent sure it is not poison hemlock. Never use just one character to make your determination. Any plant you are identifying should have at least three of the distinguishing characters shown here.

Covered here are some of the observable differences between young wild carrot and young poison hemlock, at stages when they might be confused with each other. You should know these differences like the back of your hand. And if that is hard for you, study the back of your hand more. An overview of poison hemlock is covered in its own chapter in the Poisonous Plants section. The umbels of both plants are compared here too since you might want to use carrot flowers of the mature plants for food.

Further complicating and confusing for the public is the local/regional name people use to refer to these plants. In one part of North America, Queen Anne's lace can refer to wild carrot, and in another, it can refer to poison hemlock. For this reason, I tell people to only use the common names wild carrot and poison hemlock and to never use the name Queen Anne's lace. This name confusion can lead to misunderstandings and poisonings. Queen Anne's lace is the name that should not be spoken.

Root Comparison — These are more similar than they are different

WILD CARROT ROOT

A taproot that may branch in rocky soil. Color: Off-white, not orange. Texture is often tough and fibrous, sometimes with a woody core. Aroma: Very sweet, clear, distinct carrot aroma and flavor.

POISON HEMLOCK ROOT

Taproot that may branch in rocky soil. Color: Off-white, not orange. Texture is relatively tender to cut and chew. (Don't chew it!) Aroma: Sweet, interesting, and pleasant for most people. Not exactly carrot, but has something familiar about it. Carrot "family" aroma. For roughly 10 percent of humans, it is an unbearably bad aroma. Flavor is mild, sweet, mostly pleasant with carrot-family–like tones, but not carrot. This pleasant flavor is what fools people into imagining/assuming the hemlock root is a carrot, then they die.

This name confusion all began possibly because there was once this person named Queen Anne who apparently was known for her lacy things. And for some reason people liked naming plants after her. So if you don't know a plant, and it has what you see as lacy leaves or flowers, you call it Queen Anne's lace. Sometimes that made-up name sticks with the local culture. My point is, know the plant you are referring to when in a discussions about edibility. And only refer to the common names such as wild carrot and poison hemlock, which are the names that should be spoken.

So why eat wild carrot at all? Here is a clear and strong answer: **If you are not willing to take the time to learn the differences between the two plants, I say never eat wild carrot—since you are likely to poison yourself.** However, the differences are significant and easily recognizable. As with all wild foods, you need to learn what you are doing. Only eat plants that you have positively identified and know to be edible. **Never guess.** Once you get it, once you are confident of your identification, there is no reason not to eat wild carrot if you find it desirable. But always keep vigilant about not being sloppy yourself. If you are leading novices, monitor carefully what they gather.

Umbel (Flower Head) Comparison

WILD CARROT

Wild carrot flower head, showing the intricate long branching bracts that emerge below the umbel. These unique bracts are the single most important identifier of adult carrot plants. Carrot umbels in flower are typically flat or slightly rounded.

POISON HEMLOCK

Poison hemlock flower head, showing the tiny scalelike bracts that emerge below the umbel. Poison hemlock umbels are typically more rounded, more numerous, and smaller than carrot.

Wild Carrot Gathering and Edibility

Leaves

Prior to gathering, verify that all leaf stems smell good and have hairs on them. Carrot tops of basal rosettes can provide harvestable leaves. If they are lush in growth, the youngest leaves can provide some greenery to eat. They are too tough to bother with unless you get them at a rapid growth spurt. Even small leaves can be tough. So choose carefully.

The best leaves are gathered from the upper parts of rapidly growing stalks. My guess is that growth is faster on a stalk so there is less fibering up of the top leaves. The best stage for more tender leaves is from the upper stem of a 6- to 14-inch tall plant. You can gather both the stem and upper leaves at this stage.

As with all fresh greens, place gathered parts into bags and spray-mist them until ready to use.

If you have recipes for domesticated carrot tops, you can try them with wild ones. However, most recipes will fail if you assume carrot leaves are like other greens. To use them fresh, squeegee the leaflets away from the leaf stem, removing as much of the leaf stem as possible. Finely chop the leaflets you removed—very finely. Keep chopping. Finely chopping tough leaflets renders them pre-chewed, so when they are added to things, you don't sense the fibrousness. Then you can

Above: Here is a peeled (except for the very top) stem adjacent to the kinds of leaves you would find along that stem. Leaves are younger and smaller near the top of the stem while older and larger near the base of the stem. The upper rapidly growing leaves are more desirable than the tough older leaves.

Right: Young wild carrot leaves from the tips of rapidly growing stemmed plants, prior to flower buds forming. These are often more tender than the carrot-top leaves you find on ground level plants.

judiciously add them to soups, salads, and sandwiches, or use them as a colorful green garnish. They have a nice fresh flavor, reminiscent of parsley. They likely work in smoothies, and I have seen some recipes for pesto. Toss the tough leaf stems.

Ignore this chopping thing at your own peril. Rabbits don't mind the chew, but you will. If you want to experiment, be my guest. That is where the fun is. While I have not tried it, young still-forming carrot leaves might work as a cooked green if, like fennel, you boil them for 20 to 25 minutes. Let me know how that goes. Shorter times don't seem to do it for me.

Any recipes, like one for pesto that uses a blender to shred the leaflets, will work, because you have bypassed the fiber issue. This assumes that the leaves don't jam your blender.

Wild carrot roots

Only the carrot-top stage at its prime provides a conditionally chewable raw root, so that is when you dig. Once the plant is ready to send up a flower stalk, the root becomes woody and unusable. Dig carrot roots as you would any root. Don't just pull or they will snap, you will only get part of it, and will have a dirtied broken end. Dig around the root, not into it. A long, narrow crowbar or equivalent can also work. Jam the bar deep into the earth facing one side of the plant, and pry it up. If you are in hard ground, break that ground all the way around before you pry the root up from one side. The root can be up to 9 inches long if you are lucky, so it is better to go too deep than too shallow.

Wild carrot roots are of fresh eating quality during the carrot-top stage, from germination through overwintering, and in early spring. They are as good as domesticated carrots in flavor, but more chewy, and, of course, a beautiful creamy white instead of orange. As they begin to send up a stalk (bolt), they get chewier, so there is a transition time when you have to chop them across the grain to reduce the perception of toughness. After a while, they get so tough, it's like chewing on a tree branch.

If you've ever bought older domesticated carrots, you will find that they begin to separate into a core and an outer rind. Both are chewable unless the carrot is really old. In the wild version, that core goes from tough to woody once the plant is preparing to bolt.

As the root prepares to bolt, it sends out tough lateral branches. These branches both improve the plant's ability to bring in soil nutrients and also provide a more stable base from which to support the soon-to-be-growing stem. Just seeing root branches is an indication that the root is transforming. If you see a developing stem and lots of root branches, then you are too late to use the whole root.

The carrot rind remains chewable through most of its early life and even once the core begins hardening. So even if you find a wild carrot a little late, you can often salvage the rind for use. Once the plant sends up a stalk, it is time to wistfully reminisce about any potential the root might have had as food.

Chopping carrot root into small pieces, across the grain, allows you to snack on it fresh and use it in salads, soups, and other applications that are appropriate for carrot. As you chop, put it immediately into ice water to slow browning and keep it fresh. Add a pinch of sugar to amp its sweetness. Then throw it into almost anything you are eating.

Boiling the roots for 5 minutes softens them up quite a bit, but can only do so much for developing fibrousness. They are great boiled and steamed.

An older wild carrot root, separated into its peeled outer rind (left) and woody core (right). The greater the number of side branching roots you see, the more woody the core will be.

Chopping young wild carrot roots to minimize any mild fibrousness. Try thin slices across the grain. Place in cold or ice water to reduce browning and crisp them for use.

Wild Carrot Root and Almond Butter Hummus

Makes about 1 1/2 cups

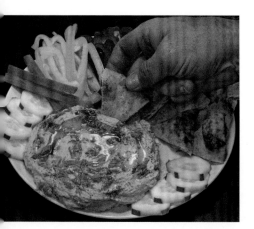

INGREDIENTS

Water, for steaming

1 1/2 cups finely chopped wild carrot roots

1/4 cup creamy almond butter

1/4 cup plus 1 tablespoon fresh lemon juice
(1 large lemon)

2 cloves garlic, minced

4 tablespoons extra virgin olive oil, plus more
for serving

3/4 teaspoon ground cumin

A pinch of salt

Chopped young wild carrot leaf tips, for garnish

Ground paprika, for garnish

DIRECTIONS

Steam the chopped carrot roots for 15 minutes and then drain, but save 1/4 cup of the cooking water; set carrots and water aside.

Mix the almond butter, 1/8 cup of the cooking water, and lemon juice in a food processor for 1 minute or until well blended. Add the garlic, olive oil, cumin, and salt and process for 30 seconds. Use a spatula to push the side splatter back in the processor bowl, and process for 30 seconds more.

Add in 1/2 cup of cooked carrots at a time to the food processor, thoroughly processing until smooth between additions. It takes about 2 minutes to completely incorporate all of the carrots.

Gradually add the remaining 1/8 cup cooking water to the hummus to smooth it out and attain the proper consistency: Dribble the water into the processor until the consistency is perfect for you. I like it thick, so I don't add all of the water. Taste and add more salt if needed.

Serve with a garnish of wild carrot leaf tips, paprika, and a drizzle of olive oil.

The peeled wild carrot stem

At the right stage of growth, the straight, rapidly growing carrot stem, prior to branching, budding, and flowering, provides one of the best fresh green foods of the wild carrot.

One problem with finding these is that at this stage of growth, they are often mixed in with a lot of other tall, open-field greenery and grasses growing at about the same height. You could walk right over one and not know it.

The other problem is that the edible stem season is very short. The stems all bolt around the same time, due to the same environmental and soil triggers. They grow fast in their quest to get past this prime eating stage to develop flowers and reproduce. You only have a couple of weeks to harvest them within any particular region. By the time they begin branching and flowering, when they are easy to spot, it is often too late. The desired part, the inner stem, gets too tough to chew. All that branching and flower development requires a sturdy stem to hold up all that weight. Fiber is sturdy and stiff, but not fun to chew.

For snacking in the field or for use in meals, you want to gather stems that are 5 to 14 inches tall and have grown under good, moist growing conditions. If you have lots to choose from, gather thick, straight stems with little zigzag. Thicker stems mean more food for less peeling (less work). Cut the stem near the ground. Leave the root at this stage, it is no longer a food, unless you just want a hit from its smell. Taking the root just adds the annoyance of dirt to your gather, which will need to be cleaned later. So leave it to feed the worms.

When gathering, keep these stems moist and protected from the sun. Better yet, put them in water to keep them fresh and crisp. Otherwise, they will wilt. If you are not going to use them right away, put them in water, covered with a plastic bag, and into the fridge to stop them from growing. Don't leave them in water at room temperature for a few days. Doing so allows them to continue to grow

Preflowering wild carrot stalks with their tough lower leaves removed. Ready for peeling. Notice all the young, underdeveloped leaves at the tips of the stems. These are the most tender leaves you will find on wild carrot.

Peeling a wild carrot stem with a knife.

in a bad way—that is, they will transfer whatever energy they can draw from the tender core into new upper growth in a futile attempt to go to flower. The stems will thin out and toughen, reducing their quality.

Prior to peeling, verify that all stems smell good and have hairs on them. Peel them at their cut point by either inserting your fingernail or a knife anywhere in the end and pulling the rind away. This should be a fairly easy process. Once all the leaves and rind are removed, place the peeled stems right into water to keep them crisp and green until you are ready to use them. Bruised areas will brown slightly. They will curl in water because long fibers on one side are slightly more formed than on the other side. Those fibers should be tender enough to chew if the plants you chose were at the proper stage of growth and you got all the rind off. Stiff areas of the peeled stem should be discarded. Some stems are more difficult to peel than others. You'll see with practice.

Left: Peeled wild carrot stems in water. The thickest ones here are about ⅜ inch in diameter. This vase is about 12 inches tall and is stored in the fridge until the stems are ready to use. They are good for about 3 days in the fridge.

Below: Peeled wild carrot stems in a salad with wild sweet fennel flowers. The smallest stems here are about ⅛ inch in diameter. They are derived from new, rapidly growing upper branching of older plants. That is why they are so thin.

Once peeled, these stems range from $^1/_8$ to $^1/_2$ inch in diameter, depending on how thick the original stem was. They are ready to eat, sweet, and mild-tasting. Snack on them, cut them into salads, and use any way you would use celery. Their tenderness goes way beyond celery.

Wild carrot buds and flowers

These are the most useful (practical, easy to use, abundant, full of uses) parts in the wild carrot's life span. From the early buds to full flowering, you have gobs of gathering options over a long period of time—months, actually. Whole plants are super easy to spot and to tell apart from other plants, including poison hemlock; easy to gather; and make a great floral arrangement until you are ready to use them. They are more likely to become a regular seasonal part of your diet than any other parts of this plant. (At least, they are more regular in mine.)

The young flower head buds of various sizes make a great vegetable to be added directly to salads or soups, and are good in the same ways you would use sprigs of broccoli, fresh or cooked. They are best mixed in with other foods and are dryer than broccoli in the raw form. They can be gathered in bags and spray-misted to keep them moist. Just pull them off the stem. They should snap cleanly from the tender stem material they arise from.

Wild carrot flower head buds, surrounded by bracts. Great added to salads or cooked like broccoli.

When you are harvesting more mature flower parts it is best to include, at least initially, enough stem material to put them in a vase of water, as you would regular flowers, or in a pitcher of water, depending on how many flower stalks you plan on gathering. This keeps them fresh and makes them easier to process. Wilted plant parts left to dry are more difficult to manage. See the fennel chapter for an example of wild flowers in water.

Wild carrot flowers, once fully open, are creamy-white. When harvesting, chose the whitest, freshest, most full flower heads you can find. If they are slightly brown or have fewer petals (are not looking real full), then they

Trimming the usable, small umbellettes off the larger unusable umbel bases. Once trimmed, they can be used for a variety of purposes.

FLOWERS CAN BE POWERFUL FOR SOME PEOPLE

Several chapters have mentioned eating flowers in quantity. Start slow. Just because your author can eat lots does not mean you can. Start out eating small amounts and pay attention to your body. Eat more if your body says you can.

have already been pollinated and will not carry as much flavor. It does not matter if the single purple flower is present or not. The first flowering blossoms of spring are the most flavorful. Later in the flowering season, their flavor wanes a bit but is still worthy.

Raw wild carrot flowers can be sharp, peppery, pungent, and mildly bitter. Alone they are more like a spice than a vegetable. There is a definite underlying carrot-family flavor. Eating the flowers dry, by themselves, leaves an itch in the back of my throat. They make a great fresh tea, which is even better to me with a little honey in it.

None of carrot's flowering stages are moist in their mouthfeel. The upshot is that when you add whole or cut-up buds to other foods that have moisture, they work great. The young flower heads have a fine, mildly spicy flavor.

Your goal is to trim the tiny upper umbellettes off of the larger umbel supporting them. These tiny umbellettes are where all the potential is. Occasionally spray-mist them so they don't dry out for fresh uses. Put them in a food dryer to use as a delicate spice, or add them to the flour of baked products for added flavor and nutrition. If you dry them, put them in sealed containers in a cool dark place to preserve their flavor. Use a food dryer at 95°F for a few hours. Vacuum-sealing the dried umbellettes in canning jars is the best way to preserve them for years.

Fresh uses include adding them to salads, sandwiches, soups, baked goods, and wherever your imagination takes you. You can even make jelly out of them.

Wild Carrot Flower Pancakes

Makes about 12 (4-inch) pancakes

Carrot flowers add a wonderful flavor to pancake batter. The flowers should retain the tiny umbels that support them, resulting in adding some lightness and structure to the finished pancakes. In preparing the batter, there is a fine balance between thick undercooked-in-the-center pancakes and overcooked thin pancakes. The pancakes should be just thick enough to cook through. Practice makes perfect with flower pancakes. Try these plain without syrup first. Eat slowly and taste every bite.

INGREDIENTS

1 cup all-purpose flour
3 tablespoons packed brown sugar
1 $^1/_2$ teaspoons baking powder
$^1/_2$ teaspoon salt
2 large eggs
$^1/_4$ cup vegetable oil
$^1/_2$ tablespoon vanilla extract
$^1/_2$ teaspoon rum extract
1 cup skim milk
1 cup firmly packed wild carrot flowers
Powdered sugar, optional

DIRECTIONS

Preheat a griddle or pan to 350°F.

In a large bowl, combine the flour, brown sugar, baking powder, and salt and mix until well blended; set aside.

In a separate bowl, beat the eggs until the yolks and whites are well blended. Add in the oil, extracts, and milk, and mix well.

Stirring gently, gradually add the liquid to the flour mixture. Don't over stir—small lumps and bits of raw flour are fine.

Loosen the flowers and gently fold them into the batter. Let the batter rest for 3 minutes.

Cook the pancakes on a well-oiled griddle or pan. DO NOT press them flat after flipping them. Who presses pancakes flat? Serve with a dusting of powdered sugar if desired.

Wild carrot flower pancakes using wild carrot flower jelly in place of syrup.

Wild Carrot Flower Jelly

Makes about 8 (6-ounce) jars

This recipe takes a lot of flower heads—over 100. But they are typically so abundant that numbers are not an issue. Clipping the tops is fun and goes by quickly. For this recipe you want to clip almost up to the flowers, removing most of the umbellette stem material. This is a tighter clipping than all the other recipes in this chapter. Don't be confused by the initial amber-brown color of the cooking liquid. By the time you add the sugar and Sure-Jell it will be a beautiful salmon color. Don't use regular Sure-Jell for this recipe; it has less pectin, so you would end up with syrup rather than jelly. (Of course, you might want syrup.) This recipe is adapted from Janet Holmes's Queen Anne's Lace Jelly recipe (Norris, 1991).

As stated before, I do not like to perpetuate the use of the name Queen Anne's Lace, so I've changed the name in my version of the recipe.

INGREDIENTS

2 cups firmly packed wild carrot flowers (measured after snipping off almost all of the supporting umbellette stems)

5 cups boiling water

3 1/2 cups granulated sugar, divided

1 package Sure-Jell fruit pectin (use the no-sugar-needed version)

4 1/2 tablespoons fresh lemon juice

DIRECTIONS

Sterilize and prepare 8 (6-ounce) jars and lids.

Place the flowers in a large bowl and cover with the boiling water. Stir to make sure all of the flowers are mixed well in the water. Cover the bowl and allow to steep for 15 minutes; then pour the mixture through a fine strainer, reserving the flower tea. Discard the used flower solids.

Pour 4 1/2 cups of the tea into a large stainless-steel pot.

Mix 1/4 cup sugar with the Sure-Jell then stir into the flower tea. Over high heat, stir until it comes to a full rolling boil. Then stir in the remaining sugar and return to a full boil for exactly 1 minute. You can either skim the foam off or leave it in. I leave mine in.

Remove the pot from the heat. Stir in the lemon juice. Then carefully pour the liquid into sterilized canning jars. If you need canning lessons, do some homework. There are tutorials available online. If you can keep yourself from eating this all in a few weeks, the jelly should last for years in the sealed jars.

Hearty version of John's Wild Carrot Blossom Soup on left; puréed version on right.

John's Wild Carrot Blossom Soup

Serves 4 to 6

This soup has a delicious, subtle, rich, savory flavor. It is good served hot or cold. You can serve it as a hearty soup where you feel the chew of the umbellettes, or blend it into a purée, which is most pleasing and could be served in the finest restaurants.

INGREDIENTS

3 cups chicken or vegetable broth

1 cup water

2 cups fresh, finely chopped wild carrot flower umbellettes

2 cups sliced leek, white and green tender parts only (about 1 large leek)

3 cups chopped celery, including the leafy parts

2 tablespoons extra virgin olive oil

Salt and pepper, to taste

Fresh lemon wedges, for serving

DIRECTIONS

In a 2-quart pot over medium-high heat, bring the broth and water to a boil. Add the carrot flower umbellettes, turn down to simmer, and cover.

In a skillet, sauté the leek and celery in the olive oil until the celery softens and the leek just begins to brown. Pour the leek mixture into the flower broth, turn up the heat, and bring to a boil; then reduce the heat, cover, and simmer for 30 minutes.

Serve as is or, even better, purée in a blender. Caution, hot stuff can explode out of the top of a blender, so do this carefully in two batches with a tightly closed lid. Or use an immersion blender and purée right in the pot. Serve the soup hot or cold

Poisonous Plants

You will not find whole sections of poisonous plants in this book, the reason being that if you know the edible species well, you don't need to know the poisonous ones, with some exceptions like poison hemlock, poison ivy, and poison oak. Some will be covered in future volumes. That is because random plants do not leap into your mouth, forcing you to swallow them: you have to actively choose to eat them. And you should not be grazing, aimlessly sampling whatever unknown plant you find. If a plant is easily confused with another, I prefer to show direct side-by-side comparisons within the edible plant chapters, rather than have whole chapters devoted to poisonous plants.

A poisonous plant compared to chickweed in volume 1 of this book series is scarlet pimpernel (*Anagallis arvensis*). Pokeweed, covered in this book, is poisonous in the raw form but certain parts become edible and wholesome once properly boiled. That is why it is not in this section. This section only covers plants that cannot be made edible no matter what processing you apply to it.

Poison hemlock is important to detail for a couple of reasons. First, for the person who knows nothing about it, young poison hemlock is easily confused with young carrot (wild or domesticated). Second, those who learn it well here can help guide others who may be curious or confused about what they are seeing in their own neighborhood or region. If more of the general public gets wind of poison hemlock, the more likely they are to refrain from eating a plant they don't really know.

And why would anyone eat a plant on a guess? Eat a plant they just *imagine* they know is edible? Finding free food accidentally is such a bonus that many people cannot help themselves. It is like finding a $50 bill on the sidewalk—they cannot pass it up. And since many poisonous plants like hemlock taste great, flavor only encourages them. Then they die. So learn your edible plants well, and you won't have to worry about the poisonous ones.

Chapter 23

FAMILY: Apiaceae
SPECIES: *Conium maculatum*

Poison Hemlock

*A very poisonous plant that can be confused
with wild carrot at its early stages.*

POISONOUS PLANT
NOT EDIBLE IN ANY WAY

A 7-foot-tall mature poison hemlock in full flower.

POISON HEMLOCK

Estimated Range

Official Species Name:
• *Conium maculatum* L.

Synonyms:
• None

Common Names:
• Poison hemlock
• Deadly hemlock
• Queen Anne's lace
• Poison parsley

Herbaceous weed naturalized from Europe. Widespread and abundant in North America, primarily where humans have invaded and where soil has been disturbed. Abandoned areas and wet meadows. Shares many habitats with wild carrot.

Edible Parts:
• None, it's all poisonous

Poisonous Parts:
• Whole plant

The main reason to learn about poison hemlock is to distinguish it from wild carrot so you will not poison yourself. There are just a few characteristics you need to know to identify this plant. If you combine what I show in this chapter with the comparisons I make in the wild carrot chapter, you should have a pretty fair chance of knowing both plants without confusion.

It is important to note that poisonous plants are not stalking you. That is, they do not recognize you as prey and try to leap into your mouth as you walk by. You have to physically insert the poisonous plant part in your mouth and swallow. So fear of just having this plant around is unwarranted unless it is in a place where infants stick everything in their mouths. I have seen no accounts where touching poison hemlock has killed anyone. I handle it myself all the time and do not typically wash my hands after doing so. It does not seem to be an issue. Beware, however; there may be people more sensitive than I am to touching it. Some members of the carrot family can irritate the skin of some people. This means: just pay attention when you handle any plant. If one is a problem, stop handling it, or get gloves.

Poisoning occurs mostly with people who have a vague idea of what carrot looks like, either from the supermarket or from seeing some in a garden, perhaps even their own garden. They do not know edible wild plants or poisonous plants. A typical scenario is the following: A person buys a property and finds what they think are carrots growing in the back lot, in or near a garden bed. They pull some up and smell the root, getting a sweet-carrot-family hit from the odor. They either assume that it is wild carrot, a strange white-rooted domesticated carrot, or a parsnip. They are pleased with the large size of the root. After enjoying a taste of it, they chop it up, throw it in a soup or stir-fry, enjoy their meal, and then die, along with anyone they fed.

Another common scenario is an adventure outfitter or guide who wants to give his customers a thrill by serving them wild foods within whatever adventure they are on. For instance, a multiday whitewater rafting group stops to cook meals periodically. They might pick berries or other easy-to-find wild foods on a regular basis. One of the guides sees what he thinks is wild carrot, adds it to that evening's dinner in an effort to impress clients, they all enjoy the flavor, and everybody dies.

It should be noted that poison hemlock plants are common and abundant. You likely pass them regularly. The reason you do not hear of regular deaths is that the great mass of the population is not putting random plants they encounter into their mouths.

Even the pollen of poison hemlock is a problem in massive amounts. In 2001 an agricultural laborer contacted me. In 2000 he had been tasked with clearing a large field of tall weeds he later learned were poison hemlock. He had some sort of thrasher attached to the front of a big farm vehicle. As he drove this machine, chopping away at the plants in full flower, the air was thick with pollen and the volatilized cut up plant juices. He was breathing it for hours. That evening, he had a hard time breathing. Within a few days he was forced to go to the hospital and collapsed due to lack of oxygen. A year later he still had a hard time breathing and was prescribed an inhaler. He called me. There was nothing I could do to help. Note that this is a massive amounts of pollen and airborne juices. Normal amounts of pollen out in the open are probably an issue for no one. I've been in fields of poison hemlock in flower and have not experienced any problem. Of course, I was not hacking away at the plants for hours. As a responsible researcher, I have to note that I never saw the original plant in this story, and only heard this story from the victim over the phone, so cannot say for a fact that it was poison hemlock that poisoned this fellow. Such is the problem with many stories on plant poisonings. This story is a cautionary note.

In ancient Greece, Socrates was sentenced to death when the powers that be concluded that he corrupted the youth with his ideas about questioning authority, among other things. The form of execution was to drink a bowl of what was long assumed to be an elixir made from the root of poison hemlock. While it might have been a simple juicing of the smashed root, no one really knows. It could have been an elixir that required some processing to get the exact effect they desired. Some are not sure Socrates was poisoned by poison hemlock; some suggest other components were added to lessen potential pain. Because of this story, the hemlock plant was used to symbolize rational suicide in the right-to-die/death-with-dignity organization called the Hemlock Society. It is only in name, though. No one uses hemlock today to commit suicide, because of the unknowns about the plant.

The symptoms of Socrates' death described by Plato don't seem to match current descriptions of hemlock poisoning. Poisonings from plants are a confusing mess of symptoms. When patients die from plant ingestion, it is often up to untrained witnesses, local physicians, or coroners to identify the plant. This is far from a perfect science, and there are rarely any real experts handy. Even poison control centers only have brief, canned explanations of poisonous plants. Conclusions by authorities are often guesses, so it is difficult to determine which plant was causing symptoms prior to the death of a person.

If you suspect poisoning from poison hemlock, this is what you might see as the initial symptom: there is numbness of the extremities, particularly the legs and feet, and walking becomes difficult. Falling happens. The symptoms will be different from those of a stroke in that they will be happening to both legs at the same time, and the brain is still fully lucid. If this happens, get to a hospital immediately.

Knowing Poison Hemlock

The seedling is similar to carrot in that the cotyledons are simply shaped and the first leaves have deeply divided leaflets. Minor differences are that the cotyledons of wild carrot are thinner and its leaflet tips have more of a canine paw look than hemlock's. Poison hemlock's first leaves are more fanlike. This finger/fan difference in the leaflets persists throughout all stages of growth. Refer back to fennel (page 328) and carrot (page 350) for a review of their seedlings.

Young poison hemlock plants are roughly similar to carrot in size, shape, and leaflet detail. The leaf blades (all the leaflets taken together) of poison hemlock have a triangular look. Poison hemlock has no hairs at any stage of growth.

The leaf stalks (petioles) of poison hemlock are long, relative to wild carrot at any stage of growth.

Poison hemlock is a vigorous grower and germinates quite well in a variety of soils. If you see one plant, there are likely others around. Plants that germinate in the spring have enough time in one year to eventually develop a stalk, complete with flowers and seed development. Plants that germinate in the fall develop a root that overwinters to get a head start on growing the next spring.

Above: Poison hemlock seedling, showing its two cotyledons and first two fanlike leaves at about 1 inch tall.

Above: Poison hemlock's first three young triangular leaves at about 6 inches tall. When the plants are this young, it is difficult to see the red speckles on the leaf stems, which I showed in the Wild Carrot chapter. They are often there, you just have to look closely.

Left: Young poison hemlock plant. Its size in this photo is about 14 inches left to right.

Many young poison hemlock plants in spring, at about 10 inches tall, too early for stalk (main stem) development. Some unfortunate person may think they've found a huge patch of wild carrot.

A young poison hemlock plant with a well-formed root just prior to stalk development. They can get much bigger than this.

Poison hemlock plants in early stalk development, but too early for flower development. Plants in this photograph range from 1 to 3 feet tall.

Plants that have overwintered grow quickly and develop large roots. Large roots provide a stable base and the nutrient storage to grow tall plants.

Once the plants store enough energy in the roots, they send up a stalk (main stem). The stalk grows quickly and is round, thick, and hollow—often more than an inch in diameter. The red speckles on the stalk and on the now larger leaf stems become much more prominent and obvious than they were on the young stalkless plant.

My friend Michael invited me to a barbecue he was hosting. When I arrived, he asked me to identify a 15-foot ornamental in his backyard. He had not planted it, but thought it was beautiful, so he nurtured it, along with all the other plants. It was poison hemlock—the most magnificent and tallest one I had ever seen! While it is capable of that height, it regularly is anywhere from 6 to 10 feet tall at maturity.

Flower heads of poison hemlock are distinctively different than those of wild carrot. Poison hemlock flower heads at their prime are smaller, convex in overall shape, and are clustered at the ends of major branching stems. The umbel gives the appearance of white fireworks that explode once (forming the umbel), whose tips explode again into miniplumes (umbellettes). This makes the flowers compound umbels, like wild carrot and fennel flowers. The umbellettes are slightly separate from each other in the poison hemlock plant. In contrast, carrot

Mature hemlock plant in full flower. The upper 2 feet of a 6 foot plant.

Rare wildlife found darting around an open field of mature poison hemlock, July 2000.

WILD CARROT

POISON HEMLOCK

Above left: The magnificent bracts below the wild carrot flower head. Above right: Mature poison hemlock flower head showing its tiny bracts.

Left: Five compound umbels at the tip of one of many branching stems of a flowering hemlock plant. Carrot flower heads don't cluster like this at the top of stems.

Right: Developing green fruits on a poison hemlock umbellette.

Below: Dead poison hemlock plants. In this photograph they range from 4 to 7 feet tall.

umbellettes are often so tightly pressed against each other that they appear as one big flower. The compound umbels of wild carrot flower heads are either flat or convex and are found singly on each branching stem.

Bracts subtending (underneath) the poison hemlock flower head are small and triangular. This is definitively different than carrot bracts, which are about ten times longer and split into threes. This is shown both here and in the carrot chapter. With all these other characteristics, it is relatively easy to distinguish between adult poison hemlock and carrot.

One fruit replaces each flower on the umbellette. The fruits look like mini-gourds with ridges, much different from the rows of spikes found on a wild carrot umbellette. The compound umbels of hemlock retain their convex form when the seeds go to maturity, rather than curling up into the bird's nest concave shape that you see in wild carrot.

In most regions, poison hemlock plants die between late spring and midsummer, soon after their seeds mature. Their tall, old, light brown stalks stand out in contrast to most other plants, which are still green. If the ground is very dry, you will see dead grass under the poison hemlocks. The dead stalks will continue to drop brown dry fruits until the umbels are empty. Most of these plants are knocked over in windy, rainy, and snowy winters.

A close-up of the flowering stem

Poison hemlock has varying amounts of reddish speckles on its leaf stems and main stems. You may have to look really close in some instances to see them, and on others the red is all over. If you find a stem that is totally red, just look to other parts of the plant to find it speckled somewhere. Speckling is not unique to poison hemlock. Other plants like cow parsnip have it too. So you cannot depend on that one characteristic. You should learn several identifying characteristics for any plant, in order to be confident of an identification.

Three of an infinite number of variations of the red speckles on the stems of poison hemlock. The center photo shows the bloom (whitish powder) that I rubbed off with my finger.

Recall that poison hemlock is hairless. It's bald, so to speak. Instead of hairs it has a whitish powder that covers the plant to varying degrees. Environmental conditions and plant variation determine how thick and obvious the powder is. When it is clearly seen, it can be rubbed off, revealing an underlying greener color on the stem.

Conclusion

Poison hemlock is a beautiful and easily spreading plant that is found all over North America and Europe. It can be mistaken for wild carrot by the uninformed. It should be easily distinguished by anyone studying my two chapters with the comparisons between wild carrot and poison hemlock. Poison hemlock is not dangerous unless you consume it. Most people will find the flavor to be pleasant. So those who assume that good flavor means edibility and nothing else will die.

Part III
The Potential of
Wild Foods

In this section, I take on the human side of the equation. How do wild foods fit into our modern world? Why pursue them, study them, eat them? How nutritious are they? How would you increase your access to wild foods in order to eat them daily, and what considerations come into play for people wanting to bring wild foods to market?

In this section I address how wild foods offer diversity in the diet that is different from common foods found in the supermarket. I also speculate on how wild foods might be a substantial food resource in times of climate change.

Amid all the fun, I take the field of wild foods very seriously, as have more and more scientific researchers. The research on wild foods takes place in a variety of disciplines with no apparent unifying agent. In this section, I collect, organize, and present some of the information here for a beginning framework for thinking about wild foods.

And while the potential of wild foods can be clearly seen throughout this book, this section helps provide the information, perspective, and motivation to foster a more active use of these plants.

Chapter 24

Nutrients in Wild Foods

The nutrients I report here are limited to those that North Americans have a difficult time obtaining in typical processed-food diets. Nutrients that are easily acquired elsewhere are not reported here.

Accuracy of values shown in this part of the book is only as good as the original source and my ability to figure out what that source was presenting. Although some scientific researchers gave me exactly what I needed here—grams, milligrams, or micrograms per 100 grams of fresh weight material—many authors did not. So for some values, great mathematical contortions were required to put the numbers in the standard forms presented here. I'm sure there are a few values that are off because of my brain exploding at times.

There are no absolutes in nutrient data

The growth media, temperature ranges, amount of sunlight, the stage of growth, the exact plant parts used, and the methods used by the analyst all cause variations in nutrient amounts. The best way to interpret this data is to assume this is the best ballpark estimate of what these plants have to offer. Since these are all averages of the data found, the more references used to determine each value, the more likely the result is a *good* ballpark figure. Much more research needs to be done regarding the nutrient content of wild foods.

Each book that I publish includes values for plants covered in that book, plus updates to values on previously covered plants. The values are not static, since new data is coming in all the time. In fact, if you are a researcher, please fill in the gaps and help verify data that is already there.

Thousands of phytochemicals that apparently serve to heal the body, work as antioxidants, and promote certain physiological processes are not covered here. Wild foods are filled with them and are a major reason that wild foods are so good for you. I often say that good health results from

The lowest things on the
food chain are plants, next
are animals that eat plants.
Carnivorous predators are
at the top of the food chain.
They eat everything that has
already eaten everything
else. A large fish eats a
smaller fish who has eaten
an even smaller fish, who
was eating seaweeds.

consuming a great diversity of foods, mostly plants, as well as animals low on the food chain. This diversity provides you with thousands of great nutrients and phytochemicals that help you.

As I said in volume 1 of this series, you should not be microanalyzing whether one food gives you 5 more micrograms of vitamin C than another. It is a waste of your time, unless you are on a special medical diet where specific nutrients have to be micromanaged. To eat well, eat a great diversity of plants. The more species you include in each meal, the better. It is that simple.

Note that three of the five domesticated species listed in Table 3 are the same species. As I will explain in Chapter 25, it is my hypothesis that once you domesticate plants, you control and restrict the natural development of phytochemicals. Wild plants, on the other hand, have no such restriction. Their arrays of phytochemicals can continue to evolve and potentially provide greater health benefits.

These nutrient tables are here because no one else is producing them specifically for wild foods. Knowing these values helps us put wild foods in perspective and provides important information to the people who need it. Ninety-nine percent of you do not need this information, other than as a curiosity. I rarely refer to this information myself unless I am collaborating or communicating with someone who has a vested interest in it.

Observations about the data

The first two tables on upcoming pages refer to leafy greens and vegetables derived from wild foods. Focusing on these kinds of foods allows some comparison to some of the most nutritious domesticated greens available today in your local supermarket. Those are leaves of broccoli, collard greens, kale, turnip leaves, and spinach. The upper table on page 392 is devoted to those leaves.

When we compare nutrients, wild foods often out-compete domesticated foods. I have outlined exceptional amounts of nutrients in red in the tables for both wild and domestic plants. In the wild foods tables, values in red are higher than the highest value of any domesticated plant. In the domesticated foods table, values are red if they are higher than any wild food values listed.

So far, fiber, vitamin C, and six of the seven minerals listed are overall higher in some of the wild foods listed. Riboflavin is relatively good in both wild and domesticated vegetables, with kale topping out at .35 milligrams. Folic acid and selenium seem to be higher in some of the domesticated vegetables.

The most nutritious of all plants listed according to the values here are garlic mustard, dwarf nettle, and wild spinach. Garlic mustard has by far more beta-carotene and overall vitamin A (as retinol equivalents) than any other plant. Dwarf nettle has, by far, more iron and calcium than any other plant. Wild spinach (lambsquarters) is a great overall food.

In my nutrient table of 2010, purslane was deemed to be the champion of omega-3 fatty acids. Purslane has been summarily bested by stinging nettle, which seems to have two to five times as much of this nutrient. Nettle stands far above all others. However, when you only see one piece of data with such an extremely high value, I do not necessarily believe it without more verification.

If you define diversity as the key to great nutrition, which I do, it helps to dispel the *superfood* concept. There are no superfoods, only super diets. Individual foods, by themselves, are always inadequate. By incorporating a great diversity of plants into your everyday diet, you end up with a super healthy diet.

Nutrient Values in 100 Grams of Wild Food: Greens, Vegetables, Shoots

Values are red if larger than the largest value for the Domesticated Greens chart.

Species	Common Name	Part / Method	Fiber gm	ω-3 mg	Oleic mg	RAE μg	β-car
Alliaria petiolata	Garlic Mustard	Greens, Raw	5.38	155	53	4,650	13,3
Amaranthus retroflexus	Green Amaranth	Greens, Raw	1.80			1,927	
Barbarea vulgaris	Wintercress	Greens, Raw				1,520	
Barbarea vulgaris	Wintercress	Bud Clusters, Raw				604	
Brassica rapa	Field Mustard	Greens, Raw					
Capsella bursa-pastoris	Shepherds Purse	Greens, Raw	2.52	248		1,500	7,4
Chenopodium album	Wild Spinach	Greens, Raw	2.31	122	59	2,095	5,3
Chenopodium album	Wild Spinach	Greens, Boiled 5 min	2.10	32	101	2,346	4,6
Cichorium intybus	Wild Chicory	Greens, Raw	3.01	19	6	743	2,3
Cichorium intybus	Wild Chicory	Roots, Raw	1.50	13	4	2	
Daucus carota	Wild Carrot	Greens, Raw	4.40				1,1
Foeniculum vulgare	Wild Sweet Fennel	Leaves, Raw	3.10	214	21		1,1
Foeniculum vulgare	Wild Sweet Fennel	Basal Shoots, Raw		181	13		
Foeniculum vulgare	Wild Sweet Fennel	Peeled Stem Cores, Raw		113	21		
Foeniculum vulgare	Wild Sweet Fennel	Flower Umbels, Raw		87	25		
Hemerocallis fulva	Tawny Day Lily	Buds, Raw				295	
Hypochaeris radicata	Cat's Ear	Leaves, Raw					1,6
Lamium amplexicaule	Henbit	Greens, Raw	5.73				
Oxalis corniculata	Wood Sorrel	Greens, Raw	.54			1,380	1,9
Oxalis stricta	Wood Sorrel	Greens, Raw					
Phytolacca americana	Pokeweed	Shoots, Raw 🕱 Poisonous	1.70			2,600	
Phytolacca americana	Pokeweed	Shoots, Boiled, 5 min/Unsp	1.50	9	12	435	5,2
Phytolacca americana	Pokeweed	Greens, Boiled, Unsp	1.50	9	13		5,1

Key to Abbreviations:

Fiber = Soluble + Insoluble Fiber (grams)	Vit C = Vitamin C (milligrams)
ω-3 = Omega-3 Fatty Acids (milligrams)	Ribo = Riboflavin (milligrams)
Oleic = Oleic Acid, Fatty Acid (milligrams)	Fol Acid = Folic Acid (micrograms)
RAE = Retinol Activity Equivalents (micrograms) Vitamin A	Ca = Calcium (milligrams)
	Fe = Iron (milligrams)
ß-car = Beta-Carotene (micrograms)	Zn = Zinc (milligrams)
a-Toc = Alpha tocopherol (milligrams) Vitamin E	Cu = Copper (milligrams)
🕱 = Poisonous in this raw form	Mn = Manganese (milligrams)
Unsp = Unspecified boiling time	Mg = Magnesium (milligrams)
	Se = Selenium (micrograms)

Compiled by John Kallas, PhD © 2022
Institute for the Study of Edible Wild Plants & Other Forageables
wildfoodadventures.com

c mg	Vit C mg	Ribo mg	Fol Acid µg	Ca mg	Fe mg	Zn mg	Cu mg	Mn mg	Mg mg	Se µg	References
	261			200	3.20	.91	.13	.99	121		24, 76
	271	.16		382	2.70	1.10	.11	.96	137		5, 9, 12, 17, 29, 47, 49, 74
	144										9, 30, 77
	163										9
				392	9.76		.10	1.00	155		20
	104			159	4.80	.55	.09	.89	84		13, 24, 35, 77
	67	.26	64	277	2.73	2.22	2.06	1.04	111	1.00	2, 5, 8, 9, 12, 14, 21, 22, 30, 31, 33, 35, 40, 41, 42, 43, 46, 47, 66, 71, 73, 75
1.85	56	.26	14	258	.70	.30	.20	.53	23	.90	35, 67
1.62	23	.10	110	115	3.24	.40	.20	.34	116	.30	9, 11, 12, 15, 19, 48, 55, 63, 70
	5	.03	23	41	.80	.33	.08	.23	22	.70	64
.35	75			240	3.50	.60			46		13, 58, 70
.63	101			180	2.24	.30			181		10, 11, 15, 58, 70
											10
											10
											10
	43										9
.19	48						10.00				14, 55, 76
											59
	154			221	9.97						4, 8, 50, 71
	1,235										13, 77
	183	.33	16	53	1.70	.24	.16	.42	18	.90	9, 13, 35, 60
.85	114	.25	9	53	1.20	19	.13	.34	14	.90	35, 61
.84	82	.25	9	53	1.20	.19	1.30		14	.90	62

tails, details, details . . .
ese charts include 12 years of additional nutrient research that was not included
our 2010 nutrient chart. If different, this new data is preferable.
lues are amounts reported in 100 grams of fresh edible material, not dry weight unless specified.
trient values above originate from the references listed at the right of the table.
anks here mean I could find no data. (Meaning that no researcher I could find has analyzed for that nutrient yet.)
aves refer to edible parts as consumed. Edible parts of leaves may vary from as little as the leaf blade stripped from
fibrous discarded main vein to whole blades plus part or whole petioles (leaf stems). No main stem material.
eens refer to edible parts as consumed. Greens can refer to leaves complete with part or whole
tioles (leaf stems) or could include tender leafy stems. Leaves are the primary material. In rapid
owth stages, some main stem material is tender enough to include with leaves.
oots refer to edible parts as consumed. Shoots refer to tender edible stem material, either arising directly from the ground or as
w stem material at the ends of more mature stems or branches. Some shoots may or may not include leaves growing on them.
res of peeled stems will be specified. Stems are the primary substance of a shoot upon which there may be some leaf material.
these values should be confirmed by more research. One or two studies is not enough to confirm reliable
mbers. Extremely high values should be viewed with suspicion until more confirmation is established.
weight, 1 gram = 1,000 milligrams = 1,000,000 micrograms. µg is an abbreviated way of saying microgram. Pronounced *mu-gram*.

Nutrient Values in 100 Grams of Wild Food—Continued: Greens, Vegetables, Shoots

Values are red if larger than the largest value for the Domesticated Greens chart.

Species	Common Name	Part / Method	Fiber gm	ω-3 mg	Oleic mg	RAE μg	β-car
Plantago lanceolata	Narrow Leaf Plantain	Leaves, Raw	3.71	152			6,7
Plantago major	Broad Leaf Plantain	Leaves, Raw	3.88	121	8	2,551	5,5
Portulaca oleracea	Purslane	Greens, Raw	1.74	241	12	2,541	4,8
Raphanus raphanistrum	Wild Radish	Leaves, Raw	1.40	171	2		1,8
Rumex acetosella	Sheep Sorrel	Leaves, Raw	1.10				
Rumex crispus	Curly Dock	Leaves, Raw	2.03			2,744	4,3
Rumex obtucifolius	Broad-Leaved Dock	Leaves, Raw	1.89				1,4
Sonchus arvensis	Perennial Sow Thistle	Greens, Raw					
Sonchus asper	Spiny Sow Thistle	Greens, Raw	2.40	279	23		8,0
Sonchus oleraceus	Sow Thistle	Greens, Raw	2.74	337	9		7,6
Stellaria media	Chickweed	Greens, Raw	2.42	113	3	492	2,4
Taraxacum officinale	Dandelion	Leaves, Raw	2.70	134	9	2,690	5,4
Taraxacum officinale	Dandelion	Buds, Raw				240	
Typha angustifolia	Narrow Leaf Cattail	Peeled Stem Shoot, Raw					
Typha latifolia	Cattail	Peeled Stem Shoot, Raw	4.50			1	
Urtica dioica	Stinging Nettle	Greens, Raw	1.73	1,250	94	2,097	2,1
Urtica dioica	Stinging Nettle	Greens, Boiled 1 min	6.15	586	32	1,021	2,0
Urtica dioica	Stinging Nettle	Greens, Boiled 7 min	4.90	611	25	1,806	3,0
Urtica urens	Dwarf Nettle	Greens, Raw	5.81				6,0

Key to Abbreviations:

Fiber	= Soluble + Insoluble Fiber (grams)	Ribo	= Riboflavin (milligrams)
ω-3	= Omega-3 Fatty Acids (milligrams)	Fol Acid	= Folic Acid (micrograms)
Oleic	= Oleic Acid, Fatty Acid (milligrams)	Ca	= Calcium (milligrams)
RAE	= Retinol Activity Equivalents (micrograms) Vitamin A	Fe	= Iron (milligrams)
		Zn	= Zinc (milligrams)
ß-car	= Beta-Carotene (micrograms)	Cu	= Copper (milligrams)
α-Toc	= Alpha tocopherol (milligrams) Vitamin E	Mn	= Manganese (milligrams)
		Mg	= Magnesium (milligrams)
Vit C	= Vitamin C (milligrams)	Se	= Selenium (micrograms)

Compiled by John Kallas, PhD © 2022
Institute for the Study of Edible Wild Plants & Other Forageables
wildfoodadventures.com

mg	Vit C mg	Ribo mg	Fol Acid mg	Ca mg	Fe mg	Zn mg	Cu mg	Mn mg	Mg mg	Se µg	References
	14			60	1.54	.58	.14	.38	49		27
	31	.28		227	3.99	.65	.14	.54	74		4, 5, 16, 21, 22, 27, 33, 75, 77
3.20	39	.04		133	3.74	.71	.24	.48	152		5, 8, 9, 12, 15, 22, 26, 33, 37, 52, 55, 71, 73, 77
89	10	.14		285	9.51	1.36	.18		99		28, 73
	53	.12		57	2.30	1.20	1.20	.92	31		31, 47
	95			54	1.37	.70	.25		51		6, 9, 13, 21, 22, 35, 54
.85	70			60	1.10	.40	10.00		52		14, 58, 70
				170	3.20						4
	63	.13		189	6.86	.67	.29	1.00	41		2, 6, 12, 23, 73
.63	46	.11		158	4.70	.78	2.19	1.00	42		3, 4, 12, 13, 14, 19, 22, 23, 33, 37, 55, 58, 70, 73, 76
	31			84	4.97	4.10	9.45	19.00	149		12, 13, 14, 15, 21, 22, 30, 33, 35, 36, 46, 54, 73, 77
3.44	56	.26	27	252	3.04	.41	.17	.34	36	.50	5, 8, 9, 13, 33, 35, 54, 68
	30										9
				225	20.30	.50	.10	2.20	69		20
	1	.03	3	54	.91	.24	.04	.76	63	.60	65
	30	.22		151	.91	2.11	1.29	.74	32		9, 13, 25, 31, 39, 41, 44, 45, 47
	1	.16	14	473	1.87	.34	.08	.78	57	.30	40, 45
	1			430	2.10						45
	45	.31		688	21.59	1.53	3.62	4.46	213		2, 14, 73

tails, details, details . . .

hese charts include 12 years of additional nutrient research that was not included
our 2010 nutrient chart. If different, this new data is preferable.
alues are amounts reported in 100 grams of fresh edible material, not from dry weight unless specified.
utrient values above originate from the references listed at the right of the table.
anks here mean I could find no data. (Meaning that no researcher I could find has analyzed for that nutrient yet.)
eaves refer to edible parts as consumed. Edible parts of leaves may vary from as little as the leaf blade stripped from
s fibrous discarded main vein to whole blades plus part or whole petioles (leaf stems). No main stem material.
reens refer to edible parts as consumed. Greens can refer to leaves complete with part or whole
etioles (leaf stems) or could include tender leafy stems. Leaves are the primary material. In rapid
rowth stages, some main stem material is tender enough to include with leaves.
hoots refer to edible parts as consumed. Shoots refer to tender edible stem material, either arising directly from the ground or as
ew stem material at the ends of more mature stems or branches. Some shoots may or may not include leaves growing on them.
ores of peeled stems will be specified. Stems are the primary substance of a shoot upon which there may be some leaf material.
ll these values should be confirmed by more research. One or two studies is not enough to confirm reliable
umbers. Extremely high values should be viewed with suspicion until more confirmation is established.
y weight, 1 gram = 1,000 milligrams, = 1,000,000 micrograms. µg is an abbreviated way of saying microgram. Pronounced *mu-gram*.

For Comparison—Leaves of Highly Nutritious Domesticated Greens

Red indicates when a domesticated green has a higher value for a nutrient than any wild food in the 3 wild food charts here.

Species	Common Name	Part / Method	Fiber gm	ω-3 mg	Oleic mg	RAE μg	β-car μg	α-Toc
Brassica oleracea var. *italica*	Broccoli	Leaves, Raw	2.6	63	29	187	361	.
Brassica oleracea var. *acephala* C	Collards	Leaves, Raw	4.0	108	29	1,506	2,990	2.
Brassica oleracea var. *acephala* K	Kale	Leaves, Raw	4.1	378	104	1,443	2,870	.
Brassica rapa var. *rapifera*	Turnip	Leaves, Raw	3.2	84	5	3,480	6,950	2.8
Spinacia oleracea	Spinach	Leaves, Raw	2.2	138	5	2,814	5,630	2.

All domesticated values above are from the Food Data Central (FDC) Nutrient Database, USDA: https://fdc.nal.usda.gov/fdc-app.html#/. The nutrient values for these plants were updated by the USDA in 2017, so may not match the ones from volume 1 of this book series.

Nutrient Values in 100 Grams of Wild Food: Pollen, Spikes, Seeds, Dried Powders

Except for the macronutrients that are not represented in the other charts, values are red if larger than the largest value for the Domesticated Greens chart above.

Species	Common Name	Part / Method	Protein gm	Fat gm	CHO gm	Fiber g
Typha domingensis	Southern Cattail	Pollen, Raw	16.00	2.30	35.00	16.
Typha latifolia	Cattail	Pollen, Raw	14.56	1.80	25.07	14.
Typha angustifolia	Narrow-Leaved Cattail	Male Spike, Raw	2.80	1.58	21.07	
Typha angustifolia	Narrow-Leaved Cattail	Male Spike, Dried	8.94	1.41	74.85	
Althaea officinalis	Marsh Mallow	Seeds, Raw		9.42		
Brassica nigra	Black Mustard	Seeds, Raw	14.42	18.7	25.92	
Lathyrus latifolius	Perennial Pea	Seeds, Raw	24.4			
Plantago major	Broad-Leaved Plantain	Seeds, Raw	18.8	15.00	14.60	
Rumex crispus	Curly Dock	Seeds, Raw	8.96	2.08	61.74	
Urtica dioica	Stinging Nettle	Seeds, Raw		7.91		
Taraxacum officinale	Dandelion	Dry Leaf Powder, Raw	15.48	3.39	58.35	47.
Urtica dioica	Stinging Nettle	Dry Leaf Powder, Raw	33.77	3.55	37.39	9.

Key to Abbreviations:

Fiber	= Soluble + Insoluble Fiber (grams)	Ribo	= Riboflavin (milligrams)
ω-3	= Omega-3 Fatty Acids (milligrams)	Fol Acid	= Folic Acid (micrograms)
Oleic	= Oleic Acid, Fatty Acid (milligrams)	Ca	= Calcium (milligrams)
RAE	= Retinol Activity Equivalents (micrograms) Vitamin A	Fe	= Iron (milligrams)
		Zn	= Zinc (milligrams)
ß-car	= Beta-Carotene (micrograms)	Cu	= Copper (milligrams)
a-Toc	= Alpha tocopherol (milligrams) Vitamin E	Mn	= Manganese (milligrams)
		Mg	= Magnesium (milligrams)
Vit C	= Vitamin C (milligrams)	Se	= Selenium (micrograms)

Compiled by John Kallas, PhD © 2022
Institute for the Study of Edible Wild Plants & Other Forageables
wildfoodadventures.com

C mg	Ribo mg	Fol Acid mg	Ca mg	Fe mg	Zn mg	Cu mg	Mn mg	Mg mg	Se µg	References
89.2	.117	63	47	.73	.41	.05	.21	21	2.5	FDC: ID 170379, NDB 11090
35.3	.130	129	232	.47	.21	.05	.66	27	1.3	FDC: ID 170406, NDB 11161
93.4	.347	62	254	1.60	.39	.05	.92	33	.9	FDC: ID 168421, NDB 11233
60.0	.100	194	190	1.10	.19	.35	.47	31	1.2	FDC: ID 170061, NDB 11568
28.1	.189	194	99	2.71	.53	.13	.90	79	1.0	FDC: ID 168462, NDB 11457

3 mg	Oleic mg	β-car µg	Vit C mg	Ca mg	Fe mg	Zn mg	Cu mg	Mn mg	Mg mg	References
56	71		173	89	6.3	.40			59	7, 32, 72
73	31			173	3.8	.30		10	147	32, 34, 51, 53, 57
									20	
									20	
83	1,600								56	
									20	
									38	
135	5,500								16	
				716	26.7	2.00	.40	3	425	20	
									25	
,173	292	13,800	53	695				470	18	
				169	227.9				1	

ails, details, details . . .

ese charts include 12 years of additional nutrient research that was not included
ur 2010 nutrient chart. If different, this new data is preferable.
ues are amounts reported in 100 grams of fresh edible material, not from dry weight unless specified.
trient values above originate from the references listed at the right of the table.
nks here mean I could find no data. (Meaning that no researcher I could find has analyzed for that nutrient yet.)
aves refer to edible parts as consumed. Edible parts of leaves may vary from as little as the leaf blade stripped from
fibrous discarded main vein to whole blades plus part or whole petioles (leaf stems). No main stem material.
eens refer to edible parts as consumed. Greens can refer to leaves complete with part or whole
tioles (leaf stems) or could include tender leafy stems. Leaves are the primary material. In rapid
wth stages, some main stem material is tender enough to include with leaves.
oots refer to edible parts as consumed. Shoots refer to tender edible stem material, either arising directly from the ground or as
v stem material at the ends of more mature stems or branches. Some shoots may or may not include leaves growing on them.
res of peeled stems will be specified. Stems are the primary substance of a shoot upon which there may be some leaf material.
these values should be confirmed by more research. One or two studies is not enough to confirm reliable
mbers. Extremely high values should be viewed with suspicion until more confirmation is established.
weight, 1 gram = 1,000 milligrams, = 1,000,000 micrograms. µg is an abbreviated way of saying microgram. Pronounced *mu-gram*.

References for nutrition tables

1. Adhikari, Bhaskar, et al. "Comparison of Nutritional Properties of Stinging Nettle (Urtica dioica) Flour with Wheat and Barley Flours." *Food Science & Nutrition* 4, no. 1 (2015): 119–124.

2. Afolayan, A. J., and F. Jimoh. "Nutritional Quality of Some Wild Leafy Vegetables in South Africa." *International Journal of Food Sciences and Nutrition* 60, no. 5 (2009): 424–431.

3. Agea, Jacob, et al. "Proximate composition, Vitamin C and Beta-Carotene Contents of Fifteen Selected Leafy Wild and Semi-Wild Food Plants (WSWFPs) from Bunyoro-Kitara Kingdom, Uganda." *Journal of Natural Product and Plant Resources* 4, no. 3 (2014): 1–12.

4. Agrahar-Murugkar, Dipika. "Interventions Using Wild Edibles to Improve the Nutritional Status of Khasi Tribal Women (India)." *Human Ecology* Special Issue No. 14 (2006): 83–88.

5. Aliotta, Giovanni, and A. Pollio. "Vitamin A and C Content in Some Edible Wild Plants in Italy." *Rivista Italiana EPPOS* 63 (1981): 47–48.

6. Anonymous. "Nutritional Composition of Greek Foods." Hellenic Health Foundation: http://www.hhf-greece.gr/tables/FoodItems, copied October 2019.

7. Arenas, Pastor, and Gustavo Scarpa. "The Consumption of Typha domingensis Pers. (Typhaceae) Pollen Among the Ethnic Groups of the Gran Chaco, South America." *Economic Botany* 57, no. 2 (2003): 181–188. (Data cited from: Charpentier, M. 1998. Valores nutricionales de las plantas ali- menticias silvestres del norte Argentino. Instituto de Cultura Popular [INCUPO], Reconquista, Argentina.).

8. Baloch, AK, and S Hujjatullah. "Nutritive Value of Edible Wild Plants in The Frontier Region of West Pakistan." *Pakistan Journal of Scientific and Industrial Research* 9 (1966): 87–90.

9. Baron, George, and Herta Lagally. Edible Plants Nutrient Data Tables. In Euell Gibbons, *Stalking the Healthful Herbs*, chapter 41: Chambersburg, Pennsylvania: Alan C. Hood, 1966, 271, 276 & 277.

10. Barros, Lillian, et al. "The Nutritional Composition of Fennel (Foeniculum vulgare): Shoots, Leaves, Stems and Inflorescences." *Food Sci Technol* 43, no. 5 (2010): 814–818.

11. Batal, Malek, and Elizabeth Hunter. "Traditional Lebanese Recipes Based on Wild Plants: An Answer to Diet Simplification?" *Food and Nutrition Bulletin* 28, no. 2 (2007): S303–S311. Supplement: June.

12. Bianco, V.V., et al. "Nutritional Value and Nitrate Content in Edible Wild Species Used in Southern Italy." *Acta Horticulturae* (ISHS) 467 (1998):71–87.

13. Burrell, R.C., and Helena A. Miller. "The Vitamin C Content of Spring Greens." *Science* 90 (2329) (1939):162–165.

14. Bvenura, Callistus, "Wild Vegetables of The Eastern Cape of South Africa: The Nutritional Value and Domestication of Solanum nigrum L." Doctoral dissertation, Department of Botany Faculty of Science and Agriculture, University of Fort Hare, South Africa, March 2014, https://core.ac.uk/download/pdf/145050122.pdf

15. Cowan, J. W., et al. Composition of Edible Wild Plants of Lebanon." *Journal of the Science of Food and Agriculture.* 14, no 7 (1963): 484–488.

16. Duke, James A. *Handbook of Medicinal Herbs, Second Edition.* CRC Press: Ann Arbor, MI, 1987.

17. Duke, James A. and A.A. Atchley. *CRC Handbook of Proximate Analysis Tables of Higher Plants.* CRC Press, Boca Raton, FL, 2017.

18. Escudero, N.L, et al. "Taraxacum officinale as a Food Source." *Plant Foods for Human Nutrition* 58, no. 3 (September 2003): 1–10.

19. García-Herrera, P., et al. "Nutrient Composition of Six Wild Edible Mediterranean Asteraceae Plants of Dietary Interest." *Journal of Food Composition and Analysis* 34, no. 2 (June 2014): 163–170.

20. Gilliland, Linda Ellen. "Proximate Analysis and Mineral Composition of Traditional California Native American Foods." Unpublished Master's thesis, Department of Nutrition Science, University of California, Davis. 1985.

21. Guil-Guerrero, José Luis, et al. "Oxalic Acid and Calcium Determination in Edible Wild Plants." *Journal Agricultural and Food Chemistry* 44, no. 7 (1996): 1821–1823.

22. Guil-Guerrero, José Luis, et al. "Nutritional and Toxic Factors in Selected Wild Edible Plants." *Plant Foods for Human Nutrition.* 51, no. 2 (1997): 99–107.

23. Guil-Guerrero, José Luis, et al. "Nutritional Composition of Sonchus species (S. Asper L., S. oleraceus L., and S tenerissimus L.)." *Journal of the Science of Food and Agriculture* 76, no. 4 (1998): 628–632.

24. Guil-Guerrero, José Luis, et al. "Nutritional Composition of Wild Edible Crucifer Species." *Journal of Food Biochemistry* 23, no. 3 (1999): 283–294.

25. Guil-Guerrero, José Luis, et al. "Fatty Acids and Carotenoids from Stinging Nettle (Urtica dioica L.)." *Journal of Food Composition and Analysis* 16 (2003): 111–119.

26. Guil-Guerrero, José Luis, et al. "Mineral Elements Determination in Wild Edible Plants." *Ecology of Food and Nutrition* 38, no. 3 (1999): 209–222.

27. Guil-Guerrero, José Luis. "Nutritional Composition of Plantago Species (P-major L., P-lanceolata, L., and P-media L.)." *Ecology of Food and Nutrition* 40, no. 5 (2001): 481–495.

28. Iyda, Júlia Harumi, et al. "Chemical Composition and Bioactive Properties of The Wild Edible Plant Raphanus Raphanistrum L." *Food Research International* 121(July 2019): 714–722.

29. Jiménez-Aguilar, Dulce, and Michael Grusak, "Minerals, Vitamin C, Phenolics, Flavonoids and Antioxidant Activity of Amaranthus Leafy Vegetables." *Journal of Food Composition and Analysis* 58 (2017): 33–39.

30. Kallman, Stefan. "Nutritive Value of Swedish Wild Plants." *Journal Svensk Bot Tidskr* 85 (1991): 397–406.

31. Kuhnlein, Harriet. "Nutrient Values in Indigenous Wild Plant Greens and Roots Used by the Nuxalk People of Bella Coola, British Columbia." *Journal of Food Composition and Analysis* 3, no. 1 (March 1990): 38–46.

32. Lee, Bung-Chan, et al. "Biological Activity and Chemical Analysis of Cattail Pollens." *Korean Journal of Agricultural Science* 36, no. 2 (2009): 185–197.

33. Liu, Lixia, et al. "Fatty Acid Profiles of Leaves of Nine Edible Wild Plants: An Australian Study." *Journal of Food Lipids* 9, no. 1 (2002): 65–71.

34. Maiden, J. H. *Useful Native Plants of Australia (including Tasmania).* Technological Museum, New South Wales, Sydney, Australia, 2012.

35. Murray, Hazel C., and Robert Stratton. "Vitamin C Content of Wild Greens." *Journal of Nutrition* 28, no. 6 (August 1944): 427–430.

36. Narzary, Hwiyang, et al. "Proximate and Vitamin C Analysis of Wild Edible Plants Consumed by Bodos of Assam, India." *Journal of Molecular Pathophysiology* 4, no. 4 (November 2015): 128–133.

37. Ogle, Britta, and Louis Grivetti. "Legacy of the Chameleon: Edible Wild Plants in the Kingdom of Swaziland, Southern Africa. A Cultural, Ecological, Nutritional Study." Department of Nutrition, University of California, Davis, California *Ecology of Food and Nutrition* 16, no. 3 (1985): 193–208, 17; no. 1 (1985): 1–64.

38. Pastor-Cavada, Elena, et al. "Nutritional Characteristics of Seed Proteins In 15 Lathyrus Species (Fabaceae) From Southern Spain." *LWT—Food Science and Technology* 44, no. 4 (May 2011): 1059–1064.

39. Paulauskiene, Aurelija, et al. "Influence of Harvesting Time on the Chemical Composition of Wild Stinging Nettle (Urtica dioica L.)." *Plants* (2021):10,686. https://doi.org/10.3390/plants10040686.

40. Phillips, Katherine, et al. "Nutrient Composition of Selected Traditional United States Northern Plains Native American Plant Foods." *Journal of Food Composition and Analysis* 34 (2014): 136–152.

41. Pradhan, S., et al., "Proximate, Mineral Composition and Antioxidant Properties of Some Wild Leafy Vegetables." *Journal of Scientific and Industrial Research* 74, no. 3 (March 2015): 156–159.

42. Prakash, Dhan, et al. "Composition, Variation of Nutritional Contents in Leaves, Seed Protein, Fat and Fatty Acid Profile of Chenopodium Species." *Journal of the Science of Food and Agriculture* 62, no. 2 (1993): 203–205.

43. Raghuvanshi, Rita, et al. "Nutritional Composition of Uncommon Foods and Their Role in Meeting Micronutrient Needs (India)." *International Journal of Food Sciences and Nutrition* 52, no. 4 (July 2001): 331–335.

44. Rai, Arun, et al. "Food Value of Common Edible Wild Plants of Sikkim." *Journal of Hill Research* 18, no. 2 (2005): 99–103.

45. Rutto, Laban, et al. "Mineral Properties and Dietary Value of Raw and Processed Stinging Nettle (Urtica dioica L.)." *International Journal of Food Science*, vol. 2013, article ID 857120, 9 pages, https://doi.org/10.1155/2013/857120.

46. Salam, Jekendra, et al. "Secondary Metabolites, Antioxidant Status and Nutritive Composition of Two Non-Conventional Leafy Vegetables— Stellaria media L. and Chenopodium album L." *Indian Journal of Agricultural Biochemistry* 24, no. 2 (2011): 136–140.

47. Samancioglu, A, et al. "Total Phenolic and Vitamin C Content and Antiradical Activity Evaluation of Traditionally Consumed Wild Edible Vegetables from Turkey." *Indian Journal of Traditional Knowledge* 15, no. 2 (April 2016): 208–213.

48. Sánchez-Mata, María de Cortes, et al. "Wild Vegetables of The Mediterranean Area as Valuable Sources of Bioactive Compound." *Genetic Resources and Crop Evolution* 59, no. 3 (March 2012): 431–443.

49. Sekeroglu, Nazim, et al., "Evaluation of Some Wild Plants Aspect of Their Nutritional Values Used as Vegetable in Eastern Black Sea Region of Turkey." *Asian Journal of Plant Sciences* 5, no. 2 (2006): 185–189.

50. Sengupta, S. R., and B. Pal. "Composition of Edible Wild Greens." *Journal of the Science of Food and Agriculture* 21, no. 4 (April 1970): 215.

51. Simms, Steven. "Acquisition Costs and Nutritional Data on Great Basin Resources." *Journal of California and Great Basin Anthropology* 7, no. 1 (1985): 117–126.

52. Simopoulos, Artemis, et al. "Common Purslane: A Source of Omega-3 Fatty Acids and Antioxidants." *Journal of the American College of Nutrition* 11, no. 4 (1992): 374–382.

53. Specter, William (ed.). *Handbook of Biological Data*. Division of Biology & Agriculture, NAS, NRC, W. B. Saunders Company, New York.

54. Stark, Philip, et al. "Open-Source Food: Nutrition, Toxicology, and Availability of Wild Edible Greens in the East Bay." *PLoS ONE* 14, no. 1 (September 2020): e0202450. https://doi.org/10.1371/journal.pone.0202450 pmid:30653545.

55. Su, Q., et al. "Identification and Quantitation of Major Crotenoids in Selected Components of the Mediterranean Diet: Green Leafy Vegetables, Figs, and Olive Oil." *European Journal of Clinical Nutrition* 56, no. 11 (2002): 1149–1154.

56. Tešević, Vele, et al. "Lipid Composition and Antioxidant Activities of the Seed Oil from Three Malvaceae Species." *Archives of Biological Sciences* 64, no. 1 (2012): 221–227.

57. Todd, Frank, and Ormond Bretherick. "The Composition of Pollens." *Journal of Economic Entomology* 35, no. 3 (1942): 312–317.

58. Trichopoulou, Antonia, et al. "Nutritional Composition and Flavonoid Content of Edible Wild Greens and Green Pies: A Potential Rich Source of Antioxidant Nutrients in the Mediterranean Diet." *Food Chemistry* 70, no. 3 (2000): 319–323.

59. Tuncturk, Murat, et al. "Chemical Characterization of Some Wild Edible Plants of Eastern Region of Anatolia, Turkey." *American Journal of Essential Oils and Natural Products* 2, no. 5 (2015): 38–41.

60. USDA, ARS. FoodData Central, Nutrient Database ID: 170432, NDB 11350—Pokeberry, Shoots Raw.

61. USDA, ARS. FoodData Central, Nutrient Database ID: 170433, NDB 11351—Pokeberry, Shoots, Boiled.

62. USDA, ARS. FoodData Central, Nutrient Database ID: 342199, NDB 72123010—Pokeberry, Greens, Boiled.

63. USDA, ARS. FoodData Central, Nutrient Database ID: 169992, NDB 11152—Chicory Greens, Raw.

64. USDA, ARS. FoodData Central, Nutrient Database ID: 169993, NDB 11154—Chicory Roots, Raw.

65. USDA, ARS. FoodData Central, Nutrient Database ID: 168994, NDB 35195—Cattail, Basal Leaf Shoots, Raw.

66. USDA, ARS. FoodData Central, Nutrient Database ID: 169244, NDB 11244—Lambsquarters, Leaves, Raw.

67. USDA, ARS. FoodData Central, Nutrient Database ID: 169245, NDB 11245—Lambsquarters, Leaves, Boiled, Drained.

68. USDA, ARS. FoodData Central, Nutrient Database ID: 169226, NDB 11207—Dandelion, Leaves, Raw.

69. USDA, ARS. FoodData Central, Nutrient Database ID: 169227, NDB 11208—Dandelion, Leaves, Boiled.

70. Vardavasa, C. I., et al. "The Antioxidant and Phylloquinone Content of Wildly Grown Greens in Crete." *Food Chemistry* 99, no. 4 (December 2006): 813–821.

71. Vishwakarma, Kanchan Lata, and Veenapani Dubey. "Nutritional Analysis of Indigenous Wild Edible Herbs Used in Eastern Chhattisgarh, India." *Emirates Journal of Food and Agriculture* 23, no. 6 (2011): 554–560.

72. Watt, George. *The Commercial Products of India: Being an Abridgment of The Dictionary of the Economic Products of India.* London: J. Murray Publishing, 1908.

73. Wehmeyer, A. S. "Edible Wild Plants of Southern Africa: Data on the Nutrient Contents of Over 300 Species." National Food Research Institute Technical Report, 1986. Council for Scientific & Industrial Research (CSIR): Pretoria, South Africa.

74. Wolfe, Wendy, et al. "Use and Nutrient Composition of Traditional Navajo Foods." *Ecology of Food and Nutrition* 17, no. 4 (1985): 323–344. Gordon and Breach Science Publishers.

75. Yildirim, Ertan, et al. "Determination of the Nutritional Contents of the Wild Plants Used as Vegetables in Upper Çoruh Valley." *Turkish Journal of Botany* 25, no. 6 (2001): 367–371.

76. Zeghichia, Sabrina, et al. "Nutritional Composition of Selected Wild Plants in the Diet of Crete." World Rev Nutr Diet. Basel, Karger. 91 (2003): 22–40. In *Plants in Human Health and Nutrition Policy*, Simopoulos A. P., Gopalan C. (eds).

77. Zennie, Thomas, and Dwayne Ogzewalla. "Ascorbic Acid and Vitamin A Content of Edible Wild Plants of Ohio and Kentucky." *Economic Botany* 31, no. 1 (January 1977): 76–79.

Chapter 25

The Richest Diet

The greatest value of wild foods, among many other things, is in the diversity they add to the diet.

DECONSTRUCTING THE MEDITERRANEAN DIET

A diet diverse in species was not all that made the Greeks healthy and long-lived in the Mediterranean diet. It was a combination of the following: great diversity in a diet of mostly plants, eating in moderation, fasting regularly, and using meats more for flavoring in larger vegetable dishes than as main dishes. Socially, the people lived in small villages in close-knit families, with multiple generations often living together, with extended family members living close by. Each person was useful, had purpose, and contributed to the family workload. Everyone was valued for who they were until their dying day. They walked everywhere, on often irregular terrain, and tended to have physical jobs. They played a lot, having regular social engagements with friends.

During research on the original Mediterranean Diet, they found that the average granny on the island of Crete knew and gathered 110 different edible wild plants throughout the year to help feed her family. That was 110 different species. That is not counting the diverse species of land animals (rabbits, snails, turtles, frogs, lizards, etc.) and marine life (clams, mussels, squid, cuttlefish, octopus, sea urchins, different species of fish, etc.) that they also ate. It is highly likely that this diversity is what helped lead to great health and a lack of degenerative diseases among the people there.

If you look at what is available to use today in a typical supermarket, the appearance is of great diversity. And if you choose wisely, you can get quite a variety of great healthy foods, both plant and animal. However, that diversity is a little deceptive and can be quite expensive.

The appearance of supermarket diversity

The vegetables commonly eaten in the United States include lettuce, spinach, carrots, cucumbers, tomatoes, broccoli, cauliflower, and cabbage, among others. Even with all these foods, there is an illusion of diversity in the produce section of the supermarket.

Make no mistake, if you select carefully and make it a mission to seek out a great diversity of plant species in the supermarket, you can achieve great diversity. Unfortunately, not everyone is a botanist and the plants displayed to you are not labeled with their scientific names. That is, you don't know what species you are eating. So what is the big deal? Why should you care?

If your goal is to add variety/diversity to your diet, you should increase the number of species you consume. Each unique species has evolved over millions of years to have its own complement of health-giving phytochemicals. Where do these phytochemicals come from? Plants in nature evolve to survive so they can have reproductive success. Unique phytochemicals develop to defend the plant from predation, damage by insects, molds, bacteria, and herbivores. They evolve in response to soil salinity, pH, wind, dryness, and other environmental conditions. They create new chemical odors to attract more and better insects for pollination, new hormones to develop underground storage mechanisms, or to better take advantage of the sun. Each wild plant has its unique challenges and creates phytochemicals to adapt and survive.

These lettuces are all derived from a single species, *Lactuca sativa.*

But what if I told you most all the lettuces in the store are the same species with the same basic array of phytochemicals? Different lettuces were selectively bred by farmers over the centuries to produce different shapes, colors, and flavors. Phytochemicals come in different colors and flavors. If you want whiter lettuce, you have to selectively breed out the colorful phytochemicals. If you want sweeter lettuce, you have to select out bitter, astringent, and sour phytochemicals. If you want to bring out and enhance certain colors, you selectively breed for that.

If I understand it correctly, you start with an original wild variety and selectively breed it into versions that are phytochemically limited to being just a subset of the

These vegetables, collards, and three types of kale, are all derived from *Brassica oleracea* leaves.

Buds of *Brassica oleracea*

original. And once the plant is cultivated and nurtured, it loses the need to continue evolving and producing new and better phytochemicals. Farming insulates plants from evolution. So as different as iceberg, butter, red leaf, green leaf, and romaine lettuces are, you are still eating from subsets of the original *Lactuca sativa* phytochemicals.

Let's use a more extreme example, *Brassica oleracea*. Known as wild cabbage, originally from southwestern Europe, it has no visible relationship with what we know today as cabbage. There is no cabbage head, it is a big-leaved mustard plant with yellow flowers on branching stalks. It is similar in appearance to *Brassica rapa* (see volume 1 of this series). But farmers have selectively bred this plant over centuries into the following supermarket varieties: cabbage (red and green), broccoli, cauliflower, Brussels sprouts, kale, collards, kohlrabi, and others. These are all very different in shape, color, and flavor. But they are all the same species originating with some subset or intentional modifications of the original phytochemicals.

Buds of *Brassica oleracea*

In fact, *Brassica rapa* itself has been selectively bred into turnip, bok choy, napa cabbage, and other variations.

The richness and diversity of phytochemicals you could benefit from are unparalleled when you invite more species in your life. While you can get some of that if you are adventurous and make a concerted effort to consume more supermarket produce, you can also do that with wild foods that are everywhere, free, and still evolving.

Leaves of *Brassica oleracea*

So join granny from Crete and me, and start eating your wild vegetables.

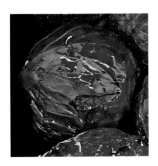

Leaves of *Brassica oleracea*

Chapter 26

Climate Change Revolution

Several things are happening due to climate change all over the world that will increase the focus on wild foods. Temperatures are rising over time and fluctuating wildly within that rise. Wind currents are migrating to produce new weather systems. Some agricultural regions are now shifting to drought areas while others are now flooding constantly. Glaciers are disappearing, reducing the year-round flow of water into streams. Lakes and rivers are drying up. Water sources for almost the whole southwestern United States are disappearing. Our agricultural breadbaskets are being threatened.

The plants we depend on through agriculture are very tied to the lands we've been growing them on and the temperatures they thrive in. Much of that will shift as heat and drought knock out a significant amount of farmland. We will be forced to adapt. Some domesticated plants will be able to make the shift to more northern climates, some will not.

In order for agriculture to provide the quantity and quality of foods necessary to feed a still-growing population, it will have to be innovative. Edible wild plants provide an amazing gene pool of resources, nutrients and phytochemicals for modern agriculture and often grow in diverse conditions, surviving in spite of many adversities. Agricultural adoption of more wild foods may be one way that the world helps to feed itself in the future.

References

Al-Snafi, Ali Esmail. 2013. The Pharmaceutical Importance of Althaea officinalis and Althaea rosea: A Review. *International Journal of Pharmacology*: 5(3):1378–1385. Tech Research CODEN (USA): IJPRIF ISSN: 0974–4304.

Alemán, Raul and Rinaldo Diaz Votto. 2003. Experiences with Lathyrus Latifolius in Agriculture of High Elevation Zones of Central America. *Lathyrus Lathyrism Newsletter*. 3:5–7.

Ali Shah, S. M., et al. 2011. Pharmacological activity of Althaea officinalis L. *Journal of Medicinal Plant Research*. 5(24): 5662–5666.

Badgujar, Shamkant B., et al. *Foeniculum vulgare* Mill: A Review of Its Botany, Phytochemistry, Pharmacology, Contemporary Application, and Toxicology. *BioMed Research International*. Volume 2014, Article ID 842674, 32 pages. http://dx.doi.org/10.1155/2014/842674.

Baranski, Rafal, et al. 2012. Towards Better Tasting and More Nutritious Carrots: Carotenoid and Sugar Content Variation in Carrot Genetic Resources. *Food Research International* 47(2):182–187.

Barnett, B. D. 1975. Toxicity of Pokeberries (Fruit of Phytolacca Americana Large) for Turkey Poults. *Poultry Science*. 54(4):1215–1217.

Barstow, Stephen. 2014. *Around the World in 80 Plants*. Permanent Publications, United Kingdom.

Bloch, Enid. 2001. Hemlock Poisoning and the Death of Socrates: Did Plato Tell the Truth? *Plato Journal*. 1:1–8.

Brackett, Babette and Maryann Lash. 1975. *The Wild Gourmet: A Forager's Guide to the Finding and Cooking of Wild Foods*. David Godine Publishing, Boston, MA.

Burrows, George and Ronald Tyrl. 2013. *Toxic Plants of North America, 2nd Edition*. John Wiley & Sons.

Callahan, R., et al. 1981. Plant Poisonings—New Jersey. CDC, *Morbidity and Mortality Weekly Report*, 30(6): 65–67.

Cheeke, Peter R. 1998. *Natural Toxicants in Feeds, Forages, and Poisonous Plants, 2nd Edition*. Interstate Publishers, Inc., Danville, IL.

Cooper, Marion and Anthony Johnson. 1984. Vetchlings and Wild Peas (Lathyrus spp) in: *Poisonous Plants in Britain and Their Effects on Animals and Man*. Ministry of Agriculture Fisheries and Food, Reference Book 161. Her Majesty's Stationery Office, London.

Couplan, François. *The Encyclopedia of Edible Plants of North America: Nature's Green Feast*. Keats Publishing Inc., New Canaan, CT, 1998.

Das, Arpita, et al. 2021. Current Perspectives on Reducing the β-ODAP Content and Improving Potential Agronomic Traits in Grass Pea (*Lathyrus sativus* L.). *Frontiers in Plant Science*. https://doi.org/10.3389/fpls.2021.703275.

Deshpande, S. S. 2021. *Handbook of Food Toxicology*. Chapters 1, 2, 10: Toxicants & Antinutrients in Plant Foods. Mercel Dekker Inc., New York.

Duke, James A. 1985. *Handbook of Medicinal Herbs*. CRC Press, Ann Arbor, MI.

Durham, Oren C. 1951. The Pollen Harvest. *Economic Botany*. 5(3): 211–254.

Edwards, N. and G. C. Rodgers. 1982. Pokeberry Pancake Breakfast—Or—It's Gonna Be a Great Day! *Veterinary and Human Toxicology*. 24(Suppl): 135–138.

FDA, HHS. 2022. Calamus and its Derivatives: Prohibited from Use in Public Food. CFR—Code of Federal Regulations Title 21, Volume 3, Section 189.110, Subpart C.

Fernald, Merritt Lyndon, et al. 1958. *Edible Wild Plants of Eastern North America, Revised Edition*. Harper & Row Publishers.

Gibbons, Euell. 1966. *Stalking the Healthful Herbs—Field Guide Edition*. David McKay Company, New York.

———. 1962. *Stalking the Wild Asparagus—Field Guide Edition*. David McKay Company, New York.

Goering, K. J. and Yolanda Alvarado Rigault. 1968. New Starches. IV. The Properties of the Starch from *Typha latifolia*. *Starch*. 20(11): 377–379. Contribution from Montana Agricultural Experiment Station, Journal Series No. 882, Montana State University, Bozeman, Montana.

Graff, Stephen. 2010. Pokeberries Provide Boost for Solar Cells. https://www.energy.gov/articles/pokeberries-provide-boost-solar-cells. U.S. Department of Energy, Washington, D.C.

Harrington, M. R. 1933. A Cat-Tail Eater. *Masterkey*. 7:147–149.

Joshi, Bhuwan Chandra, et al. 2014. Pharmacognostical Review of Urtica dioica L. *International Journal of Green Pharmacy*. 8(4): 201–209.

Kallas, John. 2005. Considerations on the Ideal Cattail Pollen Collector. *Wild Food Adventurer Newsletter*. 10(1): 1. Wild Food Adventures Publishing, Portland, OR.

———. *Edible Wild Plants: Wild Foods from Dirt to Plate*. Gibbs Smith, Layton, Utah.

———. 1999. Making Flour from Cattail's Starch Filled Rhizomes. *Wild Food Adventurer Newsletter*. 4(1): 1. Wild Food Adventures Publishing, Portland, OR.

————. 2005. Mallowmallow Takes on the Marshmallow. *Wild Food Adventurer Newsletter*. 10(2): 1. Wild Food Adventures Publishing, Portland, OR.

————. 2000. Tawny Day Lily—Unpredictably Tainted Fare. *Wild Food Adventurer Newsletter*. 5(2): 1. Wild Food Adventures Publishing, Portland, OR.

Kluger, Marilyn. 1984. *The Wild Flavor: Delectable Wild Foods to be Found in Field and Forest and Cooked in Country Kitchens*. Jeremy P. Tarcher, Los Angeles, CA.

Landers, D., et al. 1985. Seizures and Death on a White River Float Trip—Report of Water Hemlock Poisoning. *Western Journal of Medicine*. 142(5): 637–640.

Llnskens, H. F. and W. Jorde. 1997. Pollen as Food and Medicine—A Review. *Economic Botany*. 51(1): 78–86.

Lovering, F. W. 1956. Scientists Say Cattail a "Potential Goldmine." *Florida Grower and Rancher*, 64(3): 11–12, 14.

Maiden, J. H. 1889. *Useful Native Plants of Australia (including Tasmania)*. Technological Museum, New South Wales, Sydney, Australia.

Marsh, Leland C. 1955. The Cattail Story. *The Garden Journal*, New York Botanical Garden. 5(4): 114–115 & 128–129.

Matyunas, N. J. and G. C. Rodgers, Jr. 1985. Evaluation of Pokeberry Ingestion in Children. *Veterinary and Human Toxicology*. 28(4): 298.

Medsger, Oliver Perry. 1939. *Edible Wild Plants*. Macmillan Company, New York, NY.

Meredith, Leda. 2015. Foraging Plantain & Recipe for Plantain Leaf Chips. *The Forager's Feast Blog*.

Moerman, Daniel. 2010. *Native American Food Plants: An Ethnobotanical Dictionary*. Timber Press, Portland, OR.

Morton, Julia F. 1975. Cattails (*Typha* spp.): Weed Problem or Potential Crop? *Economic Botany*. 29(1): 7–29.

Murphy, Denis J. and Joanne Ross. 1998. Biosynthesis, Targeting, and Processing of Oleosin-Like Proteins, Which Are Major Pollen Coat Components in *Brassica napus*. *The Plant Journal*. 13(1): 1–16.

Nazarizadeh, Ali, et al. 2013. Therapeutic Uses and Pharmacological Properties of Plantago major L. and its Active Constituents. *Journal of Basic and Applied Scientific Research*. 3(9).

Nichols, Helena. 2020. Stay Puffed My Friends Part 1: Egypt. *Adventures in Taste and Time Blog.* https://www.adventuresintasteandtime.com/blog/stay-puffed-my-friends-h6ndj.

———. 2020. Stay Puffed My Friends Part 2: France and Pate De Guimauve. *Adventures in Taste and Time Blog.* https://www.adventuresintasteandtime.com/blog/stay-puffed-my-friends-part-2-france-and-pt-de-guimuave.

———. 2020. Stay Puffed My Friends Part 3: America. *Adventures in Taste and Time Blog.* https://www.adventuresintasteandtime.com/blog/stay-puffed-my-friends-part-3-america.

Norris, Dorry Baird. 1991. *The Sage Cottage: Herb Garden Cookbook.* Globe Pequot Press.

Ogzewalla, C. Dwayne, et al. Studies on the Toxicity of Poke Berries. Proceedings of the Oklahoma Academy of Science for 1962. pp. 54–57.

Oneto, Scott. Pokeweed: A Giant of a Weed! 2018. *UC Weed Science Blog,* Department of Agriculture and Natural Resources, University of California. https://ucanr.edu/blogs/blogcore/postdetail.cfm?postnum=27983.

Otakar, Rop, et al. 2012. Edible Flowers—A New Promising Source of Mineral Elements in Human Nutrition. *Molecules.* 17(6): 6672–6683. doi:10.3390/molecules17066672.

Que, F, et al. 2007. In Vitro and Vivo Antioxidant Activities of Daylily Flowers and the Involvement of Phenolic Compounds. *Asia Pacific Journal of Clinical Nutrition.* 16(Suppl 1): 196–203.

Reed, Ernest, and L. C. Marsh. 1955. The Cattail Potential. *Chemurgic Digest.* 14(3): 9 & 18. Council for Agricultural and Chemurgic Research. New York.

Relyea, Kie. 2010. Bellingham Man Warns Others After Poison Hemlock Scare. *The News Tribune.* http://www.thenewstribune.com/2010/05/10/1180806/bellingham-man-warns-others-after.html.

Rodriguez-Enriquez, M. J. and R. T. Grant-Downton. 2013. A New Day Dawning: *Hemerocallis* (Daylily) as a Future Model Organism. *Annals of Botany Plants.* 5: pls055. https://doi.org/10.1093/aobpla/pls055.

Sadeghpour, Nahid, et al. 2015. Study of Foeniculum vulgare (Fennel) Seed Extract Effects on Serum Level of Estrogen, Progesterone, and Prolactin in Mouse. *Crescent Journal of Medical and Biological Sciences.* 2(1): 23–27.

Sagar, G. R. and J. L. Harper. 1964. Plantago Major L., Plantago Media L., and Plantago Lanceolata L. *Journal of Ecology.* 52(1): 189–221.

Said, Amal Ait Haj, et al. 2015. Highlights on Nutritional and Therapeutic Value of Stinging Nettle (Urtica dioica). *International Journal of Pharmacy and Pharmaceutical Sciences.* 7(10):8–14.

Shimoda, M. and Yamasaki, N. *Fallopia japonica* (Japanese Knotweed) in Japan: Why Is It Not a Pest for Japanese People? In: Box, E. (ed.), *Vegetation Structure and Function at Multiple Spatial, Temporal, and Conceptual Scales, Geobotany Studies.* 2016. Springer, Cham. https://doi.org/10.1007/978-3-319-21452-8_20, pp. 447–473.

Singh, Mohar, et al. 2013. *Genetic and Genomic Resources of Grain Legume Improvement.* Elsevier, New York.

Stout, Arlow Burdette. 1933. Gum-Jum or Gum-Tsoy: A Food from the Flowers of Daylilies. *Journal of the New York Botanical Garden.* 34(401): 97–100.

Tanaka, Tyozaburo, Edited by Sasuke Nakao. 1976. *Tanaka's Cyclopedia of Edible Plants of the World.* Yugaku-sha Ltd, Tokyo, Japan.

Tatum, Billy Joe. 1976. *Billy Joe Tatum's Wild Foods Cookbook and Field Guide.* Workman Publishing Company, New York, NY.

Thayer, Samuel. 2006. *The Forager's Harvest: A Guide to Identifying, Harvesting, and Preparing Edible Wild Plants.* Forager's Harvest, Ogema, WI.

Traylor, Catey. Plant Straight Out of a B-Horror Movie Proves Nigh Invincible. The Municipal Online, 2018, #1, January 25, 2018.

USDA, ARS. 2019. Stinging Nettles, Blanched (Northern Plains Indians). FoodData Central Online Nutrient Database, FDC ID: 169819, NDB 35205, US Government.

Vandebroek, Ina, et al. 2011. Local Knowledge: Who Cares? *Journal of Ethnobiology and Ethnomedicine.* 7(35).

Wagner, H., and A. Proksch. 1985. Immunostimulatory Drugs of Fungi and Higher Plants. Chapter 4 in *Economic and Medicinal Plants Research, Volume 1*, Edited by H. Wagner, Hiroshi Hikino, and Norman Farnsworth. pp 113–153, Academic Press, New York.

Wigginton, Eliot (Editor). 1973. Spring Wild Foods. In *Foxfire 2*, pp 47–94. Spring Anchor Press/Doubleday, Garden City, NY.

Index

A

acorns (*Quercus* spp), 35–36, 295
Acorus americanus (calamus), 58–59
Acorus calamus (calamus), 58–59
agriotrophytology, 21
Alliaria petiolata (Garlic mustard), 231, 265
aloe family (*Xanthorrhoeaceae*), 232
Althaea armeniaca (marsh mallow), 118
Althaea officinalis. See marsh mallow
American Hemerocallis Society, 239
asparagus, comparison, 183, 214
axillary locations, defined, 146

B

Biology of Canadian Weeds, 10
bitter plants: flavors and cooking with, 268;
    laxative effects of, 273–274; managing
    bitterness, 270–272; nutrient information,
    274; perceptions of bitterness, 269–270;
    plantain, 289–304; wild chicory, 275–288
blue sailors, 276
blackberry, Himalayan (*Rubus bifrons*), 33–34
boiling, defined 150
Boy Scouts, 158
Brassica juncea (mustard greens), 231–232
Brassicaceae (mustard family), 231–232, 403
bullrush, 52
bull thistle (*Cirsium vulgare*), 171–186;
    background, 172–173; Canadian thistle
    as an edible look-alike, 178–179; cooking
    with, 180–186; edibility, 173, 180–186;
    flower petals, 186; flower stalk, 174–177;
    gathering, 180–186; identifying, 173–
    177; leaves, 173–174; roots, 181–183;
    spines, 172, 173, 176; sprouts, 180–181;
    stems, 183–185; taproot, 173–174

C

calamus (*Acorus americanus*), 58–59
calamus (*Acorus calamus*), 58–59
camas (*Camassia* spp), 31
Camp run-a-muck, 156

Canadian thistle (*Cirsium arvense*), 178–179
carrot. *See* wild carrot
carrot top stage: 350; defined, 355
cattail (*Typha lattifolia*), 51–92; background,
    52; cattail asparagus, 55, 71–72; cattail
    celery, 72–75; in Cattail Guacamole, 90;
    in Cattail Pollen–Banana Nut Whole
    Wheat Muffins, 88–89; in Cattail Spike
    Frittata, 89; cattail starch, 55, 66–71;
    edibility, 52–53; flower stalk, 60–62,
    75–79; gathering, 62–71; identifying,
    53–55, 60–62; nutrient information,
    52–53; pollen, 61–62, 77–78, 80, 305;
    pollen, as an ingredient, 85–86; pollen,
    collecting and refining, 80–84; rhizome
    core fibers, 66–67, 69; rhizomes, 53–55;
    rhizomes, gathering and processing,
    63–71; seeds, 62; in Soft Cattail Core
    Vanilla Pudding, 91–92; spikes, female,
    78–79; spikes, freezing, 79; spikes, male,
    77–78; squeegee processing technique,
    67–70; in Sunshine Pancakes, 87; toxic
    look-alikes, 56–59; young plants, 55
Cattail Guacamole, 90
Cattail Pollen–Banana Nut Whole
    Wheat Muffins, 88–89
Cattail Research Institute, 52
Cattail Spike Frittata, 89
Center for Disease Control, 156
chemical toxins, avoiding, 42–48
Chicorium intybus. See wild chicory
chicory. *See* wild chicory
Cirsium arvense (Canadian thistle), 178–179
Cirsium vulgare. See bull thistle
Claytonia perfoliata (Miner's lettuce), 26
clearweed (*Pilea pumila*), 104–105
climate change, 19, 308, 383, 404
common mallow (*Malva
    neglecta*), 117, 120, 129
Conium maculatum. See poison hemlock
Conley, Roy, 160–161
convergent evolution, 326

corms, defined, 53
Cream of Knotweed Soup, 219
cut-leaved purple sweet nettle, 192
cystoliths, 103

D

dandelion, 24, 95, 162, 256, 268, 276–280
Daucus carota. See wild carrot
Daylily Jam, 252
Daylily Meringue Pie, 253
decussate leaf arrangements, 98, 100
Demerath, Joseph, 115
desserts: Daylily Meringue Pie, 253; Euell
  Gibbons's Classic Knotweed Pie, 230;
  Knotweed Custard Pie, 228–229; Knotweed
  Meringue Pie, 226–227; Marshmallow
  Cream, 134–135; Marshmallows, 136–138;
  Soft Cattail Core Vanilla Pudding, 91–92
diet, diversity in, 400–403
Digitalis purpurea (foxglove), 308
dips and spreads: Fennel Tzatziki, 346; John's
  Nettle-Avocado Pesto, 110–111; Knocamole,
  224; Knotweed Pâté, 214–216; Wild Carrot
  Root and Almond Butter Hummus, 362
disclaimer, 8–9
Dixon, Carrie, 169
Doumak, Alex, 115
Dunning-Kruger effect, 37
dwarf nettle (*Urtica urens*), 96, 104

E

EDD Species Distribution Maps, 10
edibility: indicators of, 21–24,
  29–30; of noxious weeds, 33–34;
  tests, dangers of, 36–38
edible wild plants: chemical toxins on,
  avoiding, 42–48; defined, 21; and diet
  diversity, 400–403; noxious weeds
  as, 33–34; nutrient information,
  385–387; nutrient value tables,
  388–393; wild fast foods, 25–26
Euell Gibbons's Classic Knotweed Pie, 230

everlasting pea (*Lathyrus latifolius*), 307–324;
  background, 308–309; as a climbing vine,
  311–313; cooking with, 316, 318–320;
  edibility, 308, 315; flower stalk, 313–314;
  flowers, 316–318; gathering, 315–320;
  vs. grass pea, 323–324; identifying,
  309–315; and lathyrism concerns, 309,
  321–324; leaves, 310–313; peapods,
  314–315, 318–320; roots, 309–310;
  seedlings, 309; stems, 311–314; tips,
  315–316; as a wild fast food, 315

F

Fallopia japonica. See Japanese knotweed
Fallopia sachalinensis (Sakhalin knotweed),
  200–201, 209. *See also* Japanese knotweed
fennel. *See* wild sweet fennel
Fennel and Quinoa Salad, 339–340
fennel bulb, 327
Fennel Tzatziki, 346
Ferris, Melody, 86
Ferris, Michelle, 86
finocchio, 326
flower heads, defined, 177
flowers, caution in eating in quantity, 366
Foeniculum vulgare. See wild sweet fennel
food chain, 386
food jag, defined, 320
foragers, roles of, 23
foraging: vs. harvesting, 31–32; tools for, 23
foundation plants: bull thistle, 171–186;
  cattail, 51–92; flavors and cooking
  with, 50; marsh mallow, 113–138;
  pokeweed, 139–170; purple sweet nettle,
  187–196; stinging nettle, 93–112
foxglove (*Digitalis purpurea*), 308

G

garlic mustard (*Alliaria petiolata*), 231, 265
Gibbons, Euell, 12, 66, 130, 153, 230, 271
GingerRoot Wild Food Rendezvous,
  78, 86, 298, 308, 309, 318

Urtica dioica. See stinging nettle
Urtica urens (dwarf nettle), 96, 104
utility poles, avoiding gathering near, 45

W

Wagner, Florence, 246
Wagner, Herb, 246
Walls, Eva, 309
wapato (*Sagittaria latifolia*), 25, 31
weeds: noxious, 33–34; as plants
  native to humans, 24–25
wetland plants, cleaning and sanitizing, 72
Wherry, Edgar T., 246
White, Tony Joe, 143
wild carrot (*Daucus carota*), 347–370;
  background, 348–349; cooking with,
  359–361, 365–366; edibility, 348;
  flowers, 351–353, 365–366; fruits, 353;
  gathering, 359–361; identifying, 349–353;
  in John's Wild Carrot Blossom Soup,
  370; leaves, 350–351, 359–360; nutrient
  information, 349; poison hemlock as a
  look-alike to, 348–349, 354–358; roots,
  360–361; seedlings, 349–350; stalks,
  351; stems, 363–365; in Wild Carrot
  Flower Jelly, 368–369; in Wild Carrot
  Flower Pancakes, 367; in Wild Carrot
  Root and Almond Butter Hummus, 362
Wild Carrot Flower Jelly, 368–369
Wild Carrot Flower Pancakes, 367
Wild Carrot Root and Almond
  Butter Hummus, 362
wild chicory (*Chicorium intybus*), 275–288;
  background, 276–277; chicory coffee,
  276, 282–283; chicosparagus, 286–287;
  cooking with, 285–288; edibility, 276;
  flowers, 280–282; gathering, 283–284;
  identifying, 277–283; leaves, 277–281,
  284–286; nutrient information, 277; roots,
  276–277, 282–283; seedlings, 277; stems,
  280–281, 286–287; variations, 277
wild fast food, 25–26

wild food: chemical toxins on, avoiding,
  42–48; and diet diversity, 400–403; edibility,
  indicators of, 21–24, 29–30; incorporating
  into your diet, 27–28; noxious weeds as,
  33–34; nutrient information, 385–387;
  nutrient value tables, 388–393; safety, 13;
  in survival manuals, unreliability of, 35–38,
  40–41; as traditional foods, 24–25;
Wild Food Adventurer Newsletter, 117, 244
wild radish (*Raphanus raphanistrum/Raphanus
  sativus*), 257–267; background, 258–259;
  cooking with, 265–267; edibility, 259;
  flowers, 262–264, 266–267; gathering,
  265–267; identifying, 259–265; leaves,
  259–261, 265–266; roots, 266–267;
  seedpods, 264, 266–267; squeegee
  processing technique, 266; stems, 264–265
wild sweet fennel (*Foeniculum vulgare*), 325–
  346; background, 326–328; cooking with,
  336–338; edibility, 326–328, 333, 336,
  337; in Fennel and Quinoa Salad, 339–340;
  in Fennel Tzatziki, 346; flowers, 332–333,
  340–344; gathering, 333–338; hormone
  risks from seeds, 327; identifying, 328–333;
  in John's Fennel Blossom Soup, 345; leaves,
  329–331, 335–337; pollen, 343–344;
  roots, 329; seedlings, 328–329; stalks, 329,
  333–335; stems, 329–332, 334–338
wild sweet pea, 308
winged stem, defined, 311–312
woodnettle (*Laportea canadensis*), 105

X

Xanthorrhoeaceae (aloe family), 232

Y

yellow daylily (*Hemerocallis altissima*), 237
yellow daylily (*Hemerocallis lilioasphodelus*), 237
yellow iris (*Iris pseudacorus*), 56–57

Z

Zesty Knotweed Sauce, 225